THE CONCEALMENT CONTROVERSY

The idea that a claim for international protection can be rejected on the basis that the claimant behave 'discreetly' in their country of origin has remained resilient in asylum claims based on sexual orientation, but also other grounds of claim. This is significant because requiring an asylum-seeker to forgo the reason for which they are persecuted questions the very rationale of refugee protection. This book represents the first principled examination of concealment in refugee law. Janna Wessels connects the different strands of the long-standing debate in both common and civil law jurisdictions and scholarship concerning the question of whether and under which circumstances a claimant must conceal to avoid persecution. In so doing, Wessels uncovers a fundamental tension at the core of the refugee concept. This approach permits the book to cast a fresh look at central notions and core debates of refugee law, such as persecution and the Convention grounds, and their intersection with human rights.

JANNA WESSELS is an assistant professor at the Amsterdam Centre for Migration and Refugee Law, Vrije Universiteit Amsterdam. She has held research posts at the law faculties of UTS Sydney and Giessen University. Her main research interests are in the areas of migration law, human rights and refugee protection.

The Concealment Controversy

SEXUAL ORIENTATION, DISCRETION REASONING AND THE SCOPE OF REFUGEE PROTECTION

JANNA WESSELS
Vrije Universiteit Amsterdam

CAMBRIDGE
UNIVERSITY PRESS

CAMBRIDGE
UNIVERSITY PRESS

University Printing House, Cambridge CB2 8BS, United Kingdom

One Liberty Plaza, 20th Floor, New York, NY 10006, USA

477 Williamstown Road, Port Melbourne, VIC 3207, Australia

314–321, 3rd Floor, Plot 3, Splendor Forum, Jasola District Centre, New Delhi – 110025, India

103 Penang Road, #05–06/07, Visioncrest Commercial, Singapore 238467

Cambridge University Press is part of the University of Cambridge.

It furthers the University's mission by disseminating knowledge in the pursuit of education, learning, and research at the highest international levels of excellence.

www.cambridge.org
Information on this title: www.cambridge.org/9781108837095
DOI: 10.1017/9781108938402

First published 2021

A catalogue record for this publication is available from the British Library.

ISBN 978-1-108-83709-5 Hardback

Contents

Figures

Tables

Acknowledgements

The publication of this book coincides with the 70th anniversary of the Refugee Convention. On this occasion, the book pauses to reconsider the question of what, and whom, the Refugee Convention protects – and why. Many people have thought along with me about these questions over the past decade. The greatest debt of gratitude is owed to Jenni Millbank from the University of Technology Sydney and Thomas Spijkerboer from Vrije Universiteit Amsterdam, the supervisors of the PhD upon which this book is based. I am grateful for their guidance and constant and wise engagement with all aspects of my research – their input and insights created 'productive instability' at its best. I would also like to extend my sincere appreciation to the external examiners of my PhD, Gregor Noll and Hélène Lambert.

During the time at which this book was written, I was privileged to be part of inspiring groups in Sydney, Amsterdam and Giessen. For the stimulating academic and social environment they created during my time in Sydney, I am grateful to my colleagues from the Faculty of Law at University of Technology Sydney, Laurie Berg, Anthea Vogl and Starla Hargita. I am also indebted to the UTS Faculty of Law for granting me the Quentin Bryce Law Doctoral Fellowship and the International Postgraduate Research Scholarship, which enabled me to embark on this research. In Sydney, I also thank Jane McAdam and the members of the refugee law reading group at the Kaldor Centre at University of New South Wales, for discussions that were crucial in the early stages of the project.

I thank my old and new colleagues at Vrije Universiteit Amsterdam for the welcome they extended to me during my PhD and the vibrant intellectual atmosphere they created. Many have knowingly or implicitly contributed to this book. It has directly and indirectly benefitted from exchanges with Pieter Boeles, Hemme Battjes, Lieneke Slingenberg, Martijn Stronks and the late Sarah van Walsum. I am very pleased that I now have the opportunity to continue to work on issues related to those arising in this book at the Amsterdam Centre for Migration and Refugee Law.

The final stages of writing this book were completed while I was working at the University of Giessen. Particular thanks are due to Jürgen Bast for his guidance and for providing space to complete the book. I am also grateful for many insightful discussions with my other colleagues at the Chair of Public and European Law, as well as colleagues from the research group Migration and Human Rights. I thank Jelena von Achenbach and Michaela Hailbronner for their friendship and advice.

For providing cases, background information and helpful tips during my research, I am indebted to José Díaz Lafuente, Thomas Fouquet-Lapar, Leire Lasa Fernández, Claudie Lesselier, Eva Menendez, Victor Merino and Elena Muñoz. The book has also greatly benefitted from discussions with Lars Bay-Larsen, Harald Dörig and Jürgen Meng. I have had numerous exchanges valuable for the progression of my work with members of the Refugee Law Initiative and Netzwerk Migrationsrecht. A special thanks is owed to Alice Edwards, in whose office at Oxford this project started as an idea for a Master's thesis, and who nudged me to keep working on these issues.

Parts of the book have previously been published. The introduction draws on: 'The Art of Drawing Lines: Future Behaviour and Refugee Status', in Satvinder Juss (ed.) *The Research Handbook on International Refugee Law*, Cheltenham: Edward Elgar, 268–280 (2019). Sections of Chapters 4 and 5 are referred to in 'Publicly Manifested – Fatefully Determined – Invariably "Discreet": The Assessment of Sexuality-Based Asylum Claims in Germany and France' 29(2) *Canadian Journal of Women and the Law* 343–374 (2017). Chapter 9 develops some of the main arguments that appeared in '"Discretion", persecution and the act/identity dichotomy', VU Migration Law Series No. 12, Vrije Universiteit Amsterdam (2016). I am indebted to the editors and anonymous reviewers, who provided feedback on those works. I also thank Matthew Sidebotham, who provided professional editing assistance, and the team at Cambridge University Press, in particular Tom Randall and Laura Blake, for their support during the publication process.

My deepest gratitude is owed to my family, for intensive discussions on many of the arguments developed in this book, as much as for their unfaltering support, advice and patience. Without them, this book would not exist.

1

The Concealment Controversy

An Introduction

In 2010 the United Kingdom Supreme Court passed an important judgment for refugee law doctrine. The case of *HJ and HT* concerned two gay men, from Iran and Cameroon respectively, who claimed asylum based on their sexual orientation. The intention of the judgment was to settle a doctrinal dispute that had been lingering for many years: the question of 'discretion' reasoning. The Court had to decide whether claims to international protection could be denied on the basis that claimants could reasonably be required to behave 'discreetly' upon return to their country of origin in order to avoid persecution. The UK Supreme Court ruled that any such behaviour modification cannot be required, reasonably or otherwise, of a claimant. The unanimous decision also purported to provide clear guidance to judges and decision-makers on how the claimant's future behaviour should be assessed in refugee status determinations.[1]

But rather than providing a final answer, the UK Supreme Court's judgment inspired a fierce debate among refugee law scholars on the role of a claimant's acts, identity and rights.[2] James Hathaway and Jason Pobjoy prominently and severely criticised the judgment in *HJ (Iran) and HT (Cameroon)* as well as the previous Australian High Court judgment in *S395*,[3] upon which the UK Supreme Court

[1] *HJ (Iran) and HT (Cameroon)* v. *Secretary of State for the Home Department*, [2010] UKSC 31, United Kingdom: Supreme Court, 7 July 2010.

[2] See Jeffrey D. Stein (2012) 'A Brief Introduction to the Conversation', 44(2) *New York University Journal of International Law and Politics* 313–314, and the other articles of this special issue as well as the contributions to the online symposium that accompanied it at http://opiniojuris.org/2012/03/07/new-york-university-journal-of-international-law-and-politics-vol-442-opinio-juris-online-symposium.

[3] *Appellant S395/2002* v. *Minister for Immigration and Multicultural Affairs; Appellant S396/2002* v. *Minister for Immigration and Multicultural Affairs*, [2003] HCA 71, Australia: High Court, 9 December 2003, involving a gay couple from Bangladesh and a reasonable requirement to be 'discreet'.

built, for departing 'in critical ways from accepted refugee law doctrine',[4] causing 'collateral damage for applicants claiming status on grounds of religion and political opinion engendered by the confusing reasoning in these decisions' and thus risking 'doctrinal distortion'.[5] Instead, they proposed an alternative approach. While receiving praise and support from some,[6] this reaction was in turn met with strong criticism and described as 'both wrong in principle and dangerous in practice',[7] and 'on its own steam ... weaken[ing] the normative consensus that supposedly holds the regime together'[8] – or, more mildly, 'a rather curious response ... which will hardly have done protection much good'.[9] The tone of the debate indicates that the stakes are high: the role of the claimant's behaviour concerns a wider legal principle of profound significance[10] – and it is one where very different approaches clash.

1.1 THE DISPUTE

This book will show that, in many ways, the judgment in *HJ (Iran) and HT (Cameroon)*[11] and the reaction to it by Hathaway and Pobjoy[12] crystallise a broader dispute concerning 'discretion' reasoning in refugee law. This dispute centres on the following questions: what will the claimant do if returned to their country of origin? And does the question of how they will behave matter for whether they are entitled to refugee protection? If so, in what way?

4 James Hathaway and Jason Pobjoy (2012) 'Queer Cases Make Bad Law', 44(2) *New York University Journal of International Law and Politics* 315–389, 331.

5 Ibid.

6 Guglielmo Verdirame commends Hathaway and Pobjoy's approach as being based on clarity of principle and analytical rigour in Guglielmo Verdirame (2012) 'A Friendly Act of Socio-cultural Contestation: Asylum and the Big Cultural Divide', 44(2) *New York University Journal of International Law and Politics* 559–572, 567; and Richard Buxton thinks that the 'ways in which the outcome of *HJ (Iran)* appears difficult to reconcile with orthodox principles of asylum law have been set out in full and, with respect, convincing detail by Professor Hathaway and Mr. Pobjoy', Richard Buxton (2012) 'A History from across the Pond', 44(2) *New York University Journal of International Law and Politics* 391–406, 406.

7 Jenni Millbank (2012) 'The Right of Lesbians and Gay Men to Live Freely, Openly, and on Equal Terms Is Not Bad Law: A Reply to Hathaway and Pobjoy', 44(2) *New York University Journal of International Law and Politics* 497–527, 501.

8 Ryan Goodman (2012) 'Asylum and the Concealment of Sexual Orientation: Where Not to Draw the Line', 44(2) *New York University Journal of International Law and Politics* 407–446, 446.

9 Guy Goodwin-Gill (2014) 'Editorial – The Dynamic of International Refugee Law', 25(4) *International Journal of Refugee Law* 651–666, 664.

10 See Garden Court Chambers (2010) 'Future Behaviour and the Refugee Convention', *Free Movement Blog*, 12 July 2010, www.freemovement.org.uk/future-behaviour-and-the-refugee-convention (all online sources were last accessed on 29 September 2017).

11 *HJ (Iran) and HT (Cameroon)* v. *Secretary of State for the Home Department*, note 1.

12 Hathaway and Pobjoy, note 4, 315–389.

These discussions take place in the context of the refugee definition of the United Nations Convention Relating to the Status of Refugees ('Refugee Convention') from 1951. According to Article 1(A)2 of the Refugee Convention,

> the term 'refugee' shall apply to any person who ... owing to well-founded fear of being persecuted *for reasons of race, religion, nationality, membership of a particular social group or political opinion*, is outside the country of his nationality and is unable or, owing to such fear, is unwilling to avail himself of the protection of that country.[13]

The reasons for persecution (the 'Convention grounds') are not necessarily immediately visible. Political opinion, religion and ethnicity in some cases need to be expressed in one way or another to become discernible to the persecutor. This also goes for certain 'particular social groups', and has been vigorously discussed for sexual orientation.[14] Any person, therefore, has at least *some* discretion regarding what others know about such characteristics.[15] This creates a dilemma: refugee status determination is based on a future-focused analysis, but claimants can influence that future to some extent. Does this mean that claimants can be expected to hide their persecuted characteristics? If not, can claimants at the very least be required to exercise some restraint?

Judges and refugee lawyers have grappled with these questions for many years. In the United Kingdom asylum judgments have been cyclically returning to struggle with the role of the claimant's behaviour roughly every decade: the 1989 judgment of the Court of Appeal in *Mendis* expressly left the question open,[16] the 1999 Court

[13] UN General Assembly, *Convention Relating to the Status of Refugees*, 28 July 1951, United Nations, Treaty Series, vol. 189, p. 137; emphasis added.

[14] See e.g. Catherine Dauvergne and Jenni Millbank (2003) 'Before the High Court: Applicants S396/2002 and S395/2002, a Gay Refugee Couple from Bangladesh', 25 *Sydney Law Review* 97–124; Jenni Millbank (2009) 'From Discretion to Disbelief: Recent Trends in Refugee Determinations on the Basis of Sexual Orientation in Australia and the United Kingdom', 13(2/3) *International Journal of Human Rights* 391–414; Christopher Kendall (2003) 'Lesbian and Gay Refugees in Australia: Now That "Acting Discreetly" Is No Longer an Option, Will Equality Be Forthcoming?', 15(4) *International Journal of Refugee Law* 715–749; Janna Wessels (2012) 'HJ (Iran) and HT (Cameroon) – Reflections on a New Test for Sexuality-Based Asylum Claims in Britain', 24(4) *International Journal of Refugee Law* 815–839.

[15] See Eve Kosofsky Sedgwick (1990) *Epistemology of the Closet*, Berkeley: University of California Press, 75.

[16] *Mendis* v. *Immigration Appeal Tribunal and Secretary of State for the Home Department*, [1989] Imm AR 6, United Kingdom: Court of Appeal (England and Wales), 17 June 1988. The case concerned a Sri Lankan man claiming asylum on the grounds of political opinion, because of his engagement in the Tamil cause while in the United Kingdom. The judges were split on the issue: Neill LJ preferred to leave the matter open for future argument, to establish 'whether there may not be cases where a man of settled conviction may be able to claim refugee status because it would be quite unrealistic to expect him, if he were returned to a foreign country, to refrain from expressing his political views forever', whereas Balcombe LJ rejected the proposition on the basis that in his judgment 'a person is not at risk of being persecuted for his political opinions, if no events which would attract such persecution have yet taken place' as that 'is

of Appeal judgment in *Danian* was puzzled, finding that the 'learned commentaries, to the extent that they have addressed the issue, do not speak with one voice', and that 'such case-law as exists, both in this jurisdiction and abroad ... again does not point in a single direction'.[17] This had not changed much by 2010, when the UK Supreme Court noted in its judgment in *HJ (Iran) and HT (Cameroon)* that the cases reviewed revealed 'no consistent line of authority that indicates that there is an approach which is universally accepted internationally'.[18] Courts and scholars have been struggling to come to terms with the role of the claimant's potential 'discretion' for decades. The latest controversy is but the culmination of this long-standing struggle.

1.1.1 *Living Discreetly: The UK Supreme Court's 2010 Judgment*

The controversy was triggered by the UK Supreme Court judgment in *HJ (Iran) and HT (Cameroon)*.[19] The case focused on the so-called discretion requirement. It involved two gay men, HJ from Iran and HT from Cameroon, whose asylum claims had been rejected by the lower courts on the basis that they could reasonably be expected to exercise a measure of self-restraint in order to avoid coming to the attention of persecutors. The 'discretion requirement' had been widely used in decisions related to asylum claims based on sexual orientation, particularly in Australia[20] and the United Kingdom.[21] It consists of a 'reasonable expectation that persons should, to the extent that it is possible, co-operate in their own protection'.[22] The Supreme Court unanimously ruled that the 'reasonably tolerable test' was contrary to the Convention and should not be followed in the future. Instead, the judges developed a new test to be applied by lower courts and tribunals when dealing with sexuality-based claims. According to the new test, while a claimant

tantamount to saying that a person who says he proposes to invite persecution is entitled to claim refugee status' and 'could become a refugee as a matter of his own choice'. Staughton LJ in contrast thought that in certain cases such a person would qualify for refugee status, because if they had such strong convictions that they would inevitably speak out, 'it could be questioned whether the future conduct would be voluntary in any real sense'.

[17] *Danian* v. *Secretary of State for the Home Department (Appeal)*, [2000] Imm AR 96, United Kingdom: Court of Appeal (England and Wales), 28 October 1999, per Buxton LJ.

[18] *HJ (Iran) and HT (Cameroon)* v. *Secretary of State for the Home Department*, note 1, per Lord Hope at 30.

[19] *HJ (Iran) and HT (Cameroon)* v. *Secretary of State for the Home Department*, note 1.

[20] See e.g. Ghassan Kassisieh (2008) 'From Lives of Fear to Lives of Freedom: A Review of Australian Refugee Decisions on the Basis of Sexual Orientation', *Gay & Lesbian Rights Lobby*, Glebe/Australia, 64–70.

[21] See e.g. Jenni Millbank (2005) 'A Preoccupation with Perversion: The British Response to Refugee Claims on the Basis of Sexual Orientation 1989–2003', 14(1) *Social Legal Studies* 115–138, 133–134.

[22] *RRT Case No. V95/03527*, [1998] RRTA 246, Australia: Refugee Review Tribunal, 9 February 1996.

cannot be 'reasonably expected' to behave in one way or another, it is relevant to assess what the applicant would 'in fact' do.[23] The enquiry moved from a normative requirement to a factual assessment of future behaviour. In that sense, the refugee status determination procedure remains constructed around a classification of future conduct, distinguishing between 'living openly' and 'living discreetly'. According to the Court, those who will 'in fact live openly' cannot be required to change their behaviour to avoid persecution. Where the decision-maker is satisfied that applicants will in fact conceal their sexual orientation, it is necessary to enquire into the motives for such concealment. Claimants are only entitled to protection if their concealment is due to fear of persecution. If the motives for their 'discreet' behaviour are other than fear of persecution, such as personal choice or social pressures, they are not entitled to international protection.[24] As such, the analysis is dependent on the assumed future conduct of the applicant – and hinges on the motives for that conduct.

The rejection of the 'reasonable requirement' standard brought sexuality-based claims in line with claims based on other persecution grounds.[25] In fact, the approach advanced by the UK Supreme Court was explicitly distilled from previous UK and also Australian case law concerning religion and political opinion. This line of cases reveals that the claimants' conduct and their capacity for 'discretion' has been dealt with for decades, in ever more refined and more differentiated ways. In

[23] 'The tribunal must . . . consider *what the individual applicant would do* if he were returned to [his] country. If the applicant would *in fact live openly* and thereby be exposed to a real risk of persecution, then he has a well-founded fear of persecution – even if he could avoid the risk by living "discreetly". If, on the other hand, the tribunal concludes that the applicant *would in fact live discreetly* and so avoid persecution, it must go on to ask itself *why* he would do so.' *HJ (Iran) and HT (Cameroon)* v. *Secretary of State for the Home Department*, note 1, per Lord Rodger at 82; emphasis added.

[24] 'If the tribunal concludes that the applicant would choose to live discreetly simply because that was how he himself would wish to live, or because of social pressures, e.g., not wanting to distress his parents or embarrass his friends, then his application should be rejected. Social pressures of that kind do not amount to persecution and the Convention does not offer protection against them. Such a person has no well-founded fear of persecution because, for reasons that have nothing to do with any fear of persecution, he himself chooses to adopt a way of life which means that he is not in fact liable to be persecuted because he is gay. If, on the other hand, the tribunal concludes that a material reason for the applicant living discreetly on his return would be a fear of the persecution which would follow if he were to live openly as a gay man, then, other things being equal, his application should be accepted. Such a person has a well-founded fear of persecution. To reject his application on the ground that he could avoid the persecution by living discreetly would be to defeat the very right which the Convention exists to protect – his right to live freely and openly as a gay man without fear of persecution. By admitting him to asylum and allowing him to live freely and openly as a gay man without fear of persecution, the receiving state gives effect to that right by affording the applicant a surrogate for the protection from persecution which his country of nationality should have afforded him.' Ibid.

[25] See e.g. Millbank, note 7, 497–527, 500.

the first notable pair of judgments, *Mendis*[26] and *Ahmad and Others*[27] from 1988 and 1989 respectively, there was uncertainty as to whether it was acceptable to require a claimant to abstain from certain political or religious acts, with considerable disagreement amongst judges. It took ten years before the Court of Appeal was again faced with the issue, in a pair of decisions in 1999 in which it basically developed the standard that was subsequently adopted and transferred to sexuality-based claims by the UK Supreme Court in the 2010 judgment. The political opinion case of *Danian* established that fear of harm arising from *past* behaviour does not forfeit a claim to protection, even if that behaviour was engaged in order to enhance prospects for asylum ('bad faith'), if it led in fact to a genuine fear of persecution.[28] Here, the claimant's motives explicitly do not matter. Just a few weeks after the decision in *Danian*, the Court of Appeal developed this approach further, extending it also to *future* behaviour (i.e. what the claimant 'will in fact do') in the context of the religion-based case of *Iftikhar Ahmed*. The Court here for the first time distinguished between a reasonable requirement to behave in a certain way on the one hand and a factual assessment that a claimant *would* act in such a way (however unreasonable that would appear to be) on the other, finding that the latter situation would warrant protection if it led to a well-founded fear of persecution.[29]

26 *Mendis* v. *Immigration Appeal Tribunal and Secretary of State for the Home Department*, note 16.

27 *Ahmad* v. *Secretary of State for the Home Department*, [1990] Imm AR 61, United Kingdom: Court of Appeal (England and Wales), 6 October 1989.

28 The judgment concerned a Nigerian man whose claim was based on political opinion, specifically his opposition to the military regime in Nigeria. The claimant was accused of 'bad faith', as he had engaged in visible political activities in the course of his asylum application, which brought him to the attention of the Nigerian authorities. The lower court had found that his 'conduct had been wholly unreasonable and contrary to the spirit of the Geneva Convention', and was described as 'insincere', a 'charade', 'invented' and a 'sham'. The issue for the Court of Appeal was then, whether those who voluntarily 'invited persecution' and 'engaged in activity in the UK in bad faith but who nonetheless genuinely feared what would happen to [them] as a result of that activity' were protected under the 1951 Refugee Convention. The Court unanimously decided that there was no 'bad faith' exception to the Convention protection and that a fear of persecution may be well-founded irrespective of whether it followed from voluntary activity: '[T]he essential factual issue in the case [is] whether at the time of the tribunal's assessment Mr Danian, having taken the steps referred to, was then at risk of persecution, whether by reason of those steps or otherwise.' *Danian* v. *Secretary of State for the Home Department (Appeal)*, note 17.

29 The case involved a Pakistani national of Ahmadi faith, who had been persecuted in his local area for proselytising his faith. The secretary of state argued that he could relocate and avoid further persecution since it was 'not unreasonable for him to make some allowances for the situation in Pakistan and the sensitivities of others and to exercise a measure of discretion in his conduct and in the profession of his faith'. Writing for the court, Lord Justice Simon Brown concluded that '[e]ven assuming, therefore, that it would be unreasonable for this appellant on return to Pakistan to carry on where he left off . . . that still does not defeat his claim to asylum'. *Ahmed (Iftikhar)* v. *Secretary of State for the Home Department*, [2000] INLR 1, United Kingdom: Court of Appeal (England and Wales), 5 November 1999.

But the situation the UK Supreme Court faced in *HJ (Iran) and HT (Cameroon)* differed in that a factual assumption was made that the claimants would in fact *not* live 'openly'. None of the previous British asylum judgments had addressed this scenario. On this issue, the UK Supreme Court judges sought guidance from the 2003 High Court of Australia decision in *Appellant S395/2002*, a sexuality-based claim,[30] and, in particular, the subsequent decision in *NABD*, concerning a claim based on religion.[31] The judgment in *S395*, involving a gay couple from Bangladesh, which was decided by a narrow 4:3 majority, had established that in the case of a determination that a claimant *would in fact* behave 'discreetly', it was necessary to enquire into *why* they would do so.[32] Here, the claimant's motives regain relevance. That is, it was not sufficient to make a finding that a person would behave 'discreetly', and stop the analysis at that, assuming that there was therefore no risk of persecution and that their 'discretion' was uninfluenced by fear. This 'why question' acquired the quality of a test in the subsequent judgment in *NABD*, which applied *S395* to a case concerning a Christian man from Iran.[33] Here, the High Court of Australia established two alternatives in response to the 'why question': if the change of conduct was due to the fear of harm that would otherwise accrue, it would warrant protection, whereas if the changed conduct was due to personal choice, that would not warrant protection. The latter applied to the applicant in *NABD*, for whom the Court concluded that the restraint in the expression of his faith, which did not put him at risk, was freely chosen.[34] That is, while the sexuality-based case of *S395* introduced the 'why question', the religion-based case of *NABD* developed the answers to that question.

The UK Supreme Court's judgment in *HJ (Iran) and HT (Cameroon)* is clearly derived from and in line with these previous UK and Australian judgments concerning a claimant's future behaviour in cases of religion and political opinion. As a unanimous judgment, it sent a strong signal and reinforced the 'why test' that the High Court of Australia had struggled to develop: it is entirely based on what can be termed a factual assessment of the claimant's future behaviour. Though it does not prescribe certain types of conduct as protected and others as not, the assessment

[30] *Appellant S395/2002* v. *Minister for Immigration and Multicultural Affairs*; *Appellant S396/2002* v. *Minister for Immigration and Multicultural Affairs*, note 3; see on this case, Dauvergne and Millbank, note 14, 97–124.

[31] *Applicant NABD of 2002* v. *Minister for Immigration and Multicultural and Indigenous Affairs*, [2005] HCA 29, Australia: High Court, 26 May 2005.

[32] *Appellant S395/2002* v. *Minister for Immigration and Multicultural Affairs*; *Appellant S396/2002* v. *Minister for Immigration and Multicultural Affairs*, note 3, per McHugh and Kirby JJ at 51 and per Gummow and Hayne JJ at 88; see also, equally deploring the failure to ask why: Millbank, note 14, 391–414, 392 and 395–396.

[33] *Applicant NABD of 2002* v. *Minister for Immigration and Multicultural and Indigenous Affairs*, note 31.

[34] Ibid., per Hayne and Heydon JJ at 168.

depends on the classification of behaviour as 'open' or 'discreet' – in some de facto 'discreet' situations, refugee status is granted, in others it is not.[35]

1.1.2 *Protective Limits and Protected Acts: Hathaway and Pobjoy's Response*

Hathaway and Pobjoy take issue with the UK Supreme Court judgment for failing to provide a standard to determine or delimit protected acts, such that any type of conduct could lead to protection. They argue that the decision ignores the 'protective limits built into the nexus clause of the Refugee Convention'[36] by taking an 'all-embracing formulation' to action-based risks.[37] According to them, such an 'essentially boundless'[38] concept is unsustainable and there must be limits on the claimant's activities. Their concern is essentially that, on the basis of the Supreme Court's ruling, claimants could invite persecution with what they consider relatively trivial things, such as dressing a certain way or attending particular kinds of social event. In their view, the approach put forward by the UK Supreme Court in *HJ (Iran) and HT (Cameroon)* – as well as by the High Court of Australia in its 2003 decision in *S395* – is overinclusive in suggesting that there are no limits to the range of 'activity-based risks' associated with sexual orientation. In their understanding, this would come down to the Refugee Convention protecting the full range of available freedoms rather than protecting from persecution. In order to avoid this, according to the authors, 'there [is] a duty on the courts to grapple with the scope of activities properly understood to be inherent in, and an integral part of [the protected] status'.[39] They call for a kind of external or objective standard to distinguish between 'protected activities that are fairly deemed to be required to express the identity' and unprotected activities, which are trivial or marginal to the identity. To carry out this exercise of reintroducing normativity into the assessment, they advocate an approach based on the core and margins of rights. They suggest that only those acts that are reasonably necessary to reveal the sexual orientation will lead to protection. Thus, they explicitly argue *in favour* of restraint based on an external standard. This is in line with Hathaway's earlier work, in which he has proposed and defended the position that not all future *activities* might be protected by the Convention, but rather that a line should be drawn in order to define the core and the margins of the 'protected interest'. For example, Hathaway and colleagues claim that where the relevant right encompasses no public dimension, the denial of public exercise is unlikely to be within the ambit of a fear of 'being persecuted'.[40]

[35] Wessels, note 14, 815–839.
[36] Hathaway and Pobjoy, note 4, 315–389, 339.
[37] Ibid., 374.
[38] Ibid.
[39] Ibid., 335.
[40] Rodger Haines, James Hathaway and Michelle Foster (2003) 'Claims to Refugee Status Based on Voluntary but Protected Actions – Discussion Paper No. 1, Advanced Refugee Law

The core/margins approach put forth by Hathaway and Pobjoy bears many parallels with that developed by the New Zealand Refugee Status Appeals Authority, most notably in its 2004 decision in *Refugee Appeal No. 74665/03* on sexual orientation.[41] In this judgment, in which he explicitly refers to Hathaway's work, Haines QC grapples with the application of the 'human rights approach to "being persecuted"' to 'voluntary but legally protected action'.[42] Haines criticises the judgment of the High Court of Australia in *S395* for failing to offer a principled explanation as to why behaviour should not have to be modified or hidden,[43] and argues that the focus must be on the minimum core entitlement conferred by the relevant right: 'Under this approach, where the risk is only that activity at the margin of a protected interest is prohibited, it is not logically encompassed by the notion of "being persecuted."'[44]

At the heart of both Hathaway and Pobjoy's view, as well as the New Zealand Refugee Status Appeals Authority's approach, lies the concern not to protect trivial things, such as drinking cocktails or wearing tight jeans. The risk they see in the United Kingdom and Australian approaches is that they would provide protection to claimants whose situation was actually not that serious. The idea of 'refugees by choice' has overshadowed discussions on 'discretion' since the beginning,[45] and 'bad faith' considerations often underlie other arguments.

The reactions amongst scholars to Hathaway and Pobjoy's critique of *HJ (Iran) and HT (Cameroon)* were remarkably split, in particular on the aspect of future behaviour – whilst receiving wholehearted support from some, they were faced with severe criticism from others.[46] Some scholars, such as Guglielmo Verdirame[47] and

Workshop, International Association of Refugee Law Judges, Auckland, New Zealand, October 2002', 15(3) *International Journal of Refugee Law* 430–443, 438–440.

[41] *Refugee Appeal* No. 74665/03, New Zealand: Refugee Status Appeals Authority, 7 July 2004.

[42] Ibid., at 81–91.

[43] Ibid., at 116.

[44] Ibid., at 90.

[45] In *Mendis*, Balcombe LJ was of the view that granting refugee status based on future conduct 'is tantamount to saying that a person who says he proposes to invite persecution is entitled to claim refugee status' and 'could become a refugee as a matter of his own choice'. Note that Staughton LJ in contrast thought that in certain cases such a person would qualify for refugee status, because if they had such strong convictions that they would inevitably speak out, 'it could be questioned whether the future conduct would be voluntary in any real sense', *Mendis v. Immigration Appeal Tribunal and Secretary of State for the Home Department*, note 16.

[46] See in particular the contributions to the 2012 special issue in the *NYU Journal of International Law and Politics*, addressing questions around the scope of protection and human rights. David John Frank's contribution is neither critical nor supportive of the approach, but rather a broader comment on the evolving nature of LGBT rights: David John Frank (2012) 'Making Sense of LGBT Asylum Claim: Change and Variation in Institutional Contexts', 44(2) *New York University Journal of International Law and Politics* 485–495.

[47] Verdirame, note 6, 559–572, 572 ('Hathaway and Pobjoy in their article (and, to a far lesser extent, I, in my comment) have tried to show that it is possible to draw these boundaries in a principled and coherent way that accords with the legal framework of refugee law').

Richard Buxton,[48] but also Deborah Anker and Sabi Ardalan in more general terms,[49] explicitly support their analysis and conclusions. Supportive reactions generally centre on the triviality concern. According to Richard Buxton, formerly Lord Justice of Appeal at the Court of Appeal of England and Wales,[50] the UK Supreme Court adopted an approach to the Convention reasons that 'changed the nature of the protection against persecution hitherto understood in asylum law, and undervalued the serious level of feared harm that that law requires before the harm can be made the subject of international protection'.[51] Buxton agrees with Hathaway and Pobjoy that a 'critical assessment of a home state's limitations on the behaviour of the members of a protected group' must be undertaken 'if the enquiry [starts] from the proper place, by asking whether the limitations on behaviour were persecutory in the sense of being something that the applicant could not be expected to tolerate'.[52] Similarly, Verdirame, too, conflates the feared harm with the reason that triggers it when he argues that the inability to openly express affection for another man involves 'no harm-inducing or authenticity-threatening modifications or social conduct, but reasonably tolerable inconveniences'.[53]

More critical scholars take issue in particular with the construction of core and marginal acts. Jenni Millbank argues that 'acts and identities in the context of sexual orientation refugee claims cannot be separated and categorized in that way'.[54] She sees a 'very real danger' that this 'call to circumscription' would 'end up as another version of discretion'.[55] Her criticism is echoed by Ryan Goodman, who considers the distinction between protected and unprotected activities to be vague, lacking legal foundations and overlooking social realities.[56] John Tobin critically engages with the capacity of human rights law to provide clarity on the issue of protected and unprotected activities in refugee law.[57] Most importantly, human rights law knows no test to rank the seriousness of breaches, such that, despite their explicit intention and call to frame refugee law in terms of human rights, the test proposed by

48 Buxton, note 6, 391–406, 406 ('The ways in which the outcome of *HJ (Iran)* appears difficult to reconcile with orthodox principles of asylum law have been set out in full and, with respect, convincing detail by Professor Hathaway and Mr. Pobjoy').

49 Deborah Anker and Sabi Ardalan (2012) 'Escalating Persecution of Gays and Refugee Protection: Comment on Queer Cases Make Bad Law', 44(2) *New York University Journal of International Law and Politics* 529–557.

50 Richard Buxton was involved in the litigation of *HJ* as judge at the Court of Appeal – his judgment was overturned by the Supreme Court.

51 Buxton, note 6, 391–406, 392.

52 Ibid., 406.

53 Verdirame, note 6, 559–572, 572.

54 Millbank, note 7, 497–527, 512–513.

55 Ibid., 517.

56 Goodman, note 8, 407–446, 437, 442.

57 John Tobin (2012) 'Assessing GLBTI Refugee Claims: Using Human Rights Law to Shift the Narrative of Persecution within Refugee Law', 44(2) *New York University Journal of International Law and Politics* 447–484.

Hathaway and Pobjoy to distinguish between protected and unprotected activities is in fact unknown to human rights law.[58]

Moreover, these critics suggest that Hathaway and Pobjoy's concern with the 'over-inclusiveness' of the reasoning in *HJ (Iran) and HT (Cameroon)* might, in fact, be an overreaction to a misunderstood (or misread) section of Lord Rodger's opinion, in which he illustrates what equality between gay and straight people means

> with stereotypical examples from British society: just as male heterosexuals are free to enjoy themselves playing rugby, drinking beer and talking about girls with their mates, so male homosexuals are to be free to enjoy themselves going to Kylie concerts, drinking exotically coloured cocktails and talking about boys with their straight female mates. Mutatis mutandis – and in many cases the adaptations would obviously be great – the same must apply to other societies. In other words, gay men are to be as free as their straight equivalents in the society concerned to live their lives in the way that is natural to them as gay men, without fear of persecution.[59]

Hathaway and Pobjoy represented this section as meaning that trivial activities such as drinking cocktails would entitle applicants to refugee status and were concerned to 'draw a line' that would exclude such conclusions. Therefore, Millbank,[60] Goodman,[61] Anker and Ardalan[62] and Tobin[63] suggest that the whole controversy might in fact be what Millbank labels a 'tempest in a cocktail glass'.[64] Nonetheless, regardless of the role of the example in generating the controversy, recognising it does not solve the complex problems of the role of conduct, identity and rights in refugee status determination. It would, in turn, trivialise the broader implications of the debate to reduce it to an overreaction to this one section. Notably, not only did *HJ (Iran) and HT (Cameroon)* fail to settle the issue of 'discretion' reasoning for the common law jurisdictions and legal scholars, it also did not prevent Germany from making a referral to the Court of Justice of the European Union (CJEU) for a preliminary ruling on the same issue, only six months after the UK Supreme Court had handed down its judgment.[65] The continuing contentious nature of 'discretion'

58 Ibid., 473.

59 *HJ (Iran) and HT (Cameroon)* v. *Secretary of State for the Home Department*, note 1, per Lord Rodger at 78.

60 Millbank, note 7, 497–527, 522–525.

61 Goodman, note 8, 407–446, 439.

62 Anker and Ardalan, note 49, 529–557, 552–553.

63 Tobin, note 57, 447–484, 474.

64 Millbank, note 7, 497–527, 522.

65 Reference for a preliminary ruling from the Oberverwaltungsgericht für das Land Nordrhein-Westfalen (Germany) lodged on 1 December 2010, *Kashayar Khavand* v. *Federal Republic of Germany (Case C-563/10)*. Note that the UK Supreme Court did not, for its part, consider it necessary to refer the question, as Lord Hope noted: 'It was suggested by the appellants that this court should make a reference of a question arising under the Qualification Directive to the

reasoning is further evidenced by the fact that, over the following years, essentially the same question, each time a little more refined, was referred to the Court of Justice of the European Union (CJEU) on three further occasions,[66] with two judgments having been passed.[67]

As a consequence of the unresolved nature of the issue, another point of contention is the doctrinal *location* of the applicant's behaviour in the status determination analysis – is it part of the 'persecution' analysis, the 'nexus' requirement ('for reasons of'), the Convention grounds (reasons) or the assessment of well-foundedness ('real risk')? While Hathaway and Pobjoy make a case for considering the claimants' protected activities under the nexus clause, Anker and Ardalan respond that it is better addressed in the context of persecutory harm,[68] which is also where Haines QC in *Refugee Appeal* 74665/03 would place it.[69] McHugh and Kirby JJ discuss the issue of the claimant's behaviour in the context of the social group in S395,[70] whereas the dissenting judge Gleeson CJ appears to consider it as part of the well-founded fear analysis.[71] There is a general confusion as to where considerations of the claimant's conduct and motives belong. Such confusion is also reflected in the fact that in the second edition of *The Law of Refugee Status*, which Hathaway co-authored with Michelle Foster, and which proceeds by chapters separately

Court of Justice of the European Union under article 267 TFEU [*Treaty on the Functioning of the European Union*] (formerly article 234 EC). But the point that was said to require a reference was not clearly identified, and I would reject that suggestion', *HJ (Iran) and HT (Cameroon)* v. *Secretary of State for the Home Department*, note 1, per Lord Hope at 39.

66 Reference for a preliminary ruling from the Bundesverwaltungsgericht (Germany) lodged on 18 February 2011, *Federal Republic of Germany* v. *Y (Case C-71/11)*; Reference for a preliminary ruling from the Raad van State (Netherlands) lodged on 27 April 2012, *Minister voor Immigratie en Asiel* v. *X (Case C-199/12)*; and Reference for a preliminary ruling from the Sächsisches Oberverwaltungsgericht (Germany) lodged on 30 March 2015, *Federal Commissioner for Asylum Affairs* v. *N (Case C-150/15)*.

Two referrals (*Kashayar Khavand* and X) related to asylum claims based on sexual orientation, and two related to religion (Y and N), and notably *N* was a follow-up asking for clarification on the Court's ruling in *Y and Z*. The referrals in *Kashayar Khavand* and in N were however withdrawn before a decision was handed down by the CJEU, because the national authorities had granted status to the claimant in the meantime.

67 *Federal Republic of Germany* v. *Y and Z*, Joined Cases C-71/11 and C-99/11, Court of Justice of the European Union, 5 September 2012; and *X, Y and Z* v. *Minister voor Immigratie, Integratie en Asiel*, Joined Cases C-199/12, C-200/12 and C-201/12, European Union: Court of Justice of the European Union, 7 November 2013.

68 Anker and Ardalan, note 49, 529–557, 533–534 ('It may be analytically clearer to re-frame what activities should be protected under the Convention in terms of violations of core rights, rather than in terms of the scope of the sexual orientation ground.').

69 *Refugee Appeal* No. 74665/03, note 41, at 90.

70 *Appellant S395/2002* v. *Minister for Immigration and Multicultural Affairs; Appellant S396/2002* v. *Minister for Immigration and Multicultural Affairs*, note 3, per McHugh and Kirby JJ at 55–60.

71 *Appellant S395/2002* v. *Minister for Immigration and Multicultural Affairs; Appellant S396/2002* v. *Minister for Immigration and Multicultural Affairs*, note 3, per Gleeson CJ at 91–110.

addressing different elements of the refugee definition, the issue of 'discretion' is discussed in virtually all chapters.[72]

Thus, judges as well as scholars have grappled with the 'conundrum of concealment'[73] for many years. Time and again, courts are required to rule on the issue, without, apparently, being able to settle it – it stubbornly reasserts itself. The *HJ (Iran) and HT (Cameroon)* versus Hathaway and Pobjoy debate is but one expression of this long-standing riddle. Rather than dismissing the debate as much ado about nothing, it is useful to try to unravel the knot.

1.2 APPROACHING THE PUZZLE

Intrigued by the persistence of this controversial issue, this book sketches avenues for an analysis and explores 'discretion' reasoning in refugee status determinations. The aim is to examine how 'discretion' reasoning relates to and informs the scope of protection in refugee status determinations, with a particular focus on sexuality-based claims: what it is, how it plays out, what it does – and what it reveals about the concept of refugee. 'Discretion' reasoning has been haunting refugee decision-making for a long time – and for just as long has been hovering as a subject of academic engagement, though existing research into 'discretion' reasoning appears to have remained somewhat haphazard and reactive to developments in case law.

An examination of the literature on 'discretion' reveals that the phenomenon has essentially been debated in two different, largely separate, pockets. Both have developed dialectically with landmark judgments. The older, but less well-developed, debate concerns religion- and political opinion-based claims. More recent, but much more pronounced, is the discussion of 'discretion' in the context of sexuality-based claims. Interestingly, the questions have essentially remained the same as they travelled from political opinion- to religion- and, later, to sexuality-based claims. It was not until the judgment in *HJ (Iran) and HT (Cameroon)* that both discourses started to intersect.

One strand of literature focuses on political opinion and religion – and more recently also added sexuality-based claims. The relevant authors are generally refugee law scholars and the discussion remains firmly anchored in refugee law

[72] James Hathaway and Michelle Foster (2014) *The Law of Refugee Status* (2nd ed.), Cambridge: Cambridge University Press, chapter 2 'Well-Founded Fear', 168–169 (2.7 'Evidence of Individuated Past Persecution'); chapter 3 'Serious Harm', 260–261 (3.5 'Autonomy and Self-Realization) and 285–287 (3.5.6 'Privacy'); chapter 4 'Failure of State Protection', 338–339 (4.4.1 'Basis for the Internal Protection Alternative'); and chapter 5 'Nexus to Civil or Political Status', 392–394 (5.4 'The Convention Grounds'), 403 (5.7 'Religion'), 408–409 (5.8.1 'Unexpressed Political Opinion') and 445 (5.9.2 'Sexual Orientation and Gender Identity').

[73] Term borrowed from James Hathaway: James Hathaway (2014) 'The Conundrum of Concealment: Minister for Immigration and Border Protection v SZSCA [2013] FCAFC 155', *Melbourne Law School High Court Blog: Opinions on High*, 9 November 2014, https://blogs.unimelb.edu.au/opinionsonhigh/2014/11/09/hathaway-szsca-fcafc.

doctrine. The earliest standard work on refugee law, Atle Grahl-Madsen's fifty-year-old study,[74] already identified the issue of what was later to be labelled 'activity-based risks'.[75] At a time when sexuality-based asylum claims were still unthinkable, Grahl-Madsen addressed the issue in the context of asylum claims based on political opinion, which was the most pertinent Convention ground in those years. He identified the core and still controversial question: the distinction between 'simply holding' a certain opinion and the expression thereof, or in other words, the distinction between identity and acts. When it comes to expression, Grahl-Madsen refers to the expression of human rights on the one hand and actions that 'go beyond' mere expression of an opinion on the other.[76] Following Grahl-Madsen's early reflections, the subject appears to have been largely left up to the courts for many years. In the United Kingdom, a series of judgments developed the doctrine that claimants cannot be rejected merely because they could hide their political opinion or religion.[77] Overall, academic engagement with concealment in the context of religion and political opinion was sparse, and often remained at the surface, without a need to delve into the messy details of 'discretion'. In his seminal 1991 book, for example, Hathaway briefly noted that a claim cannot be simply dismissed on the basis of telling a claimant to keep quiet in order to avoid detection.[78]

A somewhat singular exception is a discussion paper that was prepared by Hathaway, together with Rodger Haines and Michelle Foster for the Refugee Law Workshop of the International Association of Refugee Law Judges in 2002. In this paper, which appeared in the *International Journal of Refugee Law* in 2003, the authors aim to 'begin the process of conceiving an analytical framework to adjudicate cases based on the risk that would follow from engaging in a voluntary but legally protected activity in the country of origin'.[79] Drawing on case law mainly from common law jurisdictions, they discuss various approaches to 'activity-based risks' in the context of religion, political opinion and also sexual orientation. As such, it is an early attempt at thinking of the different Convention grounds together under the same framework.[80] For years, however, the paper did not have the intended effect of triggering a larger debate.

74 Atle Grahl-Madsen (1966) *The Status of Refugees in International Law – Volume I: Refugee Character*, Leyden: A. W. Sijthoff, 220–253.

75 Term employed by Haines, Hathaway and Foster in: Haines, Hathaway and Foster, note 40, 430–443, 439–440.

76 Grahl-Madsen, note 74, at 248–249, see further discussion, chapter 7.

77 For case law from the United Kingdom on the matter see *Mendis* v. *Immigration Appeal Tribunal and Secretary of State for the Home Department*, note 16 and related judgments, discussion earlier.

78 James Hathaway (1991) *The Law of Refugee Status*, Toronto: Butterworths, 150.

79 Haines, Hathaway and Foster, note 40, 430–443, 430.

80 This is to be distinguished from discussions on the applicability of the listed Convention grounds to claims based on sexual orientation. On this issue see e.g. Tim Sahliu Braimah (2015) 'Divorcing Sexual Orientation from Religion and Politics: Utilizing the Convention Grounds

This may be partly due to the timing of the paper: by the time it appeared, the debate on 'discretion' had moved on. When asylum claims based on sexual orientation started to come up in the early 1990s, the debate was conducted with renewed vigour and in more depth – and largely independently from the earlier discussion in the context of political opinion and religion. While by then it was generally established that one cannot be expected to suppress one's political opinion or religious beliefs in order to avoid persecution, several sexual orientation cases gave rise to lengthy discussions on the extent to which claimants can be expected to 'discreetly' or 'safely practise' their homosexuality.[81] A small but significant body of literature has addressed 'discretion' reasoning in sexuality-based claims in particular. Authors were often not only refugee lawyers but also queer theorists or activists, which allowed them to tap into an established body of notions and concepts from queer theory outside refugee law in order to approach 'discretion' logics.

Indeed, 'discretion' chimes strongly with the 'closet', one of the key themes of queer theory.[82] The closet, a metaphor employed to describe the non-disclosure of one's sexual orientation, is such a familiar trope in the context of sexual orientation that it immediately became pertinent to sexuality-based asylum claims as well. Even some of the earliest academic contributions on sexuality-based claims mention the problem of 'discretion'.[83] Ever since, 'discretion' has been regularly discussed in works addressing such claims more broadly, spanning a timeframe of twenty years.[84]

of Religion and Political Opinion in Same-Sex Oriented Asylum Claims', 27(3) *International Journal of Refugee Law* 481–497.

81 Alice Edwards (2003) 'Age and Gender Dimensions in International Refugee Law', in Erika Feller, Volker Türk and Frances Nicholson (eds.) *Refugee Protection in International Law: UNHCR's Global Consultations on International Protection*, Cambridge: Cambridge University Press, 46–80, 66.

82 See Sedgwick, note 15, 68.

83 Jenni Millbank (1995) 'Fear of Persecution or Just a Queer Feeling? Refugee Status and Sexual Orientation in Australia', 20(6) *Alternative Law Journal* 261–265, 264–265; Kristen Walker (1996) 'The Importance of Being Out: Sexuality and Refugee Status', 18 *Sydney Law Review* 568–597, 578.

84 Jenni Millbank (2013) 'Sexual Orientation and Refugee Status Determination over the Past 20 Years: Unsteady Progress through Standard Sequences?', in Thomas Spijkerboer (ed.) *Fleeing Homophobia: Sexual Orientation, Gender Identity and Asylum*, London: Routledge, 32–54, discussing in particular 'discretion' reasoning. In addition to the early pieces cited, see e.g. Kristen Walker (2000) 'Sexuality and Refugee Status in Australia' 12(2) *International Journal of Refugee Law* 175–211, section 3.5, 203–207; Millbank, note 21, 115–138; Michael Carl Budd (2009) *Mistakes in Identity: Sexual Orientation and Credibility in the Asylum Process*, MA Thesis, The American University in Cairo [unpublished] at 30–34; Janna Wessels (2011) 'Sexual Orientation in Refugee Status Determination', RSC Working Paper Series No. 74, University of Oxford, 18–24; Toni Johnson (2011) 'On Silence, Sexuality and Skeletons: Reconceptualizing Narrative in Asylum Hearings', 20(1) *Social & Legal Studies* 57–78; Mathew Schutzer (2012) 'Bringing the Asylum Process Out of the Closet: Promoting the Acknowledgment of LGB Refugees', 13(3) *Georgetown Journal of Gender & the Law* 669–707 (part 3, 685–693); Thomas Spijkerboer (2013) 'Sexual Identity, Normativity and Asylum', in Thomas Spijkerboer (ed.) *Fleeing Homophobia. Sexual Orientation, Gender Identity and Asylum*, London: Routledge, 217–238.

Some reports for NGOs drew attention to 'discretion' reasoning over the years.[85] In particular the 2003 High Court of Australia judgment in S395, which was the first ultimate appellate court anywhere to decide on a sexuality-based asylum claim, boosted the debate with its (narrowly decided) rejection of a discretion requirement.[86] The literature addressing sexuality-based claims developed a pointed critique of 'discretion' reasoning. It was noted that decision-makers rarely spelled out what was meant by 'discretion'.[87] The term is a euphemism, as it connotes prudence and decency while actually referring to a constant state of hiding. 'Discretion' thus trivialises the cases of gay claimants, and not only semantically. Research on Anglophone cases has pointed out that 'discreet' conduct is often framed in terms of reasonableness, naturalness and the social.[88] In these logics, it is only reasonable for claimants to have some respect for the customs and mores of their country of origin. The assumption of a natural choice of discretion[89] also disregards the unreliability of concealment.[90] Moreover, heterosexist biases lead to a perception of simple expressions of gay identities as flaunting displays.[91] This is closely related to the public/private distinction and the reduction of sexual orientation to the private sphere, and essentially, sex.[92] The early literature on 'discretion' in sexuality-based claims was mainly shaped by Millbank, who summarised her extensive research[93] on 'discretion' in case law from Australia, Canada and the United Kingdom as follows:

> At its baldest, discretion reasoning entailed a 'reasonable expectation that persons should, to the extent that it is possible, co-operate in their own protection', by exercising 'self-restraint' such as avoiding any behaviour that would identify them as gay; never telling anyone they were gay; only expressing their sexuality by having anonymous sex in public places; pretending that their partner is a 'flatmate'; or indeed remaining celibate. This approach subverted the aim of the Refugee

[85] Ghassan Kassisieh, note 20, at 64–70 (chapter 7); Tim Cowen, Francesca Stella, Kirsty Magahy, Kendra Strauss and James Morton (2011) 'Sanctuary, Safety and Solidarity: Lesbian, Gay, Bisexual, Transgender Asylum Seekers and Refugees in Scotland', Glasgow: Equality Network, BEMIS and GRAMNe, online: University of Glasgow, www.equality-network.org/wp-content/uploads/2013/05/Sanctuary-Safety-and-Solidarity.pdf (chapter 3). See also a report prepared for the Canadian Immigration Board: Nicole LaViolette (2013) 'Sexual Orientation, Gender Identity and the Refugee Determination Process', report prepared for the Immigration and Refugee Board of Canada, online: Social Science Research Network, http://papers.ssrn.com/sol3/papers.cfm?abstract_id=2276049, 10–11.

[86] Dauvergne and Millbank, note 14, 97–124; Kendall, note 14, 715–749; and exploring the impact of the judgment on UK case law five years later: Millbank, note 14, 391–414.

[87] Millbank, note 7, 497–527, 503.

[88] Millbank, note 87, 32–54; see also Spijkerboer, note 84, 217–238; and Kassisieh, note 20, 64–70.

[89] Ibid., 68–69.

[90] Ibid., 69–70.

[91] Ibid., 64.

[92] Jenni Millbank (2002) 'Imagining Otherness: Refugee Claims on the Basis of Sexuality in Canada and Australia', 26 *Melbourne University Law Review* 144–177.

[93] See Dauvergne and Millbank, note 14, 97–124; Jenni Millbank (2004) 'The Role of Rights in Asylum Claims on the Basis of Sexual Orientation', 4(2) *Human Rights Law Review* 193–228; Millbank, note 21, 115–138.

> Convention – that the receiving state provide a surrogate for protection from the home state – by placing the responsibility of protection upon the applicant: it is he or she who must avoid harm. The discretion approach also varied the scope of protection afforded in relation to each of the five Convention grounds by, for example, protecting the right to be 'openly' religious but not to be openly gay or in an identifiable same-sex relationship ... The idea of discretion reflects broader social norms concerning the 'proper place' of lesbian and gay sexuality, as something to be hidden and reluctantly tolerated, a purely private sexual behaviour rather than an important and integral aspect of identity, or as an apparent relationship status. The discretion approach explicitly posited the principle that human rights protection available to sexual orientation was limited to private consensual sex and did not extend to any other manifestation of sexual identity (which has been variously characterised as 'flaunting' 'displaying' and 'advertising' homosexuality as well as 'inviting' persecution). Thus for example in 2001 the Federal Court of Australia held that the Iranian Penal Code prohibiting homosexuality and imposing a death penalty did 'place limits' on the applicant's behaviour; the applicant had to 'avoid overt and public, or publicly provocative homosexual activity. But having to accept those limits did not amount to persecution'. On appeal, the full Federal Court endorsed the view that 'public manifestation of homosexuality is not an essential part of being homosexual'. The discretion approach thus has had wide-reaching ramifications in terms of framing the human rights of lesbians and gay men to family life, freedom of association and freedom of expression as necessarily lesser in scope than those held by heterosexual people.[94]

This detailed and succinct rejection of 'discretion' was also quoted in the 2010 UK Supreme Court judgment in *HJ (Iran) and HT (Cameroon)*,[95] which could have put an end to such reasoning in claims based on sexual orientation. And in many ways, it did. The judgment, with its clear rejection of any *requirement* to be 'discreet', certainly constitutes a turning point, much more so than the previous 2003 High Court of Australia judgment in S395[96] upon which it draws. In Millbank's words, though not beyond criticism, the judgment in *HJ (Iran) and HT (Cameroon)*, along with the High Court decision in S395,

> advance[s] the development of refugee jurisprudence on sexuality in major ways. These decisions emphatically reject discretion reasoning, affirm that the experience of sexual orientation extends beyond mere private sexual conduct, and articulate the importance of equality—both as between gay and straight people in the country of origin and between sexuality claims and other categories of claimants in the receiving country—in applying the protections of refugee law.[97]

94 Millbank, note 14, 391–414, 393–394, internal references omitted.

95 *HJ (Iran) and HT (Cameroon)* v. *Secretary of State for the Home Department*, note 1, per Lord Walker at 92.

96 *Appellant S395/2002* v. *Minister for Immigration and Multicultural Affairs*; *Appellant S396/2002* v. *Minister for Immigration and Multicultural Affairs*, note 3.

97 Millbank, note 7, 497–527, 500.

This is certainly the case. At the same time, rather than being the end point of the debate on 'discretion', it constitutes a milestone that changed its character. The judgment, representing the first proper attempt to think of sexuality-based claims in the same terms as other grounds, propelled 'discretion' from the margins to the centre of refugee law doctrine. This sparked a remarkable number of responses from the refugee law community,[98] including from scholars who had not previously focused on sexuality-based claims.[99]

Two things became clear: likely thanks to the pointed criticism of 'discretion' in sexuality-based claims – and in response to the observation of discriminatory treatment of such claims vis-à-vis claims on other grounds[100] – the idea was to treat sexuality-based claims *like claims based on the other grounds*. That is, sexuality was integrated into the poorly developed framework for claims based on political opinion and religion. That did not go smoothly, and it allowed brushing over much of the detailed analysis and insights that were developed on sexuality-based claims. This is because there are two important differences: sexuality is generally assumed to be mainly an internal thing that may, in addition, have a public external dimension (or 'cause') that needs to be fought for. In that context, there is no specifically formulated human right that can be drawn on.[101] In contrast, political opinion and religion are generally assumed to be characteristics that are expressed collectively and in the public sphere. They have an internal dimension, but the activity of public expression is an essential part of both religion and political opinion, which is buttressed by specifically formulated human rights. This study will show that reflexively referring to these rights appears to allow much of the detailed analysis/reasoning necessary for sexuality-based claims to be glossed over.

Moreover, *HJ (Iran) and HT (Cameroon)*, and the debate that followed, brought to the fore the previously only looming[102] adaptive character of 'discretion'. Its flimsy, slippery nature as a concept that can adopt many shapes and forms was a key observation of the literature following *HJ (Iran) and HT (Cameroon)*.[103] It was

98 See e.g. S. Chelvan (2011) 'Put Your Hands Up (If You Feel Love)', 25(1) *Journal on Immigration, Asylum and Nationality Law* 56–66; Millbank, note 7, 497–527; Janna Wessels (2013) '"Discretion" in Sexuality-Based Asylum Cases: An Adaptive Phenomenon', in Thomas Spijkerboer (ed.) *Fleeing Homophobia: Sexual Orientation, Gender Identity and Asylum*, London: Routledge, 55–81; Wessels, note 14, 815–839; Satvinder Juss (2015) 'Sexual Orientation and the Sexualisation of Refugee Law', 22 *International Journal on Minority and Group Rights* 128–153.

99 See in particular the contributions to the 2012 special issue in the *NYU Journal of International Law and Politics* (volume 44, issue 2): Hathaway and Pobjoy, note 4, 315–389; Goodman, note 8, 407–446 Tobin, note 57, 447–484; Anker and Ardalan, note 49, 529–557; Verdirame, note 6, 559–572; Richard Buxton, note 6, 391–406; David John Frank, note 46, 485–495.

100 See e.g. Dauvergne and Millbank, note 14, 97–124, 109–114.

101 See e.g. Millbank, note 92, 144–177; and Millbank, note 93, 193–228.

102 See e.g. Millbank, note 14, 391–414, 396–398 (discussing ways of avoiding and undermining the rejection of 'discretion' in S395).

103 Millbank, note 84, 32–54; and Wessels, note 98, 55–81.

recognised that 'discretion' involves any type of reasoning in refugee status determination that builds on the notion that the claimant's persecuted characteristic will not come to the knowledge of the persecutor, or, in other words, that the claimant can pass unnoticed. Thus, 'discretion' reasoning occurs in blatant forms, such as an explicitly formulated 'reasonable requirement to be discreet' and contribute to one's own protection. But it also assumes much more subtle forms; for example, it may form the basis of an 'internal flight alternative' assessment that involves the return to a different part of the country where it is not known that a claimant is gay.[104] It has, therefore, been described as a 'many-headed monster',[105] that is 'one of, if not the, most significant and resilient barriers to fair adjudication of sexual orientation'.[106] It was found to be 'extraordinarily widespread, resistant to challenge and strongly associated with high rejection rates'.[107] Alice Edwards notes on this development that it is unclear '[h]ow discretion crept (back) into refugee claims', but that it 'has the potential to undermine one of the basic tenets of refugee law – that the Convention protects persons who possess a well-founded fear of being persecuted on account of their attributes or opinions'.[108]

In other words, it turned out that the Australian *S395* and the UK *HJ (Iran) and HT (Cameroon)* judgments could not put an end to 'discretion' reasoning. Although the judgments of these two highest courts were described and received as landmark judgments rejecting 'discretion', such reasoning remains prevalent. As noted, various cases concerning 'discretion' were also referred to the Court of Justice of the European Union (CJEU) for a preliminary ruling, two of which – a German religion-based referral and a Dutch sexuality-based referral – led to judgments.[109] The referral from Germany involved the claims of two men of Ahmadi faith from Pakistan and centred on the question of whether public manifestations of religion were protected under refugee law.[110] The Dutch referral concerned three gay men and the question of whether they could be expected to exercise restraint with regards to their sexual orientation.[111] In both cases, and partly using the exact same wording, the CJEU ruled that 'discretion' cannot be required of claimants to protection. These cases brought to light at least three points. Firstly, and arguably by coincidence (an earlier German

[104] See e.g. Millbank, note 14, 391–414, 394.
[105] Spijkerboer, note 84, 217–238, 220.
[106] Millbank, note 7, 497–527, 501.
[107] Ibid., 506.
[108] Alice Edwards (2012) 'Distinction, Discretion, Discrimination: The New Frontiers of Gender-Related Claims to Asylum', *paper delivered at the Gender, Migration and Human Rights Conference at the European University Institute*, Florence, Italy, 19 June 2012, www.refworld.org/docid/4ffd430c2.html, 9. See also very similarly: Volker Türk (2013) 'Ensuring Protection to LGBTI Persons of Concern', opinion delivered at the *Invisible in the City: Urban Protection Gaps Facing Sexual Minorities Fleeing Persecution*, HIAS LGBTI Symposium, 20–21 September 2012, 25(1) *International Journal of Refugee Law* 120–129, 123–124.
[109] On the preliminary ruling procedure see Annex I.
[110] *Federal Republic of Germany* v. *Y and Z*, note 67.
[111] *X, Y and Z* v. *Minister voor Immigratie, Integratie en Asiel*, note 67.

referral of a sexuality-based case had been withdrawn)[112] and possibly chance, the Court had to deal with religion *before* it was concerned with sexuality, which was then considered in the light of and by analogy with the ruling on religion. As in common law jurisdictions, sexuality-based claims were therefore fitted into a scheme that had been developed for another ground. Secondly, the judgments demonstrated that international judicial dialogue between the common law jurisdictions, where most of the debate on 'discretion' had been taking place, and the European civil law jurisdictions remains underdeveloped. The CJEU judgments have each triggered a wave of academic responses, though these were mostly from European lawyers interested in the development of the Common European Asylum System, with substantive analysis on 'discretion' reasoning often limited.[113] And, thirdly, little to nothing is known on 'discretion' reasoning in these jurisdictions. Although there is some research into sexuality-based claims in many European jurisdictions,[114] very little

[112] Reference for a preliminary ruling from the Oberverwaltungsgericht für das Land Nordrhein-Westfalen (Germany) lodged on 1 December 2010, *Kashayar Khavand* v. *Federal Republic of Germany (Case C-563/10).*

[113] On *Y and Z*, see e.g.: Luc Leboeuf and Evangelia (Lilian) Tsourdi (2013) 'Towards a Re-definition of Persecution? Assessing the Potential Impact of Y and Z', 13(2) *Human Rights Law Review* 402–415, at section 4, 412–414 (relevance of 'discretion' mainly assessed with a view to the potential relevance for LGBT claimants); Julian Lehmann (2014) 'Persecution, Concealment and the Limits of a Human Rights Approach in (European) Asylum Law – The Case of Germany v. Y and Z in the Court of Justice of the European Union' 26(1) *International Journal of Refugee* Law 65–81; Eleanor Drywood (2014) 'Who's In and Who's Out? The Court's Emerging Case Law on the Definition of a Refugee', 51 *Common Market Law Review* 1093–1124 (brief discussion essentially taking note that concealment was rejected at 1106–1116); Alexandra Maria Rodrigues Araújo (2014) 'The Qualification for Being a Refugee under EU Law: Religion as a Reason for Persecution – Court of Justice of the European Union (Grand Chamber), Judgment of 5 September 2012, Joined Cases C-71/11 and C-99/11, Bundesrepublik Deutschland v. Y and Z', 16(4) *European Journal of Migration and Law* 535–558; Roland Bank (2016) 'Refugee Law Jurisprudence from Germany and Human Rights: Cutting Edge or Chilling Effect?', in Bruce Burson and David Cantor (eds.) *Human Rights and the Refugee Definition – Comparative Legal Practice and Theory*, Leiden: Brill Nijhoff, 156–179.

On X, Y *and* Z see e.g.: International Commission of Jurists (2014) 'X, Y and Z: a Glass Half Full for "Rainbow Refugees"?', *The International Commission of Jurists' Observations on the Judgment of the Court of Justice of the European Union in* X, Y *and* Z v. *Minister voor Immigratie en Asiel*, ICJ, Geneva, Switzerland; Maarten den Heijer (2014) 'Persecution for Reason of Sexual Orientation: X, Y and Z', 51(4) *Common Market Law Review* 1217–1234; Alice Edwards (2014) 'X, Y and Z: The "A, B, C" of Claims Based on Sexual Orientation and/or Gender Identity?', UN High Commissioner for Refugees (UNHCR), International Commission of Jurists: Expert Roundtable on Asylum Claims Based on Sexual Orientation or Gender Identity or Expression, Brussels, 27 June 2014, www.refworld.org/docid/53bb99984.html.

For a comparative analysis of the CJEU judgments with case law of the European Court of Human Rights on these issues, see: Pasquale Annicchino (2015) 'The Persecution of Religious and LGBTI Minorities and Asylum Law: Recent Trends in the Adjudication of European Supranational Courts', 21(3) *European Public Law* 571–590.

[114] Recent studies were conducted on Norway: Deniz Akin (2017) 'Queer Asylum Seekers: Translating Sexuality in Norway', 43(3) *Journal of Ethnic and Migration Studies* 458–474; Deniz Akin (2015) 'Assessing Sexual Orientation-Based Persecution – A Closer Look at the Norwegian Practices of Asylum Evaluation of Gay and Lesbian Claimants', 1 *Föreningen*

attention has been paid to 'discretion'.[115] The 2011 *Fleeing Homophobia* report, which was the first comparative review of European jurisprudence on sexuality-based asylum claims, provides at least a glimpse. It revealed that 'discretion' reasoning was prevalent in decision-making in the majority of European jurisdictions.[116] However, the research was completed before the 'turning point' of the UK Supreme Court judgment in *HJ (Iran) and HT (Cameroon)* and the subsequent CJEU judgments on the matter.

Overall, research with a main focus on 'discretion' is surprisingly rare,[117] and is usually in response to important judgments.[118] So far, there has been no principled attempt to approach the phenomenon in a larger study. In particular, following the only recent recognition that essentially both ('discretion' and 'activity-based risks') address the same phenomenon, there is a lack of research that connects the separate camps of the discourse on 'discretion' on sexuality-based claims and claims based on other grounds. Moreover, with very few exceptions, the debate has largely taken place based on research on the English-speaking common law jurisdictions, leaving a large blind spot concerning other European civil law jurisdictions.[119]

This is where the present study picks up: the subject of analysis is 'discretion' reasoning in refugee law. It steps into the twofold research gap that emerges from the

Lambda Nordica 19–42; on Portugal: Nuno Ferreira (2015) 'Portuguese Refugee Law in the European Context: The Case of Sexuality-Based Claims', 27(3) *International Journal of Refugee Law* 411–432; and the Netherlands: Max Smeulders (2016) *Somewhere over the Rainbow: The Contemporary Situation for LGBTI Asylum Seekers in the Netherlands*, master thesis, Tilburg University, Tilburg Law School. International and European law, track International law and Human Rights, 2015–2016, http://arno.uvt.nl/show.cgi?fid=141905.

115 For rare exceptions see on the Netherlands: Hemme Battjes (2013) 'Accommodation: Sur place Claims and the Accommodation Requirement', in Thomas Spijkerboer (ed.) *Fleeing Homophobia – Sexual Orientation, Gender Identity and Asylum*, London: Routledge, 82–97 (discussing what he calls the 'accommodation' requirement for *sur place* sexuality-based claims in the Netherlands); and on the United States and Australia: Heather Kolinsky (2016) 'The Shibboleth of Discretion: The Discretion, Identity, and Persecution Paradigm in American and Australian LGBT Asylum Claims, 31(2) *Berkeley Journal of Gender, Law & Justice* 206–240.

116 Sabine Jansen and Thomas Spijkerboer (2011) *Fleeing Homophobia, Asylum Claims Related to Sexual Orientation and Gender Identity in Europe*, Vrije Universiteit Amsterdam, September 2011, 33–39.

117 See for exceptions: Venice Choi (2010) 'Living Discreetly: A Catch 22 in Refugee Status Determinations on the Basis of Sexual Orientation', 36(1) *Brooklyn Journal of International Law* 241–263 and Toni Johnson (2007) 'Flamers, Flaunting and Permissible Persecution', 15(1) *Feminist Legal Studies* 99–111. See also Gabriel Ku Wei Bin (2014) *No Freedom in a Closet: The Persistence of Discretion Reasoning in the Refugee Status Determination Process for Lesbian, Gay, and Bisexual Asylum Applications to the European Union*, master's thesis, Lund University, Faculty of Law, Spring 2014, Lund University Student Papers, https://lup.lub.lu.se/student-papers/search/publication/4500056.

118 See e.g. Nora Markard (2013) 'Sexuelle Orientierung als Fluchtgrund – Das Ende der "Diskretion" – Aktuelle Entwicklungen beim Flüchtlingsschutz aufgrund der sexuellen Orientierung', *Asylmagazin* 3/2013, 74–84.

119 For recent examples, see: Stefan Vogler (2016) 'Legally Queer: The Construction of Sexuality in LGBQ Asylum Claims', 50(4) *Law & Society Review* 856–889.

literature – on the one hand, it seeks to *broaden* the knowledge on 'discretion' by providing an assessment of decision-making practice and literature from key European civil law jurisdictions. On the other hand, it seeks to *deepen* the knowledge on 'discretion' by undertaking a principled analysis of 'discretion' reasoning in refugee law, connecting insights from sexuality-based claims and queer theory with other Convention grounds and refugee law more broadly.

The starting point of the study is the observation that although it is regularly rejected in forceful terms both in jurisprudence and in scholarship for undermining the very rationale of refugee protection, 'discretion' reasoning has proven to be astoundingly multifaceted and resilient. The guiding question is: why is 'discretion' so difficult to get rid of?

In order to explore the resilience and pervasiveness of the phenomenon, the study uses sexuality as a lens through which to look at the refugee definition more broadly. To this end, the analysis draws on queer theory, which proves to be particularly fruitful as it has dealt with many of the relevant issues before. The aim is to illustrate that much may be gleaned from sexuality claims that also applies to the Convention grounds political opinion and religion. Although to varying degrees, the other Convention grounds similarly respond to logics of revelation and free choice. If ready acceptance of the 'internal' dimension of sexuality is due to homophobia – that is, it only appears logical or 'rational' that gay people would seek to hide their sexual orientation in a generalised anti-gay climate – then by analogy, a persecutory environment may function as a 'closet' also, for example, for political opinion and religion cases. The need to hide one's 'true beliefs' from persecutors, or society at large, emphasises the internal dimension of such characteristics as well. Note that the same may apply to claims based on race or nationality as well, which must not necessarily be immediately visible in all cases. 'Discretion' – and its opposite, disclosure – are a product of the 'closet' that persecution creates. This invites the transferral of queer theory elements to understand certain dynamics in refugee law more broadly – namely, the conceptual distinction between acts and identity (act/identity dichotomy). This concept enables us to grasp the effects of 'discretion' logic which apply to all Convention grounds. Queer theorists, such as Eve Kosofsky Sedgwick[120] and Janet Halley,[121] provide the theoretical framework to conceptualise the act/identity distinction underlying 'discretion' reasoning. The adoption of this subdominant perspective enables the book to break new ground not 'just' regarding sexual orientation claims, but with a view to the refugee definition as such.

[120] Sedgwick, note 15.

[121] Janet Halley (1993) 'Reasoning about Sodomy: Act and Identity in and after Bowers v. Hardwick', 79(7) *Virginia Law Review* 1721–1780.

Looking at refugee law through the lens of the act/identity dichotomy allows for an exploration of 'discretion' reasoning even where it is not readily recognisable. And it quickly becomes clear that any discussion of 'discretion' simultaneously asks the larger question of what it is that is protected under refugee law. The scope of protection is the flipside of 'discretion' reasoning. Because it refers to the way the claimant expresses the characteristic that is the reason for persecution, 'discretion' is the site where the extent of the Convention grounds is negotiated in refugee law. An analysis of 'discretion' therefore involves an investigation of the ways in which the scope of protection is constructed and defined. In which ways is it limited? How are those limitations justified? Moreover, 'discretion' refers to the ways in which a claimant relates to the reason for persecution – their (gay, political, religious) identity and the ways in which they are expressed. Another set of questions, therefore, relates to the role of the claimant in refugee status assessment. Are they in any way responsible for their own persecution or protection? Then what role does the persecutor play?

To engage with these questions, the book proceeds as follows. The focus of the analysis is the definition of the refugee contained in the 1951 Convention as the 'cornerstone of the international refugee protection regime'.[122] While acknowledging that the separation of the different elements of the definition for analysis has been criticised as artificial,[123] this study proceeds on the basis that a 'holistic' approach risks masking error.[124] Indeed, this study reveals how the Convention grounds can be, and very often are, split into an act and an identity element which are then 'moved around' independently and affect other elements of the definition. It thus supports the necessity of a principled and systematic assessment that is conscious of the different functions and meanings of the various elements of the definition, while remaining alert to their interplay.[125]

In many ways, 'sexual orientation claims are very much at the heart of what refugee law *is* and *should be*'.[126] This is because their relatively recent advent represented particular challenges for decision-makers and refugee lawyers: sexual orientation was not foreseen as a Convention ground at the time the Refugee Convention was drafted. It was not until the early to mid-1990s that it was recognised that sexual minorities were subjected to persecution in many parts of the world.

[122] UNHCR ExCom (2005) *Conclusion on the Provision on International Protection Including through Complementary Forms of Protection*, Executive Committee of the High Commissioner's Programme, 7 October 2005, No. 103 (LVI).

[123] See e.g. *Demirkaya* v. *Secretary of State for the Home Department* [1999] Imm AR 498, United Kingdom: Court of Appeal (England and Wales), 23 July 1999, per Stuart-Smith LJ.

[124] See Michelle Foster (2007) *International Refugee Law and Socio-Economic Rights – Refuge from Deprivation*, Cambridge Studies in International and Comparative Law, Cambridge: Cambridge University Press, 25.

[125] *Refugee Appeal* No. 74665/03, note 41.

[126] David Cantor (2014) *Introductory Remarks*, ICJ Second Expert Roundtable on Asylum Claims Based on Sexual Orientation or Gender Identity, Friday 3 October 2014, London.

Dozens of countries continue to criminalise homosexuality, some of them apply the death sentence, and gay people are often subject to severe harm from non-state actors. But sexual orientation is not one of the listed Convention grounds – 'fitting' these claims into the refugee definition involved a process of 'legal gymnastics'.[127] The book argues that the struggles over understanding whether and how sexual minorities 'fit' the categories of the refugee definition have caused – or brought to light – some conceptual disruption, in particular as regards the Convention grounds. Recognising this disruption in the context of sexuality-based claims, where it comes to the fore most readily, permits deeper insights into similar dynamics in the other Convention grounds as well. The book therefore draws out what 'discretion reasoning' reveals about the concept and role of the Convention grounds and the scope of refugee protection more broadly.

Finally, the debate on 'discretion' gets muddled up with human rights arguments, where human rights are variously referred to in conflicting ways. This is usually linked to the assumption that the Refugee Convention does not guarantee the same level of rights and freedoms to all; that is, asylum seekers cannot claim a right to live 'as openly and freely' as they could in the receiving country. One of the aims of the book is, therefore, an assessment of the role and place of human rights in the context of 'discretion' reasoning.

All of these questions combine to an overarching enquiry into what is protected under refugee law and why. That is, 'discretion' reasoning is discussed as a site where the scope of protection is negotiated in refugee law.

As such, this book is a critical project. Looking at the refugee definition through the lens of the act/identity dichotomy, it seeks to draw out broader patterns and underlying assumptions that are taken for granted. And, indeed, it gets messy. A systematic assessment of 'discretion' reasoning has the potential to unsettle a series of established notions of refugee law and brings to light certain conceptual tensions. It uncovers the ways in which 'discretion' reasoning destabilises the concept of the refugee by exposing its inherent paradoxes. Consequently, the book demonstrates that 'discretion' reasoning, in some form, is inherent in the paradoxical nature of the refugee concept. The malleability that 'discretion' contains is both a necessity and a serious risk for refugee protection.

The main argument that the book advances is that the core of the dispute is, in fact, a different puzzle. The various shapes 'discretion' takes represent different ways of handling that puzzle. The dispute on 'discretion' reasoning regularly draws on two equally accepted but somewhat contradictory notions of refugee law. The first is the general acceptance that the Convention grounds are so 'fundamental to human

[127] Siobhán Mullally (2013) 'Gender and Asylum Law: Providing Transformative Remedies?', in Satvinder Juss and Colin Harvey (eds.) *Contemporary Issues in Refugee Law*, Cheltenham: Edward Elgar, 196–225, 215; see also: Thomas Spijkerboer (2000) *Gender and Refugee Status*, Aldershot: Ashgate.

identity that one should not be compelled to hide, change or renounce them in order to avoid persecution'.[128] The rationale is that to do so would 'undermine one of the basic tenets of refugee law – that the Convention protects persons who possess a well-founded fear of being persecuted on account of their attributes or opinions'.[129] The logic is clear: if it were required to hide the reasons for persecution, then there would be no need for refugee law. Precisely because the Convention reasons *can* (for the most part) be hidden, it cannot be an answer to persecution to tell claimants to forego them. This position will be referred to as the 'fundamentality principle'.

The fundamentality principle clashes with the widely accepted notion that the Refugee Convention is not there to provide a 'world wide guarantee' of freedoms[130] and, therefore, claimants cannot expect to be able to 'live as freely and openly' as they could in the country of asylum.[131] This is encapsulated in the notion of 'surrogate' protection:[132] the country of asylum steps in only if the country of origin is unable or unwilling to protect a person from persecution, defined as 'serious violations' of 'core' or 'basic' human rights.[133] This position will be referred to as the 'severity argument' – or, sometimes, the 'triviality concern'.

[128] UNHCR (2004) *Guidelines on International Protection No. 6: Religion-Based Refugee Claims under Article 1A(2) of the 1951 Convention and/or the 1967 Protocol Relating to the Status of Refugees*, 28 April 2004, HCR/GIP/04/06, www.refworld.org/docid/4090f9794.html, at 13. See also UNHCR (2002) *Guidelines on International Protection No. 2: 'Membership of a Particular Social Group' within the Context of Article 1A(2) of the 1951 Convention and/or Its 1967 Protocol Relating to the Status of Refugees*, 7 May 2002, HCR/GIP/02/02, www.refworld.org/docid/3d36f23f4.html, paragraph 6. Similarly, in internal flight or relocation cases, the claimant should not be expected or required to suppress his or her religious views to avoid persecution in the internal flight or relocation area. See UNHCR (2003) *Guidelines on International Protection No. 4: 'Internal Flight or Relocation Alternative' within the Context of Article 1A(2) of the 1951 Convention and/or 1967 Protocol Relating to the Status of Refugees*, 23 July 2003, HCR/GIP/03/04, www.refworld.org/docid/3f2791a44.html, at 19, 25.

[129] Edwards, note 108. See also McHugh and Kirby JJ in their joint submission in the Australian High Court case of *Appellant S395/2002* v. *Minister for Immigration and Multicultural Affairs; Appellant S396/2002* v. *Minister for Immigration and Multicultural Affairs*, note 3, at 13: 'The object of the signatories to the Convention was to protect the holding of such beliefs, opinions, membership and origins by giving the persons concerned refuge in the signatory countries when their country of nationality would not protect them. It would undermine the object of the Convention if the signatory countries required them to modify their beliefs or opinions or to hide their race, nationality or membership of particular social groups before those countries would give them protection under the Convention.'

[130] *Ahmad and Others* v. *Secretary of State for the Home Department*, [1990] Imm AR 61, United Kingdom: Court of Appeal (England and Wales), 6 October 1989, per Farquharson LJ.

[131] *HJ (Iran) and HT (Cameroon)* v. *Secretary of State for the Home Department*, note 1, per Lord Hope at 35: 'it would be wrong to approach the issue on the basis that the purpose of the Convention is to guarantee to an applicant who is gay that he can live as freely and as openly as a gay person as he would be able to do if he were not returned'.

[132] See Hathaway, note 78.

[133] See Ibid., 104–112; and Article 3 of the *Qualification Directive*: Directive 2011/95/EU of the European Parliament and of the Council of 13 December 2011 on standards for the qualification of third-country nationals or stateless persons as beneficiaries of international protection, for a uniform status for refugees or for persons eligible for subsidiary protection, and for the

That is, while on the one hand, claimants cannot be required to hide the characteristic they are persecuted for,[134] on the other hand they are not entitled to the same level of rights and freedoms as might be available elsewhere.[135] This creates a paradox: Where does it leave the claimant and their capacity to express or draw attention to their religion, political opinion or sexual orientation? More broadly, what does it mean for the concept of the Convention ground?

The book suggests that this is the central conflict of the debates, which leaves the claimant in a highly vulnerable position, simultaneously entitled to and restricted from the reason for persecution. As a consequent expression of that clash, the claimant's conduct, identity and rights become the focus of the analysis, while the persecutor is lost from view – and it becomes clear that the role and place of the Convention grounds has not been conceptualised to a sufficient degree in refugee law doctrine.

This conflict cuts across another, underlying tension, the two poles of which are refugee protection as a common good and limited protection capacity. As the study will show, *both* approaches subscribe to the general need for refugee protection while attempting to respond to limitation of capacity. But the assumptions as to how to legitimately limit, that is, which specific act/identity-patterns are deemed worthy of protection, are at least partly a function of the prioritisation of the fundamentality principle or the severity argument respectively. To the extent that severity/fundamentality are in an unstable relationship and the focus can be flipped, the tension of these two central notions of refugee law doctrine in fact represents a particularly powerful and dynamic mechanism to respond to limited protection capacity. The logic of this dynamic is therefore not fully grasped, encompassed or resolved by reference to a proportionality assessment or by analogy with the assessment of the scope of a positive obligation. However, it unfolds against the backdrop of limited capacity for necessary protection and needs to be read in that light.

This can be illustrated by way of the *HJ (Iran) and HT (Cameroon)* versus Hathaway and Pobjoy dispute outlined. The UK Supreme Court judgment and Hathaway and Pobjoy's approach can both be analysed in light of the tension between the fundamentality principle and the severity argument. They equally subscribe to both principles, but each side slightly prefers one over the other in a situation of conflict. Whereas both the UK Supreme Court and Hathaway and Pobjoy seek to draw lines, they draw them in different places. The UK Supreme Court – and, as it seems, the High Court of Australia – prioritises the fundamentality principle: a claimant cannot be required to forego their characteristic *in order to*

content of the protection granted (recast), oj L 337/9, 20 December 2011 (*Recast Qualification Directive*).

[134] *Appellant S395/2002* v. *Minister for Immigration and Multicultural Affairs*; *Appellant S396/2002* v. *Minister for Immigration and Multicultural Affairs*, note 3, at 489.

[135] *HJ (Iran) and HT (Cameroon)* v. *Secretary of State for the Home Department*, note 1, per Lord Hope at 35.

avoid persecution. The UK Supreme Court would allow those claims where the changed behaviour is due to fear of persecution (and not merely a 'choice' flowing from other personal considerations). Here, the limitation lies in the claimant's motives. In line with this, the UK Supreme Court undertakes a factual assessment of what the claimant will do and only accepts limitations that are not motivated by the avoidance of persecution, but rather by what they term personal choice. On its face, the UK Supreme Court thus avoids any *requirement* of 'discretion', though it can be questioned to what extent 'discretion' can be voluntary in any real sense in a persecutory environment.[136] In contrast, Hathaway and Pobjoy, and the New Zealand Refugee Appeals Authority, draw on the severity argument. They agree that those claims should not be allowed that entail a change of behaviour on the 'margins' of the 'relevant right'. Marginal – or 'trivial' – activity cannot lead to protection, precisely because refugee law is not to guarantee the same standard of rights and freedoms to all. Therefore, Hathaway and Pobjoy call for some restraint on the part of the claimants to be in line with the severity standard of the Convention.

Thus, the clash of two fundamental notions of refugee law doctrine concerning the limits of protection materialises in the debate on 'discretion' reasoning in refugee status determination. The two approaches have certain things in common on one level, but are difficult to reconcile on another. In both approaches, a sense of a need to somehow 'limit' the scope of protection in order to avoid refugees 'by choice' prevails.[137] The approaches of the UK Supreme Court and Hathaway and Pobjoy have in common that they focus on the claimants' future behaviour to achieve this. As such, they both rely on the assumption that secrecy is synonymous with safety: the rationale is that if the claimant does *not* behave in a particular way, they are not at risk. The difference lies in the conclusions drawn from this situation. In a concern to provide for a degree of objectivity, independent of the claimant's proposed future conduct, the Hathaway/Pobjoy solution considers it legitimate to prescribe conduct by classifying protected and unprotected activities, effectively excluding persecution arising from unprotected conduct from protection – and therefore, requiring restraint (or 'discretion'). The UK Supreme Court, in contrast, refuses to exclude persecution arising from certain types of conduct (and therefore, to require 'discretion'), focusing on the harm the claimant would face rather than the way in which it was triggered. But in the event that it finds that a claimant will in fact abstain from acts triggering persecution (i.e. in fact be 'discreet'), it distinguishes between the motives behind that abstention (fear versus choice).

[136] Such that the UK Supreme Court might in effect still be imposing 'discretion' without acknowledging it; see Wessels, note 14, 815–839.

[137] *Mendis* v. *Immigration Appeal Tribunal and Secretary of State for the Home Department*, note 16.

As a consequence of the clash between the fundamentality principle and the severity argument, the claimant and their capacity to exercise restraint (or 'discretion') become the focus of the analysis. Based on queer theory, the complex relationship of their acts and identity can be described as contradictory – though inherently connected, the concepts are consistently understood as separate. As a result of this arrangement, decision-makers, persecutors and scholars can make use of this unstable relation between acts and identity and play them against each other.[138] This provides opportunities for exclusion: certain identities may be deemed protected, whereas some related conduct may be understood to fall outside the scope of protection and vice versa. This reasoning places the focus on the claimant, rather than the persecutor, questioning whether they are entitled to whatever it is that triggers persecution and, consequently, making the claimant responsible for the feared persecution. If the claimant's act is found to be outside the scope of protection, then the persecutor's infliction of harm is outside the scope of refugee law. So the focus shifts away from the *act* of persecution – located with the persecutor – and to the *reason* for persecution (the Convention ground) – located with the claimant.

Framing the issue of 'discretion' as a materialisation of the clash of two fundamental notions of accepted refugee law doctrine sheds light on the persistence of the long-standing debate, the harsh tone of the latest controversy and the formation of opposing 'camps', and the perplexity as to how to deal with behaviour doctrinally. But while analysing the debate as part of a broader discussion in refugee law doctrine helps situate and untangle the different positions, it cannot 'solve' the issue. Quite the contrary: everyone will go on subscribing to the two fundamental ideas, which are in tension, so there can be no enduring solution. If the debate moves elsewhere, the instability will move with it.

The guiding question for this study is therefore: why is 'discretion' reasoning so difficult to get rid of? And what does the controversy around concealment tell us about the scope of protection in refugee law? The study explores 'discretion' reasoning as a site for the negotiation of the protective scope of the Convention in two major sections. The first part focuses on European jurisprudence, which is then tied back into international refugee law doctrine in the second part.

Specifically, the argument unfolds as follows. Chapter 2 lays out the theoretical concepts underlying the analysis as well as the methods employed for this study. The following four chapters constitute Part I, which zooms in on Europe. It is designed as an exploratory and analytical exercise that identifies and examines three different variants of 'discretion' and their adaptability in France, Germany and Spain. It consists of an empirical analysis of decision-making practice concerning sexuality-based asylum claims in these three European civil law jurisdictions. After a brief overview of the institutional and jurisprudential context that frames developments concerning 'discretion' reasoning and sexuality-based claims in the European Union

[138] Halley, note 121, 1721–1780, 1749.

in the past years (Chapter 3), the jurisdictions are addressed in turn: Chapter 4 looks at 'discretion' reasoning in sexuality-based asylum claims in France, Chapter 5 addresses Germany and Chapter 6 examines practice in Spain. Sexuality-based claims were chosen as a case study in Part I since based on the recent experience in the Anglophone common law jurisdictions, 'discretion' logics were expected to most readily appear in this subset of claims. The main objective here is to trace how these claims are constructed. In other words, the primary exercise is not to sort out which of the elements in decision-making practice are right and which are wrong applications of the law, but to explore patterns in and across decisions and to identify the consequences of the ways these claims are represented.

Part II is dedicated to the implications of these constructions for refugee law doctrine more broadly. It applies the insights drawn from Part I to scrutinise the different ways in which the scope of protection is defined through different conceptualisations of the Convention grounds. Although 'discretion' logics regularly slip into other elements of the definition, they originate at the level of the Convention grounds, as this is where the act/identity dichotomy emerges. These conceptualisations of the reasons for persecution each validate 'discretion' in their own way: the role of both the claimant's and the persecutor's motives in defining the persecuted and the protected group in the context of claims based on political opinion (Chapter 7), the long-standing controversy over how to define membership of a particular social group (Chapter 8) and the effect of a human rights-based understanding of religion as a persecution ground (Chapter 9). In other words, Part II turns the analysis around and looks at different approaches to conceptualising the Convention grounds in order to draw out where 'discretion' logics emerge before slipping elsewhere into the analysis. It assesses different approaches both across time – ranging from the earliest scholarship on refugee law to modern approaches; across Convention grounds – focusing in turn on political opinion, membership of a particular social group, and religion; and across jurisdictions, as it reconnects the European with common law perspectives. Finally, the concluding Chapter 10 draws together the findings and insights on the various conundrums and paradoxes that shape the concealment controversy and discusses their implications for the future of refugee law.

As such, while the two parts differ in approach and objectives, they complement each other to form a fuller picture of the place of 'discretion' reasoning in refugee law – and a new perspective on what refugee law protects and why. Naturally, the present study does not provide the only possible reading of decision-making practice. This approach has been chosen in the spirit that 'different perspectives provide different forms of knowledge about a phenomenon so that, together, they produce a broader understanding',[139] and can therefore be seen as a contribution to the discursive struggle within the field of refugee law.

[139] Marianne Phillips and Louise J. Jorgensen (2002) *Discourse Analysis as Theory and Method*, London: Sage Publications, 4.

2

Unpacking the Controversy

Theory and Methods

By using sexuality as a lens, this study uncovers a fundamental tension at the core of the refugee concept. It achieves this by employing queer theory elements that allow for the identification of the range of different shapes that 'discretion' reasoning adopts (in Part I). This in turn enables it to connect the different strands of the long-standing, looming debate concerning the question of whether and under which circumstances the claimant must contribute to their own protection by avoiding persecution in Part II. The adoption of this subdominant perspective thus leads not only to a fuller understanding of sexual orientation claims, but of the refugee definition generally.

2.1 DEFINITION OF KEY TERMS

Before delving any further into the topic, it is necessary to clarify the terminology used in this research. In terms of a constructionist approach, language matters because it simultaneously creates and constrains reality by providing the categories in which we are able to order it.

The core concept under study is referred to as 'discretion' reasoning, where 'discretion' is used in quotation marks. Though it has often (rightly) been criticised as being a euphemism that 'does not tell the whole truth',[1] it has remained the key term used to refer to the concept under study.[2] Other, more accurate terms have often been suggested – such as 'concealment'[3] or

[1] *HJ (Iran) and HT (Cameroon)* v. *Secretary of State for the Home Department* [2010] UKSC 31, United Kingdom: Supreme Court, 7 July 2010, per Lord Hope at 22.

[2] See for example the work of Jenni Millbank cited previously.

[3] James Hathaway (2014) 'The Conundrum of Concealment: Minister for Immigration and Border Protection v SZSCA [2013] FCAFC 155', *Melbourne Law School High Court Blog: Opinions on High*, 9 November 2014, https://blogs.unimelb.edu.au/opinionsonhigh/2014/11/09/hathaway-szsca-fcafc.

'accommodation'[4] – but none has taken hold in the way 'discretion' has. In order to connect with existing research and avoid further confusion in a field with highly disputed terminology, 'discretion' is employed despite its obvious drawbacks[5] – the quotation marks signal the insufficiency of the term.

The book uses asylum claims based on sexual orientation as a case study. In this context, it is important to note that the appropriate labels for sexual orientations are continuously debated. One of the main issues is that, regardless of which terminology is chosen, it will not accord with the self-understanding of many of those supposed to be embraced by this terminology. Concerns include the occlusion, inappropriate conflation or bifurcation and exclusion of certain identities, as well as cross-cultural issues.[6]

Fully acknowledging that the terms and categories are insufficient, the book proceeds on the basis of terminology following the Yogyakarta Principles,[7] the Media Reference Guide of the Gay & Lesbian Alliance against Defamation[8] and the International Lesbian, Gay, Bisexual, Trans and Intersex Association (ILGA) Europe.[9] Accordingly, for the purposes of this study, 'sexual orientation' is used to refer to a person's capacity for emotional, affectional and/or physical attraction to,

[4] Hemme Battjes (2013) 'Accommodation: Sur place Claims and the Accommodation Requirement', in Thomas Spijkerboer (ed.) *Fleeing Homophobia: Sexual Orientation, Gender Identity and Asylum*, London: Routledge, 82–97.

[5] An additional source of confusion is of course the fact that 'discretion' is also a technical legal term for acting on one's own authority and judgment. This is expressly *not* the intended meaning of the term used here.

[6] Sean Rehaag (2009) 'Bisexuals Need Not Apply: A Comparative Appraisal of Refugee Law and Policy in Canada, the United States, and Australia', 13(2) *International Journal of Human Rights* 415–436, 416.

[7] The *Yogyakarta Principles on the Application of International Human Rights Law in Relation to Sexual Orientation and Gender Identity* are a set of international principles relating to sexual orientation and gender identity. The document contains 29 Principles and recommendations to governments, regional intergovernmental institutions, civil society and the UN, adopted unanimously by members of the International Commission of Jurists and human rights experts from around the world at a meeting on Java from 6 to 9 November in 2006. See International Commission of Jurists (2007) *Yogyakarta Principles on the Application of International Human Rights Law in Relation to Sexual Orientation and Gender Identity*, March 2007, www.yogyakartaprinciples.org.

[8] The Gay & Lesbian Alliance Against Defamation (GLAAD) is a media-monitoring organisation that works toward public acceptance of LGBT people and to prevent the defamation of LGBT people in the media. Their activities include the publication of the 'Media Reference Guide' that promotes fair, accurate and inclusive reporting of LBGT issues. See Gay & Lesbian Alliance against Defamation (2016) *Media Reference Guide* (10th ed.), New York, October 2016.

[9] ILGA Europe is the European branch of the International Lesbian, Gay, Bisexual, Trans and Intersex Association. As an umbrella organisation, it brings together close to 500 non-governmental organisations from 45 European countries. ILGA Europe provides a regularly updated glossary with the most commonly used phrases: ILGA Europe (2015) *Glossary*, www.ilga-europe.org/media/2431.

and intimate and sexual relations with, individuals of a different gender or the same gender or more than one gender.[10] Sexual orientation means an enduring erotic, affectional or romantic attraction to individuals of a particular gender. The adjective 'gay' is used in preference to homosexual to describe people attracted to members of the same sex. 'Gay man' is used to refer specifically to male same-sex attracted individuals; 'lesbian' is used to describe same-sex attracted women. 'Gay people' refers to both men and women.[11] The term 'homosexual' is largely avoided as it is outdated and considered derogatory and offensive by many gay people.[12] The words 'heterosexual' and 'straight' will be used interchangeably to describe people whose enduring physical, romantic and/or emotional attraction is to people of the opposite sex.[13] 'Heteronormativity' refers to cultural and social practices that present heterosexuality as the only 'normal' sexuality.[14]

The term 'queer' is used as an inclusive adjective to refer to non-straight people, who are also referred to as 'sexual minorities'. Queer – a traditionally abusive term – has been reclaimed by some, though it is not universally accepted within the community.[15] However, it has become an 'academic term' for lesbians, gay men, bisexuals and trans people.[16] In particular, queer theory is established as a field of post-structuralist critical theory that challenges heteronormative social constructions of sexuality and gender.[17] As the present study is situated within that context, the term 'queer' is used in that vein.

Although in much of the literature – as well as, for example, the UNHCR *Guidelines on International Protection* – lesbians and gay men are considered at the same time as bisexual[18] and transgender,[19] and often also

10 See preamble of the Yogyakarta Principles: International Commission of Jurists, note 7.

11 Gay & Lesbian Alliance against Defamation, note 8, 6.

12 Ibid., 8.

13 Ibid., 6.

14 ILGA Europe, note 9, 6.

15 Gay & Lesbian Alliance against Defamation, note 8, 6.

16 ILGA Europe, note 9, 7.

17 Ibid., 7.

18 A bisexual person is a 'person who has the capacity to form enduring physical, romantic, and/or emotional attractions to those of the same gender or to those of another gender. People may experience this attraction in differing ways and degrees over their lifetime. Bisexual people need not have had specific sexual experiences to be bisexual; in fact, they need not have had any sexual experience at all to identify as bisexual', Gay & Lesbian Alliance against Defamation, note 8, 6.

19 Transgender is an 'umbrella term for people whose gender identity and/or gender expression differs from what is typically associated with the sex they were assigned at birth. People under the transgender umbrella may describe themselves using one or more of a wide variety of terms – including transgender ... Many transgender people are prescribed hormones by their doctors to bring their bodies into alignment with their gender identity. Some undergo surgery as well. But not all transgender people can or will take those steps, and a transgender identity is not dependent upon physical appearance or medical procedures'. Gay & Lesbian Alliance against Defamation, note 8, 10.

intersex[20] people (which has led to the acronym LGBT or LGBTI), this study looks at gay men and lesbians only. This decision has been made for the following reasons. Firstly, bisexuality tends to be less visible and there are only a very small number of reported bisexual refugee decisions.[21] Rehaag has shown in his research that bisexuals who allege persecution on account of their sexual orientation face extra obstacles that differ from those of gay men and lesbians.[22] Therefore, they are largely excluded from this study, although some references are made for illustrative purposes. Secondly, although transgender people are often mentioned in the same breath as gay people, this is in fact an 'erroneous association';[23] gender identity and sexual orientation are not the same. Transgender people may be straight, lesbian, gay or bisexual. For example, a man who transitions from male to female and is attracted to other women would be identified as a lesbian. Moreover, transgender persons often express their identity through visible physical difference, meaning 'discretion' does not play out in the same way for these claimants.[24]

2.2 THEORETICAL FRAMEWORK

Against this backdrop, the following section develops the theoretical framework for the present analysis. The core analytical tool is the act/identity dichotomy, which is drawn from queer theory, building on discourse analysis. It is related to, but distinct from, the public/private divide, another common theme in queer and gender studies. Both behaviour and identity cut across the public/private divide, though different measures of publicness and privateness may apply, depending on the location. In this sense, the act/identity distinction adds a further layer of analysis.[25]

[20] Intersex 'relates to a range of physical traits or variations that lie between stereotypical ideals of male and female. Intersex people are born with physical, hormonal or genetic features that are neither wholly female nor wholly male; or a combination of female and male; or neither female nor male. Many forms of intersex exist; it is a spectrum or umbrella term, rather than a single category', ILGA Europe, note 9, 6.

[21] See Laurie Berg and Jenni Millbank (2009) 'Constructing the Personal Narratives of Lesbian, Gay and Bisexual Asylum Claimants', 22(2) *Journal of Refugee Studies* 195–223, 213; and Rehaag, note 6, 415–436, 423.

[22] For further information see Rehaag, note 6, 415–436; Sean Rehaag (2008) 'Patrolling the Borders of Sexual Orientation: Bisexual Refugee Claims in Canada', 53 *McGill Law Journal* 59–102; and more recently for the UK context: Neva Wagner (2016) 'B Is for Bisexual: The Forgotten Letter in U.K. Sexual Orientation Asylum Reform', 26 *Transnational Law & Contemporary Problems* 205–227.

[23] Amnesty International (2008) *Love, Hate and the Law: Decriminalizing Homosexuality*, London, Amnesty International Publications, www.amnesty.org/en/documents/POL30/003/2008/en.

[24] For a study on transgender claims, see Adena L. Wayne (2016) 'Unique Identities and Vulnerabilities: The Case for Transgender Identity as a Basis for Asylum', 102 *Cornell Law Review* 241–270.

[25] For an analysis of sexuality-based refugee claims in the light of the public/private divide, see Jenni Millbank (2002) 'Imagining Otherness: Refugee Claims on the Basis of Sexuality in Canada and Australia', 26 *Melbourne University Law Review* 144–177.

Note that the terms 'behaviour', 'conduct' and 'acts' – sometimes also 'activities' – will be used interchangeably to refer to forms of expression of sexual orientation (the 'external' dimension). Likewise, 'identity' may be substituted with 'characteristic' or 'status', as such referring to the 'internal' dimension of sexual orientation.

2.2.1 *Discursive Formation: The 'Homosexual as a Species'*

Queer theory as an analytical tool is particularly suitable for the present analysis, since the logics of 'discretion' reasoning are a familiar phenomenon in this context. 'Discretion' reflects a tension in the concept of 'sexual orientation': a distinction between acts and identity is at the very core of the conceptualisation of (homo-) sexuality. In order to grasp the concept as it emerges in refugee law doctrine, therefore, the book draws on Foucault's notion of discursive formation.

In his groundbreaking research from the 1970s and 1980s, Michel Foucault developed discourse analysis as a form of understanding the role of language in our understanding of the world. Foucault advanced the concept of discourse as a culturally constructed representation of reality. According to Foucault, discourses 'define not the dumb existence of reality ... but the ordering of objects'.[26] In other words, discourse *shapes* reality by providing categories that arrange and organise the world; that is, it constructs knowledge. Along with this formation of discourse, and as a condition of its very existence, comes a *lack* – 'exclusions, limits or gaps that divide up [their] referential, validate only one series of modalities, enclose groups of coexistence and prevent certain forms of use'.[27] In Foucault's words, 'the analysis of discourse thus understood, does not reveal the universality of a meaning, but brings to light the action of imposed rarity'[28] – that is, discourse imposes certain categories of intelligibility and leaves out others. To be understood, individuals are obliged to position themselves within the discourse that is formed. In this way, the formation of discourse has 'the power of constituting domains of objects, in relation to which one can affirm or deny true or false propositions'.[29] The production of categories of knowledge defines what it is possible to talk about and what is not, and what constitutes truth. As a consequence, reality becomes comprehensible (only) through this language and the categories it contains.

As one example of the discursive formation of truth, Foucault looks at the category of 'homosexuality'. In his analysis, 'homosexuality' was constituted in European thought in the nineteenth century once it was characterised as a particular quality of sexual feeling, 'a certain way of inverting the masculine and the

[26] Michel Foucault (1972) *The Archaeology of Knowledge and the Discourse on Language*, New York: Pantheon Books, 49.

[27] Ibid., 110.

[28] Ibid., 234.

[29] Ibid., 234.

feminine of oneself', rather than as a type of sexual act that anyone might engage in.[30] Thus, a set of previously unrelated acts becomes a function of an identity.[31] Foucault calls this the 'incorporation of perversions',[32] which defines the personality structure of 'the homosexual' to such an extent that it marks them even if they do not engage in sexual acts.[33] As Foucault famously formulated in an oft-cited passage: 'Homosexuality appeared as one of the forms of sexuality when it was transposed from the *practice* of sodomy onto a kind of interior androgyny, a hermaphrodism of the soul. The sodomite had been a temporary aberration; the homosexual was now a *species*'.[34] Homosexuality was now not only an act but also an identity.

In Foucault's analysis, to give homosexuality an analytical, visible and permanent reality is not only to suppress it, but to make it into a principle of classification and intelligibility. Rather than excluding homosexuality, its specification 'strews reality' with it;[35] 'produces and fixes sexual disparity'.[36] Homosexuality is thus constituted as one of the possible sexualities, providing a 'natural order of disorder'.[37] Whereas before there was no such notion, people are now either straight or gay (or to be sorted into another of the sexuality categories that have been formed).

The basis of this discursive approach is anti-essentialist. It assumes that because the social world is constructed socially, its character is not predetermined or pregiven. Accordingly, people do not have inner 'essences', that is, authentic and immutable characteristics.[38] But once a dominant discourse is formed, it provides parameters of true and false – it simultaneously produces and constrains reality. The discourse provides rhetorical categories through which to understand and sort the world. Consequently, it is only by subscribing to this particular language that one can be understood.[39] In this vein, queer theorist Janet Halley, for example, deploys the terms 'homosexuality' and 'homosexual' as 'rhetorical categories that have real, material importance notwithstanding their failure to provide adequate descriptions of any of us'. Rather, she points out, '[s]exual-orientation identities are ... *facilities* that we use when we attempt to explain ourselves to ourselves, when we seek to situate ourselves

[30] Michel Foucault (1976) *Histoire de la sexualité I: La volonté de savoir*, Paris: Gallimard, 59.
[31] Thomas Spijkerboer (2013) 'Sexual Identity, Normativity and Asylum', in Thomas Spijkerboer (ed.) *Fleeing Homophobia: Sexual Orientation, Gender Identity and Asylum*, London: Routledge, 217–238, 227.
[32] Foucault, note 30, 58.
[33] Ibid., 58–59. See also on this point: Eve Kosofsky Sedgwick (1990) *Epistemology of the Closet*, Berkeley: University of California Press, 82–83.
[34] Foucault, note 30, 59; emphasis added.
[35] Ibid., 60.
[36] Ibid., 65.
[37] Ibid., 60.
[38] Marianne Phillips and Louise J. Jorgensen (2002) *Discourse Analysis as Theory and Method*, London: Sage Publications, 102.
[39] Spijkerboer, note 31, 217–238, 227.

in relation to others or others in relation to ourselves, and thus when we seek to gain and wield power, including the power of persuasion'.[40]

In light of these theories, 'homosexuality' can be viewed as a socially constructed category that is understood as an identity with particular characteristics in dominant discourse. In her article 'Reasoning about Sodomy',[41] Halley discusses the relation of identity and acts. She notes that some have read Foucault's periodisation of sodomitical *acts* and homosexual *persons* as follows:

> [D]epending on the equation of sodomy with homosexual identity, [their reading] assumes that sodomy (a regime of acts) was *transformed into* homosexuality (a regime of identities). Wherever this assumption operates, sodomy-the-act is thought to have been subsumed into homosexuality-the-identity; if sodomy nevertheless stubbornly reasserts its importance as a category of acts, the move is to save appearances by absorbing it into the newly invented personage of the homosexual.[42]

According to this understanding, the relevant category, or 'discourse', would thus be that of *identity*, making that of *acts* irrelevant. Halley, however, then offers

> [a]n alternative reading of Foucault's paragraph [which] assumes less, and leaves in place a more complex and more adequate set of analytic categories for understanding the reasoning of sodomy. On this reading, the rhetoric of acts has not been evaporated or transformed; it has merely been displaced, set to one side and made slightly more difficult to discern by the rhetoric of identity.[43]

This is in line with Eve Kosofsky Sedgwick's understanding of act and identity. With reference to the criminalisation of sodomy in the United States, Sedgwick finds that

> [f]or someone who lives, as I do, in a state where certain acts called 'sodomy' are criminal regardless of the gender, never mind the homo/heterosexual 'identity,' of the persons who perform them, the threat of the juxtaposition *on* that prohibition against *acts* of an additional, unrationalized set of sanctions attaching to *identity* can only be exacerbated by the insistence of gay theory that the discourse of acts can represent nothing but an anachronistic vestige.[44]

When looking at asylum claims, the present analysis understands the construction of sexual orientation, and by analogy also of political opinion and religion, as based on the coexistence of two simultaneous categories – acts and identities. It operates on the assumption that both are mutually constitutive elements of the characteristic that are sometimes difficult to discriminate.

[40] Janet Halley (1993) 'Reasoning about Sodomy: Act and Identity in and after Bowers v. Hardwick', 79(7) *Virginia Law Review* 1721–1780, 1723.
[41] Ibid.
[42] Ibid., 1739; emphasis in the original.
[43] Ibid., 1739–1740.
[44] Sedgwick, note 33, 47; emphasis in original.

2.2.2 *Exerting Power: The Act/Identity Double Bind*

Queer theorists have further examined the contradictory dynamics of this construction of homosexuality as based on a binarism of acts and identity. In her seminal book *Epistemology of the Closet*, Sedgwick drew attention to the 'plurality and the cumulative incoherence of modern ways of conceptualizing same-sex desire and, hence, gay identity', which leads to 'contradictory understandings of same-sex bonding'.[45] She deconstructs a wide range of 'binarisms', and shows how they function as double binds:

> [C]ategories presented in a culture as symmetrical binary oppositions – heterosexual/homosexual, in this case – actually subsist in a more unsettled and dynamic tacit relation according to which, first, term B is not symmetrical with but subordinated to term A; but, second, the ontologically valorized term A actually depends for its meaning on the simultaneous subsumption and exclusion of term B; hence, third, the question of priority between the supposed central and the supposed marginal category of each dyad is irresolvably unstable, an instability caused by the fact that term B is constituted as at once internal and external to term A.[46]

As Sedgwick explains, the unstable relation of these binarisms confers discursive power. She points out that

> [t]o understand these conceptual relations as irresolvably unstable is not, however, to understand them as inefficacious or innocuous … To the contrary, a deconstructive understanding of these binarisms makes it possible to identify them as sites that are peculiarly densely charged with lasting potentials for powerful manipulation – through precisely the mechanisms of self-contradictory definition or, more succinctly, the double bind.[47]

For the purposes of this research, the binary opposition that forms the basis of the analysis is that between *identity* and *acts*. In the context of sexuality-based asylum claims, in particular, the act/identity distinction is not entirely new. Several authors have noted the problem of an 'is/does' dichotomy in the past. As early as 1997, LaViolette criticised the distinction between status and conduct for permitting discrimination against people on the basis of their sexual behaviour and public sexual identity in refugee status determination in Canada.[48] Other authors have also pointed to the act/identity binarism as a problematic distinction – most notably Millbank in her work on Australia, Canada and the United Kingdom,[49] but also O'Dwyer on the United States, who pointed to the problem of the 'artificial distinction between persecution on account of homosexual

45 Ibid., 82.
46 Ibid., 9–10.
47 Ibid., 10.
48 Nicole LaViolette (1997) 'The Immutable Refugees: Sexual Orientation in *Canada (A.G.) v. Ward*', 55(1) *University of Toronto Law Review* 1–41, 33.
49 Millbank, note 25, 144–177.

status or identity, which some circuits hold warrants protection, and punishment for homosexual *acts*, which some circuits hold does not warrant such protection'.[50]

In refugee status determinations, the act/identity double bind develops a potent incoherence. It creates an 'anomalous legal situation'[51] that allows shifting from the regime of acts, which may be allowed or prohibited by whomsoever performed, to the regime of identity, which may or may not exist, irrespective of any particular acts. This split and the consequent shifts occur in claims based on sexual orientation, as well as in cases based on political opinion[52] and religion.[53]

The powerful dynamics of the act/identity dichotomy as theorised by Sedgwick and Halley are blatantly visible in the history of the adjudication of sexuality-based cases. Two examples from early case law can serve to illustrate this. Mr Gui, a gay man from China, had sought protection in Australia. He had been picked up by the police, kicked and bashed, detained for three months and subsequently harassed by the police upon being seen embracing and kissing his male partner in a park.[54] The decision-maker held that Mr Gui was not persecuted because he was gay but, rather, was punished for his conduct in a public place. In the logic of this decision, public sex was generally prohibited for anyone under Chinese law and, therefore, this was not a case of persecution. Conversely, in the case of *Re* S. *(I.Q.)*, a man from Estonia, presumably himself a sailor, had been targeted for persecution after fellow sailors had found out about an affair he had with another man. S. claimed asylum jointly with his wife and minor son, and did not see himself as gay.[55] The panel here found that the claimant had had an isolated affair, which did not indicate a gay identity that would warrant protection.

The litigation of the case of *Toboso-Alfonso* in the United States neatly reflects the dynamic potential for shifts between the regimes of acts and identity. Decided in 1990, it is one of the earliest recognitions of a gay asylum claim. Mr Toboso-Alfonso was a gay man from Cuba who had been required to appear before the police every two to three months for thirteen years, where he was detained for several hours for a

[50] Paul O'Dwyer (2008) 'A Well-Founded Fear of Having My Sexual Orientation Asylum Claim Heard in the Wrong Court', 52(2) *New York Law School Law Review* 185–212, 186. This was especially true for early decisions, such as in *In re Toboso-Alfonso*, 20 I. & N. Dec. 819 (B.I.A. 1990), United States Board of Immigration Appeals, 12 March 1990: 'The government's actions against him were not in response to specific conduct on his part (e.g. for engaging in homosexual acts); rather, they resulted simply from his status as a homosexual.'

[51] Sedgwick, note 33, 86.

[52] See e.g. the discussion in Catherine Dauvergne (2016) 'Toward a New Framework for Understanding Political Opinion', 37 *Michigan Journal of International Law* 243–298, 256–261.

[53] See e.g. the discussion of the German notion of a religious 'subsistence level' in Julian Lehmann (2014) 'Persecution, Concealment and the Limits of a Human Rights Approach in (European) Asylum Law – The Case of Germany v. Y and Z in the Court of Justice of the European Union' 26(1) *International Journal of Refugee Law* 65–81.

[54] RRT Reference No. N97/14768 (Unreported, P Thomson, 29 April 1998); case cited from: Millbank, note 25, 144–177, 145–146.

[55] *Re* S. *(I.Q.)* [1994] C.R.D.D. No. 323 (QL); case cited from LaViolette, note 48, 1–41, 35.

physical examination and questioning regarding his sex life and partners. He indicated that these actions were unrelated to any specific conduct on his part. It resulted from the fact that he was registered as gay by the Cuban government. Being gay was a criminal offence in Cuba, therefore the government maintained files on all gay men in the country.[56] The immigration judge had granted Toboso-Alfonso's claim, but the US Immigration and Naturalization Service appealed to the Board of Immigration Appeals (BIA), arguing that granting protection would be 'tantamount to awarding discretionary relief to those involved in behaviour that is not only socially deviant in nature, but in violation of the laws or regulations of the country as well'.[57] The BIA instead held that the case was not 'simply' one involving the enforcement of laws against particular homosexual acts, nor 'simply' one of assertion of 'gay rights' and ruled in favour of Toboso-Alfonso.[58] The claim is caught in a complex relationship between acts and rights – neither one nor the other alone fully encompasses it.

Clearly, then, refugee status decision-making in sexual orientation cases operates on the tension between an 'almost obsessive focus on homosexual activity'[59] on the one hand and the construction of 'homosexual *persons*, as a particular kind of person' on the other.[60] The challenge is that 'acts do not translate, one-for-one, into identities'.[61] Once the equation that sexual behaviour equals sexual identity breaks down, 'it becomes difficult to maintain the corollary assumptions that the world properly provides two and only two sexual-orientation identities, and that heterosexuality is pure of sodomitic practice and homoerotic impulse'.[62]

This instability is reflected in the fact that a heterosexual identity may be genuinely upheld, for example, by men who regularly engage in same-sex sexual acts with other men.[63] In the public health context, the term 'men who have sex with men' (and its acronym 'MSM') was coined in the early 1990s, conceived as a 'neutral' concept that would capture all those at risk of HIV infection. The rationale

[56] *In re Toboso-Alfonso*, note 50.
[57] Ibid., at 822.
[58] Ibid., at 822.
[59] See senior dissent, accusing the Court in *Bowers* v. *Hardwick*. The case concerned the constitutionality of a Georgia sodomy law criminalizing oral and anal sex in private between consenting adults; *Bowers* v. *Hardwick*, 478 U.S. 186 (1986), United States Supreme Court, 30 June 1986.
[60] Sedgwick, note 33, 86; emphasis in the original.
[61] Halley, note 40, 1721–1780, 1738.
[62] Ibid., footnote 51.
[63] Ibid., 1738–1739. Another example is the 'hype' that the 2000s saw around 'down low', a subculture of Black American men who identify as straight but secretly have sex with men. The term 'down low', also common in its abbreviated version 'DL', originated in the Black community and carries an emphasis on masculinity. A very comprehensive literature review on the topic of MSM was put together by Hudson: Jeffrey H. Hudson (2013) 'Comprehensive Literature Review Pertaining to Married Men Who Have Sex with Men (MMSM)', 13(4) *Journal of Bisexuality* 417–601.

was that it was the behaviour, rather than identities, that created the risk.[64] Comparable to the effect observed previously, however, this well-intentioned move rebounded: it quickly became apparent that this discourse, while useful in some ways, erased the *person* in public health and disregarded the social meaning of sexuality, implying 'a lack of sexual-minority identity' and an 'absence of community, networks, and relationships', which was counterproductive for their health in other ways.[65]

Queer theory has noted that a single act of same-sex sodomy is often taken to unequivocally indicate that a man is gay, whereas a man's having two children by vaginal intercourse in marriage is an uncertain indicator of heterosexual identity.[66] According to this formulation, same-sex sodomy is univocal in a way that cross-sex vaginal intercourse is not.[67] In refugee status determination, in contrast, Sean Rehaag has found in his research on sexual minorities in Canada that it was common for evidence of cross-sex sexual relations to be cited as a reason for *doubting* the asserted identity.[68] In the case of *Krystych* v. *Canada*, the claimant's long-lasting marriages with women were held to cast doubts on his contention that he was gay.[69] In her research on Australian asylum cases relating to sexual orientation, Kristen Walker found a similar incoherence in the role assigned to sexual acts. She contrasts two Australian Refugee Review Tribunal cases. In one case, the lack of sexual experience with women was seen as casting doubt on the applicant's claim to be gay. In another case, the applicant from Bangladesh had had several relationships with men and one relationship with a woman (the latter described as 'unsatisfactory'), based on which the Tribunal concluded that he was not actually gay, reasoning that youthful gay sex was common among men in Bangladesh due to the strong taboos against extra-marital sexual activity between men and women.[70]

64 Rebecca M. Young and Ilan H. Meyer (2005) 'The Trouble with "MSM" and "WSW": Erasure of the Sexual-Minority Person in Public Health Discourse', 95(7) *American Journal of Public Health* 1144–1149. For example, a 2006 population-based survey of New York City men concluded that '[m]edical providers cannot rely on patients' self-reported identities to appropriately assess risk for HIV infection and sexually transmitted diseases; they must inquire about behavior. Public health prevention messages should target risky sexual activities rather than a person's sexual identity', Preeti Pathela, Anjum Hajat, Julia Schillinger, Susan Blank, Randall Sell and Farzad Mostashari (2006) 'Discordance between Sexual Behavior and Self-Reported Sexual Identity: A Population-Based Survey of New York City Men', 145(6) *Annals of Internal Medicine* 416–425, 416.

65 Young and Meyer, note 64, 1144–1149, 1145.

66 Richard D. Mohr (1992) *Gay Ideas: Outing and Other Controversies*, Boston: Beacon Press, 11–48 (chapter 1, 'The Outing Controversy').

67 Halley, note 40, 1721–1780, 1738.

68 Rehaag, note 22, 59–102, 74.

69 *Khrystych* v. *Canada (Minister of Citizenship and Immigration)*, 2005 FC 498, Canada: Federal Court, 12 April 2004.

70 Kristen Walker (2000) 'Sexuality and Refugee Status in Australia' 12(2) *International Journal of Refugee Law* 175–211, 185–186.

To conclude with the words of Sedgwick:

> To be gay in this system is to come under the radically overlapping aegises of a universalizing discourse of acts and a minoritizing discourse of persons. Just at the moment, at least within the discourse of law, the former of these prohibits what the latter of them protects; but in the concurrent public-health constructions related to AIDS, for instance, it is far from clear that a minoritizing discourse of persons ('risk groups') is not even more oppressive than the competing, universalizing discourse of acts ('safer sex'). In the double binds implicit in the space overlapped by the two, at any rate, every matter of definitional control is fraught with consequence.[71]

In other words, whichever definition is chosen, it exerts power and has the capacity to include as much as exclude in many different ways.[72] Thus, '[s]odomy can receive its definitive characteristic from the "homosexuals" who do it, or can stand free of persons and be merely a "bad act"'.[73] It can be treated as a metonym for homosexual personhood – or not, depending on decision-maker and context. The seemingly single question turns out to be a multiple one: '"such conduct" represents not a purely act-based categorical system but an unstable hybrid one, in which identity and conduct simultaneously diverge and implicate one another'.[74]

It can be noted in this context that Walker has indicated in her research on sexuality and refugee status in Australia that heterosexuals who violate social norms concerning sex appear to receive less protection under refugee law than gay/lesbian/transgender claimants. She suggests that this is because adultery, fornication and prostitution are not seen as constituting particular kinds of people in the way that same-sex sexual activity, for example, is seen as constituting a particular kind of person, namely the 'homosexual': '"Homosexual" is something a person "is". In contrast, adultery, fornication and prostitution are viewed simply as "things a person does", and thus do not attract the operation of the Convention'.[75] This is in line with research on the Netherlands that showed that the Immigration and Naturalisation Service (IND) responsible for asylum views a gay person under the Refugee Convention as

> someone who experiences sexual or romantic feelings towards members of the same sex. This explicitly means that homosexual behaviour alone does not suffice to say that somebody is protected by the Refugee Convention. A person who only engages in same-sex activities without experiencing feelings of attraction is not persecuted

[71] Sedgwick, note 33, 86.

[72] See for example the discussion of the concept of 'behavioural bisexuality' in public health, and the distorting consequences on research that result from the ways in which the term is used in Greta Bauer and David Brennan (2013) 'The Problem with "Behavioral Bisexuality": Assessing Sexual Orientation in Survey Research', 13(2) *Journal of Bisexuality* 148–164.

[73] Halley, note 40, 1721–1780, 1747.

[74] Ibid.

[75] Walker, note 70, 175–211, 179, footnote 10.

> for who he or she is. And, according to the decision maker, the Refugee Convention principally protects people against persecution for who they are, not for what they do.[76]

Here, identity is prioritised over acts. But, as Halley points out, while the denied and submerged element in a double bind provides a point for resistance, the dominant group can at any moment make such resistance futile by flipping the system.[77] This is evidenced by the Australian asylum case of *SZJSL*. The claimant had formed a relationship with another man while in immigration detention and described their plans to marry. His application based on his bisexuality was rejected on the grounds that the relationship was found to be 'simply the product of the situation where only partners of the same sex are available and says nothing about his sexual orientation'.[78]

The objective of the present analysis is to look at refugee status determinations through the lens of an is/does dichotomy in order to reveal the ways in which a double bind is created and what consequences this has for the assessment of the claim, in particular with respect to the conceptualisation of what is protected. While drawn from and developed with respect to sexuality-based claims, this approach has explanatory force also for cases based on religion and political opinion, as will be shown in particular in Part II. As such, the aim is to expose the 'systematic ways in which acts and identities generate incoherence and instability'.[79] According to Halley:

> In everyday language, you are in a double bind when you cannot win because your victorious opponent is willing to be a hypocrite and to 'damn you if you do and damn you if you don't.' More strictly examined, a double bind involves a systematic arrangement of symbolic systems with a least three characteristics. First, two conceptual systems (or 'discourses') are matched in their opposition to one another; one is consistently understood to be not only different from but the logical alternative of the other. Second, the preferred discourse actually requires the submerged one to make it work. It is at this point that a naïve deconstructive claim is often made, that the secret inclusion of the nonpreferred discourse as a prerequisite for the smooth operation of the express one reveals the whole system to be fatally unstable. But third, that very instability can be the source of suppleness and resilience, because the two stacked discourses can be flipped: the one that was submerged and denied can become express, and it in turn can be covertly supported by the one that was preferred. The master of a double bind always has somewhere to go.[80]

76 Louis Middelkoop (2013) 'Normativity and Credibility of Sexual Orientation in Asylum Decision Making', in Thomas Spijkerboer (ed.) *Fleeing Homophobia: Sexual Orientation, Gender Identity and Asylum*, London: Routledge, 154–175, 157.

77 Halley, note 40, 1721–1780, 1749.

78 *SZJSL* v. *Minister for Immigration & Another* [2007] FCMA 313, Australia: Federal Magistrates Court, 19 February 2007.

79 Halley, note 40, 1721–1780, 1747.

80 Ibid., 1721–1780, 1748–1749.

Halley's third point is based on Sedgwick's finding that the contradictions inherent in such definitional binarisms are not necessarily immanently self-corrosive, but rather that 'discursive power can be specified as competitions for the material or rhetorical leverage required to set the terms of, and to profit in some way from, the operations of such an incoherence of definition'.[81] Sedgwick further notes: 'Nor is a deconstructive analysis of such definitional knots, however necessary, at all sufficient to disable them. Quite the opposite: I would suggest that an understanding of their irresolvable instability has been continually available, and has continually lent discursive authority.'[82]

As Halley has shown, the systematic instability of the act/identity system can be exploited by treating it as a double bind:[83] 'It is the unstable relationship between act and identity – not the preference of one to the other – that allows . . . to exploit confusion about what sodomy is in ways that create opportunities for the exercise of homophobic power'.[84] Applied to the context of refugee status determinations, this would suggest that it is the unstable relationship between act and identity that allows decision-makers to exploit confusion about *what is persecuted* in ways that create opportunities for the restriction of the scope of protection – that is, some form of 'discretion' reasoning. The extent to which that is the case is the subject of the present analysis.

To summarise, drawing on Sedgwick[85] and Halley,[86] it is possible then to conceive of acts and identity as symbolic systems that are systematically arranged in a binary opposition with the following characteristics (Figure 2.1).

1. The two conceptual systems (acts and identity) are matched in their opposition to one another in an unsettled and dynamic tacit relationship, according to which term B is not symmetrical with but subordinated to term A.
2. The preferred discourse requires the submerged term to make it work: *identity* (or acts – depending on the context, which may prioritise either one or the other) depends for its meaning on the simultaneous subsumption and exclusion of *acts* – hence, the question of priority between the supposed central and the supposed marginal discourse is irresolvably unstable because *acts* are at once internal and external to *identity*.
3. That instability can be the source of suppleness and resilience, because the two discourses can be flipped: the one that was submerged and denied can become express, and it in turn can be covertly supported by the one that was preferred.

81 Sedgwick, note 33, 11.
82 Ibid., 9–10.
83 Halley, note 40, 1721–1780, 1749.
84 Ibid., 1721–1780, 1770.
85 Sedgwick, note 33, 9–10.
86 Halley, note 40, 1721–1780, 1748–1749.

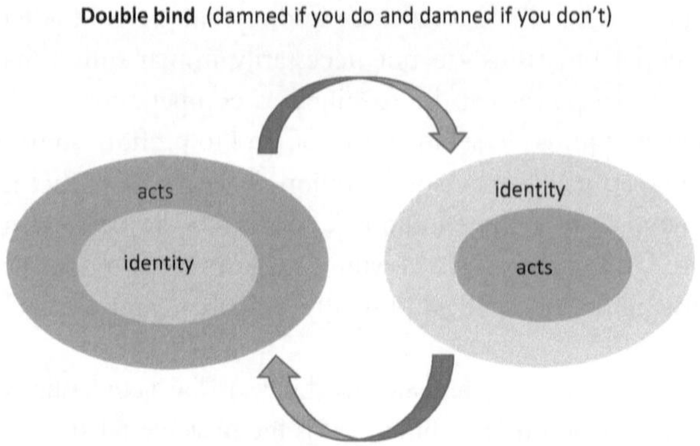

FIGURE 2.1. Act/identity double bind

As a result of this arrangement, the master of a double bind always has somewhere to go.[87] The 'master' can be anyone, ranging from the persecutor to the scholar writing on sexuality-based cases. In the status determination context, the decision-maker is in the position of master of the double bind, who may always send a claimant back to 'discretion'.

Millbank has observed one such flip: she showed how the trend has shifted from 'discretion' to 'disbelief' in Australia and the United Kingdom after the High Court of Australia rejected the notion that decision-makers could 'expect' refugee applicants to conceal their sexual orientation.[88] This shift arguably represents a flip of the discourses – after routinely relying on the absence of acts and finding that genuinely gay claimants could be expected to behave 'discreetly', the relation shifted and cases failed because of a purported absence of identity irrespective of acts that equally forced failed applicants to return to secrecy.

So an act/identity dichotomy is at the core of any 'discretion' reasoning. An 'identity per se'[89] is – consciously or subconsciously – distinguished from acts expressing or revealing this identity. It shifts the focus away from the persecutor and towards the claimant. This distinction has the potential to unfold oppressive power in refugee status determination such that it excludes claimants from protection: they are damned if they do and damned if they don't.

[87] Ibid., 1721–1780, 1749.

[88] Jenni Millbank (2009) 'From Discretion to Disbelief: Recent Trends in Refugee Determinations on the Basis of Sexual Orientation in Australia and the United Kingdom', 13(2/3) *International Journal of Human Rights* 391–414.

[89] James Hathaway and Jason Pobjoy (2012) 'Queer Cases Make Bad Law', 44(2) *New York University Journal of International Law and Politics* 315–389, 333.

2.2.3 *Coming out of the Closet: The 'Discretion'/Disclosure Binarism*

'Discretion' thus results from a distinction between acts and identity. So does its opposite, disclosure. In queer theory, disclosure takes a prominent place – more commonly referred to as 'coming out' (of the closet), it constitutes the foundational moment in queer social and political life. Sean Rehaag has neatly summarised the rationale of disclosure:

> Simply put, the logic of coming out is that, whether or not I choose to emerge from the closet, I am always already queer. When I am in the closet, I am hiding something fundamental about who I really am. It is only by acknowledging my true identity, first to myself, and later publicly, that I can begin to lead an authentic and full life. Such logic presumes that I have a 'true' identity. Lurking beneath my presumptively heterosexual public persona is an essentially queer substratum. What makes me queer is the presence of this substratum, irrespective of the sexual identity I publicly display.[90]

Together, 'discretion' and disclosure refer to a person's management of information about their sexual orientation – that is, they simultaneously evoke the person's responsibility for others' knowledge of that feature.

Reflecting on the essentialist logic of the notion of coming out, Rehaag adds that '[g]iven the reality of homophobia, many queer individuals experience their sexual identity in precisely this manner. These individuals go through long periods of being unable to publicly or even personally acknowledge what they ultimately come to see as their sexual orientation'.[91] Similarly, Sedgwick argues that '[t]he closet is still the fundamental feature of [gay] social life; and there can be few gay people, however courageous and forthright by habit, however fortunate in the support of their immediate communities, in whose lives the closet is not still a shaping presence'.[92]

This is arguably even more the case in the refugee context, where homophobia reaches the threshold of persecution in the claimants' countries of origin. In fact, a persecutory environment can generally be understood to function as a sort of 'closet' not only for gay refugees, but also for political opponents or holders of minority religions – for any of those 'fundamental characteristics' that one may attempt to hide. This is because a particular difficulty with 'fundamental characteristics', such as religion, political opinion, sexual orientation and many others, is that they are not necessarily immediately visible. Comparing homophobia with other 'modern oppressions', Sedgwick conceived of the revelation of different oppressed identities as follows:

> Racism, for instance, is based on a stigma that is visible in all but exceptional cases (cases that are neither rare nor irrelevant, but that delineate the outlines rather than

[90] Rehaag, note 22, 59–102, 81.
[91] Ibid.
[92] Sedgwick, note 33, 68.

> coloring center of racial experience); so are the oppressions based on gender, age, size, physical handicap. Ethnic/cultural/religious oppressions such as anti-Semitism are more analogous [to homophobia] in that *the stigmatized individual has at least notionally some discretion – although, importantly, it is never to be taken for granted how much* – over other people's knowledge of her or his membership in the group: one could 'come out as' a Jew or Gypsy, in a heterogeneous urbanized society, much more intelligibly than one could typically 'come out as', say, female, Black, old, a wheelchair user, or fat.[93]

To some extent, therefore, claimants can influence the ways in which they relate to the group, what they disclose to whom under which circumstances and in which context – and what they don't. That is, they can influence the future that shapes the risk they face *to some extent*. This is true not only for sexual orientation, but likewise for other 'oppressed identities', such as political opinion or religion. The act/identity dichotomy, as well as the 'discretion'/disclosure binarism, are therefore equally applied to conceive of asylum claims based on other grounds.

Importantly, there are 'multiple and complex possibilities around the way that behaviour may reflect or relate to an identity . . . An activity may *express* the identity or it may *reveal* the identity'.[94] So acts *disclose* the identity to others, and others *infer* the identity from acts. This may not always be accurate, and refugee law doctrine in principle accounts for this by accepting that protection also extends to those with an *imputed* political opinion or religion or who are *perceived as* gay by their potential persecutors.[95] This is the clearest way to illustrate that revelation (disclosure) and concealment ('discretion') are never entirely in the hands of the person concerned. As Millbank noted, the difficulty in trying to delimit the relationship between act and identity is compounded by the fact that expression and revelation can occur deliberately or inadvertently, and may be deliberate for some purposes or audiences but inadvertent for others.[96] This is particularly so in persecutory environments, where exposure of a particular characteristic may result in serious harm – and the management of that characteristic is therefore particularly delicate. This, in turn, has consequences for the understanding of that characteristic in the asylum process.

In asylum claims, 'discretion' and disclosure intersect in complex ways. This creates a predicament that has been studied by Sedgwick in the 1973 case of

93 Ibid., 75; emphasis added.

94 Jenni Millbank (2012) 'The Right of Lesbians and Gay Men to Live Freely, Openly, and on Equal Terms Is Not Bad Law: A Reply to Hathaway and Pobjoy', 44(2) *New York University Journal of International Law and Politics* 497–527, 513.

95 See e.g. UNHCR (2001) *The International Protection of Refugees: Interpreting Article 1 of the 1951 Convention Relating to the Status of Refugees*, April 2001, 25. See also: UNHCR (1979, re-edited 1992) *Handbook on Procedures and Criteria for Determining Refugee Status under the 1951 Convention and the 1967 Protocol Relating to the Status of Refugees*, HCR/IP/4/Eng/REV.1 Reedited, Geneva, January 1992, 80; Supreme Court of Canada: *Canada (Attorney General) v. Ward*, [1993] 2 S.C.R. 689, 30 June 1993, 747.

96 Millbank, note 94, 497–527, 513–514.

Acanforca. That case concerned a gay teacher from Montgomery County, Maryland, in the USA, who had been transferred to a non-teaching position, and then refused a new contract entirely after he spoke to the news media about his case. On appeal, the lower court's rationale was overruled, but its decision not to allow Acanforca to return to teaching was confirmed on the grounds that he had failed to note on his original employment application that he had been an officer of a student homophile organisation in college, which would have meant that he would never have been hired in the first place. Sedgwick notes on this case:

> It is striking that each of the two rulings in Acanforca emphasized that the teacher's homosexuality 'itself' would not have provided an acceptable ground for denying him employment. Each of the courts relied in its decision on an implicit distinction between the supposedly protected and bracketable fact of Acanforca's homosexuality proper, on the one hand, and on the other hand his highly vulnerable management of information about it. So very vulnerable does this latter exercise prove to be, however, and vulnerable to such a contradictory array of interdictions, that *the space for simply existing as a gay person who is a teacher is in fact bayonetted through and through, from both sides, by the vectors of a disclosure at once compulsory and forbidden.*[97]

The same might be true for refugees in need of protection based on their political opinion, religion or sexual orientation. Their case as a political/religious/gay person who has a valid claim for refugee protection may be made impossible by at once requiring disclosure and forbidding it on different levels and from different perspectives throughout the process: for the purposes of the claim and the decision-maker as well as in response to the persecutory environment in their country of origin. Table 2.1 illustrates the delicate position of disclosure for refugee claimants. On the one hand, the discretion/disclosure binarism serves as the 'hinge' between act and identity and makes the sexual orientation intelligible for others. On the other hand, the degrees of 'discretion' and disclosure can always be turned against the claimant.

So, much depends on the claimant's 'highly vulnerable management of information'[98] about their persecuted/protected characteristic. 'Discretion' may be expected or required at one point, disclosure at another, and sometimes both simultaneously for different reasons and purposes. Any such assessment of the degrees of disclosure and 'discretion' at the same time reveals a focus on the claimant, and assigns responsibility to claimants, at least in part. In other words, while the act/identity dichotomy turns attention away from the persecutor and toward the claimant, the discretion/disclosure binarism makes the claimant responsible for what happens to them – they are at once entitled to their sexual orientation and not. The focus shifts from protecting the claimant from the persecutor to the

97 Sedgwick, note 33, 69; emphasis added.
98 Ibid., 69.

TABLE 2.1. *Disclosure at once compulsory and forbidden*

Disclosure	Compulsory	Forbidden
Persecution	If undisclosed, the claimant has nothing to fear in home country	If disclosed, the claimant invites persecution in home country ('unreasonable')
Group membership	If undisclosed, group membership is disbelieved	If disclosed, the claimant puts themselves in real danger

claimant's management of information about their characteristic and the complex web of obligations and assumptions connected with it.

2.3 METHODOLOGICAL APPROACH

Based on these theoretical underpinnings, the book explores what 'discretion' reasoning tells us about the scope of protection in refugee law. It highlights assumptions in refugee law that expose internally inconsistent structures and tensions within the refugee definition,[99] which affect the question of what is protected and why. As such, the book shows how assumptions about the Convention and its protective scope favour certain forms of reasoning about the form and content of sexuality, but also political opinion or religion. At the same time, the book shows the opposite: how assumptions about the protected grounds inform the scope of the Convention. In order to achieve this, Part I of the study zooms in on decision-making practice regarding sexuality-based claims in the civil law jurisdictions France, Germany and Spain. Part II zooms back out and ties the insights drawn from this empirical work into doctrine and case law from common law jurisdictions and concerning other grounds of claim. The subdominant perspective adopted in the first part – both in focusing on the previously largely neglected European countries and in foregrounding sexuality-based claims – then allows for developing new perspectives on the more familiar common law doctrine and other Convention grounds (religion and political opinion). In terms of methodology, the study applies a combination of doctrinal analysis, case studies, comparative research and discourse analysis.

2.3.1 *Discourse Analysis of Legal Doctrine*

The methodology used for this study is discourse analysis of legal doctrine. The most accepted methodology in the field of law is doctrinal legal research.[100] Legal

[99] Terry Hutchinson and Nigel Duncan (2012) 'Defining and Describing What We Do: Doctrinal Legal Research', 17(1) *Deakin Law Review* 83–119, 104.

[100] Ibid., 83–119, 102.

'doctrine' can be defined as '[a] synthesis of various rules, principles, norms, interpretative guidelines and values. It explains, makes coherent or justifies a segment of the law as part of a larger system of law'.[101] Put simply, doctrinal research is research into the law and legal concepts. It requires organising 'dispersed, fragmentary, prolix and rebarbative material'.[102] This material is assessed in a synthesising process applying deductive logic, inductive reasoning and analogy.[103] It has been noted that 'it is the doctrinal aspect of law that makes legal research distinctive and provides an often under-recognised parallel to "discovery" in the physical sciences'.[104]

Discourse analysis, in turn, is a form of content analysis. All forms of content analysis involve the collection of a set of documents, reading these systematically, coding, and then drawing 'inferences and meaning' from the set.[105] The method is thus able to describe the 'landscape of decided cases'.[106] It allows researchers to deal with a large number of cases, looking for broad patterns.[107] In this sense, content analysis differs from traditional doctrinal analysis, which generally analyses issues presented in one case or a small group of exceptional or weighty cases, and 'offers distinctive insights that complement the types of understanding that only traditional analysis can generate'.[108] The functional difference between the two can be described as follows: whereas doctrinal analysis auditions 'a crowd of singers to find the best soloists', content analysts 'assemble a chorus, listening to the sound that the cases make together'.[109] To situate *discourse* analysis as a form of content analysis in this image, it can be said that it equally assembles a chorus, but is concerned with the way the sound is constructed as a song. In other words, the main concern of traditional content analysis is reliability and replicability (always ending up with the same song), aiming to emulate the natural sciences.[110] Discourse analysis, in contrast, seeks to form a coherent analytical claim that has the potential to provide new explanations (explaining how we ended up with this song): 'It is by seeing the world through a particular theory that we can distance ourselves from some of our taken-for-granted understandings and subject our material to other questions than we

[101] Ibid., 83–119, 84.

[102] Richard Posner (2007) 'In Memoriam: Bernard D. Meltzer (1914–2007)', 74(2) *University of Chicago Law Review* 435, 437, cited in Hutchinson and Duncan, note 99, 83–119, 107.

[103] Hutchinson and Duncan, note 99, 83–119, 111.

[104] Council of Australian Law Deans (2005) *CALD Statement on the Nature of Research* (May and October 2005), https://cald.asn.au/wp-content/uploads/2017/11/cald-statement-on-the-nature-of-legal-research-20051.pdf.

[105] Mark A. Hall and Ronald F. Wright (2008) 'Systematic Content Analysis of Judicial Opinions', 96(1) *California Law Review* 63–122, 64.

[106] Ibid., 63–122, 100.

[107] Terry Hutchinson (2010) *Researching and Writing in Law* (3rd ed.), Pyrmont Lawbook, 127 (chapter 5 – Social Science Methodologies for Lawyers).

[108] Hall and Wright, note 105, 63–122, 66.

[109] Ibid., 63–122, 76.

[110] See on this point the chapter on methodology guidelines in Ibid., 63–122, 100–120.

would be able to do from an everyday perspective.'[111] Discourse analysis of legal doctrine is, therefore, well suited to this study's purpose of examining the role of 'discretion' reasoning in the construction of sexuality-based asylum claims. The theoretical lens that forms the basis of this research is the act/identity dichotomy provided by queer theory in order to explore certain assumptions, dynamics and paradoxes in refugee law.

This approach is applied in two slightly different ways. Part I of the study conducts an analysis of decision-making practice in three European jurisdictions, based mainly on asylum decisions and judgments. The set of cases forming the basis for the case studies was collected from the relevant databases. Some decisions were provided to the author by lawyers or other stakeholders. The case sets for all three countries are broadly comparable in terms of number of decisions, time period covered and levels of decision-making. They each include all available relevant highest-level judgments, as well as a selection of lower-level judgments from the earliest available judgments up until the end of 2016. For France, this study works with the universal sample of all available decisions up to December 2016, which amounts to 97 decisions covering the years 1997–2016. For Germany, the case set consists of a selection of 75 decisions covering the years 1983–2016. For Spain, a total of 77 decisions were collected, from the time of the earliest Spanish sexuality-based judgment in 1998 to the end of 2016. Further details on the selection of cases are outlined shortly in the relevant chapters for each of the countries. The cases that were used for the present study are listed in Annex II. Where relevant, policy instructions that influenced the construction of claims were also included in the analysis.

There are certain inherent limitations to this approach: first, it is limited to published and accessible judgments. That means the vast majority of cases never even had the chance of being included in the sample. Accordingly, while the analysis paints a broader picture, drawing on a wider range of cases, it cannot (and does not) claim representativity.[112] Moreover, because they are not accessible, almost no administrative (first) decisions are included, even though this is where most asylum claims end. Only a small minority of administrative decisions are appealed – and they tend to be the contentious ones. This further distorts the picture. Moreover, the styles for writing judgments differ immensely between the three countries under study, greatly limiting the ability to make comparisons across the available texts. Thus, while the case collection allows for the development of fruitful analysis, it is important to keep these limitations in mind.

[111] Phillips and Jorgensen, note 38, 22–23.

[112] Note that the same limitation applies to other studies analysing case law, such as Laurie Berg and Jenni Millbank (2013) 'Developing a Jurisprudence of Transgender Particular Social Group', in Thomas Spijkerboer (ed.) *Fleeing Homophobia. Sexual Orientation, Gender Identity and Asylum*, London: Routledge, 121–153.

In light of the findings from the case studies, Part II of this book consists of a critical evaluation of a series of aspects of refugee law doctrine surrounding the Convention grounds. However, in line with the approach outlined, the aim of Part II is not to conduct a classical doctrinal analysis. Rather than looking at the 'state of the law', it seeks to trace how doctrine is constructed. That is, rather than searching for the 'right' legal answer, as classical doctrinal analysis would, it aims to show how similar issues take different discursive shape, and how they become accepted as doctrine – or do not. Therefore, the analysis is not limited to leading jurisprudence but also takes into account cases that may have been overturned on appeal. It looks for variety and different lines of reasoning, with even rare outliers of interest. The quest is for the doctrinal struggles involved in conceptualising the Convention grounds, drawing out the arguments for different approaches and exposing the tensions and paradoxes involved.

2.3.2 *Case Studies*

Given the research gap on 'discretion' reasoning in European jurisdictions outlined in the previous section, three major European states have been chosen as case studies for the analysis in Part I: France, Germany and Spain. So far, the vast majority of research has focused on the English-speaking common law jurisdictions, most notably Canada, Australia, New Zealand and the United Kingdom, with some research also into United States practice. This is true both for refugee law research generally and for sexuality-based asylum claims and 'discretion' reasoning in particular. Although this is slowly starting to change, to date Europe has received far less attention in the literature. Consequently, the general conclusions drawn to date are all from common law jurisdictions.

Several recent European research projects, such as *Fleeing Homophobia* on sexual orientation and gender identity claims[113] and *GENSEN* on gender-related claims,[114] showed that major divergences persist in asylum practice across European states.[115] The 2011 *Fleeing Homophobia* report, in particular, was the first comparative study on European state practice concerning sexuality-based claims. It turned out to be an eye-opener for cultural differences: not only did it reveal that 'discretion'

[113] Sabine Jansen and Thomas Spijkerboer (2011) *Fleeing Homophobia, Asylum Claims Related to Sexual Orientation and Gender Identity in Europe*, Vrije Universiteit Amsterdam, September 2011.

[114] Hana Cheikh Ali, Christel Querton and Élodie Soulard (2012) *Gender Related Asylum Claims in Europe – A Comparative Analysis of Law Policies and Practice Focusing on Women in Nine EU Member States* ('GENSEN report'). Brussels: European Parliament, Directorate General for Internal Policies, Department of Citizens' Rights and Constitutional Affairs.

[115] Other comparative studies followed, such as UNHCR (2013) *Beyond Proof, Credibility Assessment in EU Asylum Systems: Full Report*, May 2013; Sabine Jansen and Joël Le Déroff (2014) *Good Practices: Related to LGBTI Asylum Applicants in Europe*, International Lesbian, Gay, Bisexual, Trans and Intersex Association (ILGA), May 2014.

reasoning still occurred in the majority of European states (namely Austria, Belgium, Bulgaria, Cyprus, Denmark, Finland, France, Germany, Hungary, Ireland, Malta, Norway the Netherlands, Poland, Romania, Spain and Switzerland),[116] but also that such reasoning is subject to great diversity across different countries. That study could, however, do little more than point to the existence of such country-specific manifestations of 'discretion' – and thus effectively highlighted a large research gap in this area.

This study addresses that identified gap. It scrutinises the shapes that 'discretion' reasoning takes in European civil law countries and compares them against the Anglophone common law-dominated research findings from the literature. This helps to make the picture broader and adds another layer of insight into the functioning of 'discretion' logics. A detailed analysis and discussion of asylum judgments and academic literature from Germany, France and Spain in English is part of this exercise.

A range of countries were possible candidates for conducting in-depth analysis of sexuality-based decision-making regarding 'discretion' reasoning in European civil law jurisdictions. The *Fleeing Homophobia* report found 'discretion' reasoning in seventeen European jurisdictions. Germany, France and Spain were selected from this group for several reasons. At the time of selection, Germany and France were the two states that, while lacking external EU borders (other than airports and seaports), received the largest numbers of asylum seekers in Europe. In spite of quite different legal cultures, they are thus similarly placed within Europe. However, the *Fleeing Homophobia* report found that 'discretion' reasoning in these two countries takes very different forms. Though courts were divided on the matter, reasoning based on the claimant's capacity to hide was prevalent in Germany, whereas France had developed an '*in*discretion requirement', accepting claims only of those who had manifested their sexual orientation.[117] Spain, in contrast, receives a much lower number of asylum seekers but has external EU borders (Ceuta, Melilla, Canary Islands), which means it is often the country of entry for boat arrivals and other asylum seekers. According to the *Fleeing Homophobia* report, however, while 'discretion' reasoning takes place, it does not appear to be a very prominent phenomenon.[118] Moreover, German judges have engaged quite actively with the CJEU, whereas the same cannot be said of France and Spain. The three jurisdictions, therefore, promised a fruitful comparison relevant to a large number of different claims.[119]

[116] Jansen and Spijkerboer, note 113, 34.
[117] See Ibid., 33–39; see also Chapters 4 and 5 of this book.
[118] See Ibid., 34; and Chapter 6 of this book.
[119] Another motive is language: one of the limiting factors explaining the lack of – comparative – research on European jurisdictions to date certainly remains language. Because the author speaks German, French, Spanish and English, most countries were automatically deleted from the list of possible case studies.

Case studies are qualitative research elements that are typically used in social sciences. They are not 'samples' in the strict sense, but rather examples, and can be combined effectively with a doctrinal study. A variety of different goals can be pursued with case studies.[120] For the purposes of this research, the case studies serve two aims. Firstly, they are designed as in-depth studies exploring decision-making practice with respect to 'discretion' reasoning in sexuality-based asylum claims. Secondly, by comparing practice across these countries, the case studies serve to identify and explain the different shapes 'discretion' reasoning can take – and, consequently, the ways in which the scope of what is protected under refugee law is constructed in these jurisdictions. Obviously, the case study method is most useful when the examples allow drawing generalised principles or broader conclusions. This is achieved in the present study by comparing findings with established knowledge on 'discretion' reasoning from other jurisdictions – broadening the understanding of the dynamics of 'discretion' by adding another layer. In addition, the list of cases in Annex II provides a resource for others as an objective basis to check conclusions against.

Another advantage of the case study design is that it allows for a contextual approach, especially regarding 'time slices'.[121] A situation can be viewed before and after major events in order to document actual effects. This aspect is particularly relevant to the present study. The *Fleeing Homophobia* report documenting 'discretion' reasoning (amongst other topics) was published in 2011, shortly after the UK Supreme Court judgment in *HJ (Iran) and HT (Cameroon)* was handed down in 2010[122] and, importantly, just before the two judgments by the Court of Justice of the European Union in 2012 and 2013, also rejecting 'discretion' reasoning.[123] In addition, the *Qualification Directive* harmonising refugee status determination in the EU, which entered into force in 2006, took some time to take effect.[124] Therefore, the case studies undertake a detailed review of practice before and after these events, assessing the effect these developments have had on 'discretion' reasoning.

[120] Hutchinson, note 107, 115.

[121] Ibid.

[122] *HJ (Iran) and HT (Cameroon)* v. *Secretary of State for the Home Department*, note 1; see description, Chapter 3.

[123] *Federal Republic of Germany* v. *Y and Z*, Joined Cases C-71/11 and C-99/11, Court of Justice of the European Union, 5 September 2012; and *X, Y and Z* v. *Minister voor Immigratie, Integratie en Asiel*, Joined Cases C-199/12, C-200/12 and C-201/12, European Union: Court of Justice of the European Union, 7 November 2013; for discussion see Chapter 3.

[124] Council Directive 2004/83/EC of 29 April 2004 on minimum standards for the qualification and status of third-country nationals or stateless persons as refugees or as persons who otherwise need international protection and the content of the protection granted, oj L 304/12, 30 September 2004 (2004 *Qualification Directive*).

2.3.3 *Comparative Research*

Almost naturally, a comparative element is involved in a case study design that works with more than one example. Few researchers today examine law in one jurisdiction without considering other jurisdictions at least to some extent.[125] That is also the case in refugee law. The Anglophone common law jurisdictions, Australia, Canada, New Zealand and the United Kingdom, have long established a fruitful judicial and academic dialogue on refugee law. The common law jurisdictions lend themselves to exploring the logical parameters of the refugee definition because of the degree of comprehensive analysis their decisions require.[126] It is only since the establishment of the Common European Asylum System (CEAS) in the EU and increased adjudication of the Court of Justice of the European Union (CJEU) on issues of asylum that a refugee law dialogue has started to emerge in Europe. However, to date, there is little exchange across these pockets.[127] Looking at the use of human rights instruments, and drawing mainly on European research from the 1990s,[128] Foster noted in 2006 that the human rights approach in civil law countries tended in the past to be implicit.[129] However, European civil law jurisdictions were showing an 'increased willingness to join in the conversation' and she suggested that more explicit reference to human rights standards might occur following the then-recent enactment of the *Qualification Directive*.[130] Indeed, with the increasing establishment of the CEAS – most notably the *Qualification Directive*[131] for the purposes of the present research – and particularly the role of the CJEU in providing guidance

[125] Hutchinson, note 107, 117.

[126] See Michelle Foster (2007) *International Refugee Law and Socio-economic Rights: Refuge from Deprivation*, Cambridge Studies in International and Comparative Law, Cambridge: Cambridge University Press, 23 and 30.

[127] See in particular Hélène Lambert's work on the slowly emerging transnational judicial dialogue in the EU: Hélène Lambert (2009) 'Transnational Judicial Dialogue Harmonization and the Common European Asylum System', 58(3) *International and Comparative Law Quarterly* 519–543; see also Hélène Lambert, Jane McAdam and Maryellen Fullerton, eds. (2013) *The Global Reach of European Refugee Law*, Cambridge: Cambridge University Press; Guy Goodwin-Gill and Hélène Lambert, eds. (2010) *The Limits of Transnational Law: Refugee Law, Policy Harmonization and Judicial Dialogue in the European Union*, Cambridge: Cambridge University Press.

[128] Such as Dirk Vanheule (1997) 'A Comparison of the Judicial Interpretations of the Notion of Refugee', in Jean-Yves Carlier and Dirk Vanheule (eds.) *Europe and Refugees: A Challenge?*, The Hague: Kluwer Law International, 98–103.

[129] Foster, note 126, 30.

[130] Ibid., 30–31 (footnote 13); and Article 9(1)(a) of the *Qualification Directive*.

[131] Council Directive 2004/83/EC of 29 April 2004, note 124 (2004 *Qualification Directive*); recast in 2011: Directive 2011/95/EU of the European Parliament and of the Council of 13 December 2011 on standards for the qualification of third-country nationals or stateless persons as beneficiaries of international protection, for a uniform status for refugees or for persons eligible for subsidiary protection and for the content of the protection granted (recast), oj L 337/9, 20 December 2011 (*Recast Qualification Directive*).

to European Union member states on contentious questions,[132] engagement of European civil law jurisdictions in this cross-jurisdictional discourse has been emerging – not only with respect to human rights standards, but also regarding other aspects of refugee law doctrine. The nascent exchange regularly brings to light that, while the *Qualification Directive* provides the same legal context for all, the national contexts diverge. It remains to be explored whether and how the way the legal standards regarding sexuality-based asylum claims are transposed, interpreted and implemented at the national level will similarly differ – in particular with a view to 'discretion' reasoning.

This book undertakes comparisons at two levels. On the one hand, practice in the European states that were chosen for case studies will be compared with each other. This, in turn, will be compared with and checked against practice and doctrine in the Anglophone common law jurisdictions. While all jurisdictions apply the 1951 *Refugee Convention*, the implementation differs. In the EU, the Refugee Convention is transposed into national law via the detour of Directives (the *Qualification Directive* for the purposes of this study).[133] Therefore, even though the reference point is the same, it is important to be aware of the familial relationships of the jurisdictions; the basic separateness of the tenets of the jurisdictions can play an important role and may account for some, or even many, of the differences in the outcomes. In particular, there is a difference between common law and civil law jurisdictions that comes into a complex interplay in the European Union. The CJEU, through its preliminary rulings, 'makes' the law in ways similar to common law systems. Moreover, via the United Kingdom and the CJEU, some of the common law developments are finding entry into EU refugee law. Part of the present analysis draws out this interplay.

The limitations of comparative research include the risks of superficiality and misunderstanding the foreign law, particularly as discrepancies between theory and practice of the law may be difficult to grasp.[134] To respond to this challenge, the discussion of the case studies has been checked with refugee lawyers from each of these jurisdictions. Moreover, it is a challenge to be truly systematic in the comparison.[135] Therefore, this book does not aim to compare systematically; rather, the case studies serve as illustrations of the different ways in which 'discretion' reasoning may occur.

132 E.g. on sexual orientation: European Union: X, Y *and* Z v. *Minister voor Immigratie, Integratie en Asiel*, note 123; and A, *B*, C v. *Staatssecretaris van Veiligheid en Justitie*, Joined Cases C-148/13 to C-150/13, European Union: Court of Justice of the European Union, 2 December 2014.

133 See Annex I for a detailed description of the interplay of European and international refugee law.

134 Alan Watson (1993) *Legal Transplants: An Approach to Comparative Law* (2nd ed.), Athens: The University of Georgia Press, 10.

135 Ibid., 11.

2.3.4 *The Contribution of This Study*

Through this theoretical and methodological approach, the present study is able to explore 'discretion' reasoning at a level of breadth and depth that has not previously been achieved. The theoretical lens of the act/identity dichotomy takes account of the recognition of the multifaceted character of 'discretion' logics and allows for the identification of the range of different shapes that 'discretion' can adopt.

Applying this lens to three core European jurisdictions that have so far been largely left out of the debate shows that 'discretion' is firmly entrenched in refugee decision-making – even in jurisdictions that have not engaged to any notable extent in the transnational judicial dialogue characteristic of the common law jurisdictions. This indicates that 'discretion' logics might result from the nature of the refugee definition, which is inherently paradoxical. 'Discretion' reasoning serves as a way to 'patch' this contradictory character of the definition.

This paradox is then explored in its different dimensions in the second part, which draws out the ways in which 'discretion' logics are entrenched in the different approaches to conceptualising political opinion, membership of a particular social group and religion, not only in European doctrine, but internationally. Doctrinal analysis inspired by discourse analysis is particularly suitable to retrace the construction of the scope of protection; it explores the ways in which tensions in the refugee definition play out and are 'patched' by various versions of 'discretion'.

This combined approach leads to a fuller understanding, not only of sexuality-based asylum claims and 'discretion' reasoning, but of the refugee definition and the question of what is protected under refugee law as a whole.

PART I

Tracing 'Discretion' Reasoning

Part I focuses on 'discretion' reasoning in sexuality-based asylum claims in three core European jurisdictions. So far, there is generally little research into sexuality-based claims in these countries, and it is important to note that 'discretion' reasoning is only one aspect of relevance in the context of this set of cases. A large number of issues merits attention and discussion, such as, importantly, credibility[1] and the use of country of origin information and corroborative evidence;[2] but also the understanding and use of terms and concepts of sexuality.[3] Covering all these issues is beyond the scope of this study. The following develops an analysis of 'discretion' reasoning.

[1] The issue of credibility has sparked quite some academic interest; on that topic, see e.g. Kimberly D. Topel (2017) '"So, What Should I Ask Him to Prove That He's Gay?": How Sincerity, and Not Stereotype, Should Dictate the Outcome of an LGB Asylum Claim in the United States', 102 *Iowa Law Review* 2357–2384; Jasmine Dawson and Paula Gerber (2017) 'Assessing the Refugee Claims of LGBTI People: Is the DSSH Model Useful for Determining Claims by Women for Asylum Based on Sexual Orientation?', 29(2) *International Journal of Refugee Law* 292–322; Nicholas Hersh (2015) 'Challenges to Assessing Same-Sex Relationships under Refugee Law In Canada', 60(3) *McGill Law Journal* 527–571; Uwe Berlit, Harald Dörig and Hugo Storey (2015) 'Credibility Assessment in Claims Based on Persecution for Reasons of Religious Conversion and Homosexuality: A Practitioners Approach', 27(4) *International Journal of Refugee Law* 649–666.

[2] See e.g. David A. B. Murray (2017) 'The Homonational Archive: Sexual Orientation and Gendered Identity Refugee Documentation in Canada and the USA', 82(3) *Ethnos* 520–544; David A. B. Murray (2016) 'Queer Forms: Producing Documentation in Sexual Orientation Refugee Cases', 89(2) *Anthropological Quarterly* 465–484; Lisa Schmitz (2015) *The 'True' Homosexual Refugee – An Archaeology of the Becoming and Governing of Refugees through Scientific-Legal Categories of Sexuality in German Legal Decision-Making*, masters thesis, Lund University, Sociology of Law Department, Autumn 2015, Lund Student University Papers, https://lup.lub.lu.se/student-papers/search/publication/8568341.

[3] See e.g. Eric Fassin and Manuela Salcedo (2015) Becoming Gay? Immigration Policies and the Truth of Sexual Identity', 44 *Archives of Sexual Behaviour* 1117–1125; Stefan Vogler (2016) 'Legally Queer: The Construction of Sexuality in LGBQ Asylum Claims', 50(4) *Law & Society Review* 856–889.

The lens of the act/identity dichotomy and, building on that, the frame of the discretion/disclosure binarism, is useful to identify and explore the different ways in which 'discretion' reasoning resurfaces in asylum decision-making. The dichotomy manifests itself in refugee status determination in many different ways and itself also plays a role in questions of fact, such as in the assessment of credibility[4] and in the analysis of country of origin information, for example where a state criminalises 'homosexual conduct'.[5] But it also affects doctrinal issues, such as the analysis of the particular social group as a Convention ground,[6] the persecution analysis and the nexus requirement. The present study focuses on doctrine.

Against this backdrop, Part I traces 'discretion' reasoning. It consists of an empirical assessment of 'discretion' reasoning in three European civil law jurisdictions. So far, the literature has focused on findings from common law jurisdictions and little is known of the ways in which 'discretion' reasoning has surfaced in other jurisdictions. Decision-making practice from France, Germany and Spain is assessed in turn to explore the ways in which the notion that the claimant can pass unnoticed takes shape. A longitudinal study for each of the jurisdictions involves the earliest available decisions and explores the development of 'discretion' reasoning up until the end of 2016. While the study is chronological in principle, findings from cases are presented and discussed thematically, as broader trends are made out. Moreover, the analysis is divided into the periods before and after two major developments occurred: the Europeanisation of status determination via the *Qualification Directive* (QD), which entered into force in 2006, and the rejection of the 'discretion' requirement by high-level European courts – namely, the UK Supreme Court in 2010, and the Court of Justice of the European Union (CJEU) in 2012 and 2013. The analytical division into a pre-QD/pre-rejection and a post-QD/post-rejection phase was made under the assumption that the Europeanisation of refugee status determination and the subsequent – maybe even consequent – rejection of the 'discretion' requirement would necessarily impact upon previously established practice. The aim of the exercise is to delineate that impact.

The division is, however, not very clear-cut. The *Qualification Directive* entered into force several years before the 'discretion' requirement was rejected by the

4 A claimant may be found to lack credibility when failing to provide an account of either same-sex sexual relations (acts) or same-sex emotional and romantic attraction (identity), see e.g. Louis Middelkoop (2013) 'Normativity and Credibility of Sexual Orientation in Asylum Decision Making', in Thomas Spikerboer (ed.) *Fleeing Homophobia: Sexual Orientation, Gender Identity and Asylum*, London: Routledge, 154–175.

5 Criminal laws generally address sexual conduct rather than sexual identity, see e.g. Jenni Millbank (2012) 'The Right of Lesbians and Gay Men to Live Freely, Openly, and on Equal Terms Is Not Bad Law: A Reply to Hathaway and Pobjoy', 44(2) *New York University Journal of International Law and Politics* 497–527, 513.

6 What defines a group? Is it an innate and unchangeable characteristics? Can a group be accepted that is based on 'just acts'? See e.g. Kristen Walker (2000) 'Sexuality and Refugee Status in Australia' 12(2) *International Journal of Refugee Law* 175–211.

courts. That is, there are several years that are post-QD but pre-rejection, and, of course, the three rejections occurred over a time span of four years. These years play out differently in the three jurisdictions, and changes were triggered by the *Qualification Directive* even before the official rejection of the 'discretion' requirement. Thus, it cannot be said that there was a single 'turning point' once the 'discretion' requirement was rejected; rather, practice evolved in a gradual process that was initiated by the *Qualification Directive* and then propelled by the three judgments.

The analysis of the judgments is guided by a search for instances where acts and identities are understood or presented as separate and the ways in which disclosure and 'discretion' play a role in the decision. The rationale is that looking at case law through the lens of the act/identity dichotomy, which is the basis of any sort of 'discretion' reasoning, enables the recognition of a broader range of manifestations of the phenomenon – and allows for a reconstruction of the way in which the scope of refugee protection is conceptualised.

Part I is thus guided by a triple objective. It seeks to fill the research gap on 'discretion' reasoning in three European jurisdictions by analysing judgments concerning sexuality-based asylum claims. In order to discover the various different forms of 'discretion' reasoning, it applies the act/identity dichotomy as a lens through which to look at case law. And the overarching question that this exercise responds to is what is understood as protected, and which arguments are used to buttress that position.

3

Rejecting 'Discretion'

A Turning Point?

Before moving to the case analysis for France, Germany and Spain, it is necessary to briefly lay out the context of the major events that frame the development of national refugee jurisprudence in these countries – the establishment of the Common European Asylum System (CEAS) and the judgments of the UK Supreme Court in *HJ (Iran) and HT (Cameroon)* from 2010,[1] as well as of the Court of Justice of the European Union in *Y and Z* from 2012,[2] and *X, Y and Z* from 2013.[3] The CEAS and the *Qualification Directive* will be situated in international refugee law; and the three European decisions that rejected the 'discretion' requirement will be summarised and contextualised. This is necessary in order to appreciate the ways in which national decision-making in the three jurisdictions under scrutiny has been affected by these developments. The differential impact in each jurisdiction will then be analysed in turn in subsequent chapters.

3.1 THE INSTITUTIONAL CONTEXT: THE QUALIFICATION DIRECTIVE AND THE CEAS[4]

Like all EU member states, France, Germany and Spain are signatories to the 1951 Refugee Convention (and its 1967 Protocol).[5] This Convention constitutes

[1] *HJ (Iran) and HT (Cameroon)* v. *Secretary of State for the Home Department*, [2010] UKSC 31, United Kingdom: Supreme Court, 7 July 2010.

[2] *Federal Republic of Germany* v. *Y and Z*, Joined Cases C-71/11 and C-99/11, Court of Justice of the European Union, 5 September 2012.

[3] *X, Y and Z* v. *Minister voor Immigratie, Integratie en Asiel*, Joined Cases C-199/12, C-200/12 and C-201/12, European Union: Court of Justice of the European Union, 7 November 2013.

[4] This section focuses on a brief description of the *Qualification Directive* and the role of the CJEU. For more details on the interplay of international and European asylum law, see Annex I.

[5] UN General Assembly, *Convention Relating to the Status of Refugees*, 28 July 1951, United Nations, Treaty Series, vol. 189, p. 137; and UN General Assembly, *Protocol Relating to the Status of Refugees*, 31 January 1967, United Nations, Treaty Series, vol. 606, p. 267.

the core of the international refugee regime and states the universal definition of refugees in Article 1A(2). Until 1999, asylum was an intergovernmental matter in the EU. Thus, European states had each developed their own reception and status determination procedures, based on their own interpretations of the 1951 Geneva Convention.

The Treaty of Amsterdam instituted asylum as a community (EU) competence.[6] Since then, the European Union has been in the process of establishing a Common European Asylum System (CEAS).[7] Most relevantly for this study, the Europeanisation of asylum also involved a harmonisation of refugee status determination. This was achieved through the *Qualification Directive*.[8] The Directive lays out the standards for the recognition of refugee status, principally covering the same ground as the 1951 Refugee Convention. In that sense, it amounts to a translation of the Convention into European law. Importantly, it adds more detail and definitions in some instances, thus giving up some of the malleability that allowed for the continual reinterpretation of the key terms of the Refugee Convention.[9] In certain ways, the *Qualification Directive* 'wrest[s] international law away from the international and … reframe[s] it'.[10] It has thus been functionally compared with the UNHCR Guidelines, which provide interpretive guidance on certain issues.[11] For example, the *Qualification Directive* clarifies that persecution can emanate from private actors,[12] and that gender and sexual orientation can be grounds for persecution.[13] Both these points have obvious implications for the assessment of sexuality-based claims.

6 Treaty of Amsterdam Amending the Treaty on European Union, the Treaties Establishing the European Communities and Certain Related Acts of 2 October 1997, OJ C 340, 10 November 1997 (entry into force 1 May 1999).

7 European Commission (2015) 'Common European Asylum System', https://ec.europa.eu/home-affairs/what-we-do/policies/asylum/index_en.htm.

8 Council Directive 2004/83/EC of 29 April 2004 on Minimum Standards for the Qualification and Status of Third Country Nationals or Stateless Persons as Refugees or as Persons Who Otherwise Need International Protection and the Content of the Protection Granted, OJ L 304/12, 30 September 2004 (2004 *Qualification Directive*). The Directive was recast in the 'second phase' of the Common European Asylum System (CEAS), though most of the operative provisions, as well as the Article numbering, remain entirely or essentially unchanged: Directive 2011/95/EU of the European Parliament and of the Council of 13 December 2011 on standards for the qualification of third-country nationals or stateless persons as beneficiaries of international protection, for a uniform status for refugees or for persons eligible for subsidiary protection, and for the content of the protection granted (recast), oj L 337/9, 20 December 2011 (*Recast Qualification Directive*), transposition date 21 December 2013.

9 Catherine Dauvergne (2008) *Making People Illegal: What Globalization Means for Migration and Law*, Cambridge: Cambridge University Press, 149–150.

10 Ibid., 150.

11 Nora Markard (2007) 'Fortschritte im Flüchtlingsrecht? Gender Guidelines und geschlechtsspezifische Verfolgung', 40(4) *Kritische Justiz* 373–390, 380.

12 Article 6(c) *Qualification Directive*.

13 Article 10(d) *Qualification Directive*.

Unlike the UNHCR Guidelines however, the *Qualification Directive* is binding – if only as regards the outcome. Directives allow EU member states to decide on the means to achieve the required objective. The *Qualification Directive* had to be transposed into national legislation by EU member states by 2006. Through the transposition process, states retained substantial discretion to establish procedures for granting and withdrawing protection, which has led to much-criticised divergences across member states.[14] Even so, depending on the pre-existing asylum system in the respective countries, the *Qualification Directive* had the power to unsettle some established doctrine.[15] Whereas previously EU member states had developed their refugee law doctrine – as derived from the Refugee Convention – quite independently, their room for discretion was thereafter reduced in important ways.

The *Qualification Directive* does not address itself specifically to 'discretion' reasoning, though it does explicitly state for both religion and political opinion that public behaviour and expressions are protected.[16] But the harmonisation of refugee law doctrine via the *Qualification Directive* acquires a particular relevance through another important development that has emanated from the Europeanisation of asylum: the extension of the jurisdiction of the Court of Justice of the European Union (CJEU) to matters of asylum law.[17] Since the entry into force of the Treaty of Lisbon, national courts or tribunals can – and under certain circumstances must – request preliminary rulings on the interpretation of the *Qualification Directive*.[18] The first judgments of the CJEU on the refugee definition were passed in 2010.[19] CJEU rulings are legally binding for EU law; that is, they are authoritative for the

[14] See e.g. Catherine Teitgen-Colly (2006) 'The European Union and Asylum: An Illusion of Protection', 43(6) *Common Market Law Review* 1503–1566, 1512–1513.

[15] Note that in addition to the international protection regime, Germany and France both also guarantee a right to asylum in their national constitutions, but particularly in view of the Common European Asylum System, constitutional asylum is generally considered to have become obsolete. For a discussion see Hélène Lambert, Francesco Messineo and Paul Tiedemann (2008) 'Comparative Perspectives of Constitutional Asylum in France, Italy, and Germany: *Requiescat In Pace?*', 27(3) *Refugee Survey Quarterly* 16–32.

[16] Article 10(b) *Qualification Directive* ('the participation in, or abstention from, formal worship in private or in public, either alone or in community with others, other religious acts or expressions of view, or forms of personal or communal conduct based on or mandated by any religious belief') and Article 10(e) ('whether or not that opinion, thought or belief has been acted upon by the applicant').

[17] Article 267 *Treaty on the Functioning of the European Union (TFEU)*; see on this point: Cathryn Costello and Emily Hancox (2014) 'The UK, the Common European Asylum System and EU Immigration Law', *Policy Primer*, Oxford: The Migration Observatory, www.migrationobservatory.ox.ac.uk/wp- content/uploads/2016/04/PolicyPrimer-UK_EU_Asylum_Law.pdf.

[18] Article 267 *TFEU*. On the functioning of the preliminary ruling procedure, see Annex I.

[19] *Salahadin Abdulla and Others* v. *Bundesrepublik Deutschland*, Joined Cases C-175/08, C-176/08, C-178/08 and C-179/08, European Union: Court of Justice of the European Union, 2 March 2010; *Nawras Bolbol* v. *Bevándorlási és Állampolgársági Hivatal*, Case C-31/09, European Union: Court of Justice of the European Union, 17 June 2010; *Bundesrepublik Deutschland* v. *B and D*, Joined Cases C-57/09 and C-101/09, European Union: Court of Justice of the European Union, 9 November 2010.

member states of the EU.[20] This is the second way in which the member states' discretion in the application of the Refugee Convention was restrained through the Europeanisation of asylum, as they no longer retain the final interpretative authority. Both these developments compel states to reconsider some of their established doctrine to some extent. As regards 'discretion', two relevant judgments were handed down by the CJEU, which will be discussed further in the next section.

3.2 THE COURTS: HIGH-LEVEL REJECTIONS OF 'DISCRETION' IN EUROPE

Within this institutional context, 'discretion' has been dealt with in three landmark decisions. The UK Supreme Court addressed it in 2010 as discussed, and the CJEU ruled on 'discretion' in two closely related cases in 2012 and 2013. The following provides an overview of these judgments and situates them in the international judicial dialogue. The background and context of these judgments is important for contextualising and putting into perspective the French, German and Spanish decision-making practice.

3.2.1 *The Concealment Controversy: The UKSC Judgment in* HJ (Iran) and HT (Cameroon)

The United Kingdom has a special position in the institutional context of European and international refugee law. On the one hand, it has played an important role in the judicial dialogue of *common* law jurisdictions for years. In dialogue in particular with Australia, Canada and New Zealand, the United Kingdom has led international developments in refugee law doctrine. On the other hand, while a member state of the EU, the United Kingdom was – though somewhat reluctantly[21] – part of the Common European Asylum System and therefore bound by the *Qualification Directive*. In that sense, while still part of the system, it could be seen as a hinge between the common law and the European judicial dialogue on asylum. At the time when the issue of 'discretion' reached the UK Supreme Court in 2010 and culminated in the landmark decision of *HJ (Iran) and HT (Cameroon)*,[22] this meant two things: first, much depended on the way the United Kingdom positioned itself within that institutional framework vis-à-vis the other jurisdictions and, second, UK judgments could be assumed to carry substantial weight, as they were a point of

[20] Out of twenty-eight EU member states, Denmark is the only state that opted out entirely of the asylum package; both the United Kingdom and Ireland opted out of most of the second phase (recast) of EU legislation, but the first generation remains applicable.
[21] With the United Kingdom having left the European Union in 2020 ('Brexit'), this is now changing.
[22] *HJ (Iran) and HT (Cameroon) v. Secretary of State for the Home Department*, note 1.

reference in both 'circles'. The significance of the decision and the way it has been received must be seen against this institutional backdrop.

Following the 2003 High Court of Australia judgment in *Appellant S395/2002* v. *Minister for Immigration and Multicultural Affairs*,[23] which was faced with a similar case, the UK Supreme Court's decision in *HJ and HT* is the second landmark judgment on 'discretion' in sexuality-based asylum cases worldwide. The judges appeared to be quite aware of the potentially far-reaching implications of the judgment, as it clearly concerned a wider legal principle of profound significance.[24] Their decision was based on a 'carefully-researched debate that the Court has heard and participated in ([based on] 23 bundles of authorities containing 250 different items)',[25] in which they not only referred to previous UK case law, but also engaged quite heavily with international case law from other common law jurisdictions. Most importantly, they sought guidance from Australia and New Zealand, and also, to a lesser extent, the United States and Canada, because it is 'desirable that, so far as possible, there should be international consensus on the meaning of the Convention'.[26] Lord Hope noted that the cases reviewed revealed 'no consistent line of authority that indicates that there is an approach which is universally accepted internationally'.[27]

In tackling the open question they had thus identified, the UK Supreme Court did not seek out other European jurisprudence and explicitly decided not to make a reference for a preliminary ruling, as revealed by Lord Hope.[28] Generally, in its reasoning in this judgment, the UK Supreme Court explicitly refers to EU law only to cite the definition of persecution.[29] Otherwise, the discussion centres on

[23] *Appellant S395/2002* v. *Minister for Immigration and Multicultural Affairs; Appellant S396/2002* v. *Minister for Immigration and Multicultural Affairs*, [2003] HCA 71, Australia: High Court, 9 December 2003.

[24] See Garden Court Chambers (2010) 'Future Behaviour and the Refugee Convention', *Free Movement Blog*, 12 July 2010, www.freemovement.org.uk/future-behaviour-and-the-refugee-convention.

[25] *HJ (Iran) and HT (Cameroon)* v. *Secretary of State for the Home Department*, note 1, per Lord Walker at 87.

[26] Ibid., per Lord Walker at 127.

[27] Ibid., per Lord Hope at 30.

[28] 'It was suggested by the appellants that this court should make a reference of a question arising under the Qualification Directive to the Court of Justice of the European Union under article 267 TFEU (formerly article 234 EC). But the point that was said to require a reference was not clearly identified, and I would reject that suggestion', *HJ (Iran) and HT (Cameroon)* v. *Secretary of State for the Home Department*, note 1, per Lord Hope at 39.

[29] Ibid., per Lord Hope at 12. And there are two indirect references (per Lord Rodger at 42, and per Lord Hope at 10), when noting that sexual orientation clearly qualifies as particular social group according to the *Refugee or Person in Need of International Protection (Qualification) Regulations 2006 (SI 2006/2525)*, which implemented the necessary changes to national legislation as required by the EU Qualification Directive in the UK: UK Home Office (2006) *Explanatory Memorandum to the Refugee or Person in Need of International Protection (Qualification) Regulations 2006*, No. 2525, www.legislation.gov.uk/uksi/2006/2525/pdfs/uksi_20062525_en.pdf.

case law from common law jurisdictions and previous UK case law on the issue – and the interpretation of the 1951 Refugee Convention rather than the *Qualification Directive*.[30] Overall, it can be reasonably said that the judgment in *HJ (Iran) and HT (Cameroon)* is firmly located in the context of the common law judicial dialogue on the 1951 Refugee Convention rather than in the context of the Common European Asylum System. The extent to which it nevertheless influenced European decision-making on these matters, thus creating a bridge between common law jurisdictions and European refugee law, remains to be explored.

Substantively, the UK Supreme Court judgment addressed the question of whether gay people could be reasonably required to be 'discreet' so as to avoid persecution such that no protection would be owed. As outlined in the introduction, the judgment concerned two gay men – HJ from Iran and HT from Cameroon – whose claims to asylum had been turned down by lower courts on the basis that they could reasonably be expected to tolerate 'living discreetly' in their countries of origin in order to avoid persecution. This is not unusual: prior to this judgment, there had been a consensus in the United Kingdom that gay claimants can be reasonably expected to tolerate having to live 'discreetly' so as to avoid persecution.[31] In the leading judgment, Lord Rodger stated that '[t]he appellants take this fairly well established case law of the Court of Appeal head-on'[32] and formulated the central question of the case as being whether an applicant is

> to be regarded as a refugee for purposes of the Convention in circumstances where the reality is that, if he were returned to his country of nationality, he would have to behave discreetly in order to avoid persecution because of being gay?[33]

[30] A difference in focus is also reflected in the reasoning of the two interveners to the case: whereas the Equality and Human Rights Commission develops an EU law approach (and suggests the possibility of making a reference to the CJEU), the UNHCR in its intervention focuses on international case law, particularly common law cases, and makes no mention of the *Qualification Directive* or the CJEU. See The Equality and Human Rights Commission (2010) *HJ (Iran) and HT (Cameroon)* v. *Secretary of State for the Home Department – Case for the Equality and Human Rights Commission*, copy on file with author; and UNHCR (2011) *HJ (Iran) and HT (Cameroon)* v. *Secretary of State for the Home Department – Case for the First Intervener (the United Nations High Commissioner for Refugees)*, 19 April 2010, www.unhcr.org/refworld/docid/4bd1abbc2.html.

[31] See, for a detailed discussion of this issue based on an extensive review of case law, Jenni Millbank (2009) 'From Discretion to Disbelief: Recent Trends in Refugee Determinations on the Basis of Sexual Orientation in Australia and the United Kingdom', 13(2/3) *International Journal of Human Rights* 391–414; Catherine Dauvergne and Jenni Millbank (2003) 'Before the High Court: Applicants S396/2002 and S395/2002, a Gay Refugee Couple from Bangladesh', 25 *Sydney Law Review* 97–124; Jenni Millbank (2004) 'The Role of Rights in Asylum Claims on the Basis of Sexual Orientation', 4(2) *Human Rights Law Review* 193–228.

[32] *HJ (Iran) and HT (Cameroon)* v. *Secretary of State for the Home Department*, note 1, per Lord Rodger at 50.

[33] Ibid., per Lord Rodger at 59; though he then further refines the question at 62 to include a reference to the reasons for acting discreetly: 'is an applicant to be regarded as a refugee for purposes of the Convention in circumstances where the reality is that, if he were returned to his

The Court's unanimous answer was no: It ruled that applicants for protection cannot be required, reasonably or otherwise, to change their behaviour in order to avoid persecution.

However, the UK Supreme Court failed to put an end to the issue of 'discretion' as a whole. In fact, concealment crept back into the new test that they proposed, as it is constructed around a distinction between 'open' and 'discreet' gay people, giving considerable weight to expected or assumed future *behaviour* (or *activities*) of claimants. The assessment now turns on a 'factual' assessment of what the applicant 'will do' on return: The test states that

> the tribunal must ... consider *what the individual applicant would do* if he were returned to [his] country. If the applicant would in fact live openly and thereby be exposed to a real risk of persecution, then he has a well-founded fear of persecution – even if he could avoid the risk by living 'discreetly'. If, on the other hand, the tribunal concludes that the applicant would in fact live discreetly and so avoid persecution, it must go on to ask itself *why he would do so*.[34]

The answer to the 'why' question will determine whether protection is granted. If the appellant would behave 'discreetly' out of choice, because that is how *they chose* to live, then they would not be entitled to protection – and the presumed ensuing safety is accepted as a positive side effect. Only if they behave 'discreetly' out of fear will they be granted refugee status. The Supreme Court thus essentially stated that while 'discretion' cannot be *expected* of a claimant, it can be *accepted* as a factual basis under certain circumstances.[35]

The judgment unequivocally rejects any 'discretion' *requirement*. However, the test remains based on a classification of applicants according to their behaviour, in particular their 'discretion'. By assuming that only 'gay people who lived openly' would be liable to persecution, the Court is able to conclude that those who will 'in fact choose' to be 'discreet' are not at risk. So 'discretion logic' prevails as the persecution analysis is made dependent on the assumed future conduct of the applicant.[36] In this scenario, then, the *act* limb is the preferred one, whereas *identity* is the submerged part of the double bind. It is not sufficient to *be* gay; in addition, it requires the claimant to show and convince the decision-maker that she or he will

country of nationality, in addition to any other reasons for behaving discreetly, he would have to behave discreetly in order to avoid persecution because of being gay?'; see for a critique: Janna Wessels (2012) 'HJ (Iran) and HT (Cameroon) – Reflections on a New Test for Sexuality-Based Asylum Claims in Britain', 24(4) *International Journal of Refugee Law* 815–839.

[34] *HJ (Iran) and HT (Cameroon)* v. *Secretary of State for the Home Department*, note 1, per Lord Rodger at 82, emphasis added.

[35] See Wessels, note 33, 815–839; see also Alice Edwards (2012) 'Distinction, Discretion, Discrimination: The New Frontiers of Gender-Related Claims to Asylum', *paper delivered at the Gender, Migration and Human Rights Conference at the European University Institute*, Florence, Italy, 19 June 2012, www.refworld.org/docid/4ffd430c2.html.

[36] Wessels, note 33, 815–839, 837.

also *act* on this identity, that is, *express* their sexual orientation. Failure to do so will likely result in a negative outcome of the claim, as the claimant – though still a gay *person* and thus arguably still at risk – is not expected to display behaviour that would lead to a well-founded fear of being persecuted. As discussed in the introduction, in spite of its explicit intention, the judgment thus did not succeed in 'resolving' the issue of 'discretion' for refugee law doctrine – and continues to struggle with the limits of protection.

3.2.2 *Avoiding Trouble: The Twin Decisions of the Court of Justice of the European Union*

The fact that *HJ (Iran) and HT (Cameroon)* failed to settle the issue of 'discretion' reasoning is clearly reflected in the fact that Germany made a referral to the CJEU for a preliminary ruling on the same issue only six months after the UK Supreme Court had handed down its judgment (without for its part considering it necessary to refer the question). The referral was made by the OVG Münster, the Higher Administrative Court of Northrhine-Westphalia. The reference was lodged as *Kashayar Khavand* v. *Federal Republic of Germany (Case C-563/10)* on 1 December 2010[37] and concerned a gay man from Iran. His claim had been rejected by the Administrative Court of Düsseldorf on the grounds that gay men in Iran faced no considerable risk of persecution 'as long as they practise their orientation in secret and as long as they have not already attracted the attention of the Iranian law enforcement agencies due to their homosexual inclination'.[38] His appeal led the Higher Administrative Court of Northrhine-Westphalia to make a referral on the issue of 'discretion' to the CJEU. The relevant provision that the referral centred on is Article 10(1)(d) of the *Qualification Directive*, providing a definition of the Convention ground membership of a particular social group. Article 10(1)(d) Qualification Directive states:

> a group shall be considered to form a particular social group where in particular:
> — members of that group share an innate characteristic, or a common background that cannot be changed, or share a characteristic or belief that is so fundamental to identity or conscience that a person should not be forced to renounce it, and
> — that group has a distinct identity in the relevant country, because it is perceived as being different by the surrounding society.
>
> Depending on the circumstances in the country of origin, a particular social group might include a group based on a common characteristic of sexual orientation. Sexual orientation cannot be understood to include acts considered to be criminal in accordance with national law of the Member States. Gender related

37 Reference for a preliminary ruling from the Oberverwaltungsgericht für das Land Nordrhein-Westfalen (Germany) lodged on 1 December 2010, *Kashayar Khavand* v. *Federal Republic of Germany (Case C-563/10)*.

38 VG Düsseldorf, Urteil vom 11.3.2009, 5 K 1875/08.A.

> aspects, including gender identity, shall be given due consideration for the purposes of determining membership of a particular social group or identifying a characteristic of such a group.[39]

The last paragraph explicitly states that a particular social group may be constituted by sexual orientation. Nonetheless, the referring German Court's first question reflects doubts on this point:

> 1. Is homosexuality to be considered a sexual orientation within the meaning of the second sentence of Article 10(1)(d) of Directive 2004/83/EC and can it be an adequate reason for persecution?
> 2. If Question 1 is to be answered in the affirmative:
>   (a) To what extent is homosexual activity protected?
>   (b) Can a homosexual person be told to live with his or her sexual orientation in his or her home country in secret and not allow it to become known to others?
>   (c) Are specific prohibitions for the protection of public order and morals relevant when interpreting and applying Article 10(1)(d) of Directive 2004/83/EC or should homosexual activity be protected in the same way as for heterosexual people?[40]

Notably, the questions focused entirely on the protection of 'homosexual *activity*'. In its reasons for the referral, the Court relied on previous German case law and literature, but did not engage with other European case law, and in particular made no mention of the UK Supreme Court judgment in *HJ (Iran) and HT (Cameroon)*.[41] However, the questions remained unanswered because, before the CJEU had the opportunity to make a ruling, the case was removed from the register on 11 March 2011.[42] Since the CJEU had published the full name of the applicant, his sexual orientation had now become publicly known, and the German authorities therefore granted protection.[43] This is striking, as it reveals the extent to which the claimant's safety depends on his state of hiding, that is, his 'discretion'. As a consequence, the ruling was no longer essential for a decision in the case and therefore nugatory.

[39] Council Directive 2004/83/EC of 29 April 2004, note 8 (2004 *Qualification Directive*), this version was applicable at the time of the referral, but the provision and numbering remained unchanged in the recast version from 2011.

[40] *Kashayar Khavand* v. *Federal Republic of Germany (Case C-563/10)*, note 37. The questions referred emerged from German practice on 'discretion' reasoning (see Chapter 5).

[41] OVG Münster, Beschluss vom 23.11.2010, 13 A 1013/09.A.

[42] Order of the President of the Court of 11 March 2011 (Reference for a preliminary ruling from the Oberverwaltungsgericht für das Land Nordrhein-Westfalen, Germany), *Kashayar Khavand* v. *Bundesrepublik Deutschland* (Case C-563/10), 'Removal'.

[43] Nora Markard (2011) '60 Jahre Genfer Flüchtlingskonvention: Verantwortung für den Flüchtlingsschutz – 11. Berliner Symposium zum Flüchtlingsschutz, 21–22. Juni 2011, Berlin – Tagungsbericht', 8 *Zeitschrift für Ausländerrecht und Ausländerpolitik* 241–280, 266.

But the continuing contentious nature of the issue is evidenced by the fact that, over the following years, essentially the same question – albeit each time a little more refined – was referred to the CJEU another three times. Following *Kashayar Khavand* v. *Germany* in 2010, there were *Germany* v. *Y and Z* in 2011, *Minister voor Immigratie en Asiel* v. X, *Y and Z* in 2012 and *Federal Commissioner for Asylum Affairs* v. N in 2014.[44] Two referrals (*Kashayar Khavand* and X, *Y and Z*) related to asylum claims based on sexual orientation, and two related to religion (*Y and Z*, and N); notably, *N* was a follow-up asking for clarification on the Court's ruling in *Y and Z*. Three out of the four referrals were made by Germany and one by the Netherlands. This active role of German courts in making referrals stands in stark contrast to the reluctant UK endorsement of the CEAS and reflects Germany's wish to drive and influence European jurisprudence.[45] Only two of the four relevant referrals led to judgments – like the referral in *Kashayar Khavaand*, the case of N was withdrawn before a decision was handed down by the CJEU, because the national authorities had granted status to the claimant in the meantime.

3.2.2.1 Core Area a.k.a. 'Forum Internum': Y and Z on Religion

Even before *Kashayar Khavand* was withdrawn, the Bundesverwaltungsgericht (Federal Administrative Court of Germany) had already made two other parallel references for a preliminary ruling – closely related to the previous one, though this time not concerning sexual orientation but rather the cases of two men of Ahmadi faith from Pakistan.[46]

Both men claimed that they had been persecuted for their membership of the Muslim Ahmadiyya community. In these cases, the referring German Judges engaged explicitly with UK case law, specifically with the Court of Appeal case of

[44] *Kashayar Khavand (Case C-563/10)*; Reference for a preliminary ruling from the Bundesverwaltungsgericht (Germany) lodged on 18 February 2011, *Federal Republic of Germany* v. *Y (Case C-71/11)*; Reference for a preliminary ruling from the Raad van State (Netherlands) lodged on 27 April 2012, *Minister voor Immigratie en Asiel* v. X *(Case C-199/12)*; and Reference for a preliminary ruling from the Sächsisches Oberverwaltungsgericht (Germany) lodged on 30 March 2015, *Federal Commissioner for Asylum Affairs* v. N *(Case C-150/15)*.

[45] Markard, note 43, 241–280, 266.

[46] *Federal Republic of Germany* v. *Y (Case C-71/11)*, note 44; and Reference for a preliminary ruling from the Bundesverwaltungsgericht (Germany) lodged on 2 March 2011, *Federal Republic of Germany* v. *Z (Case C-99/11)* (2011/C 173/07). The references in Y *(C-71/11)* and Z *(C-99/11)* were joined by order of the president of the CJEU from 24 March 2011: Order of the President of the Court of 24 March 2011 (References for preliminary rulings from the Bundesverwaltungsgericht, Germany), *Federal Republic of Germany* v. *Y (Case C-71/11)* and *Federal Republic of Germany* v. *Z (Case C-99/11)*, 'Joining' [Beschluss des Präsidenten des Gerichtshofs vom 24. März 2011, 'Verbindung' in der Rechtssache C-71/11 und in der Rechtssache C-99/11].

Ahmed (Iftikhar) on religion and the Supreme Court judgment in *HJ (Iran) and HT (Cameroon)* on sexual orientation.[47] The referring court noted a difference in German and UK jurisprudence on these matters and sought to clarify:

1. Is Article 9(1)(a) of Directive 2004/83/EC1 to be interpreted as meaning that not every interference with religious freedom which breaches Article 9 of the European Convention on Human Rights constitutes an act of persecution within the meaning of Article 9(1)(a) of Directive 2004/83/EC, but that a severe violation of religious freedom as a basic human right arises only if the core area of that religious freedom is adversely affected?
2. If Question 1 is to be answered in the affirmative:
   (a) Is the core area of religious freedom limited to the profession and practice of faith in the areas of the home and neighbourhood, or can there also be an act of persecution, within the meaning of Article 9(1)(a) of Directive 2004/83/EC, in cases where, in the country of origin, the practice of faith in public gives rise to a risk to body, life or physical freedom and the applicant accordingly abstains from such practice?
   (b) If the core area of religious freedom can also comprise certain religious practices in public:
   Does it suffice in that case, in order for there to be a severe violation of religious freedom, that the applicant feels that such practice of his faith is indispensable in order for him to preserve his religious identity,
   or is it further necessary that the religious community to which the applicant belongs should regard that religious practice as constituting a central part of its doctrine,
   or can further restrictions arise as a result of other circumstances, such as the general conditions in the country of origin?
3. If Question 1 is to be answered in the affirmative:
   Is there a well-founded fear of persecution, within the meaning of Article 2 (c) of Directive 2004/83/EC, if it is established that the applicant will carry out certain religious practices – other than those falling within the core area – after returning to the country of origin, even though these will give rise to a risk to body, life or physical freedom, or is the applicant to be expected to abstain from engaging in such religious practices in the future?[48]

[47] *Ahmed (Iftikhar)* v. *Secretary of State for the Home Department*, [2000] INLR 1, United Kingdom: Court of Appeal (England and Wales), 5 November 1999; and *HJ (Iran) and HT (Cameroon)* v. *Secretary of State for the Home Department*, note 1.

[48] *Federal Republic of Germany* v. *Y (Case C-71/11)*, note 44.

German case law prior to the entry into force of the *Qualification Directive* had extended protection only to a 'core area' of the freedom of religion.[49] According to that jurisprudence, restrictions on the practice of faith in public did not infringe on the core of religious freedom and therefore could not lead to protection.[50] The questions referred to the CJEU inquired into whether that distinction is also applicable under European law. Question 1 asked whether there was a 'core' of the freedom of religion that is protected; question 2 sought to define that core; and question 3 asked on that basis whether it is reasonable to expect a claimant to abstain from activity on the 'margins'. Note that the framing of the questions referred for preliminary ruling is important. Although the Court is required to limit itself to replying to the specific questions presented, it does have latitude to rephrase them according to what it deems to be the essence of the question ('in essence, the question is . . .'). The Court frequently makes use of this possibility.

In its judgment, the Court rejected any sort of 'discretion' *requirement* – whether based on a core/margins approach or otherwise. It noted:

> None of those rules [from the Qualification Directive] states that, in assessing the extent of the risk of actual acts of persecution in a particular situation, it is necessary to take account of the possibility open to the applicant of avoiding the risk of persecution by abstaining from the religious practice in question and, consequently, renouncing the protection which the Directive is intended to afford the applicant by conferring refugee status.[51]

However, the judgment does allow for a 'factual' assessment of the claimant's future behaviour:

> It follows that, where it is established that, upon his return to his country of origin, the person concerned *will follow a religious practice* which will expose him to a real risk of persecution, he should be granted refugee status, in accordance with Article 13 of the Directive. The fact that he could avoid that risk by abstaining from certain religious practices is, in principle, irrelevant.[52]

Though it is difficult to determine to what extent the CJEU drew on previous case law from the common law jurisdictions,[53] the judgment is in that sense in line with *HJ (Iran) and HT (Cameroon)*, at least in its first step, as it does not *require* 'discretion'. Nonetheless, in passing, it considers it a 'fact' that the claimant could

49 Paul Tiedemann (2014) *Flüchtlingsrecht – Die materiellen und verfahrensrechtlichen Grundlagen*, Berlin: Springer, 60–61, and see BverfGE 76, 143, Beschluss vom 01.07.1987 at 158–159, on the religious 'forum internum'.

50 *Federal Republic of Germany* v. *Y and Z*, note 2, at 42.

51 Ibid., at 78.

52 Ibid., at 79; emphasis added.

53 The only explicit acknowledgement can be traced in a footnote reference to *HJ (Iran) and HT (Cameroon)* in Advocate General Bot's Opinion for *Y and Z*: *Federal Republic of Germany* v. *Y and Z (Opinion of Advocate General Bot)*, Joined Cases C-71/11 and C-99/11, European Union: Court of Justice of the European Union, 19 April 2012 at 104.

avoid persecution by exercising 'discretion'. But the controversial follow-up debate around what happens if the claimant will 'in fact' *abstain* from public expression was avoided – as the question was not posed.

3.2.2.2 Concealment, Restraint, Expression: X, Y and Z on Sexual Orientation

The urgency of questions around 'discretion' is borne out by the fact that, five months before the judgment was handed down in *Y and Z*, the Dutch Raad van State had already made another related referral to the CJEU. The questions referred in three joint cases, which were confusingly named *X, Y and Z*, concerned three gay men from Sierra Leone, Uganda and Senegal, respectively. In all three countries, homosexuality is a criminal offence. The Raad van State noted that the Minister had argued that 'although he did not expect foreign nationals to conceal their sexual orientation in their country of origin . . . that did not mean that they must be free to publicly express it in the same way as in the Netherlands'.[54] This statement, in a nutshell, comprises the dilemma outlined: how to solve a situation where the claimant cannot be expected to hide their characteristic, but at the same time is not entitled to the same level of freedoms under the Refugee Convention?

Further, according to the Raad van State, 'the parties in the main proceedings are not in agreement as to the extent to which fully expressing a sexual orientation, such as that shared by X, Y and Z, is protected by Articles 9 and 10 of the [Qualification] Directive'.[55] Therefore, the Raad van State decided to stay the proceedings and refer the questions to the CJEU. The questions referred were as follows.

1. Do foreign nationals with a homosexual orientation form a particular social group as referred to in Article 10(1)(d) of Council Directive 2004/83/EC of 29 April 2004 on minimum standards for the qualification and status of third country nationals or stateless persons as refugees or as persons who otherwise need international protection and the content of the protection granted (OJ 2004 L 304; 'the Directive')?
2. If the first question is to be answered in the affirmative: which homosexual activities fall within the scope of the Directive and, in the case of acts of persecution in respect of those activities and if the other requirements are met, can that lead to the granting of refugee status? That question encompasses the following subquestions:
   (a) Can foreign nationals with a homosexual orientation be expected to conceal their orientation from everyone in their country of origin in order to avoid persecution?

[54] *X, Y and Z* v. *Minister voor Immigratie, Integratie en Asiel*, note 3, at 35.
[55] Ibid., at 36.

(b) If the previous question is to be answered in the negative, can foreign nationals with a homosexual orientation be expected to exercise restraint, and if so, to what extent, when giving expression to that orientation in their country of origin, in order to avoid persecution? Moreover, can greater restraint be expected of homosexuals than of heterosexuals?

(c) If, in that regard, a distinction can be made between forms of expression which relate to the core area of the orientation and forms of expression which do not, what should be understood to constitute the core area of the orientation and in what way can it be determined?

3. Do the criminalisation of homosexual activities and the threat of imprisonment in relation thereto, as set out in the Offences against the Person Act 1861 of Sierra Leone, constitute an act of persecution within the meaning of Article 9(1)(a), read in conjunction with Article 9(2)(c) of the Directive? If not, under what circumstances would that be the case?[56]

As in *Kashayar Khavand*, the first question as to whether 'people with a homosexual orientation' can form a particular social group is somewhat surprising because Article 10(1)(d) explicitly states precisely that sexual orientation can constitute a particular social group. The context was that in the main proceedings concerning one of the claimants, the first instance court was not satisfied that all gay persons in Senegal were generally persecuted and therefore found that the applicant was not a member of a particular social group. Advocate General Sharpston, who delivered the opinion in *Y and Z*, responded that the 'EU legislator has given the clearest possible indication that persons with a shared characteristic of sexual orientation may indeed be members of a particular social group.'[57] The question of whether gay people constitute a group reflects identity reasoning. In contrast, the second question is framed around a focus on acts – it asked for persecution in respect of homosexual *activities*. The sub-questions then spell out different levels of discretion: concealment, restraint and expression. The Court ruled unambiguously, and explicitly in analogy with its previous judgment on religion in *Y and Z*, that a claimant cannot be expected to conceal or exercise reserve in the expression of their sexual orientation in order to avoid persecution.[58] As in the earlier referrals, the questions were framed around a *requirement* to be discreet, and did not consider the possibility

[56] *Minister voor Immigratie en Asiel* v. *X (Case C-199/12)*, note 44.

[57] *X, Y and Z* v. *Minister voor Immigratie, Integratie en Asiel (Opinion of Advocate General Sharpston)*, Joined Cases C-199/12, C-200/12 and C-201/12, European Union: Court of Justice of the European Union, 11 July 2013 at 35.

[58] *X, Y and Z* v. *Minister voor Immigratie, Integratie en Asiel*, note 3, at 71 and 76.

of a 'factual' finding that someone 'will be' discreet and the follow-up questions arising out of that.

3.2.3 *The Said and the Unsaid: On Thin Ice*

In both judgments, the CJEU rejected a distinction between core and marginal acts. In X, *Y and* Z, it stated that it is 'unnecessary to distinguish acts that interfere with the core areas of the expression of sexual orientation, even assuming it were possible to identify them, from acts which do not affect those purported core areas'.[59] Both of the judgments reject a requirement, or duty, to be 'discreet'.

However, the Court merely addressed the issue of 'reasonable expectation', and stopped short of considering a 'factual' finding that a claimant *will be* 'discreet'.[60] This important issue, which was dealt with in *HJ (Iran) and HT (Cameroon)* as well as in the previous High Court of Australia majority judgments in *S395* for sexual orientation[61] and *NABD* for religion,[62] therefore remains unaddressed at the European level and will, inevitably, lead to further confusion.

The fact that the Court has not achieved a settlement of the issues in both cases is revealed by a new request for a preliminary ruling by the Higher Administrative Court of Saxonia (*Sächsisches Oberverwaltungsgericht*), with questions concerning the same case that had led to the judgment in Y *and* Z, which was lodged on 30 March 2015.[63] After the judgment had been handed down in Y *and* Z, the Federal Administrative Court remitted the case back to the *Sächsisches Oberverwaltungsgericht* with instructions on how to interpret the CJEU's ruling and guidance on how to decide the case. The *Oberverwaltungsgericht*, however, did not agree with two aspects of the interpretation of the Federal Administrative Court and resubmitted the case to the CJEU, essentially asking for interpretation of its own previous rulings.

The questions referred reflect the level of detailed judicial dispute that the issue of the claimant's identity and conduct has engaged the courts in. The first question revolved around whether the prohibition of a religious act by criminal laws was to be considered persecutory only if that act was of particular importance to the claimant concerned. The second question concerned the assessment of prosecution practice and asked whether the relevant comparison was with those who did actively engage in the prohibited practice despite their criminalisation (i.e. those

59 Ibid., at 78, and by analogy: *Federal Republic of Germany* v. Y *and* Z, note 2, at 62.

60 X, Y *and* Z v. *Minister voor Immigratie, Integratie en Asiel*, note 3, at 79; *Federal Republic of Germany* v. Y *and* Z, note 2, at 81.

61 *Appellant S395/2002* v. *Minister for Immigration and Multicultural Affairs; Appellant S396/2002* v. *Minister for Immigration and Multicultural Affairs*, note 23; see Chapter 1.

62 *Applicant NABD of 2002* v. *Minister for Immigration and Multicultural and Indigenous Affairs*, [2005] HCA 29, Australia: High Court, 26 May 2005; see Chapter 1.

63 *Federal Commissioner for Asylum Affairs* v. N *(Case C-150/15)*, note 44.

'living openly'), or whether it was sufficient to establish that such laws were indeed applied in practice. The third question was whether a lower court was bound by the higher court's interpretation of the CJEU's rulings if it did not agree with it:

1. Is Article 9(1)(a) in conjunction with Article 10(1)(b) of Directive 2011/95/EU to be interpreted as follows:
   (a) that a severe violation of the freedom of religion guaranteed by Article 10(1) CFREU (Charter of Fundamental Rights of the European Union) and Article 9(1) ECHR (European Convention on Human Rights) and thus an act of persecution under Article 9(1)(a) of the Directive must be assumed when religious acts or expressions of view that are mandated by a doctrine of faith that the applicant actively professes and which form a core element of the doctrine of faith or are based on the religious convictions of the applicant in the sense that they are a pillar of his religious identity, are prohibited by criminal law in the country of origin,

   or

   (b) is it required that an applicant who actively declares his belief in a particular doctrine of faith must further prove that core elements mandated as religious acts or as or [sic] expressions of view by the doctrine of faith, which represent a prohibited religious activity subject to criminal prosecution in his country of origin, are 'particularly important' for the preservation of his religious identity and in this sense are 'essential'?
2. Is Article 9(3) in conjunction with Article 2(d) of Directive 2011/95/EU to be interpreted as follows:
   that in order to determine a well-founded fear of being persecuted and a real risk of being persecuted or subjected to inhuman or degrading treatment or punishment by one of the actors specified in Article 6 of Directive 2011/95/EU, with regard to religious acts or expressions of view that are mandated by a doctrine of faith that the applicant actively professes and are a core element of the doctrine of faith or are based on the religious convictions of the applicant in the sense that they are a pillar of his religious identity, and are prohibited by criminal law in the country of origin,
   (a) it is necessary to evaluate the relationship by comparing the number of members of the applicant's faith who practice their faith despite the prohibition to the number of actual acts of persecution of these acts of faith in the applicant's country of origin, including any possible uncertainties or unknowns regarding governmental enforcement practices,

or

(b) it is sufficient if, in the enforcement of the criminal law in the country of origin, the actual application of the laws threatening prosecution of religious acts or expressions of view that are mandated by a doctrine of faith that the applicant actively professes and which form a core element of the doctrine of faith or are based on the religious convictions of the applicant in the sense that they are a [sic] of particular importance for his religious identity can be proved?

3. Is a provision of national administrative law under which a trial court is bound by the legal judgment of the court of third instance (here: Section 144(6) VwGO (Verwaltungsgerichtsordnung) [Administrative Court Procedure Act]) compatible with the principle of the primacy of EU law if the trial court wishes to interpret a standard in EU law differently to the court of third instance but, even after implementation of a preliminary ruling procedure pursuant to Article 267(2) TFEU, is precluded from applying this interpretation of EU law by national law binding the court to the legal analysis of the court of third instance?[64]

Just a week before the hearings were scheduled in Luxembourg in the matter, however, the applicant was unexpectedly granted a residence title by the Ausländerbehörde (Aliens Authority) and the referral was, therefore, no longer essential to determine his case; the case was removed from the register on 15 April 2016.[65] The contents of the questions remain unanswered, and will likely end up before the CJEU again before long.

3.3 CONCLUSION: HALF-HEARTED DISAPPROVAL

To summarise, whereas the *Qualification Directive* itself does not address 'discretion' beyond an explicit inclusion of public expression of political opinion and religion, there have been three high-level judgments on the issue since the harmonisation of asylum in the EU. All three clearly and unequivocally reject any 'reasonable requirement' to be 'discreet'. Only the UK Supreme Court judgment goes beyond the question of a *requirement* and addresses the possibility of a 'factual' finding of 'discreet' behaviour; the CJEU has so far not pronounced a position on this variation of the issue. It is important to recall that the three judgments do not

64 Ibid.

65 Order of the President of the Court of 15 April 2016 (Reference for a preliminary ruling from the Sächsisches Oberverwaltungsgericht, Germany), *Federal Commissioner for Asylum Affairs* v. *N (Case C-150/15)*, 'Removal' [Beschluss des Präsidenten des Gerichtshofs 15. April 2016 'Streichung' In der Rechtssache C-150/15].

entirely rule out 'discretion' reasoning and remain somewhat ambiguous with regard to the role of the claimant in defining the scope of protection.

The following three chapters assess the ways in which decision-making practice in sexuality-based asylum claims in France, Germany and Spain was affected by these developments. It seeks out the shapes and forms in which 'discretion' reasoning has surfaced in these jurisdictions, and the ways in which it has possibly been altered by the Europeanisation of asylum and the judgments on 'discretion'.

The analysis shows that the three countries have very different decision-making traditions regarding sexuality-based claims, all of which draw on an act/identity dichotomy, and as such lead to 'discretion' reasoning in contrasting ways. But while established jurisprudence was affected and amended in all three jurisdictions following the entry into force of the *Qualification Directive* and the CJEU judgments rejecting a 'discretion' requirement, it does not appear to have been overturned. Rather, within their own traditions, all three jurisdictions have found ways to integrate the rulings into a reformed or rephrased version of their prior jurisprudence – in which form they continue to serve as a patch for the tension between claimant's rights and the surrogacy rationale of refugee protection.

4

Manifestly Asserted

France

In French jurisprudence regarding sexuality-based asylum claims, the act/identity dichotomy is manifest in a history of focusing on behaviour.[1] Since the very earliest judgments that accepted sexual orientation as a grounds for persecution in the late 1990s, sexuality was understood as a form of political assertion rather than in terms of its personal dimension in French jurisprudence.[2] That is, while most jurisdictions characterise sexual orientation in terms of identity, in France, the focus was upon activity. This chapter examines the ways in which this preoccupation with conduct has informed what Jansen and Spijkerboer labelled the French 'discretion reasoning in reverse'.[3] Before getting into the case law analysis, and in order to situate the findings, the following section sets out the French legal context as well as past research on sexuality-based asylum claims in France.

4.1 THE FRENCH CONTEXT: FAVOURING ACTS

Since 1946, the French Constitution has provided for asylum in its preamble: 'Any man persecuted in virtue of his actions in favour of liberty may claim the right of asylum upon the territories of the Republic.'[4] However, this so-called republican or

[1] Sections of this chapter are referred to in Janna Wessels (2017) 'Publicly Manifested–Fatefully Determined–Invariably "Discreet": The Assessment of Sexuality-Based Asylum Claims in Germany and France' 29(2) *Canadian Journal of Women and the Law* 343–374.

[2] Carolina Kobelinsky (2012) 'L'asile gay: jurisprudence de l'intime a la Cour nationale du droit d'asile', 3(82) *Droit et Société* 583–601, 589.

[3] Sabine Jansen and Thomas Spijkerboer (2011) *Fleeing Homophobia, Asylum Claims Related to Sexual Orientation and Gender Identity in Europe*, Vrije Universiteit Amsterdam, September 2011.

[4] Paragraph 4 of the preamble of the *Constitution of the IVth Republic from 1946 – 27 October* 1946 (Constitution de 1946, IVe République – 27 octobre 1946) [all translations are the author's. In the original: 'Tout homme persécuté en raison de son action en faveur de la liberté a droit d'asile sur les territoires de la République'].

constitutional asylum was never regulated in French law. Hence, despite being provided for in the Constitution, there was considered to be a 'legislative gap' regarding this provision – and therefore the Refugee Convention, which was adopted and implemented a few years later, was long considered as the implementing text of this provision.[5]

The Refugee Convention was implemented into French law by the law 52-893 in 1952.[6] This law created the Office for the Protection of Refugees and Stateless Persons (*Office français de protection des réfugiés et apatrides*, OFPRA), which is in charge of granting asylum, and the Refugee Appeals Board (*Commission de recours des réfugiés*, CRR), which decides on appeals (full legal proceedings) brought against decisions handed down by the OFPRA. The CRR became the National Court of Asylum (*Cour nationale du droit d'asile*, CNDA) as of 2008.[7] The CNDA constitutes (as did the CRR) a specialised and centralised court for asylum appeals. It reviews the asylum application and may confirm or modify the OFPRA decision. Asylum seekers have the possibility of lodging a final appeal against a CNDA decision before the *Conseil d'Etat* for legal issues only.[8] Law 52-893 stipulated in Article 2 that '[t]he office [OFPRA] recognises refugee status to any person falling within the mandate of the United Nations High Commissioner for Refugees or who meets the definitions in Article 1 of the Geneva Convention of 28 July 1951 relating to the Status of Refugees'.[9] The constitutional 'actions in favour of freedom' were merely a background presence.

The (current) Constitution of the Vth Republic from 1958 refers to the preamble of the Constitution of the VIth Republic, see *Constitution of the Vth Republic from 1958 – 4 October 1958* (Constitution de 1958, Ve République – 4 octobre 1958).

Note that asylum has been provided for since the very first French Constitution from 1793: 'It [the French people] provides asylum to foreigners banished from their country for the cause of freedom. – It refuses it to tyrants' ['Il [le peuple français] donne asile aux étrangers bannis de leur patrie pour la cause de la liberté. – Il le refuse aux tyrans.'], Article 120 of the *Constitution of the Year I – First Republic – 24 June 1793* (Constitution de l'An I – Première République – 24 juin 1793).

5 Isabelle Dodet-Cauphy (1999) 'La difficile reconnaissance du droit d'asile constitutionnel. Commentaire de la loi du 11 mai 1998 relative à l'entrée et au séjour des étrangers en France et au droit d'asile', 15(3) *Revue française de droit administratif* 469–484.

6 Law No. 52-893 of 25 July 1952 establishing a French Office for the Protection of Refugees and Stateless Persons (Loi n°52-893 du 25 juillet 1952 portant création d'un office français de protection des réfugiés et des apatrides, JORF du 27 juillet 1952, p. 7642).

7 By virtue of Article 29 of Law No. 2007-1631 of 20 November 2007 on the control of immigration, integration and asylum (Loi n° 2007–1631 du 20 novembre 2007 relative à la maîtrise de l'immigration, à l'intégration et à l'asile, JORF n°270 du 21 novembre 2007, p. 18993).

8 Hana Cheikh Ali, Christel Querton and Elodie Soulard (2012) *Gender Related Asylum Claims in Europe – A Comparative Analysis of Law Policies and Practice Focusing on Women in Nine EU Member States* ('GENSEN report'). Brussels: European Parliament, Directorate General for Internal Policies, Department of Citizens' Rights and Constitutional Affairs, 186–188.

9 Article 2 of the Law No. 52-893 of 25 July 1952: 'L'office reconnaît la qualité de réfugié à toute personne qui relève du mandat du haut commissaire des Nations Unies pour les réfugiés ou qui répond aux définitions de l'article 1er de la convention de Genève du 28 juillet 1951 relative au statut des réfugiés.'

But there was an increasing recognition that 'constitutional' and 'conventional' asylum do not cover exactly the same ground.[10] Triggered by a 1993 decision of the Constitutional Court (Conseil constitutionnel), the Aliens Act of 1998, called RESEDA,[11] finally regulated constitutional asylum and integrated it into the French asylum regime as an alternative legal basis. The RESEDA law did, however, maintain the link with the Refugee Convention, such that 'constitutional' asylum is granted by the same bodies and under the same procedure as conventional asylum, and both statuses provide for the same rights. According to Article 29 RESEDA:

> Refugee status shall be recognised by the Office to any person persecuted for their actions in favour of liberty as well as to any person . . . who meets the definitions in Article 1 of the Geneva Convention of 28 July 1951 relating to the Status of Refugees. All persons referred to in the preceding paragraph shall be governed by the provisions applicable to refugees under the aforementioned Geneva Convention of 28 July 1951.[12]

The OFPRA does not even specify whether asylum is granted under the provisions of the Refugee Convention or the French Constitution. Therefore, some authors

[10] Following a 1993 recognition of the Constitutional Court (Conseil constitutionnel) asylum was a 'fundamental right of a constitutional nature', that is, a right directly enforceable by individuals and protected by the constitutional legal order (CC, décision no. 93-325 DC du 12 août 1993), see Hélène Lambert, Francesco Messineo and Paul Tiedemann (2008) 'Comparative Perspectives of Constitutional Asylum in France, Italy, and Germany: *Requiescat in Pace?*', 27(3) *Refugee Survey Quarterly* 16–32, 19.

For a full analysis of this decision, see Catherine Teitgen-Colly (1994) 'Le droit d'asile: la fin des illusions', *L'Actualité juridique – Droit administratif* 97–114. This recognition was reaffirmed by the Constitutional Court in its judgment of 22 April 1997 (CC, décision no. 97-389 DC du 22 avril 1997). See Dodet-Cauphy, note 5, 474–475.

[11] Law No. 98-349 of 11 May 1998 on the entry and residence of foreigners in France and the right of asylum (Loi n° 98-349 du 11 mai 1998 relative a l'entrée et au séjour des étrangers en France et au droit d'asile (*RESEDA*), JORF n°109 du 12 mai 1998, p. 7087), amending Law No. 52-893 of 25 July 1952, which implements the 1951 Refugee Convention.

[12] Article 29 of the RESEDA: 'Refugee status shall be recognised by the Office to any person persecuted for their actions in favour of liberty as well as to any person over whom the Office of the United Nations High Commissioner for Refugees exercises its mandate under Articles 6 And 7 of its Statute as adopted by the General Assembly of the United Nations on 14 December 1950, or who meets the definitions in Article 1 of the Geneva Convention of 28 July 1951 relating to the Status of Refugees. All persons referred to in the preceding paragraph shall be governed by the provisions applicable to refugees under the aforementioned Geneva Convention of 28 July 1951' ['La qualité de réfugié est reconnue par l'office à toute personne persécutée en raison de son action en faveur de la liberté ainsi qu'à toute personne sur laquelle le Haut-Commissariat des Nations unies pour les réfugiés exerce son mandat aux termes des articles 6 et 7 de son statut tel qu'adopté par l'Assemblée générale des Nations unies le 14 décembre 1950 ou qui répond aux définitions de l'article 1er de la convention de Genève du 28 juillet 1951 relative au statut des réfugiés. Toutes les personnes visées à l'alinéa précédent sont régies par les dispositions applicables aux réfugiés en vertu de la convention de Genève du 28 juillet 1951 précitée.'].

have argued that constitutional asylum has played a largely symbolic role and is in fact obsolete.[13] Yet precisely the symbolic dimension of 'constitutional' asylum with its focus on 'actions in favour of liberty' may have reinforced the French preoccupation with conduct.

The transposition of the EU *Qualification Directive* into French law did not materially alter the 1998 reform. The transposition was 'anticipated' in large part by the Aliens Act of 10 December 2003 and the Immigration and Asylum Code (*Code de l'entrée et du séjour des étrangers et du droit d'asile*, CESEDA).[14] Presumably because it was transposed prematurely, that is, before its final text was adopted in April 2004, the *Qualification Directive* was integrated into the French legal framework in very broad terms, leaving out amongst other things the definition of persecution in Article 9 of the *Qualification Directive* and the criteria defining the particular social group contained in Article 10. Note that Article 10 of the *Qualification Directive* not only provides the criteria for what constitutes a particular social group in general terms, but also specifies that both gender and sexual orientation are likely candidates for such a social group:

> [D]epending on the circumstances in the country of origin, a particular social group might include a group based on a common characteristic of sexual orientation. Sexual orientation cannot be understood to include acts considered to be criminal in accordance with national law of the Member States: Gender related aspects might be considered, without by themselves alone creating a presumption for the applicability of this Article.[15]

The definition of the refugee in CESEDA art L711–1 does not reflect this: it remained essentially the same as that in the 1998 RESEDA.[16] It was not until the

[13] Lambert, note 10, 16–32; see also: Catherine Teitgen-Colly and François Julien-Laferriere (1998) 'La réforme du droit d'asile', *L'Actualité juridique – Droit administratif*, 1002–1004; Patrick Delouvin (2000) 'The Evolution of Asylum in France', 13(1) *Journal of Refugee Studies* 61–73, at 69–70.

[14] Law No. 2003-1176 of 10 December 2003 amending Law 52-893 of 25 July 1952 on the right of asylum (Loi n° 2003-1176 du 10 décembre 2003 modifiant la loi n° 52-893 du 25 juillet 1952 relative au droit d'asile, JORF n°286 du 11 décembre 2003, p. 21080); and see Virginie Fraissinier-Amiot (2011) 'Les homosexuels étrangers et le droit d'asile en France: un octroi en demi-teinte', 27(2) *Revue française de droit administratif* 291–300.

[15] Article 10(1)(d) of the 2004 *Qualification Directive*; essentially maintained in the recast version.

[16] Article L711–1 of the Code on the entry and residence of aliens and the right of asylum (Code de l'entrée et du séjour des étrangers et du droit d'asile, *CESEDA*): 'La qualité de réfugié est reconnue à toute personne persécutée en raison de son action en faveur de la liberté ainsi qu'à toute personne sur laquelle le Haut-Commissariat des Nations unies pour les réfugiés exerce son mandat aux termes des articles 6 et 7 de son statut tel qu'adopté par l'Assemblée générale des Nations unies le 14 décembre 1950 ou qui répond aux définitions de l'article 1er de la convention de Genève du 28 juillet 1951 relative au statut des réfugiés. Ces personnes sont régies par les dispositions applicables aux réfugiés en vertu de la convention de Genève susmentionnée.'

2015 *Asylum Reform Act*[17] transposed the second generation 'recast' directive[18] that an explicit reference to both Articles 9 and 10 of the *Qualification Directive* was added to the CESEDA in Article L711–2.[19] That is, only since 2015 does the French law both explicitly refer to the *Qualification Directive* definition of a particular social group and specify that gender and sexual orientation are 'duly taken into consideration' when identifying such a particular social group. The present analysis explores the impact of this situation on sexuality-based claims.

French sexuality-based asylum judgments have so far received relatively little academic attention. Two authors have looked at relevant case law in some detail. Virginie Fraissinier-Amiot conducted a legal analysis of the treatment of gay asylum

[17] Law No. 2015-925 of 29 July 2015 on the reform of asylum law (Loi n° 2015-925 du 29 juillet 2015 relative à la réforme du droit d'asile, JORF n°0174 du 30 juillet 2015, p. 12977).

[18] Directive 2011/95/EU of the European Parliament and of the Council of 13 December 2011 on standards for the qualification of third-country nationals or stateless persons as beneficiaries of international protection, for a uniform status for refugees or for persons eligible for subsidiary protection, and for the content of the protection granted (recast), oj L 337/9, 20 December 2011 (*Recast Qualification Directive*).

[19] Article L711–2 of the CESEDA: 'Acts of persecution and grounds of persecution within the meaning of Section A of Article 1 of the Geneva Convention of 28 July 1951 relating to the status of refugees shall be assessed under the conditions laid down in paragraphs 1 and 2 of Article 9 and Article 10 (1) of Directive 2011/95/EU of the European Parliament and of the Council of 13 December 2011 on standards for the qualification of third-country nationals or stateless persons as beneficiaries of international protection, for a uniform status for refugees or for persons eligible for subsidiary protection, and for the content of the protection granted.

With regard to the grounds of persecution, aspects relating to gender and sexual orientation are duly taken into consideration for the purpose of recognizing membership of a particular social group or identifying the characteristic of such a group.

In order for refugee status to be recognized, there must be a link between one of the grounds for persecution and the acts of persecution or the lack of protection against such acts.

Where the competent authority assesses whether a claimant has a well-founded fear of persecution, it is irrelevant whether the claimant actually possesses the characteristics of the persecution ground or whether these characteristics are merely attributed to him by the perpetrator of the persecution.' ['Les actes de persécution et les motifs de persécution, au sens de la section A de l'article 1er de la convention de Genève, du 28 juillet 1951, relative au statut des réfugiés, sont appréciés dans les conditions prévues aux paragraphes 1 et 2 de l'article 9 et au paragraphe 1 de l'article 10 de la directive 2011/95/UE du Parlement européen et du Conseil, du 13 décembre 2011, concernant les normes relatives aux conditions que doivent remplir les ressortissants des pays tiers ou les apatrides pour pouvoir bénéficier d'une protection internationale, à un statut uniforme pour les réfugiés ou les personnes pouvant bénéficier de la protection subsidiaire, et au contenu de cette protection.

S'agissant des motifs de persécution, les aspects liés au genre et à l'orientation sexuelle sont dûment pris en considération aux fins de la reconnaissance de l'appartenance à un certain groupe social ou de l'identification d'une caractéristique d'un tel groupe.

Pour que la qualité de réfugié soit reconnue, il doit exister un lien entre l'un des motifs de persécution et les actes de persécution ou l'absence de protection contre de tels actes.

Lorsque l'autorité compétente évalue si un demandeur craint avec raison d'être persécuté, il est indifférent que celui-ci possède effectivement les caractéristiques liées au motif de persécution ou que ces caractéristiques lui soient seulement attribuées par l'auteur des persécutions'].

seekers in French asylum practice that was published in 2011,[20] and legal anthropologist Carolina Kobelinsky undertook a review of sixty CNDA judgments concerning gay applicants spanning the time from 2001 to 2011, which appeared in 2012.[21] Both looked at sexual orientation cases in general terms, addressing the range of developments and obstacles that this class of claims has faced since they were first accepted. Around the same time these pieces appeared, the French part of the *Fleeing Homophobia* project was published. It constitutes a third piece of research on this particular type of cases in France and provides a rich source of 'raw' data, only some of which was used and discussed in the report.[22]

The present analysis has a twofold function: on the one hand, it draws and builds on this previous research to analyse how the approach towards sexuality-based asylum cases in France has developed since the publication of those findings. On the other hand, it goes beyond a general analysis, looking specifically at the issue of 'discretion' reasoning and the way it has evolved over time. Notably, although the CJEU judgment in X, *Y and* Z (and also A, *B and* C, a 2014 judgment on credibility issues[23]) were widely discussed in the French academic community and have triggered a series of comments, none of them are based on a review of, or relate the judgments to, French practice.[24] In addition, it is striking that the judgment in *Y and Z* concerning the religious 'forum internum' appears to have had fewer repercussions in France, likely because it does not reverberate as much in the jurisprudence, as will be discussed further shortly.[25]

[20] Fraissinier-Amiot, note 14.

[21] Kobelinsky, note 2, 583–601; see also her further more ethnographically oriented publications, drawing on observations of hearings and interviews with judges and decision-makers, but also referring to the same case set: Carolina Kobelinsky (2012) 'Ver o no ver al refugiado. La evaluación de las solicitudes de asilo (por motivos sexuales) en Francia', 4 *Revista Temas de Antropología y Migración* 13–29; Carolina Kobelinsky (2015) 'Judging Intimacies at the French Court of Asylum', 38(2) *Political and Legal Anthropology Review* 338–355.

[22] Thomas Fouquet-Lapar and Flor Tercero (2011) *Fleeing Homophobia Questionnaire, Best Practices on the (Legal) Position of LGBT Asylum Seekers in the EU Member States – France*, Fleeing Homophobia Project, www.rechten.vu.nl/nl/Images/France_FINAL_tcm247-240411.pdf.

[23] Because it addresses procedural questions, it is not part of the present analysis: A, B, C v. *Staatssecretaris van Veiligheid en Justitie*, Joined Cases C-148/13 to C-150/13, European Union: Court of Justice of the European Union, 2 December 2014.

[24] See e.g. Alexandre Defossez (2014) 'Arrêt "X, Y et Z": les homosexuels persécutés dans leur pays d'origine peuvent-ils bénéficier du statut de "réfugié"?', 206 *Journal de droit européen* 54–55; Caroline Lantero and Marie-Laure Basilien-Gainche (2013) 'Statut de réfugié et appartenance à un groupe social (Directive 2004/83/CE): Une victoire à la Pyrrhus pour les personnes homosexuelles', *La Revue des droits de l'homme [En ligne], Actualités Droits-Libertés*, mis en ligne le 13 novembre 2013; Marion Tissier-Raffin (2015) 'L'orientation sexuelle comme motif de persécution doit être appréciée dans la dignité', *La Revue des droits de l'homme [En ligne], Actualités Droits-Libertés*, mis en ligne le 15 janvier 2015.

[25] See for one brief note on the judgment that does not link it with French jurisprudence: Anthony Astaix (2012) 'Réfugié: le statut doit être accordé en raison de persécutions religieuses', *Dalloz Actualité* 14 septembre 2012.

The French judgments that form the basis of the present analysis were gathered from the Council of State (second instance) case law database Ariane Web, with the search terms 'homosexuel' and 'orientation sexuelle'. The first instance CNDA does not maintain a case law database but publishes annual case law collections as pdfs. These were reviewed for the years 2005 to 2015. Relevant decisions were identified with the help of the thematic index ('homosexuel' and 'orientation sexuelle' respectively). In addition, case collections from the *Fleeing Homophobia* project[26] and from the French NGO Rajfire provided further relevant judgments.[27] The overall case collection includes a total of ninety-seven French judgments, covering the years 1997–2016.[28]

The analysis of French case law faces some obstacles. Judgments do not have the discursive style typical of common law jurisdictions. Earlier judgments in particular do not generally exceed one-and-a-half pages and the motivation for a decision is usually summarised in one decisive paragraph; consequently, it is not always possible to clearly identify the reasons that motivated the decision. The jurisprudence relies on a small number of particular recurring sentences or signal words that point to the basis for the outcome. A study of 800 CRR judgments from the year 2000, for example, revealed that 41.1 per cent of rejections were based on the same single sentence.[29] In more recent years, and arguably as a (somewhat belated) consequence of the Europeanisation of asylum, this appears to be slowly changing – certainly for CNDA judgments, which now lay out both the facts of the case and the reasons for a decision in more detail. This is reflected in the length of the latest judgments, which often cover four to five pages.[30] Nevertheless, due to this French decision-making tradition, the exact wording of the respective 'codes' is of high importance, and any analysis of case law must rely on an interpretation of these.[31]

[26] Fleeing Homophobia Project, Vrije Universiteit Amsterdam, www.rechten.vu.nl/nl/onderzoek/organisatie/onderzoeksprogrammas/migratierecht/Fleeing-Homofobia/National-Questionnaires/index.aspx.

[27] Copies on file with author.

[28] Twenty-two Council of State judgments and seventy-five CRR/CNDA judgments. See Annex II for a detailed list of the analysed judgments.

[29] Hélène Perret (2000) *La Règle de droit à la Commission des recours des réfugiés*, mémoire de DEA en sociologie du droit, université Panthéon-Assas (Paris 2), 102–103. The sentence was: 'Considering, however, that [neither] the evidence in the case-file [nor the statements made in the public hearing] allow for the alleged facts to be considered as well established and the stated fear to be well-founded' ['Considérant toutefois que [ni] les pièces du dossier [ni les déclarations faites en séance publique devant la Cour/Commission] ne permettent [pas] de tenir pour établis les faits allégués et pour fondées les craintes énoncées'].

[30] See e.g. CNDA 29 octobre 2015, 15006472 C+, M. H.; CNDA 27 septembre 2016, 15004721 C, Mme T.; CNDA 18 mars 2016, 15031443 C, M. K.; CNDA 14 juin 2016, 15030258 C, Mme E.

[31] Details about the legal reasoning underlying French decisions at the CRR/CNDA are developed in the *feuilles vertes*, or preparatory documents, which are working documents for judges, see: Hélène Lambert and Janine Silga (2010) 'Transnational Refugee Law in the French Courts: Deliberate or Compelled Change in Judicial Attitudes?', in Guy Goodwin-

4.2 PUBLIC MANIFESTATION

It was not until the late 1990s that sexual orientation came to be accepted as a basis for refugee protection in France. The literature cites two early cases that were unsuccessful on the basis that sexual orientation did not fall within any of the criteria laid down by the Convention and that homosexuals did not constitute a 'particular social group'.[32] It took a 1997 Council of State judgment concerning a transsexual woman and a subsequent 1999 CRR judgment in the case of a gay man that sexual orientation was finally considered to be covered by the Convention grounds.[33] Until then, the social group ground had played no role in French asylum decision-making.

From the beginning, sexuality-based asylum claims in France centred on the claimant's past conduct.[34] In her study of sixty judgments of the CNDA, covering the years 2001–2011, Carolina Kobelinsky found that the majority of rejections were motivated by the absence of public manifestation of the sexual orientation in the country of origin.[35] The rationale was that, if the claimants had not manifested their sexual orientation, they could not be considered members of a social group that was subject to a risk of persecution.[36] Conversely, most recognitions were granted to those claimants who had manifested and asserted their sexual orientation.[37] As such, a Russian gay man who publicly campaigned for gay rights received protection,[38] as did a gay rights militant from Algeria, who had reasonable fear due to his behaviour,[39] and an Ethiopian gay rights activist, who was subject to reprisals due to his 'effeminate behaviour'.[40]

The focus on the claimant's behaviour was explicitly introduced in the French definition of 'particular social group'. The Council of State (*Conseil d'Etat*) formulated the first French social group definition in *Ourbih* in 1997, a case concerning a transsexual woman.[41] In this judgment, the Council of State defined a particular social group as 'constituting a group whose members would be at risk of persecution

Gil and Hélène Lambert (eds.) *The Limits of Transnational Law – Refugee Law, Policy Harmonization and Judicial Dialogue in the European Union*, 35–56.

32 CRR 17 décembre 1993, *Koloskov*, Documentation réfugiés no. 245, at 4, and a 1997 case concerning a lesbian woman from Iran, both cited in Fraissinier-Amiot, note 14, 293.

33 CE, 23 juin 1997, 171858, *Ourbih;* and CRR 12 mai 1999, 328310, *Djellal*, see further discussion shortly.

34 Kobelinsky, note 2.

35 Ibid., 590.

36 See e.g. CRR 12 septembre 2005, 498570, Mme. AGB.

37 Kobelinsky, note 2, 590. Note that in most cases of recognitions, homosexuality was also criminalised in the country of origin.

38 CRR 26 novembre 2002, 402381, M. T.

39 CRR 23 mai 2002, 388492, M. K. ['les craintes que peut raisonnablement éprouver le requérant *du fait de son comportement* en cas de retour dans son pays d'origine'].

40 CRR 23 juillet 2002, 394788 ['a été victime, dès son plus jeune âge, de sarcasmes, de menaces, de provocations puis d'agressions de la part de son entourage en raison de son comportement efféminé'].

41 CE, 23 juin 1997, 171858, *Ourbih*.

for reasons of common characteristics that define them in the eyes of authorities and society',[42] and thus laid the foundation for the significance of the perception of the group by persecutors in French asylum law.[43]

The 1999 CRR decision of *Djellal* applied this definition to gay people for the first time – and it is here that the focus on the claimant's behaviour came into play.[44] In its application of the general social perception definition of the Council of State to the concrete case of gay people, the CRR reasoned that, in order to constitute a particular social group, the claimant had to be gay and assert[45] their sexual orientation or manifest it in external behaviour.[46] Although the Court has never explicitly clarified this notion of external manifestation, subsequent judgments revealed that it required either that the person had publicly revealed their sexual orientation or had presented external 'signs' that rendered the sexual orientation visible and evident in the eyes of the society in which they lived.[47] Thus, in what has been termed the 'indiscretion requirement' or the 'discretion requirement in reverse',[48] those claimants who had not actively sought to publicly manifest their sexual orientation were not considered part of the particular social group based on sexual orientation.[49]

Conspicuously, this first formulation of the particular social group of gay people coincided with the integration of 'constitutional' asylum into French law in what could have led to an interesting dynamic. The Council of State judgment in *Ourbih* in 1997 preceded the 1998 law that introduced the 'actions in favour of liberty' into the definition of refugee, and the 1999 CRR judgment in *Djellal*, operationalising *Ourbih* for sexuality-based cases, followed it. It does not appear unreasonable to speculate that the focus on an active element as contained in the constitutional

42 Ibid. ['constituant un groupe dont les membres seraient, en raison des caractéristiques communes qui les définissent aux yeux des autorités et de la société algériennes, susceptibles d'être exposés à des persécutions'].

43 Caroline Lantero (2013) 'La notion de groupe social au sens de la convention de Genève dans la jurisprudence française', 41 *Actualités Juridiques – Droit Administratif* 2364–2370, 2365.

44 CRR 12 mai 1999, 328310, *Djellal*.

45 The term 'revendiquer', translated here with 'assert', does not translate into an English word that carries the same variety of meanings. It can also mean 'claim' (in the sense of 'demand'), and the French scholar Kobelinsky chose the English word 'declare' in her own translation of the definition: Kobelinsky, note 21, 349.

46 The notions in French are 'revendiquer leur homosexualité' and 'manifester [leur homosexualité] dans leur comportement extérieur', see CRR 12 mai 1999, 328310, *Djellal*. The second requirement the CRR derived from the Council of State's definition for the establishment of the social group was that *due to this behaviour*, the claimant would be exposed to prosecution, police surveillance measures or bullying, see Fouquet-Lapar and Tercero, note 22, 8.

47 Ibid. Whereas initially only state persecution was considered to lead to protection, following the introduction of subsidiary protection via the 2003 CESEDA law, this position was later developed such that persecution of non-state actors warranted refugee protection if the state was unwilling or unable to provide protection.

48 Jansen and Spijkerboer, note 3, 36.

49 See for example the cases listed at 37–38 in Fouquet-Lapar and Tercero, note 22: CRR 18 mai 2007, 589676 D.; CRR 2 mars 2007, 578257 S.; CNDA 11 avril 2008, 571886 G.; CNDA 1er juillet 2008, 571904, K.; CNDA 7 mai 2008, 605398 H.

definition ('[their] actions in favour of liberty') may have had a bearing on this conceptualisation of the particular social group. The 'militant character' of constitutional asylum was stressed by Henri Labayle, who observed that its beneficiaries, rather than being determined by their status or gender, are determined by their behaviour.[50] Inspired by the republican quest for liberty, past public expression of sexual orientation would thus be conceived as a form of past action in favour of freedom.[51] Clearly there was no necessity for this, as the courts were able to rely on the Convention definition, which had been in place since 1952 – but 'constitutional' asylum put the issue of past behaviour on the table.

In the logic of these cases, the act/identity dichotomy functions to exclude in such a way that, even though a claimant may be accepted as *being* gay, and the persecution of gay people as established in the relevant country of origin, the particular social group was understood to extend only to those who also *expressed* their sexual orientation. This interpretation reveals confusion between visibility and perceptibility – perception does *not* necessarily presuppose a visible manifestation. For example, in the 2008 case of *H*, which involved a gay man from Kosovo, the CNDA rejected the claimant's membership of the particular social group on the basis that he had not sought to ostensibly manifest his sexual orientation, even though he had been 'outed'.[52] That is, past publicised conduct was not sufficient if the sexual orientation was not actively claimed by the applicant but, rather, was passively discovered. In a particularly disturbing early case involving a gay claimant from Morocco, who had stated that he could not fully assume his sexual orientation in Morocco, this read as follows:

> Considering, however, that if Mr. N. has sincerely and convincingly expressed his inability to live his sexuality in his country of origin and his psychological distress in relation to the standards required by Moroccan society in matters of sexuality, he did not allege having sought to ostensibly manifest his homosexuality in his external behavior or having been exposed to the actual exercise of legal proceedings.[53]

[50] Henri Labayle (1997) 'Le droit d'asile en France: normalisation ou neutralisation?', 13(2) *Revue française de droit administratif* 242–269, 242. Note, however, that Viriginie Fraissinier-Amiot rejected any connection between constitutional asylum and sexuality-based claims: Fraissinier-Amiot, note 14, 292.

[51] See also Carolina Kobelinsky, who compares the conceptualisation of sexuality-based claims in France with that of claims based on political opinion: Kobelinsky, note 2, 589–590.

[52] CNDA 7 mai 2008, 605398 H.

[53] CRR 13 septembre 2001, 379319, M.N. ['Considérant, toutefois, que si M. N. a exprimé sincèrement et de façon convaincante son impossibilité de vivre sa sexualité dans son pays d'origine et sa détresse psychologique au regard des normes exigées par la société marocaine en matière de sexualité, il n'a pas allégué avoir cherché à manifester ostensiblement son homosexualité dans son comportement extérieur ou avoir été exposé à l'exercice effectif de poursuites judiciaires; que, dès lors, et en dépit de la condamnation pénale des rapports homosexuels en public telle que prévue par l'article 489 du code pénal, les craintes énoncées relatives à la réprobation familiale et sociétale à laquelle il serait nécessairement confronté ne peuvent être suffisantes'].

The Court concluded that therefore, and despite the criminalisation of homosexual acts in public by the Moroccan criminal code, the claimant's fears concerning the familial and societal reprobation with which he would necessarily be confronted were insufficient to warrant protection.[54] A gay man from Turkey, who had 'preferred to keep his homosexuality secret from his entourage', but nevertheless was subjected to severe violence at the hands of his family, was rejected in 2004.[55]

Similarly, in the case of *MS*, a Bosnian man's claim to refugee status was rejected on the basis that he did not belong to a circumscribed and sufficiently identifiable group of persons in order to constitute a particular social group because he had never 'sought to ostensibly manifest his sexual orientation in his behaviour' and had not been 'exposed to the effective exercise of prosecution in his country where the provisions of the Criminal Code punishing homosexual acts had been repealed'.[56] The Court did, however, recognise that the claimant would be 'exposed to reprisals from private actors for reasons of his homosexuality', as well as the state's inability to protect him, and granted subsidiary protection.[57] Thus, the Court found that the claimant was in need of protection. The only reason the claim to refugee status failed was the fact that he had not publicly manifested his sexual orientation and, therefore, did not establish a link to the Convention ground. In this sense, the act/identity dichotomy effectively breaks down the particular social group of 'sexual orientation' and reduces its scope to extend only to 'active' or 'open' gays.[58]

It is a particularity of the French context that 'discretion' is discussed in the social group element. Even though the act/identity dichotomy is created at the level of the Convention ground (i.e. at the level of the *reason* for persecution), the claimant's behaviour is often 'moved around' and variously – often, additionally – discussed in other elements of the refugee definition, which creates further confusion. In Germany for example, the claimant's behaviour is assessed in the context of whether the fear of persecution is 'well-founded', whereas its location is much less clear in Spain. In French practice, this seemed not to be the case. Since its decision in *Ourbih*, the Council of State has based the particular social group on 'common characteristics that define them in the eyes of authorities and society'.[59] This

[54] Note that this case predates the 2003 CESEDA law, which introduced persecution by non-state actors (transposing the *Qualification Directive*) which was not previously foreseen in France.

[55] CRR 12 octobre 2004, 483808, M. A. See for other cases in the same line: CRR 22 mai 2000 340068, M. E. (a gay man from Algeria 'qui ne revendiquait pas publiquement son homosexualité et ne la manifestait pas par son comportement extérieur'), CRR 6 février 2001, 359001, M. B. (a gay man from Jordania).

[56] CRR 12 mai 2006, 555672, MS.

[57] CRR 12 mai 2006, 555672, MS.

[58] See also the same reasoning in a very similar case concerning a gay man from Albania: CNDA, 7 mai 2008, 605398, H; and a lesbian woman from Moldova: CRR 25 mars 2005, 513547, Mlle G.

[59] CE, 23 juin 1997, 171858, *Ourbih* ['constituant un groupe dont les membres seraient, en raison des caractéristiques communes qui les définissent aux yeux des autorités et de la société algériennes, susceptibles d'être exposés à des persécutions'].

approach has later been labelled the 'social perception' approach.[60] Next to the so-called protected characteristics (or the 'ejusdem generis') approach, it remains one of two competing approaches to conceptualise membership of a particular social group at the international level, with some jurisdictions applying one or the other approach, and some applying both.[61] Both approaches are reflected in the Article 10(1)(d) of the *Qualification Directive*:

> [A] group shall be considered to form a particular social group where in particular:
>
> —members of that group share an innate characteristic, or a common background that cannot be changed, or share a characteristic or belief that is so fundamental to identity or conscience that a person should not be forced to renounce it, *and*
>
> —that group has a distinct identity in the relevant country, because it is perceived as being different by the surrounding society.[62]

The *Qualification Directive* lists the social perception and the protected characteristics approach cumulatively, linking them with an 'and', rather than with an alternative 'or'.[63] A strict reading of this definition would require that *both* elements are fulfilled in order for a particular social group to be established – and, although much criticised,[64] this was also the explicit interpretation of the CJEU.[65] In France, as

60 See T. Alexander Aleinikoff (2003) 'Protected Characteristics and Social Perceptions: An Analysis of the Meaning of "Membership of a Particular Social Group"', in Erika Feller, Volker Türk and Frances Nicholson (eds.) *Refugee Protection in International Law: UNHCR's Global Consultations on International Protection*, Cambridge: Cambridge University Press 263–311.

61 Michelle Foster (2012) *The 'Ground with the Least Clarity': A Comparative Study of Jurisprudential Developments Relating to 'Membership of a Particular Social Group'*, UNHCR Division of International Protection, Geneva, August 2012, PPLA/2012/02.

62 Article10(1)(d) Council Directive 2004/83/EC of 29 April 2004 on minimum standards for the qualification and status of third country nationals or stateless persons as refugees or as persons who otherwise need international protection and the content of the protection granted, oj L 304/12, 30 September 2004 (2004 *Qualification Directive*); emphasis added.

63 In spite of criticism, no changes have been made to this circumstance in the recast Directive, and even the proposal for a Qualification Regulation maintains the cumulative test: see ECRE (2016) *ECRE Comments on the Commission Proposal for a Qualification Regulation COM (2016) 466*, www.ecre.org/wp-content/uploads/2016/07/ECRE-Comments-EU-Asylum-Agency_July-2016-final_2.pdf, 8. See also Chapter 8.

64 See e.g. James Hathaway and Michelle Foster (2014) *The Law of Refugee Status* (2nd ed.), Cambridge: Cambridge University Press, 429–432; and Michelle Foster (2014) 'Why We Are Not There Yet: The Particular Challenge of "Particular Social Group"', in Efrat Arbel, Catherine Dauvergne and Jenni Millbank (eds.) *Gender in Refugee Law: From the Margins to the Centre*, London: Routledge, 17–45, 24.

65 In X, *Y and Z* v. *Minister voor Immigratie, Integratie en Asiel*, Joined Cases C-199/12, C-200/12 and C-201/12, European Union: Court of Justice of the European Union, 7 November 2013 at 45: 'According to that definition, a group is regarded as a "particular social group" where, inter alia, two conditions are met. First, members of that group share an innate characteristic, or a common background that cannot be changed, or share a characteristic or belief that is so

noted by Lantero, the social perception criterion clearly appeals the most to judges, who have refused to integrate the protected characteristics approach.[66]

Indeed, France has traditionally focused on the social perception approach only, and, up until 2010, the link to the *Qualification Directive* was never made. To the contrary, in the 2006 judgment of *Olena*, that is, after the *Qualification Directive* had entered into force, the Council of State reaffirmed its previous social perception approach to the social group ground, this time also explicitly applying it to cases of sexual orientation. The case involved two lesbian women from Ukraine. According to the Council of State, a particular social group was established if its 'members would be at risk of persecution for reasons of common characteristics that define them in the eyes of authorities and society'.[67] In other words, the Council of State did not see a need to revise its own definition of 'particular social group' and ignored the protected characteristics element by maintaining an approach fully reliant on 'objectified' social perception – though the Council of State here does *not* pick up the CRR/CNDA requirement of public assertion that was developed in *Djellal*, but strictly sticks with its own previous wording from the 1997 judgment in *Ourbih* without reference to manifesting or claiming the sexual orientation. As Lantero remarked, 'The social perception thus prevails over the innate or the essence.'[68]

The attraction of the social perception approach of the Council of State lies in the fact that it is designed as a way of establishing whether society and authorities – that is, potential persecutors – perceive such individuals as different generally. If people with a common characteristic that defines them in the eyes of society and authorities are subject to persecution, then they constitute a particular social group. (Perceived) membership of that group leads to the recognition of refugee status to persons who fall within its definition.[69] This interpretation appears to be a radically inclusive approach – and is not how the CNDA has in fact applied it. Rather, it has applied this social perception requirement by linking it to the individual claimant. Instead of applying the social perception requirement to establish the existence of the group (from the perspective of the persecutor) and then assessing whether the claimant was a member of that group, it applied the social perception requirement to establish the claimant's *membership* of the group. If the claimant's sexual orientation was not 'socially perceptible' through their behaviour, then they were not considered part of

fundamental to identity or conscience that a person should not be forced to renounce it. Second, that group has a distinct identity in the relevant country because it is perceived as being different by the surrounding society.'

66 Lantero, note 43, 2366.

67 CE, 23 août 2006, 272679, *Olena* ['la situation des homosexuels en Ukraine permettaient de regarder ces derniers comme constituant un groupe dont les membres seraient, en raison des caractéristiques communes qui les définissent aux yeux des autorités et de la société ukrainienne, susceptibles d'être exposés à des persécutions'].

68 Lantero, note 43, 2367 ['Le perçu social l'emporte donc sur l'inné ou l'essence'].

69 Fouquet-Lapar and Tercero, note 22, 8–9.

the persecuted particular social group.[70] In a similar vein, the claimant had to *personally* fear persecution – reference to the general treatment of gay people in their country of origin was not sufficient.[71]

Thus, in its decisions prior to the rejection of 'discretion', France had developed a well-established jurisprudence based on an act/identity dichotomy favouring acts. If a claimant could not show that they had demonstrated their sexual orientation through external behaviour – if they had been 'discreet' in the past – then they were likely to be rejected as not being a member of the particular social group and sent back, effectively returned to future 'discretion'. Though never specified, the reasoning appeared to be that those who had not manifested their sexual orientation would continue to refrain from any such manifestation in the future, such that no risk of persecution would materialise because they would not be discovered as members of the particular social group. Consequently, because they would not be *discovered* as members of the group, they *were* not members of the relevant particular social group, which was effectively limited to 'open' gays. In some cases, the reasoning was even more restrictive, such that those who *were* discovered were not members of the social group if there was no 'active element'. The split of the particular social group into 'open' and 'discreet' gays also became the basis of the UK Supreme Court judgment in *HJ (Iran) and HT (Cameroon)*. But the latter judgment went further and also considered the group of 'discreet' gay people, for which it developed the 'why' test discussed previously. In France, in turn, the analysis was neither concerned with those who had not manifested their sexual orientation, nor based on any future-focused assessment – all that counted was the claimant's *past* behaviour.

France thus extended protection on the basis of past public manifestation, without asking for limits on that behaviour in any way. Rights-based considerations did not appear to play a role in earlier French jurisprudence – it was rather based on a 'factual' assessment of past conduct that (albeit not explicitly) effectively served as a predictor for future conduct. It can be argued that, on this point, French practice was in line with the CJEU's judgments in Y *and* Z and X, Y *and* Z, which essentially rely on a 'factual' assessment of what the claimant will do. Whereas these judgments relied on a future-focused analysis, however, the scope of protection in France was limited by the fact that many had not sought to manifest their sexual orientation in the *past*. Yet the approaches are, in fact, not that different from each other, because they both effectively prescribe future conduct when they conclude that the claimant

70 See Jansen and Spijkerboer, note 3, 36. Note that this interpretation bears resemblance with the 'social visibility' approach that had been applied in some circuits of the United States since 2006, but was rejected in two Board of Immigration Appeals decisions in 2014: *Matter of* M-E-V-G-, 26 I & N December 227 (BIA 2014), United States Board of Immigration Appeals, 7 February 2014; and *Matter of* W-G-R-, 26 I & N December 208 (BIA 2014), United States Board of Immigration Appeals, 7 February 2014.

71 Fraissinier-Amiot, note 14, 297.

has not manifested or will not manifest, respectively, their sexual orientation. In contrast, discussions on the reason for 'discretion' (fear of persecution?) or discovery against the claimant's will did not play much of a role, although such considerations were not entirely absent, as the following section shows.

4.3 *CLAIMING* SEXUAL ORIENTATION

Even before the rejection of the 'discretion requirement', the well-established French preoccupation with public manifestation of sexual orientation was not without criticism and inconsistencies. There were some early cases of recognition of sexuality claims without the requirement of asserting sexual orientation through active external behaviour – but these exceptions were limited to cases where the claimant had in fact been 'outed' against their will and therefore suffered persecution. For example, in a case from 2000 involving an Iranian claimant *M. M.*, the particular social group was established without reference to public manifestation but by reference to his 'reasonable fear' following his denunciation. The circumstances of the case were that the claimant had ended his secretly maintained same-sex relationship with another Iranian man in order not to jeopardise his marriage when his Romanian wife and their son relocated to Iran. His former partner threatened to denounce him to the authorities, who indeed looked for him at his home when he was not there. Fearing for his life due to being accused of homosexuality, he left the country.[72] Even though the claimant never actively sought to publicly assert his sexual orientation, the court appears to have taken the view that discovery through others could warrant protection in this case.[73] The same reasoning could arguably apply to most (or even all) of the other cases that were rejected based on a failure of public expression – particularly, but certainly not exclusively, in countries where homosexuality is criminalised. Another early recognition without public manifestation was that of *M. K.*, a gay man from Ukraine in 2001. In *M. K.*, the Court explicitly noted that 'despite his discreet behaviour concerning his private life',[74] and although homosexuality had been decriminalised in Ukraine in 1991, the claimant had been subject to violence committed by law enforcement agents outside the framework of the law and therefore could not rely on state protection.[75]

Yet such reasoning was initially very sparse, with a few more cases to be found since 2008 – that is, following entry into force of the *Qualification Directive*. For example, in the case of *K.*, a Ugandan claimant who did not publicly assert his sexual orientation but, rather, secretly maintained a same-sex relationship over

72 CRR 4 octobre 2000, 330627, M. M.

73 See Kobelinsky, note 2, 590. But see the 2008 case of *H.* from Kosovo, who had been 'outed' but whose group membership was not recognised on the basis that he had not sought to ostensibly manifest his sexual orientation.

74 CRR 29 juin 2001, 367645, M. K. ['malgré un comportement discret quant à sa vie privée'].

75 Ibid.

several years that was subsequently discovered by accident, the Court first cited the *Djellal* definition of particular social group requiring manifestation in external behaviour. It then went on to find without further discussion that 'the claimant's reasonable fear because of his homosexuality if returned to his country must be regarded as resulting from his membership of a particular social group' in the sense of the Refugee Convention.[76] Here, the Court did not address, let alone solve, the evident contradiction. In a similar case from 2009 concerning C., a gay man from Tunisia, however, the CNDA went further. In that case, the claimant had been discovered with his partner, but had never sought to assert or manifest his sexual orientation. On the basis that homosexuality is criminalised in Tunisia, the Court here came to the conclusion that

> [t]he situation of homosexuals in Tunisia is such that, even if they have neither ostensibly asserted nor manifested their sexual orientation, they may be considered a collection of people that is circumscribed and sufficiently identifiable in order to constitute a group whose members are at risk of being exposed to persecution for reasons of common characteristics that define them in the eyes of the Tunisian authorities and society.[77]

A very similar case involved M. N., a gay man from Cameroon from 2011, whose sexual orientation had been discovered and who had already served two years in prison. Here, the Court found that, due to criminalisation, there was no requirement of assertion or manifestation of sexual orientation in order to form a particular social group.[78] Just two months later, in a very interesting judgment, the CNDA decided the case of M., a gay man from Guinea who had also been discovered with a lover and imprisoned, without even raising the question of public assertion or manifestation. The Court outlined that not only were homosexual acts criminalised in Guinea, but also the claimant's sexual orientation transgressed the customs and laws of his country of origin and that no state protection would be available upon return. Therefore, M. belonged to a 'group whose members are likely, *simply because of their sexual orientation*, to be exposed to activities of such gravity that they can amount to persecution'.[79]

76 CNDA 1er juillet 2008, 571904, K. ['les craintes que peut raisonnablement éprouver le requérant du fait de son homosexualité en cas de retour dans son pays d'origine doivent être regardées comme résultant de son appartenance à un groupe social au sens des stipulations de l'article 1er, A, 2, de la Convention de Genève'].

77 CNDA 7 juillet 2009, 634565/08015025, C. ['la situation des homosexuels en Tunisie quand bien même ils n'auraient ni revendiqué, ni manifesté leur orientation sexuelle de manière ostensible, permet de les regarder comme un ensemble de personnes circonscrit et suffisamment identifiable pour constituer un groupe dont les membres sont, en raison des caractéristiques communes qui les définissent aux yeux des autorités et de la société tunisiennes, susceptibles d'être exposées à des persécutions'].

78 CNDA 10 janvier 2011, 09012710 C+, M. N.

79 CNDA 7 mars 2011, 10002367 M.; emphasis added ['la communauté homosexuelle guinéenne se trouve actuellement régulièrement victime de graves violences perpétrées en toute

The unifying feature of the cases that diverted from the public manifestation standard up to 2011 is that homosexuality was criminalised in the claimant's country of origin and the claimant's sexual orientation had been discovered by accident. As such, there seemed to be an increasing awareness of the possibility of risk even if the claimant had sought to hide their sexual orientation – but only if there had indeed been past persecution. Claimants from countries where homosexuality was not criminalised, however, continued to be unlikely to receive protection if they had not somehow externalised their sexual orientation.[80] Note that this distinction between claimants who have suffered persecution in the past – and hence, where 'discretion' had in fact failed – and those who have not – and thus where 'discretion' still appeared as an option – correlates strongly with the distinction between past persecution ('Vorverfolgung') and un-persecuted departure ('unverfolgte Ausreise'), which is particularly well established in German jurisprudence. For the former case, that is, where a claimant has already suffered harm for the Convention reason, a more lenient risk assessment applies. In the context of sexual orientation, this involves already having been 'outed' and therefore having come to the knowledge of the persecutor, a situation that could still be avoided if it has not already happened. These logics rely on the 'secrecy = safety' equation, which can also be found in *HJ (Iran) and HT (Cameroon)*.

The 'public manifestation' requirement had been developed independently in French jurisprudence by the CNDA and does indeed appear to be unique in this formulation – although, as shown, it relies on the same assumptions that are found in other jurisdictions. Michelle Foster noted in 2012 that, in spite of the introduction of the *Qualification Directive* in 2004, France had not changed its approach at all with regards to the particular social group in the previous decade.[81] This was arguably facilitated by the patchy transposition in the CESEDA law, which skipped over the criteria for membership of a particular social group. Indeed, the first explicit reference to the social group definition from the *Qualification Directive* appears in a CNDA decision from 3 November 2010, following the UK Supreme Court's judgment in *HJ (Iran)*, although there is no reference to this judgment. The case involved O., a gay man from Nigeria.[82] In this judgment, the Court dropped its own 'public manifestation' definition. Instead, it referred to Article 10(1)(d) of the

impunité; que, dans ces conditions, l'orientation sexuelle de l'intéressé doit être admise comme étant transgressive à l'égard des coutumes et des lois en vigueur dans son pays d'origine et qu'il s'ensuit dès lors que l'intéressé ne pourra, en cas de retour et pour cette raison, solliciter efficacement en cas de besoin une quelconque protection des autorités; qu'il suit de là que la situation des homosexuels, telle qu'elle prévaut aujourd'hui dans la République de Guinée permet de regarder M. comme appartenant à un groupe dont les membres sont susceptibles, du simple fait de leur orientation sexuelle, d'être exposés à des agissements d'une gravité telle qu'ils peuvent être assimilés à des persécutions au sens de la convention de Genève'].

80 Fouquet-Lapar and Tercero, note 22, 39.

81 Foster, note 61, 36.

82 CNDA 3 novembre 2010, 09018078 O.

Qualification Directive, but then linked it to the French Council of State's traditional definition of particular social group from *Ourbih* in 1997 and *Olena* in 2006, requiring for the establishment of a particular social group that its members be at risk of persecution for reasons of common characteristics that define them in the eyes of authorities and society. Even though the Council of State's definition of particular social group does bear similarities with the definition in the *Qualification Directive*, and might appear as a reformulation of the public perception approach, it continues to leave out the 'immutable or unchangeable' requirement that is unknown to French decision-making practice.

In subsequent decisions from 2011 onwards, the CNDA no longer applied its 'public manifestation' requirement. It seems to have practically disappeared at least from the publicly available decisions.[83] For example, in the case of *M. D.*, which concerned a gay man from Georgia (where homosexuality is not criminalised), the CNDA found that, due to a particularly homophobic environment, the *simple suspicion* of same-sex sexual orientation would put a person at risk of harm.[84] There is no reference in this judgment to external manifestation or even assertion.

With this change in practice, the CNDA anticipated an explicit change in guidance from the Council of State. In two judgments from 27 July 2012, the Council of State also unambiguously rejected the CNDA's 'public manifestation' requirement.[85] Note that this overturn of practice occurred six weeks before the CJEU first rejected the 'discretion' requirement in *Y and Z* on 5 September 2012. The Council of State referred to the *Qualification Directive* definition and then added its own social perception approach in slightly revised terms:

> Therefore, in the event that a person seeks the benefit of refugee status on the basis of sexual orientation, it is necessary to assess whether, given the conditions in the country of his nationality, it is possible to assimilate people *claiming* the same sexual orientation in a social group because of the view that the surrounding society and institutions have of these people and whose members have well-founded fear of being persecuted because of the simple fact of their membership of that group.[86]

[83] See for example CNDA 29 juillet 2011, 09004056 C, M. B.; CNDA 21 novembre 2011, 11010494 C, Mlle M.; CNDA 11 juillet 2011, 10020448 C, M. M.; CNDA 4 juillet 2011, 11002234 C, M. K.; CNDA 3 novembre 2011, 11010972 C, M. A.; CNDA 1er mars 2011, 09023968 C, M. I.; CNDA 1er juin 2011, 10015959 C, Mlle N.

[84] CNDA 4 mai 2012, 11009260 C, M. D.

[85] CE, 27 juillet 2012, 349824, A. B. and CE, 27 juillet 2012, 342552, O. A. Note that any criminalization requirement was also rejected.

[86] CE, 27 juillet 2012, 349824; emphasis added ['il convient d'apprécier si les conditions existant dans le pays dont elle a la nationalité permettent d'assimiler les personnes se revendiquant de la même orientation sexuelle à un groupe social du fait du regard que portent sur ces personnes la société environnante ou les institutions et dont les membres peuvent craindre avec raison d'être persécutés du fait même de leur appartenance à ce groupe'].

On its face, this definition appears to be substantially broader than the previous CNDA definition. It rigorously takes the persecutor's perspective in defining the particular social group. The Court goes on to explain that

> the granting of refugee status because of persecution due to membership in a social group based on common sexual orientation should not be subordinated to the public manifestation of the sexual orientation of the person seeking the benefit of refugee status ... [because] the social group is not established by those who compose it, nor even because of the objective existence of characteristics attributed to them, but by the surrounding society's and institutions' view of these people.[87]

As such, the group does not depend on any preconceived notions of what it can comprise nor does it distinguish between the claimant's acts and identity. Rather, it depends on the persecutor's view as to who is persecuted and on which basis. Lantero observed of this definition that '[t]he criterion of social perception can prove to be very protective insofar as it does not require from group members the slightest claim to belonging'.[88]

However, in the time period under review until the end of 2016, the inclusive potential of this definition had not yet been put to the test in practice. Subsequent judgments of the CNDA regularly referred to the wording of the slightly varied test but in all available judgments until that date the claimant had been 'outed' against their will and suffered past persecution.[89] Nevertheless, on this basis, some preliminary observations can be made on the new definition, which point to two possible ways in which this seemingly broad approach might be circumscribed.

First, much depends on what is attributed to the persecutor's perception. This becomes evident, for example, in the intensive discussion in Germany in the context of the question of whether criminal laws sanctioned gay 'identity' or 'merely homosexual acts'. The answer to this question may lead to differently defined groups. In the case of O. A., concerning a lesbian woman from Mongolia, the Council of State itself appears to have allowed for such limiting distinctions. In this judgment, it further specified that the assessment must 'be sufficiently precise and take into account, where appropriate, any specific features of [the society's and

[87] CE, 27 juillet 2012, 349824. ['L'octroi du statut de réfugié du fait de persécutions liées à l'appartenance à un groupe social fondé sur des orientations sexuelles communes ne saurait être subordonné à la manifestation publique de cette orientation sexuelle par la personne qui sollicite le bénéfice du statut de réfugié dès lors que le groupe social n'est pas institué par ceux qui le composent, ni même du fait de l'existence objective de caractéristiques qu'on leur prête mais par le regard que portent sur ces personnes la société environnante ou les institutions'].

[88] Lantero, note 43, 2367 ['Le critère de la perception sociale peut s'avérer très protecteur en tant qu'il n'exige pas des membres du groupe la moindre revendication d'appartenance'].

[89] See for example CNDA 18 octobre 2012, 12013647 C, M. B. N.; CNDA 29 novembre 2013, 13018825 C, M. A.; CNDA 10 juillet 2014, 13025005 C, M. J-J.; CNDA 19 décembre 2014, 14017576 C, Mme W.

institutions'] view of the different components of this group'.[90] In other words, this opens up the possibility of finding that if the criminal law merely sanctions homosexual acts, but not the 'identity per se', then the group is made up of gay people who engage in same-sex sexual conduct only. Likewise, it could, for example, lead to findings such as that only gay men formed a particular social group, because lesbian women remained invisible – or because the criminal law sanctions same-sex sexual acts between men, but not between women.

A second way to curtail this broad notion of particular social group lies in one notable and confusing addition to the new definition. While the Council of State explicitly rejected the CNDA's requirement of public manifestation, it introduced the notion of 'revendication' ('claim' or 'assertion').[91] This term had not previously been used by the Council of State.[92] It had been an invention of the CNDA in the 1999 decision in *Djellal*, mentioned earlier,[93] and it could easily have been left out – there was simply no need for the Conseil Constitutionnel to pick it up.[94] One interpretation of this addition is that it could be a concession by the Council of State to the two-limbed 'particular social group' definition from the *Qualification Directive*, with the 'claim to be gay' having to be corroborated in order to determine the inner essence of the fundamental characteristic.

Whatever the motivation for its inclusion, the function of the term in the new definition remains obscure, not least because it can have several meanings. It can refer to public assertion. That is how it was applied in previous case law, where it was often used interchangeably with 'manifestation', connoting some sort of outwardness, usually linked with qualifications such as 'ostensibly'. But the more likely meaning in this context is 'claiming' in the sense of applying a category to oneself, as in 'claiming to be gay', which connotes doubts as to the veracity of the alleged

90 CE, 27 juillet 2012, 342552, O. A.

91 See: 'whether . . . it is possible to assimilate people *claiming* the same sexual orientation in a social group because of the view that the surrounding society and institutions have of these people . . .', CE, 27 juillet 2012, 349824.

92 Recall that the Council of State had defined the notion of particular social group generally as 'constituting a group whose members would be at risk of persecution for reasons of common characteristics that define them in the eyes of authorities and society' ['constituant un groupe dont les membres seraient, en raison des caractéristiques communes qui les définissent aux yeux des autorités et de la société algériennes, susceptibles d'être exposés à des persécutions'], CE, 23 juin 1997, 171858, *Ourbih*.

93 Recall that the CRR's definition of the social group of gay people from *Djellal* relied on asserting the sexual orientation or manifesting it in external behaviour, CRR 12 mai 1999, 328310, *Djellal*, and see earlier discussion.

94 It suffices to look at the Council of State's own previous *Ourbih/Olena* definition, which avoided any such a term: 'homosexuals . . . constitute a group whose members are at risk of being exposed to persecution due to their common characteristic which defines them in the eyes of the authorities and society', ['homosexuels constitu[ent] un groupe dont les membres seraient, en raison des caractéristiques communes qui les définissent aux yeux des autorités et de la société ukrainienne, susceptibles d'être exposés à des persécutions'], CE, 23 août 2006, 272679, *Olena*.

identity.[95] Both meanings reflect the claimant's own position towards the characteristic – and, as such, in some ways undermine the very core of the definition based on public perception that the Council of State proposed, namely the fact that the claimant does *not* have to claim membership in any way.[96] In that capacity, the notion of 'se revendiquer' might develop into a back door through which the 'discretion requirement in reverse' might slip back in; those who have not 'claimed' their sexual orientation in the past could be rejected. But since the term also suggests the doubt of an unproven allegation, it could also serve to encourage disbelief concerning the sexual orientation of claimants who *have* claimed their sexual orientation.

Given that the claimants in all most recent judgments under review had been 'outed', their sexual orientation was known and in that sense presumably 'asserted' or 'claimed'.[97] A 2014 decision by the CNDA concerning W., a lesbian woman from the Democratic Republic of the Congo (DRC) is noteworthy in this context for two reasons. First, it made reference for the first time to the CJEU's decisions on sexuality-based claims. It noted that X, Y *and* Z stipulates that 'discretion' or 'reserve in the expression' of sexual orientation cannot be required of a claimant and that A, B *and* C outlines the criteria of assessment and the elements of proof to establish a claimant's sexual orientation.[98] These judgments appear to have influenced the reasoning in the decision,[99] although the Court did not later explicitly engage with them in the assessment of the facts of the case. Second, the CNDA rejected the claimant on the basis of disbelief of both her alleged sexual orientation and – consequently – the past persecution she suffered for that reason: even though the Court found that a particular social group of 'homosexuals' who 'hide their sexual orientation for fear of reprisals' exists in the DRC, it reasoned that the claimant's vague and confusing evidence did not establish her sexual orientation. Among others, the Court criticised that her evasive account lacked details and did not provide evidence about the ways in which she would, or would not, have sought to hide her sexual orientation.[100] Given this definition of 'particular social group', it would be interesting to know what the outcome would have been if the claimant had established in a credible manner that she had *not* sought to hide her sexual

95 Note the further linguistic difficulties linked to the difference between 'revendiquer' (as it was used in the earlier CNDA definition) as opposed to the reflexive use 'se revendiquer de' (in the new Council of State definition), the latter in fact being an – albeit common – barbarism resulting from a confusion with 'se réclamer' ('to invoke').

96 Lantero, note 43, 2367.

97 See for example: CNDA 18 octobre 2012, 12013647 C, M. B. N.; CNDA 29 novembre 2013, 13018825 C, M. A.; CNDA 10 juillet 2014, 13025005 C, M. J-J.; CNDA 19 décembre 2014, 14017576 C, Mme W.

98 CNDA 19 décembre 2014, 14017576 C, Mme W.

99 The credibility assessment is carried out on the basis of the claimant's account and no further evidence is required, and the Court accepts that 'discretion' cannot be required.

100 CNDA 19 décembre 2014, 14017576 C, Mme W.

orientation in the past. Would she have been found not to fall within the particular social group of 'homosexuals who hide their sexual orientation for fear of reprisals' and therefore rejected? This would come down to a complete reversal of the traditional approach in France.

Similarly, in a 2016 judgment concerning a Nigerian man, the Council of State had to overrule the CNDA's finding of disbelief of the claimant's homosexuality, arguing that all declarations were in fact corroborated, clear and coherent.[101] In a 2016 judgment concerning a lesbian woman, Mme E, from the DRC, the CNDA went to great lengths to lay out the reasons why the claimant was a credible witness.[102] Previously, disbelief of the sexual orientation itself had been very rare in the decision-making practice of the CNDA, but, on the basis of the few available decisions, it appears to have become more common since the rejection of the public manifestation requirement.[103] Kobelinsky found in her examination of judgments from 2001–2011 that, where there were findings of disbelief, they were mostly linked to the claimed past persecution. Her interviews with decision-makers did, however, reveal that doubts concerning the sexual orientation of the claimant often underpinned the assessment of the cases.[104] The fact that the explicit 'public manifestation' requirement as an alternative grounds for rejection no longer applies might have led to an increased reliance on disbelief concerning the sexual orientation itself. Even though the small number of published decisions does not allow for broader conclusions, these findings might indicate a trend similar to that found in Millbank's study of UK and Australian case law, of shifting from 'discretion' to 'disbelief' after the 'discretion requirement' had been rejected by the majority of the High Court of Australia.[105]

Based on the reviewed cases, in which all of the claimants had been 'outed', it is not possible to assess how the new definition is conceived of in cases where a claimant has in fact successfully kept their sexual orientation secret in the past and would likely seek to continue to do so in the future. It is in such a situation that the function of the term 'se revendiquer' would have to prove (and would likely reveal) itself. It is also the situation that the CJEU judgments do not address, and for which *HJ (Iran) and HT (Cameroon)* and Hathaway and Pobjoy have developed different answers – and it is precisely around this question that the debate has revolved in Germany.

[101] CE, 17 juin 2016, 391534.

[102] CNDA 14 juin 2016, 15030258 C, Mme E.; see also the similar case of Mme T. from Cameroon who was found to have presented a plausible and lively account: CNDA 27 septembre 2016, 15004721 C, Mme T.

[103] See for example: CNDA 28 novembre 2011, 10019216 C, M. C.; CNDA 29 juillet 2011, 09004056 C, M. B.; CNDA 24 juin 2011, 10025142 C, M. V. [sexual orientation established, but past persecution disbelieved]; CNDA 3 novembre 2011, 11010972 C, M. A.

[104] Kobelinsky, note 2, 597.

[105] Jenni Millbank (2009) 'From Discretion to Disbelief: Recent Trends in Refugee Determinations on the Basis of Sexual Orientation in Australia and the United Kingdom', 13(2/3) *International Journal of Human Rights* 391–414.

4.4 CONCLUSION: FRANCE – 'DISCRETION' UPSIDE DOWN

A series of insights emerge from an analysis of French sexuality-based asylum judgments through the lens of an act/identity dichotomy. Firstly, 'discretion' reasoning is well established in case law, in spite of the fact that it is not always recognised as such. It surfaces in the shape of the opposite, requiring outwardness rather than silence. It turns 'classical discretion reasoning' on its head by refusing protection to those claimants who have *not* publicly claimed their sexual orientation. But, even upside down, the underlying reasoning is the same – if they have been 'discreet' in the past, they can continue to exercise 'discretion' in the future.

Secondly, there is no visible reception of the judgment in *HJ (Iran) and HT (Cameroon)* in France. It is true that the CNDA dropped its 'public manifestation' requirement in late 2010 – that is, after the UK Supreme Court's judgment. Given that there is no explicit engagement with the judgment, and that its connection with the French 'particular social group' definition is rather indirect, this could be a mere coincidence. The style of the French judgments reveals so little of the underlying considerations that it cannot be excluded that the Supreme Court's judgment was read and received, although, given that there was no wide recognition of 'discretion' reasoning in France, it could have been considered irrelevant to French jurisprudence.[106] Likewise, the judgment in Y *and* Z has not impacted sexuality-based claims in France. It was acknowledged for claims based on religion,[107] but no link seems to have been made with claims based on sexual orientation. Only those CJEU judgments that explicitly engage with sexuality-based claims (X, Y *and* Z and A, B *and* C) were applied in France accordingly. No links or transferrals were made between the Convention grounds.

In turn, the *Qualification Directive* – though somewhat belatedly – and, to a lesser extent, the CJEU judgment in X, Y *and* Z have both had an impact on French jurisprudence regarding this group of cases. Because French 'discretion' reasoning in reverse was based on its specific notion of particular social group – and that notion was changed when Article 10 of the *Qualification Directive* finally found its way into French decision-making – the *Qualification Directive* led to dropping the 'public manifestation' requirement that had formed the basis of French 'discretion' logics. In contrast, the French adoption of the *Qualification Directive* definition has maintained the focus on the persecutor's perspective, which still comprises the potential for 'discretion' reasoning in reverse – *if* it is applied as a social visibility requirement linked to the particular claimant, as it has been in the past. Moreover, the addition of the term 'claim' to the sexual orientation remains obscure and creates the risk of both another manifestation requirement (for those who have

[106] It is in the nature of CNDA judgments that there are very few express references to case law, although they may have influenced the decision, see Lambert and Silga, note 31, 47–48.

[107] See e.g.: CNDA 12 février 2013, 11029513 C, M. M.; CNDA 4 novembre 2013, 13007332 C, M. F.

not been persecuted in the past) and disbelief (for those who have suffered harm). As such, while integrating international guidance into its doctrine, French jurisprudence appears to have managed to maintain its traditional approach to 'discretion' in a revised form.

Thirdly, the doctrinal *location* of 'discretion' reasoning in France is the particular social group analysis. Instead of moving the 'act' element to another place in the assessment, French jurisprudence conceives of 'discretion' considerations as part of the Convention ground. When digging deeper, it becomes clear, however, that the rationale is the assumption that secrecy is synonymous with safety, such that considerations of likelihood of risk underlie the definition of particular social group.

Fourthly, the judgments do not frame their reasoning in terms of human rights. However, Kobelinsky found some evidence in her interviews that rights-based considerations are present. For example, she cites one decision-maker who said at an interview that the case concerning a Tunisian gay man who had never publicly manifested his sexual orientation 'ultimately raises the question of whether the protection provided by the CESEDA encompasses the right to a normal personal life, that is, to a non-clandestine sexual life'.[108] That is, whereas jurisprudence clearly relied on a 'factual' assessment of behaviour, rejecting those who had led a clandestine life, some evidence of doubts as to whether human rights claims of the claimant had to be taken into account appear to be present. The scope of refugee protection in France is limited by 'discretion' reasoning relying on the claimant's acts, not on their rights.

Though there are some parallels with German jurisprudence to be found in French cases, the primary approach to sexuality-based claims is the opposite. Whereas France has traditionally focused on the claimant's behaviour, Germany has always concentrated on the claimant's identity. As the following discussion shows, both reasonings work with the act/identity double bind, but in different manners. While the underlying discourse is the same, the reasoning is not. Ultimately, however, claimants are damned if they do and damned if they don't.

[108] Kobelinsky, note 2, 592.

5

Irreversibly Determined

Germany

In sexuality-based asylum decisions in Germany, the act/identity dichotomy materialises in the preference of identity over acts.[1] Since the earliest judgments accepting gay claimants – which were amongst the earliest worldwide to grant refugee protection to people persecuted for their sexual orientation – German courts have developed the notion of a fatefully determined gay identity. This concept emerged from the context in which it was developed, which is why the following discussion examines the legal and institutional system before delving into the case analysis.

5.1 THE GERMAN CONTEXT: FAVOURING IDENTITY

Like France, Germany provides for asylum in its Constitution. Since 1949, the Basic Law (Grundgesetz, GG) stipulates that 'politically persecuted persons enjoy the right to asylum'.[2] Its initial purpose was limited to extradition proceedings, providing a subjective right of political offenders not to be expelled.[3] Refugee protection in turn was foreseen under the international regime – in 1953, the Refugee Convention was ratified in Germany. In this context, the first asylum procedure was established.[4]

1 Sections of this chapter are referred to in Janna Wessels (2017) 'Publicly Manifested–Fatefully Determined–Invariably "Discreet": The Assessment of Sexuality-Based Asylum Claims in Germany and France', 29(2) *Canadian Journal of Women and the Law* 343–374.

2 Article 16(2); since the 1993 'asylum compromise' Article 16a(1) of the *Basic Law for the Federal Republic of Germany of 23 May 1949* (Grundgesetz für die Bundesrepublik Deutschland vom 23. Mai 1949 (BGBl. S. 1)) ['Politisch Verfolgte genießen Asylrecht'].

3 Hélène Lambert, Francesco Messineo and Paul Tiedemann (2008) 'Comparative Perspectives of Constitutional Asylum in France, Italy, and Germany: Requiescat in Pace?', 27(3) *Refugee Survey Quarterly* 16–32, 26; see also Paul Tiedemann (2014) *Flüchtlingsrecht – Die materiellen und verfahrensrechtlichen Grundlagen*, Berlin: Springer, 9.

4 By virtue of the *Act concerning the Legal Status of Refugees of 1 September 1953* (Gesetz betreffend das Abkommen vom 28. Juli 1951 über die Rechtsstellung der Flüchtlinge vom 1. September 1953, BGBl. II 559) and the *Order on the Recognition and Distribution of Foreign Refugees (Asylum Ordinance) of 6 January 1953* (Verordnung über die Anerkennung und die

But in 1959, the Federal Constitutional Court (Bundesverfassungsgericht, BVerfG) in obiter distinguished between the scope of protection of constitutional asylum (which it held to be wider) and that of conventional protection, which was at the time still limited to refugees whose displacement was caused by events in Europe prior to 1 January 1951.[5] This distinction was regulated in law in the 1965 *Aliens Act*, which explicitly referred to two separate legal bases for protection: convention refugees and 'other foreigners' who were politically persecuted persons within the meaning of Article 16(2) of the Constitution.[6] This triggered the 'progressive and gradual implementation of a national scheme of refugee protection that was to be entirely separate from the developments of refugee law standards in the international law arena'.[7] By prioritising constitutional asylum over the Refugee Convention, the Federal Constitutional Court adopted interpretative authority concerning asylum in Germany[8] and developed a comprehensive jurisprudence on 'political persecution', whereas refugee status according to the Convention played practically no role. Liberal at first, the Court's approach became much more restrictive in the 1980s, when it developed certain doctrinal positions that both reduced the scope of asylum and were contrary to the jurisprudence of most states party to the Refugee Convention. Among other developments, the BVerfG ruled that *sur place* claims were not protected,[9] developed the doctrine of 'more likely than not' ('überwiegend wahrscheinlich') for the risk assessment, requiring a likelihood of risk exceeding 50 per cent,[10] and decided that persecution had to emanate from the state in order to warrant protection.[11] Importantly for this study, it also developed the doctrinal figure of the 'religious subsistence level' ('religiöses Existenzminimum'), which is defined as the 'religious forum internum', according to which religious life is protected only in private.[12]

A 1990 reform of the Asylum Procedures Act revived asylum under the Refugee Convention by stipulating that, in all asylum cases, both legal bases had to be considered. This simultaneously revived the role of the Federal Administrative Court, which is the last instance for appeals under the Refugee Convention. But, rather than developing its own jurisprudence or considering developments

Verteilung von ausländischen Flüchtlingen (Asylverordnung) vom 6. January 1953, BGBl 1953 Abs. 1 3).

5 Lambert et al., note 3, 27.

6 Article 28 of the *Aliens Act of the Federal Republic of Germany of 28 April 1965* (Ausländergesetz der Bundesrepublik Deutschland vom 28. April 1965; BGBl. I 1965 353).

7 Lambert et al., note 3, 27. In a 1980 judgment, the Court reaffirmed its position that the scope of protection of constitutional asylum can be broader than that of the Refugee Convention, without however specifying in which ways: BVerfGE 54, 341, Urteil vom 02.07.1980.

8 For asylum under the Refugee Convention, the Federal Administrative Court is responsible in its capacity as final instance in non-constitutional public law cases.

9 BVerfGE 74, 51, Urteil vom 26.11.1986.

10 BVerfGE 76, 143, Beschluss vom 01.07.1987.

11 BverfGE 80, 315, Urteil vom 10.07.1989.

12 BVerfGE 76, 143, Beschluss vom 01.07.1987.

concerning the interpretation of Article 1(A)2 of the Refugee Convention abroad, the Court transferred and applied the Federal Constitutional Court's jurisprudence on Article 16(2) of the GG to the interpretation of conventional asylum. As such, it adopted the 'more likely than not' standard for the risk assessment,[13] confirmed the rejection of non-state persecution[14] and embraced the 'religious subsistence level' doctrine.[15]

All of these positions were contrary to international consensus and guidance regarding the Refugee Convention – and contrary to the dispositions of the *Qualification Directive*. Therefore, the transposition of the *Qualification Directive* into German law had quite a disruptive effect,[16] even though, as in France, the transposition was initially selective. It was integrated into the established, complicated system based on cross-references between different laws, which were each amended various times throughout the following years. In particular, the relevant provisions were split between the Law of Residence (*Aufenthaltsgesetz, AufenthG*) and the Asylum Procedures Act (*Asylverfahrensgesetz, AsylVfG*). A very long article, *AufenthG* art 60(1), titled 'Prohibition of Deportation', essentially covered the material provisions concerning refugee status, in particular specifying that persecution may emanate from private actors. Other provisions are merely mentioned to the effect that '[i]n order to determine persecution [within the meaning of this article], Article 4 (4) and Articles 7 to 10 of the [*Qualification Directive*] are to be applied in addition'.[17] Much like in France, it was not until the transposition of the recast *Qualification Directive* that the contents of Article 9 on persecution and Article 10 on the Convention grounds were explicitly integrated into German law.[18] In particular, Article 1(1) of the *AsylVfG* was amended to reflect the refugee definition from the *Qualification Directive* and Article 3 was amended with a verbatim repetition of Article 9 and 10 *Qualification Directive*, including the specific reference to sexual orientation and gender as a particular social group and to public religious acts.

[13] BVerwGE 88, 367, Urteil vom 23.7.1991, 9 C 154/90, at 377.
[14] BVerwGE 95, 42, Urteil vom 18.01.1994, 9 C 48/92.
[15] BVerwGE 92, 278, Urteil vom 13.05.1993, 9 C 49/92.
[16] By virtue of a 2004 reform that replaced the previous Aliens Act with the Residence Act (*Law on the Residence, Employment and the Integration of Foreigners in the Federal Territory of 30 July 2004 (Residence Act)* (Gesetz über den Aufenthalt, die Erwerbstätigkeit und die Integration von Ausländern im Bundesgebiet vom 30. Juli 2004 (*Aufenthaltsgesetz, AufenthG*); BGBl. I 2004 1950)), which entered into forced on 1 January 2005 and reformed the Asylum Procedures Act; as well as the *Act Implementing the European Union Directives on Residence and Asylum of 19 August 2007* (Gesetz zur Umsetzung aufenthalts- und asylrechtlicher Richtlinien der Europäischen Union vom 19. August 2007, BGBl. I 2007 1970, '*Richtlinienumsetzungsgesetz*').
[17] Article 60(1) Residence Act ['Für die Feststellung ob eine Verfolgung nach Satz 1 vorliegt, sind Artikel 4 Abs 4 sowie die Artikel 7 bis 10 der [Qualifikationsrichtlinie] ergänzend anzuwenden'].
[18] *Act Implementing the Directive 2011/95/EU of 28 August 2013* (Gesetz zur Umsetzung der Richtlinie 2011/95/EU vom 28. August 2013, BGBl. I 2013 3473).

In terms of procedure, the 1965 Aliens Act created the Federal Office for the Recognition of Foreign Refugees (Bundesamt für die Anerkennung ausländischer Flüchtlinge, BAFl),[19] which became the Federal Office for Migration and Refugees (Bundesamt für Migration und Flüchtlinge, BAMF) in the course of the reform that transposed the *Qualification Directive*. The BAMF, which falls under the responsibility of the Ministry of the Interior, is the administrative body responsible for the asylum procedure. Appeals against BAMF decisions are litigated within the administrative jurisdiction of the federated states (Bundesländer) as follows: first instance appeals go to the responsible regional Administrative Court (Verwaltungsgerichte, VG), appeals against these judgments are dealt with at Higher Administrative Courts (Oberverwaltungsgerichte, OVG/ Verwaltungsgerichtshöfe, VGH),[20] which are the highest instance administrative courts at the level of the *Bundesländer* (federal states). Further appeals then address the Federal Administrative Court (Bundesverwaltungsgericht, BVerwG), the last instance national court for administrative matters. As a result of this situation, asylum jurisprudence in Germany evinces more regional divergence than in France and Spain with their centralised appeals system. In particular, this judicial set-up allows controversial issues and disagreement over doctrinal questions to persist longer, before they reach the central final instance court. As the discussion to come shows, this is what happened with the question of 'discretion' in sexuality-based claims.

In comparison with the situation in France and Spain, German sexuality-based asylum claims have received quite a bit of attention, in particular in the context of 'discretion' reasoning. Two book chapters have examined German practice with a view to sexuality-based claims more broadly,[21] but the German refugee law community was primarily concerned with the issue of concealment, which was discussed with respect to both religion and sexual orientation in a series of publications in the years between 2011 and 2013 – that is, at the time that the three high-level judgments were handed down.[22] Some of these contributions engage with German jurisprudence, but – due to the date of their publication – they cannot assess the effect of the

[19] *Aliens Act of the Federal Republic of Germany of 28 April 1965* (Ausländergesetz der Bundesrepublik Deutschland vom 28. April 1965; BGBl. I 1965 353).

[20] For historical reasons, depending on the Bundesland, the name of the Court is either 'Oberverwaltungsgericht' or 'Verwaltungsgerichtshof'.

[21] Jerzy Szczensny (2009) 'Sexuelle Selbstbestimmung und das Recht auf Asyl in Deutschland', in Claudia Lohrenscheit (ed.) *Sexuelle Selbstbestimmung als Menschenrecht*, Berlin: Nomos, 169–181; Rainer Keil (2016) 'Sexuelle Orientierung im Flüchtlingsrecht und im allgemeinen Migrationsrecht der Bundesrepublik Deutschland', in Claus Dieter Classen, Dagmar Richter und Bernard Łukanko (eds.) *'Sexuelle Orientierung' als Diskriminierungsgrund: Regelungsbedarf in Deutschland und Polen?*, Tübingen: Mohr Siebeck, 293–315.

[22] See Nora Markard and Laura Adamietz (2011) 'Keep It in the Closet? Flüchtlingsanerkennung wegen Homosexualität auf dem Prüfstand', 44(3) *Kritische Justiz* 294–302; Nora Markard (2013) 'Sexuelle Orientierung als Fluchtgrund – Das Ende der "Diskretion" – Aktuelle Entwicklungen beim Flüchtlingsschutz aufgrund der sexuellen Orientierung', *Asylmagazin* 3/2013, 74–84; Anngeret Titze (2012) 'Sexuelle Orientierung und die Zumutung der

rejection of 'discretion' in case law. The same goes for the German contribution to the *Fleeing Homophobia* project, which – as for the other jurisdictions under review – provides a rich source of information.[23] The following discussion draws on these earlier findings to develop an assessment of 'discretion' reasoning in German jurisprudence prior to the Europeanisation of asylum and the rejection of the 'discretion' requirement, and builds on it to examine in which ways these developments are reflected in more recent jurisprudence.

Germany has a slightly more liberal publication system for judgments than France. The case law that forms the basis of this examination principally consists of all judgments tagged with 'homosexuell' in the case law database asyl.net. In order to cover gaps in the case collection (mainly for the years before 2006 and for the most recent judgments, i.e. since 2014), additional cases were gathered from the case law database Beck-Online. The overall case collection thus includes a total of seventy-five German judgments, covering the years 1983–2016.

Unlike their French counterparts, German judgments have a more discursive style, laying out both the facts of the case and the motivations for a decision in detail. Judgments have a very clear, consistently recurring structure, as German judges stringently apply an established evaluation scheme. This makes it easier both to put single judgments into context and to analyse the reasoning underlying the decision than in the case of French (and Spanish; see next chapter) judgments, as it involves less deduction and speculation.

5.2 INESCAPABILITY AND FATEFUL DETERMINATION

In contrast to France, Germany has a tradition of favouring identity over acts. In this sense, German practice was closer to 'classical' 'discretion' reasoning. This is ironic, as the earliest recorded rejection of 'discretion' worldwide was a 1983 case of the Administrative Court of Wiesbaden: the Court compared the 'discretion' requirement to a requirement that someone would have to change their skin colour in order to evade persecution.[24] On appeal, the VGH of Hesse confirmed this

Diskretion', *Zeitschrift für Ausländerrecht und Ausländerpolitik* 2012, 93–102; on religion see Anna Lübbe (2013) 'Flüchtlingsanerkennung in Verhaltenslenkungsfällen nach den Ahmadi-Entscheidungen des BVerwG', *Zeitschrift für Ausländerrecht und Ausländerpolitik* 2013, 272–278; Anna Lübbe (2012) 'Verfolgungsvermeidende Anpassung an menschenrechtswidrige Verhaltenslenkungen als Grenze der Flüchtlingsanerkennung?', *Zeitschrift für Ausländerrecht und Ausländerpolitik* 2012, 7–13; Anna Lübbe (2011) 'Zielgerichtetheit des Akteursverhaltens und Unterlassen im Flüchtlingsrecht', *Zeitschrift für Ausländerrecht und Ausländerpolitik* 2011, 164–167.

23 Michael Kalkmann (2011) *Fleeing Homophobia Questionnaire, Best Practices on the (Legal) Position of LGBT Asylum Seekers in the EU Member States – Germany*, Fleeing Homophobia Project, www.rechten.vu.nl/nl/Images/Germany_questionnaire_tcm247-240406.pdf.

24 VG Wiesbaden, Urteil vom 26.4.1983, IV/I E 06244/81, as discussed in Maryellen Fullerton (1990) 'Persecution Due to Membership in a Particular Social Group: Jurisprudence in the Federal Republic of Germany', 4 *Georgetown Immigration Law Journal* 381–444 at 408–410.

rejection, arguing that it could not reasonably be required of the applicant to avoid prosecution by abstaining from sexual acts.[25] The case was further appealed and led to a 1988 judgment of the German Federal Administrative Court that remained the leading case concerning sexuality-based claims in Germany for two decades. In this judgment, the Court developed the distinction between – variously – 'irreversible', 'fateful' or 'inescapable' homosexuality on the one hand, and 'latent' homosexuality on the other.[26] In the former case, a person is thought to be 'fatefully determined' ('schicksalhafte Festlegung') by their sexual orientation to such an extent that they have no choice but to satisfy their same-sex sexual urges ('homosexuelle Triebbefriedigung'), in the latter case, they have a 'mere inclination' ('bloße Neigung') towards same-sex sexuality and can choose whether or not to engage in same-sex sexual acts.[27] Based on this classification, for years, only those claimants who could convince courts that their identity was sufficiently and irreversibly determined by their sexual orientation would regularly be granted protection. It is precisely the idea of innateness that is inherent in likening sexual orientation to race rather than religion or political opinion that defined German pre–*Qualification Directive* jurisprudence on sexuality-based claims. In this reasoning, the act/identity dichotomy functions to limit the scope of protection in such a way that even though a claimant might engage in same-sex behaviour, it would not warrant protection if their identity was not considered to be sufficiently determined by the same-sex sexual orientation.

The 1988 BVerwG judgment stands out in several ways. Firstly, it reveals that Germany accepted sexuality-based claims more than a decade earlier than Spain and France, and indeed many other jurisdictions.[28] But, secondly, this was possible only because the judgment was explicitly *not* based on the Refugee Convention, but on Article 16(2) of the constitution. Rather than subsuming sexual orientation under membership of a particular social group, the Court argued that sexual orientation was not covered by the Convention grounds. It even explicitly doubted that 'homosexuals' can be considered members of a particular social group,

[25] Hess. VGH, Urteil vom 21.08.1986, 10 OE 69/83. See also the discussion in Titze, note 22, 100–101.

[26] BVerwG Urteil vom 15.3.1988, 9 C 278/86.

[27] See also Sabine Jansen and Thomas Spijkerboer (2011) *Fleeing Homophobia: Asylum Claims Related to Sexual Orientation and Gender Identity in Europe*, September 2011, 50.

[28] Some common law jurisdictions started to accept sexuality-based claims in the early 1990s; the USA in 1990 (*In re Toboso-Alfonso*, 20 I. & N. December 819 (B.I.A. 1990), United States Board of Immigration Appeals, 12 March 1990); Canada in *obiter dicta* in 1993 (*Canada (Attorney General)* v. *Ward*, [1993] 2 S.C.R. 689, Canada: Supreme Court, 30 June 1993); New Zealand in 1995 (*Re GJ, Refugee Appeal* No. 1312/93, New Zealand: Refugee Status Appeals Authority, 30 August 1995). For a discussion see Kristen Walker (2000) 'Sexuality and Refugee Status in Australia', 12(2) *International Journal of Refugee Law* 175–211, 181–183. For a discussion of the earliest Australian cases from 1994, see Jenni Millbank (1995) 'Fear of Persecution or Just a Queer Feeling? Refugee Status and Sexual Orientation in Australia', 20(6) *Alternative Law Journal* 261–265.

although it refrained from coming to a conclusion on this point.[29] Rather, it ruled that Article 16(2) GG[30] was broader in scope as it was not limited to the Convention grounds of the Refugee Convention, such that 'other personal characteristics and behaviours can also be relevant to asylum [under this provision], for example, if someone is irreversibly and fatefully homosexual and is therefore threatened with persecution in Iran – to the point of death penalty'.[31] This is an important point: sexual orientation was protected in Germany *not* in the framework of the Refugee Convention, but under constitutional asylum provisions. A year later, the Federal Administrative Court (BVerwG) confirmed its previous ruling and extended it also to bisexual people.[32] The Federal Administrative Court clarified that irreversibility of a homosexual predisposition did not require that same-sex sexual contact was the *only* possibility for sexual activity. Rather, a 'homosexual drive' that is present alongside a heterosexual orientation, which the person concerned does not have the strength to resist or avoid permanently, and which therefore always leads to homosexual acts, is irreversible.[33]

Despite this clarification, due to the notion of irreversibility, the claims of bisexual claimants, or claimants who the Court found were not entirely sure about their same-sex sexuality, regularly failed. This reasoning is exemplified in a case concerning a gay man from Ethiopia from 2000. In this case, the Administrative Court of Ansbach rejected the claim for protection on sexuality grounds on the basis that he was clearly not a 'determined homosexual', because he admitted to having had sexual contacts with women after having discovered his homosexuality.[34] Eight years

[29] BVerwG Urteil vom 15.3.1988, 9 C 278/86: 'There is no need to determine whether, as the applicant argues, this list of personal characteristics and properties was meant to be conclusive in the view of the States Parties to the Geneva Convention on Refugees, and whether, as the Court of Appeal has assumed, homosexuals could be regarded as belonging to a particular social group, which indeed seems doubtful.' ['Es kann dabei dahinstehen, ob – wie der Beteiligte vorträgt – diese Aufzählung persönlicher Merkmale und Eigenschaften nach Auffassung der Vertragsstaaten der Genfer Flüchtlingskonvention abschließend sein sollte und ob unter dieser Voraussetzung – wie das Berufungsgericht angenommen hat – Homosexuelle als Angehörige einer bestimmten sozialen Gruppe angesehen werden könnten, was in der Tat zweifelhaft erscheint'].

[30] Which stipulates: 'Politically persecuted persons enjoy the right to asylum.'

[31] BVerwG Urteil vom 15.3.1988, 9 C 278/86 ['Keine Begriffsbeschränkung bei asylerheblicher politischer Verfolgung nach Article 15 Abs. 2 Satz 2 GG auf die persönlichen Merkmale, die in Article 1 A Nr. 2 der Genfer Konvention genannt sind. Deswegen können auch andere persönliche Eigenschaften und Verhaltensweisen asylrechtlich relevant sein, wenn etwa jemand irreversibel und schicksalhaft homosexuell geprägt ist und ihm darum im Iran Verfolgung droht – bis hin zur Todesstrafe'].

[32] BverwG, Urteil vom 17.10.1989, 9 C 25/89, at 104–106.

[33] Ibid. ['Auch eine neben einer heterosexuellen Orientierung vorhandene homosexuelle Triebrichtung, welcher der Betreffende aus eigener Kraft auf Dauer und immer erneut nicht zu widerstehen bzw. auszuweichen vermag und die deshalb immer wieder zur Vornahme homosexueller Handlungen führt, ist irreversibel']; and see the discussion in Keil, note 21, 300–301.

[34] VG Ansbach, Urteil vom 11.10.2000, AN 3 K 00.31628 [ein 'geprägter Homosexeller'].

later, the same court found in a case concerning a married man with a child that his sexual orientation towards same-sex contacts with men did not have a grave influence on his identity. The claimant had stated that his homosexuality was not unambiguous and irreversible, although he tended more towards men than women. The Court concluded that the claimant was apparently not determined to a sufficient degree by his homosexuality, 'which may possibly be present in addition to his heterosexuality'.[35] Such erasure of bisexuality is in line with Rehaag's findings from Canada, the United States and Australia.[36] It results from the focus on identity; France would arguably have much less difficulty accepting bisexual claims.

In the German asylum decision-making tradition overall, the distinction between cases of claimants who have suffered past persecution ('Vorverfolgung') and those who have not plays an important role. A more lenient risk assessment applies to applicants who have already suffered harm.[37] Accordingly, in German practice concerning sexuality-based claims, if a claimant could establish the alleged past persecution, the claim would regularly succeed. In such cases, 'discretion' was not an option – since the claimants had already been 'outed'. Therefore, for this group of cases, rejections tended to be based on disbelief. That is, such claims could still fail if the claimant's past (public) behaviour leading to the persecutory harm was disbelieved. For example, the Administrative Court of Frankfurt/Oder quoted from (and disagreed with) a decision from the BAMF concerning a gay man from Cameroon: 'The applicant's claim to having lived his sexual orientation openly during the past years in Cameroon is not credible as this would have meant to expose himself to danger.'[38] In the case of a Sunni Arab man from Mosul, Iraq, the BAMF found the claimed past persecution implausible on the grounds that 'if he had been known, resp. persecuted, for homosexual activities, he would have been convicted under Section 400 of the Iraqi Penal Code'.[39] If gay applicants claimed past persecution, therefore, there was a tendency to move from 'discretion' to

35 VG Ansbach, Urteil vom 21.8.2008, AN 18 K 08.30201.

36 Sean Rehaag discussed the difficulties of bisexuals in Canada, the United States and Australia: Sean Rehaag (2009) 'Bisexuals Need Not Apply: A Comparative Appraisal of Refugee Law and Policy in Canada, the United States, and Australia', 13(2) *International Journal of Human Rights* 415–436; and Sean Rehaag (2008) 'Patrolling the Borders of Sexual Orientation: Bisexual Refugee Claims in Canada', 53 *McGill Law Journal* 59–102.

37 Such a distinction has also found entry into the *Qualification Directive* in Article 4(4): 'The fact that an applicant has already been subject to persecution or serious harm, or to direct threats of such persecution or such harm, is a serious indication of the applicant's well-founded fear of persecution or real risk of suffering serious harm, unless there are good reasons to consider that such persecution or serious harm will not be repeated.'

38 Quote from the BAMF decision as cited by the VG Frankfurt in its judgment: VG Frankfurt/Oder, Urteil vom 11.11.2010, VG 4 K 772/10.A. See also VG Bremen, Urteil vom 28. 4.2006, 7 K 632/05.A, where the Court cites an expert opinion according to which measures by the State are not to be expected as homosexuals would keep a low profile 'in their own interest' (though the case failed on credibility grounds).

39 VG Sigmaringen, Urteil vom 26.04.2010, A 1 K 1911/09. The Administrative Court disagreed.

disbelief as a basis for rejections. Like the findings on France, these findings from Germany reveal a repetition of the theme first observed by Millbank for the United Kingdom and Australia;[40] if 'discretion' is not an option for the rejection of a claim, the judge will revert to the other malleable element, that is, credibility.

However, the situation was different in cases where the claimant had *not* suffered persecution in the past. In such cases, the decisive element was the claimant's disposition, or 'sexual identity'. This is explained in a somewhat confusing statement issued by the German government (the Ministry of Interior is responsible for the administrative decision-making body BAMF) as follows:

> In the prediction of the likelihood of persecution the asylum seeker's own future conduct in his home state that would trigger that persecution should not generally be taken into account. The situation is different if that behaviour is more or less inevitable and thus the risk must be classified as an imminent danger (Federal Administrative Court, judgment of 15 March 1988 9 C 278/86). It therefore depends on whether the asylum seeker is determined by his sexuality in such a way that corresponding acts are to be expected, and whether there is the necessary degree of likelihood that these will be known to the Iranian authorities.[41]

The statement was issued in response to a parliamentary inquiry on BAMF decision-making practice a few weeks *before* the UK Supreme Court's judgment in *HJ (Iran) and HT (Cameroon)* was handed down. Therefore, it refers to German practice prior to the high-level rejections of 'discretion' reasoning. According to this statement, the BAMF would grant protection for reasons of sexual identity if there was a considerable degree of likelihood ('beachtliche Wahrscheinlichkeit') that persecution would ensue.[42] In other words, in cases where claimants had not yet suffered persecutory harm, the outcome of the asylum procedure depended on whether the asylum-seeker would behave in a manner that would lead to persecution after their return – but only if such behaviour resulted from a corresponding inescapable sexual

[40] Jenni Millbank (2009) 'From Discretion to Disbelief: Recent Trends in Refugee Determinations on the Basis of Sexual Orientation in Australia and the United Kingdom', 13 (2/3) *International Journal of Human Rights* 391–414.

[41] Bundestags-Drucksache 17/1505, 'Antwort der Bundesregierung auf die Kleine Anfrage der Abgeordneten Ulla Jelpke, Jan Korte, Dr. Barabara Höll, weiterer Abgeordneter und der Fraktion DIE LINKE: Aufnahme von Flüchtlingen aus dem Iran und Umgang mit homosexuellen Flüchtlingen', Deutscher Bundestag 17. Wahlperiode, 2010, at 7 ['Bei der Prognose über die Wahrscheinlichkeit einer Verfolgung ist ein die Verfolgung erst auslösendes zukünftiges eigenes Verhalten des Asylsuchenden in seinem Heimatstaat grundsätzlich nicht zu berücksichtigen. Etwas anderes gilt, wenn dieses Verhalten mehr oder weniger zwangsläufig zu erwarten ist und damit die Gefährdung des Asylsuchenden in so greifbare Nähe gerückt ist, dass sie wie eine unmittelbar drohende Gefahr als asylrechtlich beachtlich eingestuft werden muss (Bundesverwaltungsgericht, Urteil vom 15. März 1988, 9 C 278/86). Es kommt also darauf an, ob der Asylsuchende sexuell so geprägt ist, dass im Einzelfall eine entsprechende Betätigung zu erwarten ist, die den iranischen Behörden mit der erforderlichen Wahrscheinlichkeit bekannt werden wird'].

[42] Ibid., at 7.

disposition. It was therefore this disposition – the fateful, irreversible determination – that the claimant had to prove in order to reach the reasonable degree of likelihood standard.[43]

Against this background, the question of whether 'discretion may reasonably be required' of a claimant was considered to be irrelevant in BAMF practice.[44] The assessment was rather treated as a 'factual' examination establishing whether the claimant had a sufficiently stable sexual identity or not. As such, it was possible for the Administrative Court of Köln to accept a claim by an Iraqi man three years after his arrival. The Court found that the claimant explained in a credible manner that he could only decide to publicly admit to his homosexuality after a lengthy inner process and a difficult inner struggle, the end of which was marked by the finding of his own sexual identity.[45] As long as the claimant's identity appeared straightforward, stable and final, the German decision-makers were comfortable with accepting a claim. In French pre-2011 practice, in contrast, due to the lack of past public manifestation, this case would likely have had no chances of success.

But if the claimant's identity was not sufficiently determined by the sexual orientation, their same-sex sexual activity was considered an engagement in frivolous behaviour.[46] The latter was not deemed to be protected; a right for claimants to live their sexual orientation openly was not recognised.[47] That is, in such a case, while the identity as 'somewhat gay' was accepted and even deemed protected, 'discretion' *was* effectively reasonably required on the basis that what was persecuted was 'merely' the claimant's voluntary acts, from which they could choose to abstain. This position reflects the triviality concern: protection cannot be granted if the situation is not sufficiently serious.

In this sense, 'discretion' reasoning did play a role in German practice, although it took place in a different doctrinal location. Unlike the French context, where it is located in the particular social group, in Germany it determines the well-founded fear analysis: the risk was only well-founded if the sexual orientation 'will become known'. This was usually deemed to be the case for 'fatefully determined' gay people who could not resist their sexual urges. But sometimes, and particularly from the early 2000s onwards, the likelihood of discovery was treated as a separate element in addition to 'irreversible homosexuality'. For example, in the 1998 case of an Iranian gay man before the Higher Administrative Court of Munich, a medical examination had come to the conclusion that the claimant – even though he was irreversibly gay – was in a position to control his sex drive, as evidenced by the fact that he had not had any homosexual sexual contacts for about one and a half years. The court

43 Ibid., at 9–10.
44 Ibid., at 10.
45 VG Köln, Urteil vom 8.9.2006, 18 K 9030/03.A.
46 Jansen and Spijkerboer, note 27, 62.
47 Klaudia Dolk and Andreas Schwandtner (2007) 'Homosexualität und (Abschiebungs)schutz in Deutschland', 7–8 *Amnesty International – asyl-info* 4–15, 4.

further noted that by his own account, the claimant was able to abstain from sexual acts for long periods of time, and that he had the option of satisfying his urges through masturbation. Further, he had no disease that prevented him from controlling his sex drive and possible depressive moods could be treated by masturbation or medical therapies.[48] The court concluded that there was no risk of discovery *in spite of* his irreversible sexual identity. In 2002, the Administrative Court of Würzburg argued that, even though the Iranian man had convinced the court that he was gay, his story of past persecution was disbelieved and the Court did not see that he faced a concrete personal risk.[49]

A similar distinction between an accepted homosexual identity and risk of persecution was applied to the assessment of well-founded fear based on criminalisation. In a case before the Administrative Court of Ansbach, the Court found that, even though same-sex sexual relationships between men would be liable to prosecution and even the death penalty, the same was not true if merely a homosexual *inclination* became known.[50] In this way, German courts were able to reject a series of cases of irreversibly gay men on the basis essentially that claimants would hide their sexual orientation and not engage in sexual acts. This approach is also reflected in a resolution by the Administrative Court of Münster that the Cameroonian penal sanctions were understood to relate not to the 'sexual disposition as such', but to a particular external behaviour;[51] therefore, there was no risk of persecution on account of 'sexual identity' alone.[52] Besides, 'homosexuals in Cameroon don't usually make their sexual orientation public in order to avoid social and criminal sanctions'.[53] This idea that a protected fixed sexual identity is not affected by criminal sanctions targeting sexual acts can be traced back to the leading Federal

[48] VGH München, Beschluss vom 12.11.1998, 19 ZB 98.33916 ['Ein auf Beweisantrag des Bevollmächtigten hin beauftragter Gutachter ist – aufgrund der Angaben des Klägers – zwar zu dem Ergebnis gelangt, daß dieser irreversibel homosexuell festgelegt sei, hat jedoch sowohl in dem Gutachten vom 20. Mai 1998 als auch bei seiner Befragung in der mündlichen Verhandlung vom 21. Juli 1998 jeweils festgestellt, daß der Kläger in der Lage sei, seinen Sexualtrieb zu steuern, da er seit ca. eineinhalb Jahren keine homosexuellen Sexualkontakte mehr gehabt habe und nach eigenen Angaben auch in der Lage sei, auf sexuelle Handlungen über einen längeren Zeitraum zu verzichten; der Kläger habe die Möglichkeit, seinen Trieb durch Selbstbefriedigung zu befriedigen und es liege keine Krankheit vor, die ihn daran hindern würde, seinen Sexualtrieb zu steuern bzw. es sei möglich, eventuelle depressive Verstimmungen durch Selbstbefriedigung oder eine entsprechende Behandlung zu therapieren'].

[49] VG Würzburg, Urteil vom 16.7.2002, W 7 K 01.30170.

[50] VG Ansbach, Urteil vom 21.8.2008, AN 18 K 08.30201.

[51] VG Münster, Beschluss vom 4.7.2007, 9 L 381/07.A ['Auch wenn Homosexualität in Kamerun mit Gefängnis zwischen 6 Monaten und 5 Jahren sowie einer Geldstrafe bis zu 200.000,00 CFA bestraft werden kann, knüpft die strafrechtliche Verfolgung nicht an die sexuelle Veranlagung als solche an, sondern an ein bestimmtes äußeres Verhalten. Mit Verhängung und Vollstreckung einer Strafe soll nicht die homosexuelle Veranlagung an sich getroffen, sondern allein die Aufrechterhaltung der öffentlichen Moral bezweckt werden'].

[52] See also concerning Iran: Bundestags-Drucksache 17/1505, note 41, at 7.

[53] VG Münster, Beschluss vom 4.7.2007, 9 L 381/07.A.

Administrative Court decision from 1988, which first formulated that criminalisation of 'certain external behaviour' is not in itself a 'targeted intrusion' into the homosexual *disposition*.[54] The principle is reflected in a series of cases from countries with criminal laws in force, such as Algeria or Iran. On the basis that these criminal laws are not aimed at the 'disposition' but, rather, at 'certain sexual practices if these become known', the Court found that the claimant 'can be reasonably required to live his orientation without attracting attention'.[55] A fierce supporter of this distinction between irreversibility and likelihood of discovery can be found in the Administrative Court of Düsseldorf. In a series of decisions, the Court sent claimants back to 'discretion'. In the case of a claimant from Morocco, the Court found that if he relocated,

> overall, it can be assumed that the claimant is not at risk of persecution as long as he maintains reasonable discretion. The fact that the claimant will be required not to make his sexual orientation and practices known but rather confine it to the area of his closest personal environment is not unreasonable.[56]

The Administrative Court of Regensburg similarly found a relocation alternative for a claimant from Algeria, who could live his sexual orientation 'in strict privacy', 'as he does even here in Germany', because the penal provisions are 'not aimed at the immutable orientation but ultimately punish "only" certain sexual practices'.[57] Support for this sort of reasoning also came from the Administrative Court of Berlin, which found no real risk of persecution for an 'irreversibly homosexual' man in Iran if he has 'practised discreetly' in the past.[58] In a case concerning a gay claimant from Egypt, the Düsseldorf Court reiterated this position, although 'discretion' was deemed impossible for this particular 'evidently homosexual' man:

[54] BVerwG Urteil vom 15.3.1988, 9 C 278/86 ['Allerdings stellen die im Iran bestehenden, die Homosexualität betreffenden Verbotsnormen als solche noch keinen hierauf abzielenden Eingriff dar. Nach ihrem vom Berufungsgericht festgestellten Inhalt knüpfen sie eindeutig nicht schon an die homosexuelle Veranlagung, sondern an ein bestimmtes äußeres Verhalten an'].

[55] VG Trier, Beschluss vom 9.9.2010, 1 L 928-10.TR. The Court further found a relocation alternative: 'There is a certain tolerance for this in big cities, where a homosexual scene has established itself in a discreet manner.'

[56] VG Düsseldorf, Urteil vom 14.01.2010, 11 K 6778/09.A. See also: VG Düsseldorf, Urteil vom 11.3.2009, 5 K 1875/08.A, finding no considerable risk of persecution 'as long as they practise their orientation in secret and as long as they have not already attracted the attention of the Iranian law enforcement agencies due to their homosexual inclination'. Note that this case later gave rise to the referral for a preliminary ruling to the CJEU in *Khashar Khavand*: Reference for a preliminary ruling from the Oberverwaltungsgericht für das Land Nordrhein-Westfalen (Germany) lodged on 1 December 2010, *Kashayar Khavand* v. *Federal Republic of Germany (Case C-563/10)*, see Chapter 3.

[57] VG Regensburg, Urteil vom 15.09.2008, RN 8 K 08.30020; emphasis in original.

[58] VG Berlin, Urteil vom 3.12.2008, 23 X 30.06.

> While the claimant may be reasonably expected to live his homosexual orientation only in the closest private environment upon return and to make an effort not to make it publicly known, the court is convinced that the Egyptian authorities will very quickly become aware of the actual disposition of the applicant because it is obvious.[59]

In its earlier jurisprudence, Germany had thus developed its decision-making practice around the act/identity favouring identity; if claimants could not show that their identity was determined to a sufficient degree by their sexual orientation then they would not face a risk of persecution and be required to return and remain 'discreet'. The reasoning is that claimants will not come to the attention of persecutors if they conceal their sexuality – which is deemed possible for those people whose identity as a gay person is not determined to a sufficient degree. Compared with France, German jurisprudence adds another layer of complexity: both agree that it will be the claimant's conduct that will bring attention to them as gay people. But rather than merely asking for past (or future) behaviour, German decision-makers focus on the identity from which such conduct is understood to logically flow. Unlike in France, this can mean that even those people who have manifested their sexual orientation in the past would *not* be granted protection, because they merely have a homosexual inclination which they are deemed to be able to withstand. Conversely, claimants who have *never* manifested their sexual orientation in the past would not be granted protection in France, but might in Germany, if their sexual orientation is judged to be 'fateful' such that it would inevitably be discovered. In Germany, therefore, the level of risk was determined by the degree of determination of the identity. But even some 'irreversibly gay' people were rejected in Germany if, in their particular case, they were deemed able to 'control' their sex drive. A particularly restrictive interplay of the act/identity double bind was thus in place in Germany.

In case law prior to the rejection of the 'discretion requirement', even though the elements appear to be inverted between Germany and France at the outset, the outcome is ultimately he same: the act/identity distinction functions as a double bind that allows for exclusion of claimants who would otherwise be entitled to protection. But the scope of protection was limited differently. Whereas Germany favoured the claimant's identity and France focused on the claimant's behaviour, both sent claimants back to 'discretion'.

5.3 *IMPORTANCE* FOR IDENTITY

Just as in France, the established concepts concerning sexuality-based claims, and, in particular, the 'discretion' reasoning, did not go unchallenged in Germany. The implementation of the *Qualification Directive* and, subsequently, the rulings from

[59] VG Düsseldorf, Urteil vom 21.02.2008, 11 K 2432/07.A.

the CJEU[60] and also the UK Supreme Court,[61] unsettled established practice and appear to have led to some uncertainties and debates.

The entry into force of the *Qualification Directive* triggered debate around the extent to which established jurisprudence and prevailing opinions conformed to the Directive. One such point of contention was the issue of 'discretion'. As early as 2007 and 2008, the Administrative Courts of München and Düsseldorf engaged in a 'duel' concerning this concept.[62] Düsseldorf's strong support of 'discretion'[63] was countered by a fierce rejection from München.[64] In the case of a gay man from Nigeria, the Administrative Court of München rejected 'discretion' reasoning both on fundamental rights grounds, stating that the claimant has a 'right to live his homosexuality freely and openly', as well as on the grounds that it is ill-conceived, as there is a permanent risk of discovery.[65] Moreover, contrary to the prevailing opinion in Germany, it understood Nigerian criminal provisions as sanctioning 'homosexual being' ('homosexuelles Sein'), rather than simply 'acts'. According to the Court, the fact that there was no evidence of the effective application of these provisions did not preclude the possibility that the claimant could be the first to whom they might be applied as long as the sanctions remained in place.[66]

München was joined by judgments critical of 'discretion' from Frankfurt/Oder,[67] Chemnitz[68] and Neustadt/Weinstraße.[69] Interestingly, however, these judgments criticised 'discretion' on the basis of the old 'irreversibility' test. In a case concerning an Iranian lesbian, the Administrative Court of Neustadt an der Weinstraße remained very close to previous practice and relied on a psychiatric report, which had confirmed that the claimant's sexual orientation was irreversible with respect to her 'sexual structure, sexual practice and sexual identity'. The Court went on to

60 Particularly *Federal Republic of Germany* v. *Y and Z*, Joined Cases C-71/11 and C-99/11, Court of Justice of the European Union, 5 September 2012, concerning the distinction between forum internum and externum in the context of religion and *X, Y and Z* v. *Minister voor Immigratie, Integratie en Asiel*, Joined Cases C-199/12, C-200/12 and C-201/12, European Union: Court of Justice of the European Union, 7 November 2013 concerning 'discretion' and criminalisation in the context of sexuality-based claims; and more recently *A, B, C* v. *Staatssecretaris van Veiligheid en Justitie*, Joined Cases C-148/13 to C-150/13, European Union: Court of Justice of the European Union, 2 December 2014 concerning credibility and evidence in sexuality-based claims.

61 *HJ (Iran) and HT (Cameroon)* v. *Secretary of State for the Home Department*, [2010] UKSC 31, United Kingdom: Supreme Court, 7 July 2010.

62 Commenting the dispute between the courts: Klaus Dienelt (2008) 'Vermeidungsverhalten zur Abwendung von Verfolgung – Vereinbarkeit mit der Qualifkationsrichtlinie', *Nachrichten zum Schwerpunkt Asylrecht, Migrationsrecht.net*, www.migrationsrecht.net/nachrichten-asylrecht/1178-eu-qualifikationsrichtlinie-rl-200483eg-religion-verfolgung.html.

63 VG Düsseldorf, Urteil vom 21.02.2008, 11 K 2432/07.A.

64 VG München, Urteil vom 30.1.2007, M 21 K 04.51494.

65 Ibid.

66 Ibid.

67 VG Frankfurt/Oder, Urteil vom 11.11.2010, VG 4 K 772/10.A.

68 VG Chemnitz, Urteil vom 11.7.2008, A 2 K 304/06.

69 VG Neustadt/Weinstraße, Urteil vom 8.9.2008, 3 K 753/07.NW.

reject the 'discretion requirement' both as being contrary to human dignity and in the terms of the original 1988 judgment, according to which homosexual behaviour would inescapably follow in cases of an irreversible determination of identity and as such put the claimant at risk.[70] The Administrative Court of Chemnitz, equally applying the old 'irreversibility test' from the 1988 BVerwG judgment to the case of two gay men from Afghanistan, agreed with München and Chemnitz that secrecy, and even denial, could not only not be reasonably required but were simply not safe. The claimant would permanently face the risk of discovery of his sexual orientation and the consequences of this discovery. The Court therefore conducted the risk assessment on the basis of a 'discovered' sexual orientation.[71] Notably, common to all these decisions is that the claimant's (irreversible) sexual *identity* was not in doubt. On the basis that acts would necessarily ('inescapably') follow, the claimants were accepted.

In subsequent judgments, the 'irreversibility test' started to lose ground. In its 2010 judgment concerning a gay man from Cameroon (after the United Kingdom's *HJ (Iran)* judgment, though the case was not acknowledged in any way), the Administrative Court of Frankfurt/Oder diverged from the old test, finding that, in contrast to the previously prevailing opinion, gay men *can* constitute a 'social group' according to Article 1A(2) of the Refugee Convention. The Court argued that previous jurisprudence had focused on 'inescapability', considering sexual orientation as an 'immutable' characteristic like race or nationality. According to the Court, however, the *Qualification Directive* does not conceive of sexual orientation as an 'immutable' characteristic, but rather as one that is so fundamental to human identity that it cannot be changed. That is, sexual orientation was now to be considered under the social group ground and to be conceived in analogy with the other 'fundamental' characteristics such as religion or political opinion. The Court based this view on the explanatory statement of the European Commission's proposal for the Directive.[72] On this basis, the Court concluded that it was no longer relevant whether a claimant was able to maintain sexual abstinence. Rather, according to the *Qualification Directive*, repression of their sexual orientation cannot be required of a claimant, even – and precisely – if this were 'in fact possible' for them.[73] Even the Administrative Court of Düsseldorf, previously such a strong supporter of 'discretion reasoning', took a much more inclusive view in a 2012 judgment involving a Guinean gay man.[74] Noting that the 1988 judgment had been overruled by the *Qualification Directive* and that sexual orientation was now capable

70 Ibid.

71 VG Chemnitz, Urteil vom 11.7.2008, A 2 K 304/06. This judgment is also notable for its rejection of psychiatric reports for the establishment of the claimant's sexual orientation.

72 VG Frankfurt/Oder, Urteil vom 11.11.2010, VG 4 K 772/10.A., citing Reinhard Marx, *Handbuch zur Flüchltingsanerkennung*.

73 VG Frankfurt/Oder, Urteil vom 11.11.2010, VG 4 K 772/10.A.

74 VG Düsseldorf, Urteil vom 23.3.2012, 13 K 1217/11.A.

of constituting a particular social group based on a fundamental (rather than immutable) characteristic, the Court rejected a 'discretion' requirement as well as a relocation alternative on the grounds of human dignity. The Court held that sexual orientation involves not only sexual behaviour but also influences a person's 'social existence', such that a sexual orientation may become evident even on the basis that a man has no apparent relationships with women.[75]

This conceptual change, which was triggered by the *Qualification Directive* and moved sexual orientation from the 'immutable' to the 'fundamental' characteristics, allowed German judges to apply established doctrine on religious cases also to sexual orientation, most notably the *forum internum/forum externum* distinction. This distinction, which is the religious version of 'discretion' reasoning in German practice, was the main issue in *Y and Z*, the religion case referred by Germany – and it was rejected by the CJEU. Accordingly, in a 2012 letter to a member of parliament, written *after* the judgment in *Y and Z* was handed down, the president of the BAMF logically transferred the *Y and Z* judgment on religion to cases concerning sexual orientation.[76] Noting that sexual orientation is generally considered under the Convention ground of 'particular social group', he stated that the BAMF abstains from any assessment of sexual orientation, 'particularly as the latter can only be assumed by the persecutor as well'.[77] He further noted that, following the CJEU's judgment of *Y and Z*, the BAMF had changed its instructions for decision-making practice to the extent that the decisive element is now whether and to what extent there is a risk of sanctions: 'As a matter of principle, it is now irrelevant which component of sexual self-determination – the sexual orientation as such or certain, including public, activities – are affected.'[78] The President of BAMF concluded: 'In principle, a claimant cannot be reasonably required to avoid dangerous behaviour in order to avoid persecution which would otherwise occur due to his sexual orientation.'[79] In its application of the *Y and Z* judgment to sexuality-based claims, the BAMF thus anticipated the CJEU's subsequent decision in *X, Y and Z*.

This brief moment of opening up seemed like a chance to overcome established practice based on the act/identity dichotomy. In its application of the CJEU's judgment in *Y and Z* to the cases of the Ahmadi men that had caused the referral for a preliminary ruling in its decisions from 20 February 2013, however, the BVerwG saw a chance to defend its previous approach.[80] In its judgments, the

75 Ibid.

76 Manfred Schmidt (2012) 'Kriterien der Flüchtlingsanerkennung. Hier: Sexuelle Orientierung', 424 –7313/05 – 12 (5506046-286) *Brief an Volker Beck MdB*, Nürnberg, 27 December 2012.

77 Ibid., 1–2.

78 Ibid., 4.

79 Ibid., 4.

80 Four judgments: BVerwG Urteile vom 20.2.2013, 10 C 20.12; 10 C 21.12; 10 C 22.12; 10 C 23.12. See on these judgments: Lübbe, note 22.

BVerwG strongly emphasised one particular section in the reasons of the CJEU's judgment. The section in *Y and Z* states:

> In assessing such a risk [of being prosecuted[81] or subject to inhuman or degrading punishment], the competent authorities must take account of a number of factors, both objective and subjective. The subjective circumstance that the observance of a certain religious practice in public, which is subject to the restrictions at issue, is of particular importance to the person concerned in order to preserve his religious identity is a relevant factor to be taken into account in determining the level of risk to which the applicant will be exposed in his country of origin on account of religion, even if the observance of such a practice does not constitute a core element of faith for the religious community concerned.[82]

The Federal Administrative Court took this to mean that a finding that a certain religious behaviour will lead to a real risk of persecution is only relevant if that behaviour is subjectively of particular importance to preserve religious identity.[83] Thus, the act/identity dichotomy – and 'discretion' – persists in this reading; the fact that the renunciation of a particular behaviour (that is, 'discretion') cannot be required is undermined by the fact that this *behaviour* must be important for the claimant's *identity*. This has strong correlations with the previous 'irreversibility' requirement. If the claimant cannot convince the Court that their *identity* is such that the *behaviour* is 'indispensible' ('unverzichtbar'), they are likely to be rejected. Note that this interpretation was one of the main motives for the referral in N, since the Sächsisches Oberverwaltungsgericht did not agree with the BVerwG on this point.[84]

In its decision concerning a gay man from Nigeria, the Higher Administrative Court of Baden-Württemberg was the first to apply the CJEU judgment of *Y and Z* to a case on sexuality grounds.[85] Before even the Federal Administrative Court had published the reasons for its judgments applying *Y and Z* to the cases that had led to the referral to the CJEU,[86] and in spite of the fact that the Dutch request for a preliminary ruling concerning three gay men was pending before the CJEU,[87] the Higher Administrative Court of Baden-Württemberg handed down its judgment. It was of the view that the Dutch preliminary ruling was not necessary. The Court

81 Sic; see paragraph 69 of *Federal Republic of Germany* v. *Y and Z*, note 60.

82 *Federal Republic of Germany* v. *Y and Z*, note 60, at 70.

83 BVerwG Urteil vom 20.2.2013, 10 C 20.12 at 17. The Court also indicated that this might not be the case for the cases at hand and remitted the cases partly on these grounds; see paragraphs 27–28.

84 Reference for a preliminary ruling from the Sächsisches Oberverwaltungsgericht (Germany) lodged on 30 March 2015, *Federal Commissioner for Asylum Affairs* v. *N (Case C-150/15)*, see Chapter 3.

85 VGH Baden-Württemberg, Urteil vom 7.3.2013, A 9 S 1873/12.

86 *Federal Republic of Germany* v. *Y and Z*, note 60; BVerwG Urteil vom 20.2.2013, 10 C 20.12 (only the press release had been published).

87 *X, Y and Z* v. *Minister voor Immigratie*, note 60.

reasoned that sexual orientation could be subsumed under 'privacy' within the meaning of Article 8 of the *European Convention of Human Rights* (ECHR)[88] such that the 'freely chosen sexual determination' was to be viewed as decisive rather than an 'inescapable inclination'.[89] According to the rationale that sexual orientation is a fundamental characteristic like religion, the Court found that no particular acts could be excluded from the outset; '[O]nly the identity determining characteristic as such' is decisive: 'the behaviour concerned must be significant and particularly important for the identity of the claimant'.[90] The Court linked this 'importance' argument to the UK Supreme Court's decision in *HJ (Iran) and HT (Cameroon)*, which had introduced the 'why test', rejecting protection if 'discretion' was due to personal reasons or familial or social pressures or considerations.[91] Indeed, though not explicitly, the German interpretation of the CJEU judgment emerges as another, even broader, version of the 'why' test. If the claimant's behaviour is not important enough for their identity to resist social pressure, then it cannot be important enough to lead to protection. The judgment was indeed received as such in subsequent judgments, as for example by the Administrative Court of Braunschweig:

> Nor does the case-law of Baden-Wurttemberg (v. 07.03.2013 – A 9 S 1873/12) lead to a different assessment, according to which an entitlement to protection is warranted only if the person seeking protection conceals his sexual orientation in order to avoid imminent sanctions, and does not abandon a public mode of conduct for personal reasons.[92]

But, unlike the UK Supreme Court, which limited the why test to the forward-looking analysis of a situation where it is established that a person will in fact live 'discreetly', the German courts can expect 'discretion' (whether or not the claimant will in fact apply it) whenever the court considers that the relevant conduct is not 'of particular importance' to the claimant. In this respect, the German approach is closer to the pre–*HJ (Iran)* 'reasonable expectation'. The German Courts thus appear to have combined the narrowest possible interpretations of both *Y and Z* and the *HJ (Iran) and HT(Cameroon)* judgment to formulate this new version of a 'reasonable requirement to be discreet', now testing 'how the applicant would

[88] European Convention for the Protection of Human Rights and Fundamental Freedoms, as amended by Protocols Nos. 11 and 14, 4 November 1950, ETS 5 (*European Convention of Human Rights, ECHR*).

[89] VGH Baden-Württemberg, Urteil vom 7.3.2013, A 9 S 1873/12.

[90] Ibid., at 21.

[91] Ibid., at 21–22.

[92] VG Braunschweig, Urteil vom 2.9.2015 – 7 A 68/15, at 12 ['Zu einer anderen Bewertung führt auch nicht die Rechtsprechung des VGH Baden-Wurttemberg (Urt. v. 07.03.2013 – A 9 S 1873/12), wonach ein Schutzanspruch nur dann besteht, wenn der Schutzsuchende seine sexuelle Ausrichtung zur Vermeidung drohender Sanktionen verheimlicht, er also nicht aus persönlichen Motiven auf eine öffentliche Verhaltensweise verzichtet'].

behave with regards to his sexual orientation upon return and how important this behaviour is for his identity'.[93]

For the risk assessment, the Higher Administrative Court of Baden-Württemberg formulated the following standard: 'The more a claimant makes their sexual orientation public, and the more important this behaviour is for them, the higher is the likelihood of risk.'[94] The Court conceded that there were some reported cases of the persecution of persons who had 'not lived their homosexual orientation in a publicly noticeable manner', but it then conducted a sort of mathematical assessment to establish that the low number of reported cases of imprisonment of 'discreet' gay men and lesbians (an Amnesty International report cited in the judgment mentions seventeen cases for the period of March 2011 to March 2012) in relation to the assumed total number of gay people in Cameroon (estimated by the judges at 100,000 by reference to a clinical lexicon) was insufficient to establish a 'real risk' since the 'persecution density' was not high enough.[95] The Court came to this conclusion after listing several pages of evidence testifying to the persecutory environment that exists for 'openly' gay people in Cameroon,[96] noting in particular that gay people have to hide their sexual orientation and live in constant fear of denunciation and further persecution by persons from their immediate environment such as neighbours, landlords and acquaintances[97] and that gay people often abstain from reporting theft, robbery or harassment due to their fear that the persecutors may reveal their sexual orientation to the police.[98] In a judgment from the same year, the Administrative Court of Berlin repeated these standards for the assessment of sexuality-based claims that were derived from *Y and Z*.[99]

Germany thus developed these reconceived 'discretion' standards essentially based on the 'importance' clause in paragraph 70 of *Y and Z*. However, when the judgment in *X, Y and Z* was handed down, and even though the CJEU explicitly referred back to its own previous judgment in *Y and Z* and repeated the two subsequent paragraphs verbatim, precisely this section was missing.[100] Significantly, there is no reference to the subjective 'importance' requirement as derived from paragraph 70 in *Y and Z*, that resonated so strongly in German practice – and, as noted, the judgment did not deal

93 VGH Baden-Württemberg, Urteil vom 7.3.2013, A 9 S 1873/12, at 21.
94 Ibid., at 25.
95 Ibid., at 36–37.
96 Ibid., at 24–35.
97 Ibid., at 26 and 29.
98 Ibid., at 29. In the case of the claimant from Nigeria before it, the Court concluded that the claimant's sexual orientation was 'evident' and that he wished to enter same-sex relationships and possibly live with a partner, though it was not apparent that 'any further publicly noticeable homosexual behaviour' was of particular importance for him. He was granted protection on the basis of a risk of persecution from non-state actors.
99 VG Berlin, Beschluss vom 29.10.2013, 34 L 89.13 A, at 3–4.
100 *X, Y and Z* v. *Minister voor Immigratie*, note 60, at 72–74.

with the issue of claimants who will 'in fact' remain 'discreet'. This was also observed by Harald Dörig, judge of the German Federal Administrative Court, who concluded:

> The Court, however, does not say anything regarding the situation where an asylum seeker faces the risk of persecution only if he demonstrates his homosexuality in public. In such cases, the criterion of the CJEU Judgment on religion should apply. That would mean that an individual can only be recognised as a refugee if the freedom to demonstrate such behaviour in public is of particular importance to him to preserve his sexual identity. I would use the same standard to define persecution by interference in a person's political opinion. The subjective criterion in all these cases should be the particular importance of a certain religious, sexual or political behaviour for the applicant's personal identity.[101]

As such, there appears to have been a sense in Germany that there was no need to change its newly developed 'expectation of discretion', which was essentially not that different from the old requirement. 'Irreversibility' was simply substituted by 'importance'. Following X, Y *and* Z, the notion of 'importance' was dropped in sexuality-based claims and transformed into the requirement that their sexual orientation had to be 'identity-defining' ('identitätsprägend') for the claimant. This requirement was derived from the two-pronged social group definition of the *Qualification Directive*. The Administrative Court of Frankfurt/Oder, for example, reasoned that 'it no longer matters whether the applicant can sustain sexual abstinence in the long term' in order to determine whether their sexual orientation is 'inescapable', because according to the *Qualification Directive*, sexual orientation is a 'fundamental characteristic', repression of which cannot be required even if it were in fact possible.[102] Rather, in order to establish membership of a particular social group, the claimant's sexual orientation must be a defining feature of their identity, and gay people must constitute a clearly defined group that is regarded as different by the surrounding society.[103]

This transformation invites at least three observations. First, due to the new legal basis, it appears that 'discretion' reasoning moved from the well-founded fear assessment to the social group analysis. In this context, Germany clearly adopts the cumulative – and therefore more restrictive – interpretation of the social group criteria listed in the *Qualification Directive*.

Second, the first element concerning the fundamentality of the characteristic is interpreted as an inquiry into whether the sexual orientation is identity-defining for the claimant – in other words, 'important' – which appears to be a prerequisite in order for them not to be expected to forego it, since only then will it be contrary to

[101] Harald Dörig (2014) 'German Courts and Their Understanding of the Common European Asylum System (Opinion)', 25(4) *International Journal of Refugee Law* 768–778, 772.
[102] VG Frankfurt/Oder, Urteil vom 19.11.2015, 4 K 109912.A at 8.
[103] Ibid., at 8.

human dignity within the meaning of Article 1(1) Basic Law.[104] This is the repetition of a theme that has been observed in several contexts, namely that, rather than holding that nobody should be compelled to forsake their sexual orientation (or religion) in general terms, the requirement is made personal, such that it results in an inquiry into whether *this particular person* should not be expected to give up this feature. Based on these logics, the Administrative Court of Saarland, in a particularly noteworthy 2015 judgment, found that a bisexual man could return to Algeria and continue to live his same-sex orientation in secret. According to the Court the case was different from those decided by the CJEU in X, Y *and* Z, where the claimants were compelled to *completely* deny their sexual orientation or live it in secret in order to escape persecution.[105] For example, such was the case of a gay claimant from Iran, decided by the Administrative Court of Würzburg, who was granted protection because he had been forced to 'entirely abandon, suppress and conceal' his homosexuality in view of the risk of persecution.[106] In its 2015 case, the Administrative Court of Saarland, in contrast, maintained the reasoning that those who successfully conceal their sexual orientation will have no problem with government agencies or other actors – and because this claimant was attracted not exclusively to men, but could enter a relationship with a woman in order to live his sexuality, this situation is not unreasonable for him.[107] In other words, his same-sex attraction was not such an essential part of him that he could not make up for it by reverting to the opposite sex.[108] While the notion of 'importance' is substituted with 'constitutive element of personality', the judgment indicates the persistence (or revival) of the theme of a stable identity and fateful determination that will inescapably lead to a situation of persecution. As a consequence, twenty-six years after the BVerwG judgment on bisexuality, German judges still struggle with such claims. Strikingly, whatever the label, this approach bears strong parallels with the 'reasonable requirement' to be 'discreet' that was applied in the United Kingdom prior to the UK Supreme Court Judgment in *HJ (Iran) and HT (Cameroon)* to the extent that it deems 'discretion' to be 'reasonable' if it does not require a claimant to 'entirely negate' their sexual orientation.[109]

Third, the second element of the membership of a particular social group definition concerning the society's perception regularly relies on an assessment of

[104] Article 1 of the *Basic Law for the Federal Republic of Germany of 23 May 1949* (Grundgesetz für die Bundesrepublik Deutschland vom 23. Mai 1949 (BGBl. S. 1)).
[105] VG Saarland, Urteil vom 23.1.2015, 5 K 534/13, at 11–12.
[106] VG Würzburg, Urteil vom 1.7.2016, W 6 K 15.30116, at 15.
[107] VG Saarland, Urteil vom 23.1.2015, 5 K 534/13, at 11–12.
[108] The court sees evidence for this in the fact that the claimant is the father of a child in Germany.
[109] Note that in addition, the explicit link with 'human dignity' within the meaning of Article 1(1) *Basic Law* also suggests parallels with Hathaway and Pobjoy's human rights approach, although any core/margins distinction remains implicit at most. It is hidden underneath notions of reasonableness and 'entirely abandon, suppress and conceal' – and emerges from the sense that *some* adaptation can be expected of a claimant; see further discussion in Chapter 9.

criminalisation in the country of origin. In X, Y *and* Z, the CJEU had ruled that criminal laws are an indicator for the existence of a particular social group that is regarded as different. In earlier German judgments, this ruling was misunderstood to *require* criminalisation in order for a particular social group to be established.[110] But even those judgments that did not interpret criminal laws as a requirement still considered it relevant to assess precisely *what* is persecuted by the laws: whether they prohibit 'homosexuality as such' or merely homosexual acts. In the case of the gay man from Cameroon before the Administrative Court of Frankfurt/Oder cited earlier, the Court observed that the Cameroonian judiciary and other government bodies in fact misapplied their own criminal code, because persons were arrested and prosecuted not because of a homosexual act but because of the presumed sexual orientation 'as such': 'This erroneous application of the law makes it clear that it is not just the criminalisation of homosexual acts, but ultimately … the same-sex orientation as such is persecuted'.[111] In other words, the act/identity dichotomy persists in the context of criminalisation in addition to the 'identity-defining' requirement. Hence, the CJEU judgment in X, Y *and* Z, which is regularly referenced in recent sexuality-based decisions,[112] appears to have changed the wording, but not the substance of the reconceived German 'discretion' standards.

Up until the most recent judgments under review until the end of 2016, this new jurisprudence does not yet appear to be entirely settled. Indicative of a lingering dispute within Germany is the fact that the Oberverwaltunsgericht Sachsen did not agree with the requirement of an 'importance' criterion that the Bundesverwaltungsgericht deduced from the CJEU's judgment in Y *and* Z and resubmitted the matter to the CJEU for another preliminary ruling to clarify this point.[113] However, the reference was subsequently removed from the register

[110] See e.g. VG Potsdam, Urteil vom 13.5.2014, VG 6 K 3802/13.A (holding by reference to X, Y *and* Z that the claimant was not a member of a particular social group because even though homosexual acts were sanctioned with fourteen years imprisonment in Kenya, there was no evidence that these criminal laws were actually applied, 'which is however a prerequisite in order to distinguish a relevant social group'); also VG Düsseldorf, Urteil vom 13.12.2013, 13 K 3683/13.A. But see VG Aachen, applying X, Y *and* Z to Nigeria to find that criminalisation is evidence for the existence of a social group, without any reference to 'importance' and noting that the low number of reported cases for the application of criminal laws is sufficient to constitute 'actual enforcement' and therefore real risk. VG Aachen, Urteil vom 12.12.2014, 2 K 1477/13.A.

[111] VG Frankfurt/Oder, Urteil vom 19.11.2015, 4 K 109912.A at 12.

[112] See e.g. VG Düsseldorf, Urteil vom 13.12.2013, 13 K 3683/13.A; VG Potsdam, Urteil vom 27.2.2014, VG 6 K 435/13.A; VG München, Urteil vom 24.4.2014, M 4 K 13.30114; VG Potsdam, Urteil vom 13.5.2014, VG 6 K 3802/13.A; VG Würzburg, Beschluss vom 21.8.2014, W 1 S 14.30384; VG Augsburg, Urteil vom 31.10.2014, Au 3 K 14.30222; VG Aachen, Urteil vom 12.12.2014, 2 K 1477/13.A.

[113] Reference for a preliminary ruling from the Sächsisches Oberverwaltungsgericht (Germany) lodged on 30 March 2015, *Federal Commissioner for Asylum Affairs* v. N *(Case C-150/15)*. The first question of the referral read: '1. Is Article 9(1)(a) in conjunction with Article 10(1)(b) of Directive 2011/95/EU 1 to be interpreted as follows: (a) that a severe violation of the freedom of

because the claimant had been granted status by the administrative authorities – so the question remains open and will likely be resubmitted before long.[114]

5.4 CONCLUSION: GERMANY – 'DISCRETION' RELOADED

The application of the act/identity dichotomy to an analysis of German sexuality-based jurisprudence reveals that 'discretion' reasoning is highly prevalent – both before and after the implementation of the *Qualification Directive* and the judgments rejecting the 'discretion requirement'. In well-established and firmly entrenched pre–*Qualification Directive* jurisprudence, 'discretion' was required unless a claimant was inescapably determined by their sexual orientation, such that they would inevitably come to the attention of the persecutors and suffer harm. Since the Europeanisation of asylum, and much more so – or at least more visibly – than their French counterparts, German judges engaged with *HJ (Iran) and HT (Cameroon)* and later the CJEU twin judgments. In fact, it was the fact that the German Bundesverwaltungsgericht disagreed with the judgment handed down by the UK Supreme Court that led to the referral in *Y and Z* in the first place. Contrary to earlier findings, which identified a lack of engagement with foreign jurisprudence in German decision-making practice, this is a remarkable example of transnational dialogue between the German courts and the UK Supreme Court, and then the CJEU.[115] The fact that the CJEU did not pronounce itself on the question of a 'factual' finding that a claimant will behave 'discreetly' in the future permitted German judges to maintain a reconceived notion of 'discretion', requiring sexual orientation to be an 'identity-defining' feature. In essence, the changes therefore allowed for the maintenance of the previous approach.

religion guaranteed by Article 10(1) CFREU (Charter of Fundamental Rights of the European Union) and Article 9(1) ECHR (European Convention on Human Rights) and thus an act of persecution under Article 9(1)(a) of the Directive must be assumed when religious acts or expressions of view that are mandated by a doctrine of faith that the applicant actively professes and which form a core element of the doctrine of faith or are based on the religious convictions of the applicant in the sense that they are a pillar of his religious identity, are prohibited by criminal law in the country of origin, or (b) is it required that an applicant who actively declares his belief in a particular doctrine of faith must further prove that core elements mandated as religious acts or as or expressions of view by the doctrine of faith, which represent a prohibited religious activity subject to criminal prosecution in his country of origin, are "particularly important" for the preservation of his religious identity and in this sense are "essential"?'

[114] Order of the President of the Court of 15 April 2016 (Reference for a preliminary ruling from the Sächsisches Oberverwaltungsgericht, Germany), *Federal Commissioner for Asylum Affairs* v. *N* (Case C-150/15), 'Removal' [Beschluss des Präsidenten des Gerichtshofs 15. April 2016 'Streichung' In der Rechtssache C-150/15].

[115] Paul Tiedemann (2010) 'The Use of Foreign Asylum Jurisprudence in the German Administrative Courts', in: Guy Goodwin-Gil and Hélène Lambert (eds.) *The Limits of Transnational Law – Refugee Law, Policy Harmonization and Judicial Dialogue in the European Union*, 57–84.

In the process, the doctrinal location of 'discretion' appears to have shifted, or become more unstable. Whereas in earlier jurisprudence, 'discretion' logics were relevant for the assessment of the well-foundedness of the risk, the institutional and jurisprudential developments have now tied it to the social group analysis. Conspicuously, while 'discretion' reasoning was always considered under the social group ground in France, the underlying rationale that informs the definition of the group is also based on considerations relating to risk. Both jurisdictions subscribe to the idea that claimants are safe if they do not express their sexual orientation (the secrecy = safety equation).

Finally, unlike French jurisprudence, human rights arguments are drawn on in German sexuality-based jurisprudence. Not only did the VGH Baden-Wurttemberg draw a parallel between Article 8 of the ECHR (privacy) for sexual orientation and Article 9 ECHR (freedom of religion) for religion-based cases[116] but, more importantly, the social group assessment based on an identity-defining feature is based on the rationale that negating this feature would be contrary to human dignity as provided for in the German Basic Law. This is interesting for several reasons. Firstly, the reference here is to a fundamental right in the national constitution, rather than to a human right, for example, from the *European Convention on Human Rights*[117] (as suggested by the VGH Baden-Wurttemberg), or from the *EU Charter*.[118] Secondly, in combination in particular with the example of the VG Saarland judgment that rejected the bisexual claimant, such reasoning allows for findings of situations of 'discretion' that do *not* infringe on human dignity, for example, if sex does not have to be forsaken *entirely*. As such, German jurisprudence turns out to be closer to Hathaway and Pobjoy's core/margins approach than first appearances suggest. However, since sexual orientation raises issues not neatly linked to one single right, but to a plurality of rights, if applied in a principled manner, human dignity as an umbrella concept could indeed have positive potential in cumulating the losses incurred in a fragmented reasoning where each right is analysed separately.

Taken together, the jurisprudence in Germany and France thus presents a neat exemplification of the subtle workings of the double bind emerging from the act/identity dichotomy that was outlined in Chapter 2: claimants are damned if they do, and damned if they don't.

[116] Articles 8 and 9 of the European Convention for the Protection of Human Rights and Fundamental Freedoms, as amended by Protocols Nos. 11 and 14, 4 November 1950, ETS 5 (*European Convention of Human Rights, ECHR*).

[117] European Convention for the Protection of Human Rights and Fundamental Freedoms, as amended by Protocols Nos. 11 and 14, 4 November 1950, ETS 5 (*European Convention of Human Rights, ECHR*).

[118] Charter of Fundamental Rights of the European Union, 26 October 2012, 2012/C 326/02 (*EU Charter*).

Spanish jurisprudence is much more difficult to locate in this debate. Its jurisprudence has developed largely 'undisturbed' by international influences and is therefore messy and somewhat unexpected in many respects. The following chapter attempts to order it for the purpose of comparing it with German and French practice and with Common law cases. The analysis shows that Spanish jurisprudence on sexuality-based claims relies on a 'singling out' requirement, which bears parallels with the French focus on public manifestation.

6

Singled Out

Spain

In Spanish asylum decision-making regarding sexual orientation cases, the act/identity dichotomy is not as clearly identifiable as in Germany and France. Spanish asylum jurisprudence generally appears to have evolved entirely independently from international developments, as there is little to no engagement with foreign jurisprudence or international guidance. Yet, even though it is not immediately recognisable, a closer analysis of Spanish case law reveals that it, too, is constructed around a distinction between the claimant's identity and behaviour, limiting the scope of protection to those claimants who have been 'singled out' for persecution – in other words, who have presented 'something extra' that led to persecution.

6.1 THE SPANISH CONTEXT: THE GHOSTLY SUBSTANCE OF SOMETHING EXTRA

Due to the Franco dictatorship, the modern Spanish refugee regime is substantially more recent than those in France and Germany. Spain ratified the 1951 Refugee Convention in July 1978, following the death of Franco in 1975. In the same year, the present Spanish constitution was adopted. The Constitution stipulates in Article 13(4) that '[t]he law will establish the terms under which citizens of other countries and stateless persons may enjoy the right to asylum in Spain'.[1] It was debated whether this provision provided for a constitutional right to asylum; whether it implied an obligation to provide for asylum in law; or whether it was a materially void precept, entirely dependent on a legislative decision.[2] When Law 5/84

[1] Article 13(4) of the *Spanish Constitution of* 1978 (Constitución española de 1978; B.O.E. núm. 311, de 29 de diciembre de 1978, páginas 29313 a 29424).

[2] See José Díaz Lafuente (2014) *Refugio y asilo por motivos de orientación sexual y/o identidad de género en el ordenamiento constitucional español*, doctoral thesis, Faculty of Law, University of Valencia, 372.

implemented the Refugee Convention into Spanish law in 1984,[3] it initially distinguished between refugee status according to the Refugee Convention and asylum according to the Constitution. Following several Tribunal Supremo judgments, however, this distinction was abolished when the law was amended ten years later by Law 9/94.[4] Since then, there is only one status and Spanish 'constitutional' asylum was never developed into a significant concept based on an independent definition.

The applicable law prior to the *Qualification Directive* was, therefore, Law 5/84 from 26 March amended by Law 9/94 of 19 May. For the refugee definition, Article 3(1) of Law 5/84 made reference to 'the requirements of international instruments ratified by Spain, and in particular the Convention relating to the Status of Refugees'.[5] The 1994 amendment introduced, among others, a two-stage assessment process that provided for the exclusion of claims deemed abusive or unfounded (Article 5.6).[6] Reasons not to admit a case according to Article 5.6 of Law 5/84 were, most notably, that the claimant did not refer to any of the Convention grounds ('ninguna de las causas') and the estimation that the facts, dates or allegations related by the claimant were manifestly false or implausible.[7] This two-stage admissibility

3 *Law 5/1984, of 26 March, regulating the right of asylum and refugee status* (Ley 5/1984, de 26 de marzo, reguladora del derecho de asilo y de la condición de refugiado; B.O.E. núm. 74, de 27 de marzo de 1984, páginas 8389 a 8392).

4 *Law 9/1994, of 19 May, amending Law 5/1984, of 26 March, regulating the right to asylum and refugee status* (Ley 9/1994, de 19 de mayo, de modificación de la Ley 5/1984, de 26 de marzo, reguladora del derecho de asilo y de la condición de refugiado; B.O.E. núm. 122, de 23 de mayo de 1994, páginas 15796 a 15800); see Díaz Lafuente, note 2, 373–375.

5 Article 3(1) of the *Law 9/1994, of 19 May, amending Law 5/1984, of 26 March, regulating the right to asylum and refugee status* ['Se reconocerá la condición de refugiado y, por tanto, se concederá asilo a todo extranjero que cumpla los requisitos previstos en los Instrumentos internacionales ratificados por España, y en especial en la Convención sobre el Estatuto de los Refugiados, hecha en Ginebra el día 28 de julio de 1951, y en el Protocolo sobre el Estatuto de los Refugiados, hecho en Nueva York el 31 de enero de 1967'].

6 Article 5.6 of *the Law 9/1994, of 19 May, amending Law 5/1984, of 26 March, regulating the right to asylum and refugee status.*

7 Other reasons for inadmissibility of a claim were: (a) exclusion according to Article 1F or 33(2) of the 1951 Convention; (c) the mere repetition of a claim rejected in an earlier decision; (e) cases where Spain is not responsible for processing the claim; and (f) cases where the claimant passed through a third country where they could have sought protection:

(a) Las previstas en los artículos 1.F y 33.2 de la Convención de Ginebra sobre el Estatuto de los Refugiados de 1951.

(b) Que en la solicitud no se alegue ninguna de las causas que dan lugar al reconocimiento de la condición de refugiado.

(c) Que se trate de la mera reiteración de una solicitud ya denegada en España, siempre y cuando no se hayan producido nuevas circunstancias en el país de origen que puedan suponer un cambio sustancial en el fondo de la solicitud.

(d) Que la solicitud se base en hechos, datos o alegaciones manifiestamente falsos, inverosímiles o que, por carecer de vigencia actual, no fundamenten una necesidad de protección.

(e) Cuando no corresponda a España su examen de conformidad con los Convenios Internacionales en que sea Parte. En la resolución de inadmisión a trámite se indica al process has become a central and contested element of Spanish refugee law and has affected doctrinal developments.

The *Qualification Directive* was transposed in Spain in Law 12/2009.[8] However, the transposition deadline had passed on 10 October 2006, following which the Directive had direct effect. That is, during the time between October 2006 and October 2009, even though Law 5/1984 remained applicable, an individual could rely on the *Qualification Directive* in court. Moreover, appeals reaching the Audiencia Nacional and Tribunal Supremo are decided on the basis of the law applicable at the time of the first instance decision, such that this transition phase persisted up to 2014 for some cases. That is, for a transition period of up to eight years, the old Law 5/1984 effectively had to be applied in the light of the *Qualification Directive*. The transition was much more reluctant than in the other jurisdictions under review, which is further evidenced by the fact that, years after Law 12/2009 entered into force, the Implementing Asylum Regulation ('Reglamento de asilo') has not been updated: the asylum regulation is an instrument issued by the government that contains interpretations and rules of application for the Law of Asylum. The regulation that remains in force is the one developed in 1995 for the previous Law of Asylum (Law 5/84 as amended by Law 4/94).[9] With a view to assessing possible effects of the *Qualification Directive* on Spanish jurisprudence concerning sexuality-based asylum claims, the following will therefore first analyse case law roughly up to the end of 2006. In a second step, an analysis will be conducted of case law from the years roughly from 2006 to 2016.

In line with the *Qualification Directive*, Law 12/2009 explicitly mentions both gender and sexual orientation as examples of particular social groups. While there

solicitante el Estado responsable de examinar su solicitud. En este caso, dicho Estado habrá aceptado explícitamente dicha responsabilidad y se obtendrán, en todo caso, garantías suficientes de protección para su vida, libertad y demás principios indicados en la Convención de Ginebra, en el territorio de dicho Estado.

(f) Cuando el solicitante se halle reconocido como refugiado tenga derecho a residir o a obtener asilo en un tercer Estado o cuando proceda de un tercer Estado cuya protección hubiera podido solicitar. En ambos casos, en dicho tercer Estado no debe existir peligro para su vida o su libertad ni estar expuesto a torturas o a un trato inhumano o degradante y debe tener protección efectiva contra la devolución al país perseguidor, con arreglo a la Convención de Ginebra' (Law 9/94, Article 5.6).

8 *Law 12/2009 of October 30, regulating the right of asylum and subsidiary protection* (Ley 12/2009 de 30 de octubre, reguladora del derecho de asilo y de la protección subsidiaria; B.O.E. núm. 263 del 31 de Octubre de 2009).

9 *Royal Decree 203/1995, of 10 February, which approves the Regulation implementing Law 5/1984, of 26 March, regulating the right to asylum and refugee status, as amended by Law 9/1994, of 19 May* (Real Decreto 203/1995, de 10 de febrero, por el que se aprueba el Reglamento de aplicación de la Ley 5/1984, de 26 de marzo, reguladora del derecho de asilo y de la condición de refugiado, modificada por la Ley 9/1994, de 19 de mayo; B.O.E. núm. 52, de 2 de marzo de 1995, páginas 7237 a 7246).

was some research into gender-related persecution in Spain, led in particular by the NGO Spanish Commission for Refugee Aid (Comisión Española de Ayuda al Refugiado, CEAR),[10] Spanish jurisprudence regarding sexuality-based asylum claims has so far never been subjected to academic scrutiny in significant detail. The 2009 CEAR report addressed gender-related issues and subsumed LGBT claims under a broad notion of 'gender', though the analysis focused effectively on gender rather than sexuality.[11] José Díaz Lafuente briefly discussed Tribunal Supremo judgments on sexuality-based claims in one chapter of his doctoral thesis from 2014, but addressed the issue broadly, without discussion of 'discretion' reasoning.[12] In this context, the Spanish contribution to the *Fleeing Homophobia* project in the form of the national questionnaire constitutes a rare resource.[13] More generally, it appears that Spanish lawyers and scholars take part in the transnational judicial dialogue on asylum to a much lesser extent: the twin CJEU judgments concerning 'discretion' were received with minimal, and delayed, discussion.[14] This state of disconnectedness also emerges from the Spanish sexuality-based asylum jurisprudence.

The present analysis is based on a selection of sexuality-based decisions from the *Audiencia Nacional* and all available published sexuality-based decisions from the *Tribunal Supremo* up until the end of 2016. The Spanish asylum system foresees three instances. Administrative decisions are taken by the *Oficina de Asilo y Refugio* (OAR, Asylum and Refuge Office), which is assisted by the *Comisión*

[10] Leire Lasa, Izaro López de Lacalle, Estefanía Pasarín and Iñaki Ramírez de Olano (2009) *Persecución por motivos de género y derecho de asilo: del contexto global al compromiso local – El sistema de asilo español frente a la violación de los derechos humanos de las mujeres y de lesbianas, gays, bisexuales y transexuales*. Comisión Española de Ayuda al Refugiado en Euskadi (CEAR-Euskadi), Bilbao. See also on gender-related claims in Spain (not touching on sexual orientation): Victor Merino Sancho (2012) *Tratamiento Jurídico de las Demandas de Asilo por Violencia contra las Mujeres en el Ordenamiento Jurídico Español: Perspectivas y Prospectivas*, Pamplona: Thomson Reuters.

[11] Lasa et al., note 10.

[12] Díaz Lafuente, note 2, Chapter X. An earlier version of the chapter was published as: José Díaz Lafuente (2014) 'Estudio de la doctrina jurisprudencial española sobre la protección internacional por motivos de orientación sexual e identidad de género', *Libertad de circulación, asilo y refugio en la Unión Europea* 69–92. See also by the same author, on sexuality-based asylum claims in Europe generally, José Díaz Lafuente (2014) 'El Derecho de Asilo por Motivos de Orientación Sexual e Identidad de Género', 89 *Revista de Derecho Público* 345–388.

[13] Arsenio Cores (2011) *Fleeing Homophobia Questionnaire, Best Practices on the (Legal) Position of LGBT Asylum Seekers in the EU Member States – Spain*, Fleeing Homophobia Project, www.rechten.vu.nl/nl/Images/Spain_questionnaire_tcm247-240407.pdf.

[14] There is one comment for each judgment, though neither of them puts the rulings into perspective with Spanish doctrine or jurisprudence: Almudena Rodríguez Moya (2015) 'Asylum and Religious Freedom: The ECJ Position', 94 *Revista de Derecho Político* 115–140 (on *Y and Z*, in English) and Claribel de Castro Sánchez (2015) 'La condición sexual como razón de la concesión de asilo. ¿Una nueva puerta de entrada a Europa? Reflexiones a la luz de la sentencia del Tribunal de Justicia de la UE de 7 de noviembre de 2013, Minister Voor Inmigratie en Asiel/X, Y y Z. (RI §415704)', 35 *Revista General de Derecho Europeo* 3–25 (on *X, Y and Z*).

Interministerial de Asilo y Refugio (CIAR, Interministerial Commission on Asylum and Refuge). Appeals against these decisions can be filed at the Audiencia Nacional. Under the current asylum law, two types of appeal are possible against OAR decisions: an administrative appeal for reversal ('recurso de reposición') can be lodged before the OAR. Such appeals are optional and limited to points of law. Alternatively, a judicial appeal can be submitted at the Audiencia Nacional, which also extends to the facts; therefore the Court may re-examine evidence submitted at first instance and new evidence may be submitted.[15] The Audiencia Nacional has the power to grant status and does not have to remit the case for review. A further onwards appeal in cassation is possible in front of the Tribunal Supremo, which can also grant status.[16]

Spain maintains a general case law database under poderjudicial.es. The search terms 'asilo' in combination with 'homosexual' yielded 433 decisions for the years 1998–2016. Seventy-seven judgments were randomly selected across the entire time-frame to roughly equal the number of judgments selected for the other jurisdictions. In general, it is difficult to analyse Spanish judgments because decision-makers are not very specific in articulating their reasons and the analysis is not systematic. There is minimal discussion and reasons are often generic, such that it is difficult to identify the exact basis for a rejection. It is very common to read in decisions that the Chamber 'finds no grounds for believing the existence of persecution, or a well-founded fear of the same, for reasons of race, religion, nationality, membership of a particular social group or political opinion'.[17] According to a representative of the Spanish Commission for Refugee Aid (Comisión Española de Ayuda al Refugiado, CEAR) this practice of issuing generic and imprecise judgments is a way of avoiding appeals.[18] Despite these difficulties, a closer reading may sometimes suggest the background and reasoning behind the decision, such that some indicative trends can be identified – in particular, the reliance on the ghostly substance of 'something extra'.

6.2 THE SINGLING OUT REQUIREMENT

In Spain, cases based on sexual orientation started to appear in the late 1990s, around the same time as they started to come up in France, and substantially later

15 Article 29(1) of the *Law 12/2009 of October 30, regulating the right of asylum and subsidiary protection*.

16 ECRE (2014) *Agentes de Protección y Aplicación de la Alternativa de Protección Interna – Informe de País España*, APAIPA, www.refworld.org.es/pdfid/543bc5424.pdf, 4.

17 See e.g. SAN 5372/2008 de 10 de diciembre de 2008; SAN 1003/2009 de 25 de febrero de 2009 ['no apreciando la Sala motivos que acrediten la existencia de persecución, o su temor fundado a padecerla, por motivos de raza, religión, nacionalidad, pertenencia a determinado grupo social u opiniones políticas ... procede desestimar el recurso'].

18 Personal interview with Elena Muñoz, CEAR Madrid, 18 June 2013.

than in Germany. Prior to the *Qualification Directive*, the claimants' sexual orientation was very rarely disbelieved, but claims tended to be rejected on the basis that the claimant did not have a well-founded fear of persecution for this reason.[19]

6.2.1 *Sexual Orientation as a Convention Ground*

The early cases reveal that the non-acceptance of sexual orientation as a particular social group continued for longer than in the other countries under discussion. A number of claims were not admitted on the basis that sexual orientation was no grounds for protection according to Article 5.6.b.[20] In SAN 6483/1999, concerning a trans woman from Ecuador, the Audiencia Nacional made reference to a series of decisions from the time between 21 April 1998 and 25 June 1999 concerning sexuality-based claims that were declared inadmissible on the basis that 'either that the fact [sexual orientation] as such is not a ground for persecution or that the allegations were unfounded'.[21] Notably, however, even in those early cases decision-makers were hesitant to entirely reject sexual orientation as a grounds for persecution. For example, in SAN 4388/1998 the court concluded: 'We will not question the [claimant's] homosexual condition here, but we do question that this is a cause for asylum ... we would *almost* say that there is not even a ground to claim [asylum], with *possible* application of article 5.6.b [no Convention ground alleged] to these facts'.[22] As it was never clearly answered, the idea that sexual orientation might not even qualify as a Convention ground lingered for years. Whereas in a 2001 decision concerning a bisexual man from Romania, the Audiencia Nacional found that 'persecution for membership of a particular social group, in this case that of homosexuals' is encompassed by the situations to which asylum extends,[23] a decision from 2003 confirmed the non-admissibility of the claim of a Cuban gay man based on Article 5.6.b, as his claim was 'founded on an objectively unsuitable cause'.[24]

19 Cores, note 13, 11.

20 See e.g. SAN 4388/1998 de 6 de noviembre del 1998; SAN 6483/1999 de 29 de octubre del 1999; SAN 1890/2001 de 23 de marzo de 2001; SAN 2628/2003 de 11 de noviembre de 2003.

21 SAN 6483/1999 de 29 de octubre del 1999 ['se ha considerado o que el hecho en sí no es motivo de persecución, o que se trata de alegatos infundados']. Also note the conflation of sexual orientation and gender identity in this case.

22 SAN 4388/1998 de 6 de noviembre del 1998; emphasis added ['La condición de homosexual no vamos a cuestionarla aquí pero lo que si cuestionamos es que ello sea causa de asilo ... casi diríamos nosotros, que no hay ni siquiera causa de pedir, con aplicación posible del articulo 5.6.b con respeto a los mismos hechos'].

23 SAN 1890/2001 de 23 de marzo de 2001. Also note the lacking distinction between bisexual and gay men.

24 SAN 2628/2003 de 11 de noviembre de 2003 ['el resultado lógico y ajustado a Derecho tenía que ser y fue el de la inadmisión a trámite de una solicitud fundada en una causa objetivamente inidónea para alcanzar el fin pretendido'].

6.2.2 *Mere Membership and 'Personal' Persecution*

For those sexuality-based claims that *were* considered admissible, that is, where sexual orientation was considered as falling within Convention grounds, Spanish jurisprudence had developed the notion that protection is not required when homosexuality is 'in fact' tolerated by the authorities. In those cases, where there was found to be no persecution 'in general terms', belonging to the particular social group was not 'by itself' sufficient to grant asylum; the claimant had to provide evidence of concrete, personal and individual persecution.[25]

This requirement to prove 'individual' persecution was already present in the earliest available decision on sexual orientation from 29 September 1998.[26] It concerned a gay man from Kazakhstan whose claim was rejected on the basis of a 'lack of reliable evidence that the claimant belongs to a social, ethnic, political or religious group targeted for persecution'.[27] The decision referred to a 1996 UNHCR report stating that '*homosexuality "per se" is not persecuted* in Kazakhstan as it is "de facto" tolerated by the authorities and society in general'.[28] For such situations, the Audiencia Nacional developed the following doctrine:

> [P]ersons unjustly persecuted in their country of origin for belonging to a particular ethnic group or for professing ideas or beliefs that in a given historical moment are not well regarded by the politically dominant position, *mere membership* of such ethnic group or ideological stance is not sufficient for their recognition, but it must be translated into *a real and personal persecution* or at least a well-founded fear of such persecution at a personal level.[29]

For sexuality-based claims, the relevant social group was that of gay people. In much the same way that 'gender' was considered too broad a concept to be accepted in many jurisdictions, such that it had to be narrowed down through further

[25] Cores, note 13, 16.

[26] According to a 2002 judgment, the Audiencia Nacional had first accepted a social group of 'Romanian homosexuals' in a judgment from 24 September 1996, see: SAN 4464/2002 de 12 de julio de 2002.

[27] SAN 3500/1998 de 29 de septiembre del 1998 ['El recurso interpuesto debe ser desestimado ... faltando constancia fehaciente de su pertenencia a grupo social, étnico, político o religioso objeto de persecución'].

[28] SAN 3500/1998 de 29 de septiembre del 1998; italics added ['la homosexualidad "per se" no está perseguida, siendo tolerada "de facto" por las autoridades y por la sociedad en general'].

[29] SAN 4388/1998 de 6 de noviembre del 1998 concerning a gay man from Ecuador, appealing the inadmissibility of his claim; emphasis added ['personas injustamente perseguidas en su país por pertenencia a étnia concreta, o por profesar ideas o creencias que en un momento histórico determinado no son bien vistas por la posición políticamente dominante, no basta para su reconocimiento la pertenencia simple a tal etnia o postura ideológica sino que es preciso que ello se traduzca en una real y personalizada persecución o al menos en un muy fundado temor de sufrirla a título individual'].

qualifications,[30] the particular social group of 'gay people' was distinguished further. The doctrinal 'device' for this purpose in Spain was the doctrine of requiring 'personal' persecution. It translated into the following reasoning:

> Currently the group of homosexuals cannot be considered as a social group at risk in Cuba *for the fact of being gay*. While it is true that in the past they had problems, today they are tolerated by the authorities (if they have problems with the authorities, these are usually due to added circumstances) and *not persecuted only for that status*.[31]

It remains unclear what these 'added circumstances' are and whether, and how, they relate to the claimant's sexual orientation. Decision SAN 4388/1998 may give an indication of the reasoning behind the distinction between homosexuality 'per se' and personal persecution:

> As far as we know, there is no specific legislation in Ecuador criminalising these situations, and in any event the claimant only refers to police harassment. We are unaware for which concrete manifestations of homosexuality this alleged harassment occurs or whether – which we doubt – it occurs for the simple differential fact [of being gay].[32]

This statement implies that it is not sufficient to simply *be* gay. If persecution ensues, it must have been caused by 'something extra'; the claimant must have done something to bring attention to his sexual orientation and cause the harm – in other words, they must have manifested their sexual orientation through an activity that triggered the risk of harm.

6.2.3 *Criminalisation*

In this context, the issue of criminalisation is another contentious element. In Spanish pre–*Qualification Directive* practice, laws criminalising homosexuality

[30] An oft-cited example is the US case of *Kasinga*, a woman who fled from the risk of female genital mutilation (FGM) in Togo. The relevant social group was found to be that of 'young women of the Tchamba-Kunsuntu Tribe who have not had FGM, as practised by that tribe, and who oppose the practice', rather than simply 'women in Togo'; see *In re Fauziya Kasinga*, 21 I. & N. December 357 (B.I.A. 1996), United States Board of Immigration Appeals, 13 June 1996.

[31] SAN 1790/2005 de 30 de marzo de 2005; emphasis added ['Actualmente no cabe considerar al colectivo de homosexuales como grupo social de riesgo en Cuba por el hecho de serlo. Si bien es cierto que en el pasado tuvieron problemas, en la actualidad son tolerados por las autoridades (si tienen algún problema con dichas autoridades suele ser por circunstancias añadidas) y no sufren persecución solo por tal condición'].

[32] SAN 4388/1998 de 6 de noviembre de 1998 ['En lo que sepamos no hay normativa específica en Ecuador represora de estas situaciones, o al menos no se nos habla más que de acoso policial. Ignoramos por qué manifestaciones concretas de la homosexualidad se produce ese supuesto acoso o si es, que no creemos, por el simple hecho diferencial . . .'].

were not generally considered serious enough to constitute persecution; conversely, *absence* of criminalisation was deemed sufficient to reject claims.[33]

This trend appears to have remained relatively consistent over the pre–*Qualification Directive* years. The earliest available decision from 1998 referred to a 1992 Amnesty International report according to which, even though same-sex sexual acts were criminalised in Kazakhstan, the penal sanctions were not implemented if the acts were consensual, among adults and conducted in private.[34] The claim failed for 'lack of sufficient circumstantial evidence'.[35] Ten years later, the 2008 decision in SAN 5321/2008 similarly rejected the claim of an Algerian gay man after noting that criminal sanctions apply to same-sex sexual acts according to three different articles of the Algerian Penal Code. The Court reasoned that 'none of the consulted sources [Google search 'homosexuals in Algeria' and 2004 Home Office Country Report on Algeria] states that anyone has recently been charged with these crimes in Algeria'.[36] The Court concluded: 'That is: a homosexual in Algeria can have no problems, the situation is not such as to consider that anyone is automatically subject to persecution in Algeria for [their] mere sexual orientation.'[37] In both these examples, the analysis stops short of a discussion of whether the existence of criminal sanctions indicates a broader persecutory environment and whether this means that the claimant has to exercise 'discretion' or hide their sexual orientation entirely in order 'not to have any problems'. The rationale is clearly that if a claimant is deemed able to pass unnoticed, they should. Indeed, as noted by Díaz Lafuente, the prevalent doctrine in Spanish jurisprudence regarding countries sanctioning homosexuality with imprisonment or death is a requirement to provide at least presumptive evidence for the effective application of these laws *to the person claiming asylum*.[38] In other words, the claimant must provide evidence that they are directly and individually threatened with the effective application of these laws.

The absence of criminal laws, on the other hand, was initially considered to indicate an absence of persecution. In the case of a Croatian gay man, for example, the Audiencia Nacional argued in 2007:

> If the appellant came to our country and did so, according to his account, for fear of persecution in his home country because of his homosexuality, we do not understand the reason because in Croatia homosexuality is decriminalised and recently

33 Cores, note 13, 19.
34 SAN 3500/1998 de 29 de septiembre del 1998 ['si bien la legislación de ese país prohíbe las prácticas homosexuales, éstas no son castigadas si son consentidas, entre adultos y en privado'].
35 Ibid.
36 SAN 5321/2008 de 7 de noviembre de 2008 ['ninguna de las fuentes consultadas informa si recientemente en Argelia ha sido alguien condenado por alguno de estos delitos'].
37 Ibid. ['Es decir: un homosexual en Argelia puede no tener problemas, la situación no es tal como para considerar que por la mera orientación sexual alguien es, automáticamente, objeto de persecución en Argelia'].
38 Díaz Lafuente, note 2, 471.

> even a bill has been presented in Parliament to legalise civil unions between persons of the same sex.[39]

Similarly, according to Cores, the Asylum Office waited for the mid-2008 reform of the Nicaraguan Penal Code, which decriminalised homosexuality, in order to reject all sexuality-based claims from this country that had been submitted after that reform had been announced.[40] Indeed, no sexuality-based Nicaraguan claims appear to have reached the Audiencia Nacional before May 2010.[41] Thus, criminalisation and state persecution of the individual claimant were required in pre–*Qualification Directive* practice for a sexuality-based claim to succeed.

However, just as 'mere group membership' was not sufficient, it was also not sufficient that there were criminal laws that were effectively applied in the country of origin. The claimant had to show 'something extra' that would demonstrate that they *personally* were at risk of imprisonment or other criminal sanctions for their sexual orientation. Rather than engaging in a future-focused analysis, Spanish jurisprudence, therefore, effectively required past state persecution based on having been identified as gay. As a consequence, the doctrinal *location* of 'discretion' reasoning is less clear in Spanish case law than in the other jurisdictions under discussion. Though judgments do not lay out their reasons in a principled manner that allows for such clarity, 'discretion' logics appear to have a double function, influencing both the social group assessment ('mere' membership is not sufficient) and the well-founded fear analysis ('singled out' for 'personal' persecution).

6.2.4 *Pre-qualification Directive 'Discretion' Reasoning*

The review of Spanish pre–*Qualification Directive* jurisprudence on sexuality-based claims reveals some trends and lines of reasoning. Before the implementation of the *Qualification Directive* via Law 12/2009, it was widely accepted that only those sexuality-based claims would be successful that presented cases of past state persecution. In this sense, there was some coherence, even though it was clearly contrary to international guidance. In this context, two notions of particular importance are 'mere membership' and 'singling out'. These are related but different concepts: whereas the former looks at the claimant and asks whether they have manifested their sexual orientation, the latter looks at the persecutor and the question of whether the claimant has been specifically targeted. Both result from earlier Spanish practice and essentially deny protection to those who have maintained a

[39] SAN 3139/2007 de 4 de julio de 2007 ['Si el recurrente llegó a nuestro país y lo hizo, según su relato, por temor a ser perseguido en su país de origen por razón de su homosexualidad no se entiende la razón ya que en Croacia la homosexualidad esta despenalizada e incluso recientemente se ha presentado en el Parlamento una proposición de Ley para legalizar las uniones de hecho entre personas del mismo sexo']. See also Díaz Lafuente, note 2, 470.

[40] Cores, note 13, 19.

[41] Search on poderjudicial.es on 17 June 2015.

low profile and have been able to pass under the persecutors' radar. That in and of itself is paradox; according to the Refugee Convention, a person is entitled to protection if they are persecuted for reasons of membership of a particular social group. Spain's jurisprudence states that 'mere' membership (i.e. identity) is not sufficient, but persecution must also be 'personal'. So, a claimant must be singled out from their group for persecution – even though persecution must be for membership of that group. The Audiencia Nacional does not offer a solution for this paradox and it remains unexplained what this ghostly expectation of 'something extra' refers to.

It is only possible to speculate that the requirement of 'personal persecution' implies that all gay people have the *potential* of being persecuted but have the possibility of passing unnoticed,[42] for example by only *privately* engaging in consensual same-sex sexual acts among adults, as was described for Kazakhstan. In addition to *being* gay, the claimant must have somehow drawn attention to themselves or stand out as a particular member of this particular group. Though not explicit, this notion implements an act/identity dichotomy that is effectively based on 'discretion' reasoning. To posit that the simple 'differential fact' of being gay is not persecuted enables decision-makers to easily accept the claimant's sexual identity – even if only a limited idea of identity in the sense of an inclination entirely separated from its links with behaviour. Seen in this light, the Spanish reasoning bears surprising parallels with French practice requiring assertion; if past persecution could be established for a country that criminalises homosexuality, then the claimant had obviously not only been 'outed' but also stood out from the gay masses. If, however, no past state persecution could be established, then it was unlikely in Spanish pre–*Qualification Directive* practice for a sexuality-based claim to succeed – and the claimant was returned to a state of continued 'discretion'. Unlike, for example, UK jurisprudence prior to *HJ (Iran) and HT (Cameroon)*, such 'discretion' was never explicitly required, but implicitly expected. As such, there was no need to engage with the meaning and consequences of such 'discretion'. Like in France, absence of past persecution was taken as a predictor in Spain for absence of future persecution based on a 'factual' finding derived from past conduct. The scope of protection was not defined by a notion of protected identity and rights but, rather, by a focus on the perceptibility of the claimant as gay in the past and their assumed ability to (continue to) pass unnoticed.

Hence, it appears that in pre–*Qualification Directive* times the group of potentially successful sexuality-based claims in Spain was clearly defined and narrow. It was limited to claimants from countries that criminalised homosexuality, and who had personally been prosecuted under these laws in the past or who had been threatened with such prosecution. The *Qualification Directive* represented a rupture in this tradition and gave way to a more varied range of approaches as attempts

[42] Cores, note 13, 12.

were made to integrate established Spanish practice with European standards. Specifically, Spanish judges struggled to come to terms not only with the clarification that sexual orientation comes under Convention protection, but also – and particularly – with the relevance of non-state actors for the assessment of persecution, which consequently meant that criminalisation of homosexuality was not a prerequisite.

6.3 SIGNIFICANT TRANSCENDENCE OF HARM

Following the entry into force of Law 12/2009, the Technical Office of the Administrative Litigation Section of the Tribunal Supremo published a 'chronicle' of jurisprudence concerning international protection covering the years 2009 to 2012, 'reviewing and systematising' its own case law.[43] One of the stated aims of this chronicle was a comparative review of existing doctrine with the provisions of Law 12/2009, in an effort to detect what jurisprudential lines were still valid and which could be considered superseded by the new law.[44] Tribunal Supremo decisions up to 2012 almost exclusively still applied the old law.[45] In its chronicle, the Tribunal Supremo essentially took the view that there were no conceptual differences between the 1984 Law and the 2009 Law with respect to the refugee definition, given that both refer to the 1951 Refugee Convention. Therefore, the Court argued that the doctrine developed in application of the old law concerning the reasons for persecution, the assessment of credibility or the required standard of proof, could substantially be extended to the new law.[46] Indeed, it seems that many of the aspects where Spanish jurisprudence and the *Qualification Directive* diverged had, for the most part, been adapted in Spanish practice under Law 5/1984 by the time the Technical Office published its reviews.

6.3.1 *From Non-admissibility to Disbelief*

While the new law was understood not to affect the refugee definition – though, significantly, it explicitly introduced 'gender' and 'sexual orientation' as grounds for Convention protection – it provided some changes with respect to the admissibility process, which was maintained in a slightly revised version (Articles 20; 21; 25).[47] Most notably, the new law no longer foresees non-admissibility for claims that 'do

43 Pedro Escribano Testaut and Margarita Diana Fernández Sánchez (n.d.) *Doctrina jurisprudencial sobre protección internacional (asilo, y refugio, protección subsidiaria y autorización de permanencia en España por razones humanitarias) 2009–2012*. Tribunal Supremo, Sala de lo Contencioso-Administrativo, Gabinete Técnico, 2.

44 Ibid., 3.

45 Ibid., 2.

46 Ibid., 10.

47 Articles 20, 21 and 25 of the *Law 12/2009 of October 30, regulating the right of asylum and subsidiary protection*.

not refer to any of the Convention grounds'. The Law now distinguishes between claims submitted at the border (Article 21), where the admissibility phase is mandatory, and claims submitted on territory (Article 20), where the admissibility phase is optional. Reasons for non-admissibility also differ; for claims made on territory, they are limited to cases where Spain is not responsible for processing the claim (Article 20), whereas in the case of claims made at border posts, claims can in addition be declared non-admissible if the claimant raises 'only issues that do not qualify for the examination of the requirements for the recognition of refugee status' (Article 21.2.a in conjunction with Article 25.1.c), and when the applicant has made

> inconsistent, contradictory, implausible, insufficient arguments, or arguments which contradict sufficiently verified information about their country of origin ... so as to clearly reveal that his application regarding the fact of holding a credible fear of persecution or serious harm is manifestly unfounded.[48]

The term 'manifestly unfounded' in this context is contested and has been defined by the Tribunal Supremo in two decisions on 27 March 2013.[49] Law 12/2009 also explicitly incorporates both 'gender' and 'sexual orientation' in the refugee definition.[50] Following entry into force of the *Qualification Directive*, which stipulates that sexual orientation can constitute a particular social group, in a series of decisions from 2006 and 2007 the Tribunal Supremo had finally addressed the long-standing uncertainty on this issue in Spain, stating that

> the applicant alleges persecution for reasons of their *sexual orientation, which is incorporated among those covered by the 1951 Geneva Convention and the Asylum Law 5/1984 itself,* and this is sufficient for the application to be admissible (regardless of whether the facts are true or not, then this should be justified during the procedure).[51]

48 Article 21.2.b of the *Law 12/2009 of October 30, regulating the right of asylum and subsidiary protection* ['cuando la persona solicitante hubiese formulado alegaciones incoherentes, contradictorias, inverosímiles, insuficientes, o que contradigan información suficientemente contrastada sobre su país de origen, o de residencia habitual si fuere apátrida, de manera que pongan claramente de manifiesto que su solicitud es infundada por lo que respecta al hecho de albergar un fundado temor a ser perseguida o a sufrir un daño grave']. Another reason for inadmissibility are cases of exclusion or rejection outlined in Articles 8, 9, 11 and 12 (equivalent to the exclusion clauses in the 1951 Convention and national security reasons; Article 21.2.a in conjunction with Article 25.1.f).

49 STS 1957/2013 de 27 de marzo de 2013 and STS 1971/2013 de 27 de marzo de 2013.

50 Sancho, note 10, 255.

51 STS 8650/2006 de 14 de diciembre de 2006; emphasis added ['En el caso examinado, el interesado alega una persecución por causa de su orientación sexual, incardinable entre las contempladas en la Convención de Ginebra de 1951 y en la propia Ley de Asilo 5/1984, y ello es suficiente para que la solicitud haya de ser admitida a trámite (con independencia de que los hechos expuestos sean o no ciertos, pues ello deberá justificarse durante el procedimiento)']. See also STS 5650/2007 de 25 de julio de 2007; STS 6674/2007 de 4 de octubre de 2007 ['en este caso se ha producido la vulneración del artículo 5-6-b) de la Ley 5/84, ya que el solicitante sí describió unos hechos que encierran una persecución por motivos de orientación sexual

It appears that this put an end to the non-admissibility of sexuality-based claims on the basis of Article 5.6.b and it was accepted that, in principle, sexual orientation qualifies as a particular social group. Law 12/2009 does not leave any room for doubt in this respect. The refugee definition in Article 3 states:

> Refugee status is extended to any person who, owing to well founded fear of being persecuted for reasons of race, religion, nationality, political opinions, membership of a particular social group, *of gender or sexual orientation*, is outside the country of their nationality.[52]

While it might seem at first glance that gender and sexual orientation are established as separate Convention grounds, the law in fact systematises them as criteria for establishing a social group.[53] In that sense, it does not go further than the *Qualification Directive*, though the latter does not include gender and sexual orientation in the refugee definition under Article 2 but, rather, mentions them as examples of social groups under Article 10, which provides some context and explanations on the Convention grounds.

Ignoring the previous uncertainties as to this issue, and referring back to decisions from 2006 and 2008, in which the Court stated in passing that sexual orientation could constitute a Convention reason,[54] in the view of the Tribunal Supremo this explicit reference did nothing but lay down in positive law what had already been declared in case law in the interpretation and application of the old law.[55] It cites cases such as STS 5907/2012, still applying law 5/1984, which stated: 'In principle, persecution by government authorities against a person because of their homosexuality can find protection under the 1951 Geneva Convention and Asylum Law 5/84, of 26 October, as we have declared in numerous judgments.'[56]

The general acceptance of sexual orientation as protected under the Convention notably coincides with an increased tendency to disbelieve identity. For decisions from 2006 onwards, rather than not admitting sexuality-based claims it appears to have become much more common to indicate disbelief with respect to the

incardinable entre las que dan derecho al reconocimiento de la condición de refugiado, aunque después, en la tramitación del expediente administrativo, acaso se revelen como inciertos']; STS 8251/2007 de 13 de diciembre de 2007.

52 Article 3 of the *Law 12/2009 of October 30, regulating the right of asylum and subsidiary protection*; emphasis added ['La condición de refugiado se reconoce a toda persona que, debido a fundados temores de ser perseguida por motivos de, raza, religión, nacionalidad, opiniones políticas, pertenencia a determinado grupo social, de género u orientación sexual, se encuentra fuera del país de su nacionalidad . . .'].

53 Sancho, note 10, 256. See also Díaz Lafuente, note 2, 449–450.

54 STS 4511/2003 de 29 de septiembre de 2006 and STS 5265/2005 de 28 de noviembre de 2008.

55 Testaut and Fernández Sánchez, note 43, 10.

56 STS 5907/2012 de 21 de septiembre de 2012 ['En línea de principio, una persecución desarrollada por las autoridades gubernamentales contra una persona por razón de su homosexualidad puede encontrar amparo en la Convención de Ginebra de 1951 y en la Ley de Asilo 5/84, de 26 de octubre, como así lo hemos declarado en numerosas sentencias'].

applicant's sexual orientation, particularly for those claims that would otherwise have chances of success due the existence of criminal laws in the respective countries of origin. For example, in SAN 2533/2014, a Nigerian gay man's story was disbelieved as being vague, imprecise, ambiguous and generic, and 'lacking reliable evidence of his membership of a social, ethnic, political or religious group subject to persecution'.[57] As is typical for Spanish decision-making, this disbelief was often formulated implicitly rather than clearly found and stated, and tended to be backed up by disbelief regarding their story of past persecution. According to Spanish doctrine, disbelief of past persecution essentially came down to a rejection of the claim. In SAN 1584/2011, concerning a gay man from Iran, the decision-maker disbelieved the entire story, including the claimant's sexual orientation:

> [T]he applicant's account does not offer minimum guarantees of credibility and on the contrary, everything leads to believe that the applicant has recreated a story using as a basis a grounds of persecution that in view of the extensive experience of this Office is quite susceptible to being appealed given the difficulty of proving its existence or not.[58]

In the 2014 case of a Cameroonian claimant, the Court found in its individual assessment that the claimant 'bases his application on his homosexual condition which he maintained in secret during many years out of fear' before he was discovered and outed by a friend, beaten up at his place of work and searched for by the police, who came to his home to arrest him when he was not there.[59] The court concluded that 'the applicant claims not to have had any problems due to his sexual orientation before November 2010, even though at least since 2005 he maintained stable and continuing homosexual relationships with two different men', and disbelieved his story.[60]

Moreover, reasons for disbelief were often expressed not only on an individual basis but also on a group basis. This trend is unique to Spain and, at first glance, appears to contradict the 'individual assessment' as established in Spanish jurisprudence. The case of a Cameroonian claimant in SAN 2340/2014 provides a good illustration of this. In this case, the court first cited the Asylum Office's individual assessment, finding that 'neither has it been demonstrated, not even circumstantially,

[57] SAN 1832/2014 de 30 de abril de 2014 ['faltando constancia fehaciente de su pertenencia a grupo social, étnico, político o religioso objeto de persecución'].

[58] SAN 1584/2011 de 24 de marzo de 2011 ['Por tanto, a la vista de todo lo señalado esta Instrucción considera que el relato del solicitante no ofrece las mínimas garantías de credibilidad y por el contrario, todo lleva a pensar que el solicitante ha recreado una historia utilizando como base de la misma una causa de persecución, que a la vista de la amplia experiencia de esta Oficina, es bastante recurrible dado la dificultad que existe de probar o no su existencia'].

[59] SAN 2793/2014 de 12 de junio de 2014 ['El recurrente fundamenta su solicitud en su condición de homosexual que mantuvo en secreto durante muchos años por miedo'].

[60] Ibid. ['el interesado no alega haber tenido problema alguno a causa de su orientación sexual antes de noviembre de 2010, a pesar de que al menos desde 2005 mantenía relaciones homosexuales estables y continuadas con dos hombres distintos'].

that his sexual orientation is ultimately that which he claims it to be', on the basis of considering his coming-out story banal and noting a lack of 'feelings'.[61] In addition to this problematic individual assessment, the Asylum Office also disbelieved the claimant's story on the basis that it was too similar to the stories of other claimants, from which it concluded that it could not be true:

> In short, his story is full of commonplaces: indeed, it should be noted that the applicant's allegations are very similar, or at least going in the same line, as those brought forward on the same dates by other asylum seekers in Ceuta and Melilla, also alleging to be Cameroonians citizens and gay.[62]

In SAN 2530/2014, concerning a gay man from Cameroon, the court found the claimant's entire story vague, incoherent and contradictory, also disbelieving his sexual orientation on the basis that it bore too many parallels with the stories brought forth by similarly situated claimants: 'The episode in which his wife suddenly enters and discovers him while in bed with another man "is another commonplace among the arguments of those who claim to be Cameroonian citizens and also homosexuals."'[63] Similarly, in SAN 379/2014, the Iranian claimant's identity is disbelieved not

[61] SAN 2340/2013 de 12 de mayo de 2014. Note that this individual assessment itself is already problematic on several levels, as it is full of stereotyped notions concerning sexuality and in its attempt to detect implausibilities presents contradicting reasoning itself: 'Particularly striking is the ease with which he describes the discovery of his sexual orientation, as we say, reducing it to joining the others in the practice of homosexuality, as if it were something completely banal, which is of course incompatible with the real situation of the people who are homosexual in Cameroon, and who are deeply rejected by the mainstream society. Moreover, he has not named anyone in particular who he had a relationship with, nor have we detected in the account of the applicant any hint of affection or feeling of any kind. Also, absolutely nothing happened to him until his mother surprised him [in his room making love with a partner] . . . It is also surprising that after this incident the applicant returned to his school . . . Since it appears that he did return . . . it appears strange that he would have felt embarrassed at school, where he had a large group of friends who had the same sexual orientation as him, and who logically would have protected him'. ['Llama la atención la ligereza con la que describe el descubrimiento de su orientación sexual, como decimos, reduciéndolo a unirse a los demás en la práctica de la homosexualidad, como si se tratara de algo completamente banal, desde luego incompatible con la situación real de las personas que son homosexuales en Camerún, profundamente rechazadas por el común de la sociedad. Tampoco nombra alguien en concreto con quien tuviera una relación, ni se aprecia en el relato del solicitante ningún viso de afecto o de sensación de ningún tipo. Tampoco le ocurre absolutamente nada hasta que su madre le sorprende. . . También es sorprendente que después de este incidente el solicitante vuelva a su colegio . . . Puesto que parece ser que volvió . . . resulta extraño que sintiera vergüenza en el colegio, donde tenía un nutrido grupo de amigos que tenían la misma orientación sexual que él, y que lógicamente le hubieran protegido . . .'].

[62] SAN 2340/2013 de 12 de mayo de 2014 ['En definitiva su relato está lleno de tópicos: es más, es necesario destacar que las alegaciones del interesado son muy similares, o al menos van en la misma línea, a las formuladas en esas mismas fechas en Ceuta y Melilla por otros solicitantes de asilo que alegan igualmente ser ciudadanos cameruneses y homosexuales . . .'].

[63] SAN 2530/2014 de 30 de mayo de 2014 ['El episodio en el que estando en la cama con otro hombre su esposa entra de improviso y los descubre 'es otro elemento tópico habitual entre las alegaciones de quienes afirman ser ciudadanos cameruneses y además homosexuales'].

only on individual grounds[64] but also based on the fact that the story cannot be true due to its similarity with other stories, such that the claimant does not stand out: 'it [is] appropriate to draw attention to a phenomenon that has been observed throughout this year related to asylum applications made by citizens of Iran. Indeed . . . the applicants are starting to tell, all of them – a story of persecution related to sexual identity'.[65]

This trend towards considering 'the appearance of many similar stories alleged by several asylum seekers . . . an element that points to the implausibility of the claimed persecution',[66] has been developed and established from 2005 onwards. While it is no longer possible to refuse to admit sexuality-based claims to procedure, it has become much more common to disbelieve the claimants' sexual orientation, and consequently the past persecution they claimed to have suffered on that basis. The reasons for disbelief are often twofold: not only do decision-makers disbelieve the claimants' sexual orientation on an individual basis, but also on a group basis. Even though it appears counter-intuitive, because the argument for rejection is group-based, the latter chimes with the concept of the 'singling out' criterion. Just like the 'personal persecution' assessment, it requires 'something extra'. While it would appear not only possible but likely that stories of the same group of persecuted people would bear similarities, as they are subjected to the same situation, the 'usual' story is not sufficient in Spain.

Much like in France and Germany, then, for those who claimed to have been 'outed' in the past, meaning that 'discretion' was no longer an option, there has been an increase in disbelief since the entry into force of the *Qualification Directive*. Unlike the other two jurisdictions, however, the shift in Spain was not from

[64] SAN 379/2011 de 31 de enero de 2011. Again, this individual assessment demonstrates a blatant lack of sensitivity towards and understanding of concepts of sexuality that create implausibility where there is not necessarily one: the claimant is found to be no witness of truth because he 'begins his story . . . indicating that he is gay. When [asked] for his sexual practices, the claim of being gay is not true. Indeed, the applicant states literally that since the age of 11 or 12 he has sex with both, men and women' ['. . . comienza su relato al formular su petición y al realizar la entrevista con la Instrucción indicando que es gay. Cuando esta Instrucción pregunta al solicitante por sus prácticas sexuales, la alegación de ser gay no es cierta. En efecto, el solicitante refiere literalmente que desde los 11–12 años practica sexo con todo, hombres y mujeres']. Note that this judgment also contains the same paragraph cited previously from a case concerning another Iranian claimant.

[65] SAN 379/2011 de 31 de enero de 2011 ['En este sentido, esta Instrucción considera procedente hacer una llamada de atención sobre un fenómeno que se viene observando a lo largo del presente año relacionado con las solicitudes de asilo realizadas por ciudadanos procedentes de Irán. En efecto, . . . los solicitantes comienzan a referir, todos, – un relato de persecución relacionado con la identidad sexual'].

[66] SAN 2793/2014 de 12 de junio de 2014 ['Recordemos que la Audiencia Nacional . . . establece que la aparición de diversos relatos similares alegados por varios solicitantes de asilo es un elemento que apuntan a la inverosimilitud de la persecución relatada'].

'discretion' to disbelief, but from non-admissibility to disbelief. 'Discretion' logics continued to apply for those claimants who had faced prosecution under anti-gay laws – and for those who had faced harm beyond prosecution that was not 'significantly transcendent'.

6.3.2 *'Without These Aspects Alone'*

The trend to require 'something extra' in the case of sexuality-based claims was explicitly reinforced by Law 12/2009. The 2004 *Qualification Directive* provides for a 'something extra' requirement for social groups based on gender when it states that gender-related aspects 'by themselves alone' cannot lead to refugee protection. Article 10(1)(d) reads:

> [D]epending on the circumstances in the country of origin, a particular social group might include a group based on a common characteristic of sexual orientation. Sexual orientation cannot be understood to include acts considered to be criminal in accordance with national law of the Member States: Gender related aspects might be considered, *without by themselves alone* creating a presumption for the applicability of this Article .[67]

In its transposition of the *Qualification Directive* into national law, the Spanish legislature also explicitly extended this provision to sexuality-based claims. According to Article 7.1.e of the Spanish Law 12/2009:

> Depending on the circumstances in the country of origin, the concept of social group includes groups based on the common characteristic of *sexual orientation or gender identity*, and/or age, *without these aspects alone* giving rise to the application of this article. Under no circumstances shall be understood as sexual orientation, any conduct that is criminalised in the Spanish legal system.
>
> Also, depending on the circumstances in the country, it includes people who flee their countries of origin due to well-founded fear of persecution on grounds of *gender* and/or age, *without these aspects alone* resulting in the application of this article.[68]

[67] Article 10.1.d *Qualification Directive*; emphasis added.

[68] Article 7.1.e of the *Law 12/2009 of October 30, regulating the right of asylum and subsidiary protection; emphasis* added ['En función de las circunstancias imperantes en el país de origen, se incluye en el concepto de grupo social determinado un grupo basado en una característica común de orientación sexual o identidad sexual, y, o, edad, sin que estos aspectos por sí solos puedan dar lugar a la aplicación del presente artículo. En ningún caso podrá entenderse como orientación sexual, la realización de conductas tipificadas como delito en el ordenamiento jurídico español. Asimismo, en función de las circunstancias imperantes en el país de origen, se incluye a las personas que huyen de sus países de origen debido a fundados temores de sufrir persecución por motivos de género y, o, edad, sin que estos aspectos por sí solos puedan dar lugar a la aplicación del presente artículo'].

Adding the 'without these aspects alone' condition to sexuality-based cases is in line with and confirms Spanish jurisprudence. In a 2012 decision, the Tribunal Supremo summarised its own previous case law regarding sexuality-based claims since 2006, as having developed two criteria: the existence of a 'social context of severe vulnerability and persecution' because of the claimant's sexual orientation; and the requirement of an 'individual analysis' ('análisis casuístico') to determine whether it may be concluded to the required level of evidence that such persecution exists for the claimant.[69] In other words, jurisprudence emphasised the importance of the individual case analysis requiring that the individual circumstances of each situation are addressed when it comes to establishing sufficient evidence of the existence of persecution on grounds of sexual orientation.[70] If the concrete personal situation of the claimant was not such that the claimant stood out from the (gay) masses, then they could be rejected in spite of a social context of severe vulnerability and persecution. For claims from countries with laws criminalising homosexuality, the jurisprudence developed the 'mere' membership doctrine and the 'singling out' criterion to limit the scope of protection at the level of the well-founded fear of persecution. Concerning countries that do not criminalise homosexuality, the focal point of the assessment became the nexus requirement, that is, the requirement that the harm is feared *because of* the Convention ground. Spanish jurisprudence developed the doctrinal figure of 'significant transcendence' for this analysis.

6.3.3 *Establishing Nexus: 'Significant Transcendence' of Past Persecution*

With the *Qualification Directive*, the previously established general rejection of claims of persecution concerning countries that do not criminalise same-sex sexual acts started to lose ground from 2005 onwards.[71] In a case in that year concerning a gay man from Moldova, the Court found that 'even after the repeal of repressive laws on homosexuality, the citizens of Moldova with this sexual orientation are still abused by security forces, besides being discriminated against in different areas of social life'.[72] This idea of the possibility of persecution in the absence of laws

[69] STS 5907/2012 de 21 de septiembre de 2012 ['Resulta determinante a estos efectos, un contexto social de grave desprotección y persecución por razón de su orientación homosexual (SSTS de 29 de septiembre de 2006, RC 4511/2003, y 28 de noviembre de 2008, RC 5265/2005), por lo que se ha de examinar cada caso, de forma individualizada, y determinar si, en definitiva, puede considerarse acreditada (al nivel indiciario requerido en esta materia según constante jurisprudencia y a la vista de los elementos probatorios aportados por el solicitante de asilo) una persecución por tal razón que merezca el reconocimiento de la condición de refugiado'].

[70] Díaz Lafuente, note 2, 468.

[71] See ibid., 470.

[72] STS 7098/2005 de 30 de noviembre de 2005 ['aun después de la derogación de las leyes de represión de la homosexualidad, los ciudadanos de Moldavia con esta orientación sexual siguen siendo objeto de malos tratos por las Fuerzas de Seguridad, además de resultar discriminados en diferentes ámbitos de la vida social'].

criminalising homosexuality was quickly linked in Spanish case law with the notion of 'significant transcendence'.

This notion, also referred to as 'the objective element', was developed by the Tribunal Supremo mainly to assess whether the harm suffered amounted to persecution in cases from countries that do not criminalise homosexuality. According to the Technical Office of the Tribunal Supremo, 'purely episodic events, isolated and/or of little relevance, lack the capacity to merit consideration of a protectable persecution'.[73] In essence, the issue of 'significant transcendence' is an issue of establishing the nexus to a Convention ground. Examples of this new standard include findings that the reason or motive for the harm suffered is unclear;[74] that there is no 'precise and direct link' between the harm and the Convention ground;[75] or that the harm suffered is only a single incidence or an isolated act by the police.[76] At the same time, all of these elements reveal a continuous presumption of state protection in countries that do not criminalise homosexuality.[77]

The 'significant transcendence' requirement is well reflected in SAN 2122/2014, still applying law 5/1984, concerning a gay man from Venezuela, for which it is worth repeating the facts as related by the decision-maker in full.

> The appellant bases his request on the account of the following facts: In the situation of public insecurity in Venezuela, he was subjected to threats, insults and even physical attacks for being a homosexual; he was forced to leave his country because they were harassed by a marginal group when his partner came to live at the applicant's parents' house. He tried to report these incidents to the police station in Ocumare del Tuy, being expelled from the same with insults. In July 2012, on the occasion of returning home with his partner in a van, they were followed by a group of bikers who threw a case at the windshield of the vehicle, which caused an accident where they hit a wall, receiving insults because of their sexual condition. They received threats from the same group if they voted against the party in power.[78]

[73] Testaut and Fernández Sánchez, note 43, 13.
[74] E.g. SAN 200/2007 de 30 de enero de 2007.
[75] E.g. SAN 2122/2014 de 22 de mayo de 2014.
[76] E.g. SAN 2530/2014 de 30 de mayo de 2014.
[77] See e.g. SAN 2122/2014 de 22 de mayo de 2014.
[78] Ibid. ['El recurrente fundamenta su solicitud en la narración de los siguientes hechos: La situación de falta de seguridad ciudadana en Venezuela, que provoca que, por su condición de homosexual se vea sometido a amenazas, insultos e incluso agresiones físicas por dicha condición sexual, viéndose obligado a salir de su país, debido a que su pareja fuera a vivir con el solicitante a casa de los padres del mismo, sufriendo acoso por parte de un grupo marginal. Que intentó formular denuncia de tales hechos ante la Comisaría de Ocumare del Tuy, siendo expulsado de la misma con insultos. Que en julio de 2012, con ocasión de dirigirse el recurrente y su pareja a casa en una camioneta fueron seguidos por un grupo de moteros y que arrojaron un caso al cristal delantero del vehículo, lo que provoco un accidente al chocar contra un muro, recibiendo insultos por su condición sexual. Que recibieron amenazas del mismo grupo si votaban en contra del partido en poder'].

The decision-maker rejected the claim based on a lack of 'minimal consistency' of the claimant's story and a presumption of state protection based on the absence of 'political or legislative persecution', noting that the Venezuelan constitution protects homosexuality. He further reasoned:

> [E]ven accepting, despite the lack of evidence, that the appellant holds the alleged homosexual condition, this is no evidence at all that he has been persecuted for membership of this group nor that, moreover, this persecution, which should have been manifested in concrete facts or behaviours that the claim should have referred to with a minimum of detail, can be attributed to the authorities of his country, either as protagonists of the persecution towards his person, or by evidence of passivity or abstention vis-à-vis the alleged reports [to the police] of which it is not certain that they have been made; the documentation concerning the accident cannot rebut that conclusion, since *there is no precise and direct link between the alleged persecution suffered and the claimed accident.*[79]

In other words, the Court – despite doubts regarding this aspect – was ready to accept the claimant's sexual orientation as well as the harm that he suffered, but the claim failed because the Court was not convinced that the persecutor's motive was to punish his homosexuality, regardless of the homophobic insults that they received.

In a particularly disturbing 2007 case, a Cuban gay man laid out a very detailed account of having been subjected to radical mastectomy against his will at the age of 15 because his mammary glands possessed feminine characteristics. The chief of the local police had claimed that with 'a woman's tits' ('tetas de mujer') it was not fitting for the claimant to mingle with 'virtuous men' ('hombres integros'). During surgery, his areolas, nipples and part of the pectoral muscle tissue were arbitrarily removed, leaving enormous scars and causing psychological problems. Again, the court found that the nexus between the Convention ground and the harm suffered had not been established because the motivation for the surgery was not clear:

> [T]here is no evidence that this surgery, of which we do not doubt the existence because photographs of scars on each breast and the removal of the nipples and areolas were provided, was an imposition by the Cuban authorities for his

[79] SAN 2122/2014 de 22 de mayo de 2014; emphasis added ['A lo expuesto se añade que aun aceptando, pese a la falta de prueba, que el recurrente ostentase la alegada condición de homosexual, no consta tampoco en modo alguno que haya sufrido persecución por razón de la pertenencia a ese colectivo ya que, además, esa persecución, que debería haberse manifestado en hechos o conductas concretas a las que tendría que haberse referido la demanda con un mínimo de detalle, provenga de las autoridades de su país, bien por ser los protagonistas de la persecución hacia su persona, bien por evidencia de pasividad o abstención frente a supuestas denuncias que no constan formuladas, sin que la documentación aportada relativa al accidente de tráfico pueda enervar dicha conclusión, pues no existe enlace preciso y directo entre la supuesta persecución padecida y el accidente que se dice sufrido'].

> homosexual condition or rather a medical necessity for some kind of anomaly or specific problem.[80]

This case, which has been characterised as 'torture' by CEAR,[81] failed because the claimant could not provide proof of the persecutors' motives – even though the sexual orientation and the harm were established. The same reason led to rejection in the case of a Cameroonian claimant (SAN 2530/2014). The facts are recounted as follows:

> In 2010, he met another man at a party, they saw each other regularly and went out together. On 21 May 2011 his wife came home unexpectedly, and found him in bed with his friend, she began to shout, creating a scandal that the whole neighbourhood heard. His friend ran away and the appellant was beaten and insulted by the neighbours, the police arrived, arrested him and took him to the police station Dobon in Douala.[82]

The Court concluded in this context that the arrest was only an isolated act by the police for which the motive was unclear:

> [R]egarding the problems he claims to have had in his city for being homosexual, he relates *but an isolated act of the police and it is unclear what the reasons for his arrest were*, since the arrest was linked to the commotion caused by his wife, supposedly when she returned home and found him in bed with a man.[83]

A similar conclusion was reached in SAN 1584/2011, concerning a gay man from Iran who had submitted evidence of his arrest at a park. The Asylum Office had found that the document submitted could not be considered as proof or indication of persecution because it only demonstrated that he was detained, not the motive for this detention.[84]

In SAN 1790/2005, in contrast, the Audiencia Nacional did speculate on the persecutor's motive. The decision concerned a gay man from Cuba who had been

80 SAN 200/2007 de 30 de enero de 2007 ['no existe prueba alguna de que dicha operación, de la que no se duda de su existencia pues se aportaron fotografías de cicatrices en cada pecho y de la extirpación de los pezones y aureolas [sic], fuera una imposición de las autoridades cubanas por su condición de homosexual o una necesidad medica de algún tipo de anomalía o problemática específica'].

81 Lasa et al., note 10, 162.

82 SAN 2530/2014 de 30 de mayo de 2014 ['En el 2010 conoció a otro hombre en una fiesta, se veían con regularidad y salían juntos. Llegó a su casa el 21 de mayo del 2011 su esposa de forma imprevista, le encontró en la cama con el amigo, empezó a gritar, creó un escándalo que se enteró todo el barrio. Su amigo se escapó y al recurrente le pegaron, le injuriaron los vecinos, llegó la policía, le detuvieron y le llevaron al puesto de policía de Dobon en Douala'].

83 Ibid.; emphasis added ['en cuanto a los problemas que dice haber tenido en su ciudad por ser homosexual, no relata sino una actuación aislada de la policía y no resulta claro cuáles fueron los motivos por los que fue detenido, pues su arresto fue ligado al alboroto que organizó su esposa, supuestamente cuando regresó a casa y le encontró en cama con un hombre'].

84 SAN 1584/2011 de 24 de marzo de 2011 ['solo se deduce del mismo que se encuentra en manos del poder judicial pero no el motivo'].

registered as gay by the authorities and was regularly humiliated in public and detained. The decision-maker concluded:

> All his problems seem to be limited to the alleged occasional 'retentions' (which is how the Cubans refer to detentions of a few hours at the police station). Besides not being established, rather than representing a personal and specific persecution, this fact is due to an attitude of excessive control that the Cuban authorities have over the great majority of the population.[85]

A reference to the general situation in the country was also the grounds for the rejection of the case concerning a gay couple from Russia before the Audiencia Nacional (SAN 842/2011). Here the Court found that

> even though it is true that the Russian society is homophobic and situations arise in which homosexuals are subject to aggression, blackmail and humiliation ... the current situation of homosexuals in Russia is not so extreme as to consider that the mere fact of being it [gay], represents a risk for the integrity and security of claimants.[86]

Concerning the claimants, the Court found that what they faced was not persecution for reason of their sexual orientation but simply the Russian standard for all: 'Regarding the attitude of the police, taking into account the Russian parameters, [their behaviour] was no more derogatory or more humiliating than that bestowed on any citizen, homosexual or not.'[87] The same assessment applies to the treatment the claimants received from a doctor: 'what happens to the applicants is, unfortunately, something very common and, again, there is no homophobic component in the attitude of the doctor'.[88] This judgment demonstrates that the 'individual assessment' of the claimant's personal circumstances allows decision-makers to reject claims on the basis that the harm they faced was no different than that inflicted on 'normal' people. If the treatment is bad for all, then 'something extra' is required to prove that the harm was inflicted due to the Convention ground. Generally, it appears that decision-makers were prepared to accept the nexus

[85] SAN 1790/2005 de 30 de marzo de 2005 ['Todos sus problemas parecen haberse reducido a supuestas "retenciones" (así se refieren los Cubanos a las retenciones de unas pocas horas de duración en la estación de policía) ocasionales. Hecho que, además de no quedar establecido, obedece más que a una persecución personal y concreta a una actitud de excesivo control que las autoridades cubanas ejercen sobre la gran mayoría de la población'].

[86] SAN 842/2011 de 18 de febrero de 2011 ['si bien es cierto que la sociedad rusa es homófoba y se dan situaciones en que los homosexuales pueden ser objeto de agresión, chantaje o humillaciones ... la situación actual en Rusia no es tan extrema como para considerar que el solo hecho de serlo supone un peligro para la identidad y la seguridad de los solicitantes'].

[87] Ibid. ['Respecto a la actitud de la policía, teniendo en cuenta los parámetros rusos, no fue ni más despectiva ni más humillante que la dispensada a cualquier ciudadano, homosexual o no'].

[88] Ibid. ['lo que le sucede a los solicitantes es algo, desgraciadamente, muy común y, de nuevo, no hay ningún componente homófobo en la actitud del médico'].

between Convention ground and persecutory harm emanating from both private actors and state actors (if they were not merely applying anti-gay laws) only if the claimant was able to produce a document that explicitly stated the reason for the particular treatment suffered. Conversely, there was an increased readiness to assume that the suffered harm had nothing to do with the Convention ground – even if there were indications in the evidence that this was the case. Spanish jurisprudence opted for the narrowest possible approach to the nexus requirement based on assumptions regarding the persecutor's motives. As noted, a similar tendency is inherent in the Spanish approach to criminalisation, where absence of criminal laws was taken to mean absence of persecution whereas the opposite did not apply.

To some extent, the 'significant transcendence' requirement also transcends 'discretion' reasoning; under this notion, it does not matter whether or not the claimant has been outed, because it assumes that, in any case, the persecutor was not influenced by the sexual orientation, whether or not they were aware of or suspected it – whatever happened to the claimant was unrelated to their sexual orientation. The transcendence assumption develops a great exclusionary potential, because it allows for rejections *even though* it is established that the claimant had been outed to the persecutor *and* suffered harm. The claim only fails because the decision-maker disbelieves those elements of the story that link the two.

Very rarely is there any legal discussion to be found in judgments. The 2011 judgment concerning the Russian couple (whose past persecution involved discrimination and harassment by the police and a doctor) was unusually explicit in providing a glimpse of the underlying reasoning for this restrictive doctrine:

> The applicants mainly allege that they could not openly live their homosexuality, as they can, for example, in Spain. But this is not sufficient reason to consider them refugees. If we applied this principle (as the UNHCR wants us to), any citizen who comes from a dictatorial country would be a refugee for the simple fact that, for example, they cannot openly express their opinions or they are deprived of their freedom of information.[89]

Though it is not acknowledged in any way, the discussion giving rise to this paragraph bears a resemblance to the UK Supreme Court judgment in *HJ (Iran) and HT (Cameroon)* and its concern about living freely and openly, which had been handed down half a year earlier. It thus similarly reflects the severity concern. This engagement with the issue of living 'openly' remains a rare exception, however (and

[89] Ibid. ['Sobre todo lo que los solicitantes alegan es que no podían vivir abiertamente su homosexualidad como la pueden vivir, por ejemplo, en España. Pero se considera que esto no es motivo suficiente para considerarlos refugiados. Si aplicamos este principio (como lo quiere el ACNUR), tendríamos que cualquier ciudadano que provenga de un país dictatorial seria un refugiado por el simple hecho de que, por ejemplo, no puede manifestar abiertamente sus opiniones o se le está sustrayendo de la libertad de información'].

even here, it is quickly rejected), although the core rationale in Spanish jurisprudence is the notion of passing under the persecutor's radar.

For claims concerning countries of origin that do not have anti-gay laws in force, the nexus had become the focal point in post–*Qualification Directive* case law. However, the past prosecution requirement also saw an improbable resurrection – inspired in particular by the CJEU judgment in *X, Y and Z*.

6.3.4 *International Guidance and the Resilience of the State Persecution Requirement*

Even though the *Qualification Directive*, and the new Spanish Asylum Law, explicitly provide for the possibility of non-state persecutors, the requirement of past prosecution under the criminal laws of the state (that is, by *state* actors) appears not to have been entirely overcome in Spanish jurisprudence. Decision-makers seem to be hesitant to accept private actors and 'private' harms in the context of sexuality-based claims. In its 2012 review of case law, the Technical Office of the Tribunal Supremo stated that 'normally, protectable persecution proceeds from political authorities of the country of origin, though that need not necessarily be so'.[90] In other words, state persecution is considered the norm, non-state persecution is exceptional. The Asylum Law 12/2009 provides at Article 13:

> Article 13. Actors of persecution or serious harm.
> Agents of persecution or serious harm may be, among others:
> (a) The State;
> (b) parties or organisations controlling the State or a substantial part of its territory
> (c) Non-state actors, when the actors mentioned in the above, including international organisations, are unable or unwilling to provide effective protection against persecution or serious harm.[91]

The Technical Office went on to claim that the case law in connection with the 1984 Law had already developed the same view, and shall therefore apply to disputes arising under the new Law.[92] Indeed, following entry into force of the *Qualification Directive*, twelve Audiencia Nacional decisions from 2008 onwards – the vast majority of which by the same decision-maker – contain one paragraph concerning non-state actors that is derived from the UNHCR Guidelines. This is particularly

[90] Testaut and Fernández Sánchez, note 43, 40.

[91] Article 13 of *the Law 12/2009 of October 30, regulating the right of asylum and subsidiary protection* ['Articulo 13. Agentes de persecución o causantes de daños graves.

Los agentes de persecución o causantes de daños graves podrán ser, entre otros: (a) El Estado; (b) Los partidos u organizaciones que controlen el Estado o una parte considerable de su territorio; (c) Agentes no estatales, cuando los agentes mencionados en los puntos anteriores, incluidas las organizaciones internacionales, no puedan o no quieran proporcionar protección efectiva contra la persecución o los daños graves'].

[92] Testaut and Fernández Sánchez, note 43, 40.

notable as there are very few other references to any of the UNHCR Guidelines in Spanish sexuality-based case law. The paragraph, which also found its way into a 2011 Tribunal Supremo judgment,[93] developed an approach for the persecution assessment in the case of non-state persecutors by reference to the UNHCR Social Group Guidelines[94] and the UNHCR Gender Guidelines.[95] It highlighted in particular that the causal nexus may be established:

> a) where there is a real risk of persecution by non-state actors for reasons related to one of the Convention grounds, whether the failure by the State to protect the applicant is related to the Convention or not; or b) if the risk of persecution by non-state actors is unrelated to a Convention ground, but the inability or unwillingness of the State to offer protection is for a Convention reason.[96]

It further noted that 'individual cases of abuse motivated by sexual orientation' can be analysed in this context.[97] This conceptualisation of the causal nexus by reference to the Guidelines is one of the rare moments of engagement with international guidance in Spanish case law, but it has not brought an end to the rejection of non-state actors.

As noted by Díaz Lafuente, while prior to the 2009 Law the Audiencia Nacional had at least *considered* the possibility of granting asylum to persons persecuted for their sexual orientation by non-state actors, it did so only if the authorities of the country of origin remained 'totally passive'.[98] Otherwise, a level of state protection was assumed to exist. Díaz Lafuente based this assessment on two decisions in particular. In SAN 2491/2007, the Audiencia Nacional rejected the claim of a Georgian gay man based on the following reasoning:

> The appellant acknowledges that when he was beaten up on October 17, 2002 the police intervened in the incident, but did not take all the forceful measures that were necessary. Police also intervened when strangers entered his house and beat his mother (File 5.7 of the record). It means, therefore, that *the police have not remained entirely passive* towards events related by the appellant and which he aims to build his asylum claim on.[99]

93 STS 3901/2011 de 16 de junio de 2011.
94 UNHCR (2002) *Guidelines on International Protection No. 2: 'Membership of a Particular Social Group' within the Context of Article 1A(2) of the 1951 Convention and/or Its 1967 Protocol Relating to the Status of Refugees*, 7 May 2002, HCR/GIP/02/02, www.refworld.org/docid/3d36f23f4.html.
95 UNHCR (2002) *Guidelines on International Protection No. 1: Gender-Related Persecution within the Context of Article 1A(2) of the 1951 Convention and/or Its 1967 Protocol Relating to the Status of Refugees*, 7 May 2002, HCR/GIP/02/01, www.refworld.org/docid/3d36f1c64.html.
96 SAN 5372/2008 de 10 de diciembre de 2008.
97 Ibid.
98 Díaz Lafuente, note 2, 460.
99 SAN 2491/2007 de 23 de mayo de 2007; emphasis added ['El propio recurrente reconoce que cuando fue golpeado en fecha 17 de Octubre de 2002 la policía intervino en el incidente, aunque no tomó medidas todo lo contundentes que eran precisas. La policía también intervino

In the case of the Cuban gay man who had been subjected to the mutilation of his breasts, the Audiencia Nacional concluded that the claimant had not shown that he had 'suffered a systematic and personal persecution by the authorities of his country, or that they have consented to it or remained passive'.[100] Notably, in both these cases, the claim failed precisely because the authorities were *not* entirely passive – and in the cases reviewed there was no example where this was considered to be the case.

The explicit inclusion of persecution by non-state actors in the new Law 12/2009 has not materially altered this approach. The decision in SAN 1832/2014, applying this law, is a good example of this inconsistency. The judgment extensively cites the very poorly drafted Asylum Office decision (amongst others, it contains the same text block twice, and this slip is repeated in the judgment), which presented the facts of the case as follows:

> He claims ... to be a national of Nigeria, who is homosexual, stating that he was persecuted in his country for a political and family issue, for maintaining a relationship with a college guy named Luis Antonio, when he was twelve. Luis Antonio was found dead, so the claimant feared for his life, because Luis Antonio's family came looking for him, killing his mother ... that following the death of his mother, his father, a political opponent of Luis Antonio's family, took the law into his own hands, resulting in a clash between families. That his father went to prison, and warned him to leave the country or he would kill him. That he has not suffered persecution for his sexual orientation.[101]

The Asylum Office concluded that the claimant 'states with absolute clarity that the alleged persecution stems from his family or social environment which cannot be considered persecution',[102] and that 'for the reasons why he left his home country, he said that he is gay, that he has had problems with his family for this reason, who rejected him, however, that he has not suffered any persecution for his sexuality, nor

cuando unos desconocidos entraron en su casa y golpearon a su madre (folio 5.7 del expediente). Quiere decir, pues, que la policía no se muestra del todo pasiva ante los sucesos que relata el recurrente y que pretende tomar como base de la petición de asilo'].

100 SAN 200/2007 de 30 de enero de 2007 ['hubiera sufrido una persecución sistemática y personal por parte de las autoridades de su país, o que estas la hayan consentido o mostrado pasivas'].

101 SAN 1832/2014 de 30 de abril de 2014 ['Alega ... es nacional de Nigeria, que es homosexual, manifestando que fue perseguido en su país por un tema político y familiar, al mantener una relación sentimental con un chico universitario, llamado Luis Antonio, cuando tenía doce años. Que a Luis Antonio lo encontraron muerto, por lo que temió por su vida, pues los familiares de Luis Antonio le fueron a buscar, matando a su madre ... Que tras la muerte de su madre, su padre, adversario político de la familia de Luis Antonio, se tomó la justicia por su mano, produciéndose un enfrentamiento entre familias. Que su progenitor fue a prisión, y le advirtió que se fuera del país o le mataría. Que no ha sufrido persecución por su condición sexual'].

102 Ibid. ['el solicitante manifiesta con absoluta claridad que la persecución alegada proviene de su familia o entorno social lo que no se puede considerar persecución'].

that he has reported any threats against him to the Nigerian authorities'.[103] In essence, the Audiencia Nacional agreed with this reasoning in its judgment and stated:

> In fact, the existence of specific and individualised persecution against the person of the applicant does not emerge from the account given, moreover, it does not offer any data or elements that specify persecution in the ambit of the situation described, because the applicant himself states in his application that the reason for leaving his country is that his family does not accept his homosexuality.[104]

Next to the resistance regarding non-state actors, the past persecution requirement also lingered. Two decisions from 2011 concerning Iranian gay men both contain the same paragraph from the respective Asylum Office's decision, which appears to interpret the 2002 UNHCR Gender Guidelines as requiring past persecution for cases based on sexual orientation. Citing to page 5, the Asylum Office claims that the 'UNHCR itself' ('el propio ACNUR') requires 'that these requests must be assessed not only in light of the existing regulations in the country of origin but applicants must show that they have been victims of acts of persecution (including discrimination) on grounds of their sexuality or sexual practices'.[105] While this constitutes another of the few attempts to engage with international guidance at all, not only is it surprising that the Asylum Office referred to the Gender Guidelines rather than the Guidance Note on sexuality-based claims which had been published in 2008,[106] but it also misinterpreted the guidance, which states at paragraph 16:

> Refugee claims based on differing sexual orientation contain a gender element. *A claimant's sexuality or sexual practices may be relevant to a refugee claim where he or she has been subject to persecutory (including discriminatory) action* on account of his or her sexuality or sexual practices. In many such cases, the claimant has refused to adhere to socially or culturally defined roles or expectations of behaviour

[103] Ibid. ['En cuanto a los motivos por los que abandonó su país de origen, manifestó que es homosexual, que ha tenido problemas con su familia por este motivo, que le rechazó, sin embargo, no ha sufrido persecución alguna por su condición sexual, ni ha denunciado ante las autoridades nigerianas amenazas contra su persona'].

[104] Ibid. ['En efecto, del relato ofrecido no se desprende la existencia de una persecución concreta e individualizada en la persona del recurrente, sin que, por otra parte, se ofrezcan en la demanda datos o elementos que particularicen una persecución en el ámbito de la situación que describe, pues el propio solicitante refiere en su demanda que el motivo para salir de su país es que su familia no acepta su condición de homosexual'].

[105] SAN 379/2011 de 31 de enero de 2011 ['En este contexto es muy importante remarcar siguiendo lo señalado por el propio ACNUR en sus Directrices sobre protección internacional: la persecución por motivos de género, en el contexto del artículo 1A de la Convención de 1951 sobre el Estatuto de los Refugiados y/o su Protocolo de 1957 [sic], Pag. 5, que estas peticiones deben ser valoradas no solo a luz de la regulación existente en el país de origen sino que los solicitantes deberán demostrar que han sido víctimas de acciones persecutorias (incluyendo la discriminación) por razones de su sexualidad o prácticas sexuales']. See also the same paragraph in SAN 1584/2011 de 24 de marzo de 2011.

[106] UNHCR (2008) *UNHCR Guidance Note on Refugee Claims Relating to Sexual Orientation and Gender Identity*, 21 November 2008, www.refworld.org/docid/48abd5660.html.

> attributed to his or her sex. The most common claims involve homosexuals, transsexuals or transvestites, who have faced extreme public hostility, violence, abuse, or severe or cumulative discrimination.[107]

The formulation in past tense appears to be open to an interpretation requiring past persecution. Clearly, however, this was not the intended meaning, and other guidance, such as the 2008 Guidance Note, confirm this. In both cases, the Audiencia Nacional judges cited the Asylum Office's decisions extensively without themselves engaging with any of the facts or reasoning in the cases, let alone correcting the misinterpretation of the UNHCR Gender Guidelines. However, these two decisions appear to be outliers, as they represent the only ones to be found with this interpretation of the Gender Guidelines. Nevertheless, they illustrate the strong resilience of the notion that past state persecution is a prerequisite of refugee status on sexuality grounds. As the following paragraphs demonstrate, support for a past persecution requirement was also found in the interpretation of the CJEU judgment in *X, Y and Z*.

Whereas the CJEU judgment in *Y and Z* on religion has not found entry into Spanish decisions on sexuality-based asylum claims – likely because, as in France, it did not resonate in Spanish case law with its focus on perceptibility rather than protected identity – the judgment in *X, Y and Z* was widely received and was (wrongly) understood in Spanish jurisprudence to confirm the requirement of past personal persecution. The Tribunal Supremo judgment from 12 February 2014 was the first to adopt the CJEU judgment and summarised it as follows:

> The obligation of national authorities ... is to determine whether '[...] in the applicant's country of origin, the term of imprisonment provided for by such legislation is applied in practice', as well as whether, based on this premise, 'in fact the applicant has a well-founded fear of being persecuted on return to his country of origin within the meaning of Article 2(c) of the Directive, read together with Article 9(3) thereof'.[108]

When faced with the case of a Nigerian gay man who had stated that he could not return to his country of origin because 'if his father sees him, he will kill him, in his country one cannot walk down the street with one's boyfriend, they can only be in closed places, if the police sees them in this situation they arrest them',[109] the

[107] UNHCR, note 95, paragraph 16, 5; emphasis added.

[108] STS 376/2014 de 12 de febrero de 2014 ['La obligación de las autoridades nacionales ante estas solicitudes, consistirá en determinar tanto si "[...] en el país de origen de la persona que solicita asilo, se aplica en la práctica la pena privativa de libertad prevista por una legislación de ese tipo" como si, a partir de la premisa anterior, "efectivamente, la persona que solicita asilo tiene fundados temores a ser perseguida al regresar a su país de origen, en el sentido del artículo 2, letra c), de la Directiva, en relación con el artículo 9, apartado 3, de la misma"'].

[109] SAN 2523/2014 de 18 de mayo de 2014 ['si lo ve su padre le mata, en su país no se puede ir por la calle con su novio, solo pueden estar en sitios cerrados, la policía si les ve en esa situación les arresta'].

Audiencia Nacional referred to the Tribunal Supremo's judgment and rephrased it as follows:

> In accordance with the recent judgment of the Tribunal Supremo dated February 12, 2014, citing the judgment of the Court of Justice of the European Union of November 7, 2013 (Case C-199/12) interpreting Directive 2004/83/EC Council, with respect to countries of origin, it is necessary to distinguish between 'legislation that merely classifies homosexual acts as an offence or misdemeanour . . . and legislation which punishes homosexual acts classified as a criminal offence with terms of imprisonment', establishing the obligation of a twofold examination on the courts: whether terms of imprisonment are applied in practice in the country of origin and whether the asylum seeker 'has well-founded fear of being persecuted on return to their country of origin'.[110]

Represented in this way, the decision appears to allow for an interpretation that requires not only legislation punishing homosexual acts with imprisonment but also that the claimant needs to individually and *personally* face such imprisonment. This seems to be the interpretation preferred by the Audiencia Nacional judge, who concluded:

> Well, from this perspective . . . we must conclude that such fear has not been established in this case. Not only due to the lack of credibility of the story, as stated above, but also because no persecution by the authorities of his country can be deduced from the applicant's own account, since the latter refers exclusively to threats within his home environment.[111]

Notably, the applicable law in this judgment is also Asylum Law 12/2009, which had explicitly provided for the possibility of persecution by non-state actors in Article 13.

In a very similar judgment, SAN 2533/2014, also applying Law 12/2009, the same conclusion was reached without reference to the Tribunal Supremo or the CJEU. The decision concerned another gay man from Nigeria whose father had denounced him to a homophobic group and whom the police did not protect but instead also persecuted for that sexual orientation. The decision cited extensively

[110] Ibid. ['Conforme a la reciente sentencia del Tribunal Supremo de fecha 12 de febrero de 2014, que cita la sentencia del Tribunal de Justicia de la Unión europea de 7 de noviembre 2013 (asunto C-199/12) interpretando Directiva 2004/83/CE del consejo, debe diferenciarse, respecto del país de origen, la "mera legislación que tipifique como delito o falta los actos homosexuales . . . y la legislación que castiga con penas privativas de libertad los actos homosexuales tipificados como delitos" estableciendo la obligación de los tribunales de examinar una doble vertiente: si se aplica en el país de origen en la practica la pena privativa de libertad y si la persona que solicita asilo "tiene fundados temores a ser perseguida al regresar a su país de origen"'].

[111] Ibid. ['Pues bien, desde esta perspectiva, aparte lo dicho anteriormente, debemos concluir que dicho temor no ha quedado establecido en el presente supuesto. No solo por falta de verosimilitud del relato, conforme hemos expuesto, sino también por cuanto del propio relato del actor no se deduce persecución por las autoridades de su país, pues se refiere exclusivamente a amenazas dentro de su entorno familiar'].

the poorly drafted decision of the Asylum Office, without engaging with it. The Asylum Office had mainly found that his allegations concerning his sexual orientation were vague and ambiguous and that his claim had to fail because the risk emanated only from his father, a non-state actor. It reasoned that the claimant could have changed residence to avoid the risk 'since his father does not dominate completely and effectively the entire national territory'[112] – a finding that might hint at the possibility of an internal relocation alternative, though there is no assessment to this end.

Conversely, in the case of SAN 1584/2011 (a judgment still applying the old Law 5/1984) concerning a gay man from Iran who was generally disbelieved, the fact that homosexuality is sanctioned with the death penalty, which 'does not exist only on paper but is practised and enforced', was held against the claimant who stated among other elements that he was caught having sex with his boyfriend by team members of his soccer club, resulting in his exclusion from the soccer team. The decision-maker reasoned that the described persecutor behaviour is implausible: 'Clearly, if the applicant had been "caught" having sex with another man in the restrooms of the club and reported to the police, the issue would not have been settled with a simple dismissal from the team as can reasonably be understood from the situation described in the applicant's country of origin.'[113] Here, too, the claimant had not reported a past (threat of) prosecution under the criminal laws of his country of origin, and his claim was dismissed.

Subsequent Tribunal Supremo judgments regularly made reference to the judgment in *X, Y and Z*.[114] One judgment in particular stands out in this context as the applicant, a gay man from Senegal, appealed the rejection of his case on the grounds that a requirement of personal and individualised persecution was not applicable to him.[115] The Audiencia Nacional had held that the persecution alleged by the claimant did not deserve international protection because he had not suffered personal and individualised persecution at the hands of one of the agents indicated in Article 13 of the Law of Asylum. By reference to the CJEU judgment in X, *Y and* Z as well as the Tribunal Supremo judgment of 12 February 2014, the claimant appealed on the grounds that the Senegalese criminal code foresees imprisonment for homosexual acts, such that gay people in Senegal can be considered a social group – without a requirement of personal and individualised persecution. He

[112] SAN 2533/2014 de 30 de mayo de 2014 ['puesto que su padre no domina de una forma total y con plena eficacia la totalidad del territorio nacional'].

[113] SAN 1584/2011 de 24 de marzo de 2011 ['Es evidente que si el solicitante hubiese sido "pillado" practicando sexo con otro hombre en los servicios del club y denunciado a la policía, el hecho no hubiese quedado en un simple despido del equipo como se puede razonablemente entender de la situación descrita en el país de origen del solicitante'].

[114] STS 4492/2015 de 2 de noviembre de 2015; STS 124/2016 de 25 de enero de 2016; STS 3847/2016 de 18 de julio de 2016.

[115] STS 4492/2015 de 2 de noviembre de 2015.

further argued that the decrease in convictions under these laws was due to the fact that gay people had gone into hiding.[116]

The Tribunal Supremo noted that the applicant's claim was based entirely on his 'sexual inclination (he claims to be homosexual) and the persecution that he suffered for that reason by his relatives and neighbours in his country of origin, as well as the fear that if he returns to his country he would be prosecuted, tried and sentenced to prison terms for his homosexual tendency'.[117] The Court then went on to rule that:

> In any case, the individualised nature of the acts of persecution derived from their homosexual status must be accredited, at least indicatively, and they must reach a certain degree of seriousness, such that they constitute a serious violation of fundamental human rights, and for this purpose it is necessary to examine the rules of the country of origin on the punishability of homosexual conduct, in order to determine whether the asylum seeker has effectively proven to have been persecuted and there are serious indications of well-founded fears of persecution in the event of return to their country of origin.[118]

After citing several sources stating that prosecutions under the Senegalese anti-gay laws have not been reported in recent years, the Court concluded:

> This shows, according to the case law cited above [X, Y *and* Z and STS of 12 February 2014], that there is no solid basis on which to base a well-founded fear of being prosecuted or sentenced by the authorities of the country of origin. In fact, despite the fact that according to his account, his homosexual tendency was publicised, being known by his family and neighbours, he has never been persecuted by the police nor were criminal proceedings instructed against him, which guarantees the inexistence of a well-founded fear of suffering persecution by the authorities of his country.[119]

[116] Ibid.

[117] Ibid. ['Todo su relato destinado a obtener la protección internacional como refugiado se basa en su inclinación sexual (afirma ser homosexual) y la persecución que por tal motivo sufrió en su país de origen por sus familiares y vecinos y en el temor de que si vuelve a su país sea perseguido, juzgado y condenado a penas de cárcel por su tendencia homosexual'].

[118] Ibid. ['En todo caso, debe acreditarse, siquiera indiciariamente, el carácter individualizado de los actos de persecución derivados de su condición de homosexual, y que éstos alcancen cierta gravedad, de modo que constituyan una grave violación de los derechos humanos fundamentales, y para ello es preciso examinar la reglamentación del país de origen sobre la punibilidad de las conductas homosexuales, a los efectos de determinar si efectivamente la persona que solicita el asilo ha demostrado haber sido objeto de persecución y existen indicios serios de los temores fundados de sufrir persecución en el supuesto de que regrese a su país de origen'].

[119] Ibid. ['Lo cual evidencia, conforme a la jurisprudencia antes apuntada, que no existe una base sólida en la que fundar un temor fundado a sufrir una persecución o condena penal por las autoridades de su país de origen. De hecho pese a que, según su relato, era publica su tendencia homosexual, siendo esta conocida por su familia y vecinos, nunca se le ha perseguido por la policía ni se instruyó causa penal contra él, lo que avala la inexistencia de un temor fundado a sufrir persecución por las autoridades de su país'].

This case is notable for a series of reasons. First, it maintains the interpretation that *X, Y and Z* requires a personal and individualised threat of prosecution. Whereas some German judges had adhered to the notion that *X, Y and Z* requires that criminal laws are actually applied either to establish the social group or to establish persecution in earlier applications of the judgment,[120] the Spanish approach is even more restrictive in linking that requirement to the particular claimant personally. The Tribunal Supremo, as the court of final instance in the Spanish system, thus proclaims an interpretation of the CJEU judgment that allows for the maintenance of the previous Spanish notion of 'personal and individualised' persecution.

Second, and related, the judgment entirely excludes persecution emanating from private actors – which the claimant *had* suffered in the past, but which is ignored in the assessment. The claim was specifically *not* limited to prosecution under criminal laws, but also extended to persecution from private actors, which is not further assessed by the Tribunal Supremo.

Thirdly, Spanish jurisprudence is largely devoid of human rights reasoning, or any considerations of rights and identity. This judgment makes reference to the definition of persecution (arguably derived from the *Qualification Directive*) based on a serious violation of fundamental human rights – but then does not apply this standard to assess the harm feared by the claimant once it is established that the criminal laws are not enforced.

Finally, and significantly, the judgment is one of the first to even *mention* the future-focused element of the risk assessment; Spanish jurisprudence entirely hinges on past persecution (further conditioned – variously – by the past prosecution requirement or the 'significant transcendence' requirement). The well-founded fear element is simply absent in Spanish asylum decision-making. Here, the claimant had explicitly formulated his fear of being prosecuted under the criminal laws *upon return*. The Court takes the fact that his sexual orientation was known to his neighbours and family – who had submitted him to harm for that reason – as a 'guarantee' of the 'inexistence of a well-founded fear of suffering persecution by the authorities of his country'. After all, he had not been prosecuted so far. The distinction between different standards of risk assessment for claimants who have suffered persecution in the past and those who have not is not taken into account in Spain simply because those who have not suffered persecution in the past will not succeed. Any future-focused assessment remains implicit and is derived from the question of whether the claimant has managed to avoid harm in the past. Therefore, the complicated questions linked to a claimant's ability to influence the future through their management of 'discretion' and 'disclosure' are avoided in Spain; that debate achieves a level of detailed legal reasoning that is far beyond Spanish jurisprudence.

[120] E.g., VG Düsseldorf, Urteil vom 13.12.2013, 13 K 3683/13.A (persecution only if criminal laws are applied), or VG Potsdam, Urteil vom 13.5.2014, VG 6 K 3802/13.A (no social group if criminal laws are not applied), and see discussion in previous chapter.

This does not, however, mean that 'discretion' logics do not apply in Spain – to the contrary, the core rationale concerning sexuality-based asylum claims is the presumption that claimants can evade the persecutor's attention, that is, remain 'discreet', and protection is only owed if that evasion has already failed – but only sometimes.

6.4 CONCLUSION: SPAIN – 'DISCRETION' IMPLICIT

The review of Spanish case law on sexuality-based claims reveals that while 'discretion' logics are active, they remain implicit, hidden underneath a pile of doctrinal approaches that are not in line with international guidance. Spain pursues an extremely restrictive approach to the refugee definition, which hinges on past persecution. It must also be noted in this context that Spain adopts an exceptionally limiting approach generally, such that out of the pool of cases, status was granted in only one appeal.[121] Eight appeals against inadmissibility were successful[122] and, in the case where it applied the CJEU judgment in X, *Y and* Z for the first time, the Tribunal Supremo remitted the case to the Audiencia Nacional[123] – though these cases then still had to be decided. All other claims were rejected. Prior to the *Qualification Directive*, the relevant notions were that 'mere' membership of the social group of gay people was not sufficient in order to be granted international protection, but rather, the claimant had to have been 'singled out' for persecution. In other words, the claimant had to have been identified as a group member by the persecutor (though there is rarely any inquiry into this process, such as considerations concerning expression of sexuality), *and* have been persecuted for that fact. Such persecution was taken to be synonymous with prosecution under criminal laws in pre–*Qualification Directive* doctrine.

When the *Qualification Directive* and the new Asylum Law 12/2009 provided for non-state persecutors, Spanish case law held on to the requirement of past persecution and developed the 'objective element', which required 'significant transcendence' of that past harm emanating from private actors; if the relevant persecutory harm was not related to prosecution under anti-gay laws, the claimed harm was only accepted if the claimant could provide clear evidence (ideally in the form of a document) stating that the reason for that harm was their sexual orientation.

Either way, the analysis in Spain always focuses backwards; the future-focused element of fear of harm upon return *now* is not addressed. If anything, lack of past

[121] STS 8251/2007 de 13 de diciembre de 2007, a case concerning a gay man from Cuba, who was found to have suffered personal persecution for that reason.

[122] At the time when non-admissibility to procedure on the basis that no Convention ground had been alleged was given up: SAN 4464/2002 de 12 de julio de 2002; SAN 5515/2006 de 30 de noviembre 2006; STS 7098/2005 de 30 de noviembre de 2005; STS 2331/2006 de 21 de abril de 2006; STS 8650/2006 de 14 de diciembre de 2006; STS 8248/2006 de 22 diciembre de 2006; STS 5650/2007 de 25 de julio de 2007; STS 6674/2007 de 4 de octubre de 2007.

[123] STS 376/2014 de 12 de febrero de 2014.

prosecution, or of significantly transcendent persecution, were taken as guarantees that the same would apply in the future.

The questions of what the claimant 'will do' upon return, let alone which aspects of their identity are protected, are not addressed in Spanish jurisprudence; there is no analysis as to what will happen to the claimant upon return. Accordingly, both the judgments in *HJ (Iran) and HT (Cameroon)* and in *Y and Z*, which developed approaches for this type of question, have not found their way into Spanish jurisprudence. This is unsurprising to the extent that there is generally a lack of reference to case law both from other EU countries and the CJEU in Spanish jurisprudence.[124] Even *X, Y and Z*, which pronounced itself on the question of restraint regarding expression of sexuality, had no repercussions in Spain regarding this element. It was only received concerning the aspect of criminalisation, effectively misunderstood to confirm a requirement of *past personal prosecution*. The logics are simple in Spain; if the claimant has so far avoided prosecution or significantly transcendent harm (be that because they have hidden their sexual orientation or for any other reason), they are not entitled to protection and can be returned to continue to avoid persecution.

The doctrinal location of these 'discretion' logics in Spain is less clear than in the other jurisdictions – not least because there is no systematic assessment of all the different elements. Whereas the nexus has become the focal point of the analysis for claims of persecution beyond prosecution, it usually serves to reject claims of those claimants who *have* already been 'outed' and suffered harm. The social group is usually quite easily accepted under the proviso that 'mere' membership is not enough. 'Discretion' logics are hidden in the 'singling out' criterion which refers to the risk of persecution, as it leads to rejection for those who have maintained a low profile and have been able to pass under the persecutors' radar.

Rights considerations play no role in Spanish case law generally, and certainly not with respect to defining the Convention ground. The jurisprudence focuses on the persecutor and their persecutory intent; if the persecutor has aimed at punishing this particular claimant for their sexual orientation, they are entitled to protection. What role the claimant and their ability to express the sexual orientation they are persecuted for plays in this context is not the subject of discussion. The scope of protection is thus restricted to those who not only have been 'outed' to the persecutor, but who have also already been subjected to harm due to this discovery. Spanish jurisprudence is, therefore, quite disconnected from international practice. The closest parallels are with the French 'discretion' reasoning in reverse, which – though still more liberal – likewise depends on the claimant having been identified as gay in the past, with a reduced future-focused assessment.

[124] María-Teresa Gil-Bazo (2010) '"Thou Shalt Not Judge" . . . Spanish Judicial Decision-Making on Asylum and the Role of Judges in Interpreting the Law', in Guy Goodwin-Gil and Hélène Lambert (eds.) *The Limits of Transnational Law – Refugee Law, Policy Harmonization and Judicial Dialogue in the European Union*, 107–124.

PART I

Conclusions

Acts or Identity – Invariably 'Discreet'

Research on the common law jurisdictions has described 'discretion' reasoning as an 'adaptive phenomenon',[1] that is 'extraordinarily widespread, resistant to challenge and strongly associated with high rejection rates'.[2] Likewise, this is reflected in those high-level European judgments that rejected a 'discretion' requirement. They maintained 'discretion' logics by allowing for a 'factual' finding that a claimant 'will' maintain secrecy. This study of asylum judgments concerning sexuality-based claims in Germany, France and Spain suggests that the same conclusions are true of these three civil law jurisdictions.

'Discretion' reasoning was prevalent in all countries (albeit in very different forms) before the *Qualification Directive* Europeanised refugee law, even where it was not immediately visible. The act/identity dichotomy revealed the very different shapes of 'discretion' logics in the three jurisdictions: France required a level of martyrdom by focusing on past expression; Germany required victimhood by focusing on internal suffering; and Spain required distinctiveness by focusing on individuals standing out from others. In other words, both France and Spain focused on the claimant's acts, whereas Germany was closer to common law jurisprudence in putting the identity and the 'quality' of the protected characteristic at the centre of the analysis. In both France and Spain, future-focused analysis was effectively absent; along with these different foci, France and Spain tended to look backwards for past discovery and persecution. Both jurisdictions thus escaped the complicated question of future discovery and merely by default relied on the claimant's ability to continue to conceal their sexual orientation from potential persecutors. The German analysis

[1] Janna Wessels (2013) '"Discretion" in Sexuality-Based Asylum Cases: An Adaptive Phenomenon', in Thomas Spijkerboer (ed.) *Fleeing Homophobia. Sexual Orientation, Gender Identity and Asylum*, London: Routledge, 55–81.

[2] Jenni Millbank (2012) 'The Right of Lesbians and Gay Men to Live Freely, Openly, and on Equal Terms Is Not Bad Law: A Reply to Hathaway and Pobjoy', 44(2) *New York University Journal of International Law and Politics* 497–527, 506.

was more forward-looking, deducing the risk of future discovery from the intensity of the characteristic – if it was deemed particularly important for the claimant, the likelihood that it would be revealed to the persecutor was deemed as given, otherwise, it was assumed that the claimant would be able and willing to continue to hide their 'inclination' from the persecutor.

Established practice was clearly unsettled by the *Qualification Directive*, and also, to some extent, by the CJEU judgments – especially in Germany. It is clear that there have been improvements. But they are hard-won and only pertain to some of the most prominent issues, such as the clarification that sexual orientation can constitute a social group, which was particularly doubted in Spain. But, at the same time, there are some indications that Germany and France moved from 'discretion' to disbelief in cases of past persecution while maintaining an adapted version of their previously established 'discretion' reasoning for those who have not suffered persecution in the past – that is, those who have not yet been 'outed' (to the persecutor). In that sense, France moved from externally manifested to 'claimed' sexual orientation, while Germany moved from a 'fateful determination' to an 'importance' (or 'identity-defining') criterion. Much as 'discretion' reasoning was transformed rather than eliminated by the judgment in *HJ (Iran) and HT (Cameroon)* in the United Kingdom, this study thus indicates that 'discretion' logic is deeply entrenched in German and French asylum practice – when challenged, it tends to reappear in a different guise, with similarly far-reaching consequences. This is striking because Germany and France have opposite approaches to 'discretion' at the outset; France focuses on the act and the Convention ground, whereas Germany assesses the claimant's identity and discusses it in the context of the well-foundedness of the fear.

This review is thus a clear illustration of the workings of the act/identity double bind. Both approaches are grounded in a common core, namely the assumption that secrecy is synonymous with safety – the fear of persecution is well founded only if the claimant externalises their identity and can no longer pass unnoticed by the persecutor. For Germany, the question then becomes that of assessing when claimants *can* or *must* or *should* refrain from such externalisation. In addressing this question, Germany has developed the notion that protection is owed when the sexual orientation is 'identity-defining' for the applicant, such that having to give it up would be contrary to human dignity as a fundamental right. In French jurisprudence, on the basis of the reviewed judgments, this latter question has so far been avoided as claimants had already been outed. One possible approach is the interpretation that the claimant must 'claim' their sexual orientation in the sense of adopting and expressing it.

While Spain runs counter to French and German jurisprudence in many respects, it builds on the same concern: namely, the question of whether the claimant has passed underneath the persecutor's radar. In Spain, this assessment was derived from the notion that 'mere' group membership was not sufficient; a claimant had to have been 'singled out' for prosecution under anti-gay laws or subject to 'significantly transcendent' harm. In other words, they had to have been *identified* as a group member by the persecutor *such that harm was inflicted* (mere identification was not sufficient) – demonstrating some parallels to French jurisprudence in this respect.

Neither France nor Spain had formulated a 'reasonable requirement' for the claimant to be 'discreet'. This was, however, in essence the contentious question for all three high-level European judgments rejecting 'discretion' reasoning. Germany in contrast, had operated on the basis of a core/margins distinction, considering only the 'sexual forum internum' to be protected. The extent to which the three judgments affected jurisprudence in the three case studies therefore differs substantially. Germany proved to be the most receptive, likely for two main reasons. Firstly, German judges and scholars appear to take part in the refugee law dialogue more actively than their Spanish and French counterparts. This is evidenced by, inter alia, the fact that three of the four 'discretion'-related transferrals for preliminary rulings proceeded from Germany. Secondly and importantly, as a consequence the issues discussed in the judgments made more sense in the German context than in the other two due to the focus on limiting the claimant's future expression of *identity*. Although 'discretion' reasoning does play a role in both France and Spain, it is neither constructed around the question of *why* the claimant 'will behave' in a particular way (*HJ (Iran) and HT (Cameroon)* – social reasons vs fear), nor around the question of what the claimant is *entitled* to do (both CJEU judgments – core/margins distinction or expecting restraint). Instead, 'discretion' logics are grounded in the act of manifestation which leads to the discoverability of the claimant by the persecutor. Ultimately, however, both paths lead to the same destination – because both rely on the assumption that the claimant will only be subjected to harm if they actively externalise their sexual orientation in one way or another.

As a result of the different approaches, the location of 'discretion' differed in the three jurisdictions, and was not necessarily stable; in the decision-making process, different elements of the definition are the focus of analysis at different points. In France, 'discretion' reasoning took place at the level of the Convention ground, whereas in Germany it has traditionally influenced the risk assessment, though more recently it appears to have spilled over into the establishment of the social group. In Spain, in contrast, 'discretion' logics were implicit in the 'singling out' criterion, though it is unclear whether that was understood to relate to the group or the risk assessment; and in the 'significant transcendence' requirement that was linked to the nexus clause. This finding also chimes with observations concerning the common law jurisdictions, where there was much uncertainty as to where to locate the question of 'discretion'. States link the 'discretion' logics to different elements of the refugee definition, such that it changes locus depending on which jurisdiction we look at. Once the sexual orientation of the claimant is conceptually separated into sexual *identity* and related *conduct*, only one of them is required for the establishment of the Convention ground, while the other can move around freely and play into other elements of the definition. In Germany, for example, the 'act' element is moved to the well-founded fear analysis. The stable identity signals the claimant's group membership, but the consequent expression is considered in the context of the risk assessment. Simultaneously, this means that Germany effectively breaks down the particular social group into a protected group of those with an irreversible identity and an unprotected group of those with merely an 'inclination'. The justification for this breakdown is found in the well-foundedness of the fear, which is reasoned to be a necessary corollary of a fixed and stable identity because the claimant is unable to pass unnoticed. Such processes thus lead to further confusion about what the Convention grounds are, and the ways in which the dichotomy is employed create exclusionary potential.[3]

More generally, the case studies suggest a number of broader conclusions. Firstly, it has become clear that 'discretion' reasoning is an issue for refugee law overall. It is not limited to any particular jurisdiction or any particular type of doctrinal construction. Rather, it emerges in very different forms. Even the clear rejection of the 'discretion' *requirement* (in accordance with the judgments from CJEU and the UK Supreme Court) has not put an end to calls to circumscription both in jurisprudence and in scholarship. Germany continues to require restraint based on the importance of the characteristic for the claimant, whereas Hathaway and Pobjoy maintain a core/margins approach to determine which types of concealment are acceptable. France and Spain circumvent the question of the claimant's identity and rights by cutting the analysis short, skipping the future-focused risk assessment and requiring that a claimant has already been outed and suffered harm. Otherwise they are sent back – to (continued) 'discretion' by default. In these jurisdictions, the paradox that the claimant is at once entitled to engage in (religious, political, social group-constituting) expression of the Convention ground – and not – is brushed over through the backward-looking analysis.

Secondly, although it is not always analysed in that context, 'discretion' reasoning is *created* at the level of the Convention ground. It splits the *reason* for persecution into acts and identity. Once that move is made, the elements can float around independently and influence other parts of the status assessment analysis. The consequences are far reaching and distorting for the entire analysis of the different elements in status determination. When act and identity are moved around independently between the different elements of the definition, they are difficult to trace and create a legal mess. Due to assumptions of immutability, this process is likely particularly pronounced for sexuality-based cases, where the invitation to establish the 'essence' of a person or their group may be stronger than for other grounds of claim. In contrast, it is generally more accepted that political opinion, for example,

[3] Janet Halley (1993) 'Reasoning about Sodomy: Act and Identity in and after Bowers v. Hardwick', 79(7) *Virginia Law Review* 1721–1780, 1770; building on Eve Kosofsky Sedgwick (1990) *Epistemology of the Closet*, Berkeley: University of California Press.

can be fleeting. However, a similar distinction between act and identity also occurs for other Convention grounds. The example of the religious forum internum in German practice and the *Y and Z* judgment are evidence of this. In order to understand the resilience of 'discretion', it is therefore worth exploring the ways in which the Convention grounds are conceptualised in refugee law doctrine more closely.

Thirdly, 'discretion' reasoning is at the core of the question of what is protected under refugee law: the justifications of 'discretion' logics, as well as the place where they are located, reveal the ways in which jurisdictions grapple with the scope of protection – the places where they draw lines. It is a result of the tension, identified in Chapter 1, between the fundamentality principle and the severity argument. 'Discretion' reasoning functions as the patch for the tension within the refugee definition that emerges from the fact that persecution constitutes a very serious situation created by the persecutor, which must be feared for a reason, concerning which the claimant has some leverage. The materialisations of 'discretion' logics in Germany, France and Spain are evidence of attempts to find more or less principled approaches to reconciling the fundamentality principle with the severity argument to determine the scope of what it is that is protected under the Refugee Convention.

Part II explores these points in more detail and conducts an exploration of the various tensions involved in conceptualising the Convention grounds: how is it determined *what* is protected in general terms, and *who* is protected more specifically? What is the role of the claimant, the strength of their identification with the impugned characteristic and the ways they express it (or not)? To what extent does the persecutor define the parameters of *what* – and therefore *who* – is persecuted, and hence, protected? Which standards are drawn on to determine the scope of protection and with which consequences? And, in particular, do human rights help us to answer any of these questions?

PART II

Exploring the Limits of Protection

Part I explored decision-making practice concerning sexuality-based asylum claims in France, Germany and Spain. The different countries' jurisprudence revealed that 'discretion' reasoning was prevalent in all three jurisdictions, and remained resistant to challenges over time, albeit with significant differences in focus. France, for example, granted protection only to those who had manifested their sexual orientation, whereas Germany limited protection to those with a determined identity. Either act or identity can stand in for the group, while the respective counterpart can be assessed as part of another aspect of the Convention definition. The fact that it is sometimes the act that counts for the Convention ground, and other times the identity, makes the reasoning more difficult to reconstruct.

Taking together the insights from Part I, it emerges that it is necessary to take a closer look at the workings of the Convention grounds. The conceptualisation of the Convention grounds has so far often been somewhat neglected in refugee law doctrine as the focus has been on persecution, commonly understood to be the core notion of the refugee definition. In order to more fully grasp the ways in which 'discretion' logics emerge and persist, Part II therefore turns the analysis around and looks at the way Convention grounds are conceptualised, both within the jurisdictions under review and in the common law jurisdictions. This is based on the understanding that, although 'discretion' logics are attached to a range of different elements of the refugee definition, the act/identity dichotomy – which is at the root of this process – is created at the level of the Convention grounds. As illustrated in Part I, the modification of behaviour or the stability of the identity always relate to the Convention ground, even if the discussion revolves around other technical elements. For example, when the argument is made that a claimant has no well-founded fear of persecution because they can or will hide, this 'hiding' refers to the Convention ground. 'Discretion' reasoning thus originates in the Convention ground, and then variously slips into the persecution assessment, the nexus requirement and the well-founded fear analysis. As part of the analysis in Part II, the points where such slips from the Convention grounds to other elements of the definition take place will be drawn out.

The paradoxical situation that the Convention protects fundamental characteristics that should not be foregone (the fundamentality principle) whereas refugee protection is not designed to provide the same level of rights and freedoms for all (the severity argument) is at the core of the conceptualisations of the Convention grounds. The different approaches to defining the persecuted (or protected) groups exhibit the struggles over reconciling this paradox, which is exacerbated by the fact that claimants do have a degree of control over 'discretion' and disclosure – though, as Sedgwick reminds us, it is never to be taken for granted how much.[1] Consequently, the analysis gets caught up in considerations concerning the claimant, their identity, past and future behaviour and the motives for their conduct, as well as their rights and entitlements.

Part II explores different approaches to conceptualising the Convention grounds and draws out the ways in which they are particularly susceptible to 'discretion'. It is divided into three chapters, addressing political opinion, membership of a particular social group and religion in turn. The first draws on Grahl-Madsen's early approach to conceptualising political opinion to illustrate the clash between applying an external, general standard of what can comprise the *protected* group on the one hand and going with the persecutor's definition of what is the *persecuted* group on the other (Chapter 7). Chapter 8 juxtaposes the competing definitions for 'membership of a particular social group', which is the ground which is most commonly used for sexuality-based claims, and draws out how each of them responds to the central tension between fundamentality and triviality. The final chapter of this part focuses on religion, to explore the ways in which human rights are drawn on to establish the parameters of the Convention grounds and the scope of protection (Chapter 9). All three chapters ultimately reflect on the question of what is protected and why, and reveal that the issue is far from settled – rather, the central tension that a claimant is simultaneously entitled to the expression of the persecuted characteristic, and not, cuts across time, from 1960s refugee law scholarship to modern human rights–based approaches to refugee law doctrine, as well as across Convention grounds, ranging from political opinion to membership of a particular social group and religion.

[1] Eve Kosofsky Sedgwick (1990) *Epistemology of the Closet*, Berkeley: University of California Press, 75, and see Chapter 2.

7

Drawing Lines

Distinguishing *Protected* Groups from *Persecuted* Groups

According to the Refugee Convention definition, persecution must be feared *because* the claimant is of a particular race, religion, nationality, particular social group or political opinion. Much like the concept of persecution, the Convention grounds are not further defined in the Refugee Convention. There are no clear indicators to determine under which circumstances the persecution feared is for one of the stated reasons. What does political opinion mean for the purposes of the refugee definition? What does religion involve in this context? Even more confusingly, what constitutes a 'particular social group' – and, importantly, what does not? The definition of the Convention grounds is essential to 'discretion' reasoning. In general terms, a definition lays out what a notion includes and, significantly, what it excludes; it sets the boundaries of a concept. This chapter is the first of three to explore the ways in which attempts to grasp and define the Convention grounds are linked to 'discretion' reasoning. The rationale that spans the three chapters is that any definition of the persecuted characteristic puts limits on the Convention grounds that enable 'discretion' reasoning, because any form of behaviour/act (e.g. 'trivial') or type of identity (e.g. 'mere inclination') that is deemed to be beyond the scope of the so-defined Convention grounds would be beyond the scope of protection. Remarkably, the tension between the notion that the Convention grounds should not be hidden on the one hand, while refugee protection is only available for particularly serious situations on the other, remains stable – both across time and across Convention grounds and approaches. This chapter traces this tension in Grahl-Madsen's reflections on the political opinion ground in his 1966 standard work; the subsequent chapters identify it in the continuously competing approaches to particular social group (Chapter 8) and in the most recent attempts to define the Convention grounds by recourse to human rights with a particular focus on religion (Chapter 9).

7.1 THE CONVENTION GROUNDS AND THE PROBLEM OF CATEGORIES

Though the fact that protection is extended to one of five reasons can be seen as making the Refugee Convention an anti-discrimination instrument in some ways, the list of specified grounds is notably shorter than that of human rights instruments generated in the same era.[1] This more limited coverage is generally considered to be a result of recent experience at the time of drafting the Convention – it was initially intended only to provide protection to those displaced as a result of persecution under the Nazi regime and the emerging Cold War.[2] Consequently, the Convention grounds refer to characteristics that are difficult to describe in general terms. Scholars tried to 'categorise' or 'group' them early on. In his groundbreaking 1966 book *The Status of Refugees in International Law*, Atle Grahl-Madsen made a first attempt.[3] His early contribution to refugee law scholarship is surprisingly revealing with respect to the ongoing challenges connected with the conceptualisation of the Convention grounds; few scholars have explicitly engaged with them in a similar way since.[4] Therefore, it is worthwhile to explore Grahl-Madsen's reflections and assess their validity for current debates.

In his considerations on the Convention grounds, Grahl-Madsen proposed a distinction between Convention reasons that are 'beyond the control of the individual' on the one hand and reasons of an 'individual character' on the other. Grahl-Madsen viewed race, nationality, membership of a particular social group and certain aspects of religion as falling in the former group and political opinion and 'active religion' as falling in the latter.[5] Even at that early stage, Grahl-Madsen noted that 'race' in the context of the Refugee Convention referred to 'social prejudice rather than a more or less scientific division of mankind'.[6] Accordingly, the concept of race must be understood as a social rather than an ethnographic concept.[7] This approach takes the perspective of the persecutor into account – it does not matter either whether 'genetics' assign a person to a particular ethnic group or whether the persons themselves identify with that group, as long as they are faced with persecution based on the respective *assumption* of the persecutor. Similarly, according to

1 Nora Markard (2007) 'Fortschritte im Flüchtlingsrecht? Gender Guidelines und geschlechtsspezifische Verfolgung', 40(4) *Kritische Justiz* 373–390, 374.

2 See e.g. Efrat Arbel, Catherine Dauvergne and Jenni Millbank (2014) 'Introduction', in Efrat Arbel, Catherine Dauvergne and Jenni Millbank (eds.) *Gender in Refugee Law: From the Margins to the Centre*, London: Routledge, 1–16, 3.

3 Atle Grahl-Madsen (1966) *The Status of Refugees in International Law – Volume I: Refugee Character*, Leyden: A. W. Sijthoff, 220–253.

4 A rare and recent exception can be found here: Catherine Dauvergne (2016) 'Toward a New Framework for Understanding Political Opinion', 37 *Michigan Journal of International Law* 243–298.

5 Grahl-Madsen, note 3, 217.

6 Ibid., 218.

7 Ibid.

Grahl-Madsen, 'nationality' as used in the refugee definition 'applies also to persecution because of an alleged – as contradistinguished from a real – nationality'.[8] Again, both the persecutor and the claimants themselves can attribute the characteristic. In that sense, group membership can be established in two ways, either via the attribution of the persecutor or via 'actual' membership of the claimant.

In Grahl-Madsen's understanding, membership of a particular social group also belongs to the category of characteristics 'beyond the control' of a claimant, such that they would be faced with persecution 'merely because of [their] background'.[9] However, some of the social groups he mentions by way of example are clearly not beyond the individual members' control:

> Nobility, capitalists, landowners, civil servants, businessmen, professional people, farmers, workers, members of a linguistic or other minority, even members of certain associations, clubs or societies, all constitute social groups of various kinds.[10]

The fact that the social group ground sits uncomfortably with Grahl-Madsen's categorisation speaks to its lack of clarity[11] – but in combination with the fact that the subchapter on 'Membership of a Particular Social Group' barely covers one page in Grahl-Madsen's important work, it also indicates that the social group ground simply did not play a major role at the time, and he did not devote much thought to it.[12]

To Grahl-Madsen, religion and political opinion were different characteristics in the sense that they are 'individual' in character. The exact meaning of the term 'individual' remains nebulous. Given that it was put forth as the counterpart to characteristics 'beyond the control' of the individual, it can only be speculated that it refers to the fact that a person has some control over their beliefs, in contrast to categories such as race or nationality. On this basis then, the Convention ground religion

> covers persecution on a variety of different grounds, notably: (1) membership of a religious community (church, sect, order, [etc.]; (2) personal faith or private worship; (3) participation in or insistence on certain forms of public worship; (4) religiously motivated acts or omissions (e.g. refusal to do military service).[13]

8 Ibid., 219.
9 Ibid., 220.
10 Ibid., 219.
11 Global Consultations on International Protection (2003) *Summary Conclusions: Membership of a Particular Social Group*, adopted at the expert roundtable organized by the United Nations High Commissioner for Refugees and the International Institute of Humanitarian Law, San Remo, Italy, 6–8 September 2001, www.refworld.org/pdfid/470a33b40.pdf, 312; see also: Michelle Foster (2012) *The 'Ground with the Least Clarity': A Comparative Study of Jurisprudential Developments Relating to 'Membership of a Particular Social Group'*, UNHCR Division of International Protection, Geneva, August 2012, PPLA/2012/02.
12 Grahl-Madsen, note 3, 219–220.
13 Ibid., 218.

It is remarkable that the CJEU judgment in *Y and Z* had to deal essentially with points (3) and (4). Half a century after Grahl-Madsen's exploration of these questions, the extent to which claimants could live their religion in public remained a controversial issue in refugee law.[14] Though Grahl-Madsen limited his discussion of religion to half a page, he referenced the section on 'political opinion and expression thereof', which extensively discusses similar points for the political opinion ground and arguably applies in analogy. It is in this section that he attempted to develop a principled approach to conceptualising what is protected under the Refugee Convention – and what is not.

At the height of the Cold War, political opinion was the most significant Convention ground. Grahl-Madsen engaged in a detailed effort to define political opinion, which extends over thirty-four pages.[15] Such efforts to conceptualise the Convention grounds appear to have been superseded (or at least moved sites) since political opinion and religion have been mapped onto the respective human rights. This is because reference to a human right appears to nullify the requirement for a complicated conceptualisation, as the discussion in Chapter 9 will show. Possibly because there is no 'easy way out' for sexual orientation claims (namely, mapping sexual orientation onto a 'freedom of sexual orientation'[16]) – and many other social group claims – much of the controversy as laid out by Grahl-Madsen in the context of political opinion is repeated in the contemporary debate surrounding sexuality and particular social groups, as will be outlined in Chapter 8. This chapter first lays out the fundamentals of Grahl-Madsen's discussion concerning the Convention ground of political opinion and then maps them onto similar arguments and concerns in the jurisdictions and case law reviewed in this study.

The main aim of this chapter is to draw out the ramifications of the question of whether one focuses on the claimant or the persecutor to define the persecuted group and establish membership. In line with queer theory, the analysis ties in with the insight that, while 'discretion' and disclosure are partly in the hands of the claimant, the decision is never fully theirs. The 'cause' for the attribution of a characteristic may lie in the genuine identity of the claimant or in a misunderstanding or misinterpretation by the persecutor, either based on a particular conduct of the claimant, or entirely unrelated to the claimant. These issues neatly emerge from Grahl-Madsen's exploration of political opinion as a grounds for persecution.

14 *Federal Republic of Germany* v. *Y and Z*, Joined Cases C-71/11 and C-99/11, Court of Justice of the European Union, 5 September 2012.

15 Grahl-Madsen, note 3, 220–253.

16 See Tobin's critique that in their concern to frame sexuality-based claims in terms of human right, both Hathaway and Pobjoy and the UK Supreme Court refer to a series of invented 'rights': John Tobin (2012) 'Assessing GLBTI Refugee Claims: Using Human Rights Law to Shift the Narrative of Persecution within Refugee Law', 44(2) *New York University Journal of International Law and Politics* 447–484.

7.2 DEFINING POLITICAL OPINION: 'THREE REALISATIONS'

Grahl-Madsen defined political opinion within the Convention as including people who are 'alleged or known to hold opinions contrary to or critical of the policies of the government or ruling party' and, 'without stretching the term . . . also . . . that the person . . . has more or less publicly expressed such opinions'.[17] As with religion, Grahl-Madsen identified an act/identity distinction for political opinion, and he clearly considered the public expression aspect as problematic. He made out three types of 'realisation' of political opinion that are relevant for the Convention:

(1) 'simply because he *holds* – or is alleged to hold – certain political opinions'
(2) 'only because of their *exercise* of their *right to freedom* of opinion and expression and the similar rights set forth in the Universal Declaration of Human Rights'
(3) '*actions* which go beyond the mere expression of political opinion'[18]

The first two categories – holding and exercising their right to freedom of political opinion – are defined broadly and deemed straightforward. Although Grahl-Madsen made reference to the 'right to freedom of opinion and expression' and the Universal Declaration of Human Rights more generally at this point, he did not further engage with that right when defining political opinion. Rather, Grahl-Madsen applied a very expansive notion of 'political', further specifying that

> any real, alleged or implied opinion which leads to persecution in violation of the Universal Declaration of Human Rights, may qualify as a 'political opinion' in the sense of the Refugee Convention . . . *because the very fact that he is threatened with persecution implies that the persons in power consider his opinion 'political' in the existing circumstances*. This is but another facet of what we have pointed out in another connexion, namely that *the behaviour of the persecutors determines what persons shall be considered refugees*.[19]

In other words, the crucial factor was not whether the claimant held an opinion that could be considered political, or that was captured by the freedom of opinion and expression, but that the persecutor interpreted it as such. In principle, Grahl-Madsen considered that the persecutor's perspective defined the meaning of 'political'. The notion that it is the persecutor who determines who is a refugee is central to Grahl-Madsen's thinking. According to this principle, Grahl-Madsen noted:

> If a person has *committed some act* and as a result is liable to persecution because the *authorities of his home country read a political motivation into his action*, we

[17] Grahl-Madsen, note 3, 220.
[18] Ibid., 250; emphasis added.
[19] Ibid.; emphasis added.

> have a repetition of the theme that the behaviour of the persecutors is decisive with respect to which persons shall be considered refugees: he is in fact a (potential) victim of persecution for reasons of (alleged or implied) political opinion and may consequently invoke the Convention on an equal footing with those who were motivated by true political beliefs.[20]

Much as with race and nationality, Grahl-Madsen identified two alternatives: 'true' political beliefs, and imputation by the persecutor. The 'theme' that the persecutor is decisive for refugeehood is a thread that runs through Grahl-Madsen's book. Among other things, it informs his understanding of the unreliability of 'discretion' in the context of 'Political Opinion and Expression Thereof' – even if a claimant tries to keep their opinion to themselves, they may be discovered and persecuted:

> A person living under a regime which exercises 'thought control' may keep his political opinions to himself, or at least try to do so, yet he may become a victim of persecution 'for reason of political opinion' . . . Firstly, his past may catch up with him . . . Secondly, persons may be provoked to show their non-conformity with the existing regime . . . Thirdly, a person may – in private – express a political opinion or act in some way which indicates a certain political attitude; yet he may be denounced by his own child, by his closest 'friend' or associate, or by some passing stranger.[21]

Such considerations have more recently been put forth in strikingly similar terms for claims based on sexual orientation by a series of authors.[22] In the context of discussing the concept of 'persecution', Grahl-Madsen also reiterated the notion that 'it is the persecutor who determines what persons shall be considered refugees', citing a 1957 German case that held that it does not matter whether the expected persecution would be the reaction of the authorities to a preceding 'active behaviour' of the refugee (this somewhat tautological expression underlines the active element on the part of the claimant).[23]

20 Ibid., 251–252; emphasis added.

21 Ibid., 224–225.

22 See e.g. Catherine Dauvergne and Jenni Millbank (2003) 'Before the High Court: Applicants S396/2002 and S395/2002, a Gay Refugee Couple from Bangladesh', 25 *Sydney Law Review* 97–124, 122 ('even an individual who wishes to hide, who desperately wishes – and takes all possible steps – to remain closeted does, in fact become increasingly "visible" with the passage of time'); or Ghassan Kassisieh (2008) 'From Lives of Fear to Lives of Freedom: A Review of Australian Refugee Decisions on the Basis of Sexual Orientation', *Gay & Lesbian Rights Lobby*, Glebe, at 70 ('Most importantly, the decision [to disclose one's sexuality] is often out of the applicant's control. Sexual minorities may choose to disclose their sexuality to close friends who later betray their trust. Rumours are readily circulated in close-knit societies, especially where applicants contravene cultural and gender norms, such as by refusing to get married or remaining single in older age'); and discussion further shortly.

23 Grahl-Madsen, note 3, 192, citing Ansbach Court case 2753-54II/56 (10 September 1957) ['Ob die erwartete Verfolgung die Reaktion des Gewalthabers auf ein vorausgehendes aktives Verhalten des Fluechtlings bilden mochte, darauf kommt es beim Vollzug der G[enfer] K[onvention] nicht an'].

However, this principle has a limit in Grahl-Madsen's reasoning – under certain circumstances, he considers that it *does* matter whether persecution was the reaction to a preceding 'active behaviour'. In addition to holding and expressing an opinion, Grahl-Madsen identified the differently situated case of an 'act beyond mere expression'.

7.3 ACTS 'BEYOND MERE EXPRESSION': GRAHL-MADSEN'S TWO SCHOOLS OF THOUGHT

In Grahl-Madsen's analysis, the holding and expression of a political opinion is unproblematically encompassed by the notion of political opinion – and the meaning of what is 'political' is defined by the persecutor. But Grahl-Madsen does not extend this principle fully to what he terms acts beyond mere expression:

> If, on the other hand, a person is liable to sanctions, not merely because he holds or expresses certain opinions, but because of certain acts which he has committed, the situation is different. Here, the person concerned must show the political relevance of his motives.[24]

Inconsistent with his earlier approach, Grahl-Madsen considers that there *are* limits to what can be considered 'political' beyond what the persecutor may perceive as such – and in such cases, he argues that the claimant's motives (their identity) become the decisive factor. Difficulties inevitably impose themselves. It remains unclear on what basis Grahl-Madsen distinguishes between political opinion 'pure and simple' and expression thereof on the one hand, and acts 'going beyond' on the other. The examples he lists for expression of political opinion include the waving of a particular flag, the construction of a road on one side of the river and not the other and voting for a particular candidate.[25] Active resistance, desertion and draft evasion, unauthorised departure or absence from the home country and political activities abroad, in contrast, were considered as acts going beyond the mere expression of an opinion. But what is the substantive difference between waving a red flag and 'active resistance'? This is particularly unclear in view of Grahl-Madsen's observation that any act can be an expression of an opinion if it is understood as such.[26] Such a blurry distinction is clearly echoed in Hathaway and Pobjoy's attempt to distinguish between acts reasonably required to express sexual orientation on the one hand versus acts 'on the margins' on the other.[27] Whereas Hathaway and Pobjoy sought guidance in human rights law in order to determine the boundaries, which will be discussed further shortly, Grahl-Madsen reviewed refugee law scholarship from

24 Ibid., 250.
25 Ibid.
26 Ibid., 251–252.
27 James Hathaway and Jason Pobjoy (2012) 'Queer Cases Make Bad Law', 44(2) *New York University Journal of International Law and Politics* 315–389.

the time and identified two schools of thought for the treatment of acts beyond mere expression. Grahl-Madsen labelled them the 'restrictive school' and the 'liberal school'.

7.3.1 *The 'Restrictive Doctrine': Focus on the Persecutor*

According to the so-called restrictive doctrine, acts beyond the mere expression of political opinion become relevant for refugee law if they are met with a politically motivated sanction. That is, the state must attach an (assumed) political opinion to the claimant's act, which must be decisive for the nature and severity of the punishment that is imposed. According to Grahl-Madsen, this view is 'best in keeping with the wording of Article 1A(2)'.[28] The focus here is not on the claimant's identity and the question of the genuineness of their motives, but on the persecutor and *their* motives. Put differently, the *harm* must be inflicted due to the political opinion that the persecutor attaches to the claimant.[29] Many of Grahl-Madsen's examples refer to situations concerning laws of general application, in particular draft evasion. For example, in the logics of this approach, punishment for conscientious objection amounts to persecution only if it is influenced by the fact that the conscientious objector was (assumed to be) guided by political or religious reasons.[30] This influence must be evidenced by a more severe punishment. In other words, the persecutor must apply a more severe punishment due to the political motivation they read into the claimant's act.

But the approach can also be applied more broadly, in the sense that it is the imagination of the persecutor that defines what and who is persecuted. Rather than 'restrictive', such a broader persecutor perception approach can in fact be very inclusive, as it does not require that group members identify with the persecuted characteristic in any way[31] – and it strongly resonates with Grahl-Madsen's basic theme that it is the persecutor who defines who is a refugee.

It can be argued that both Spain and France applied a version of the persecutor's perspective, although, rather than applying it to define the persecuted group generally (*what* is persecuted), both applied it to establish each claimant's *membership* of the group (*who* is persecuted), based on the perceptibility or visibility of the claimant as a holder of the characteristic. Likewise, the Spanish 'significant transcendence' criterion can be described as a perverted version of this approach; only if the claimant could prove that the persecutor committed the harm because of their sexual orientation were their claims admitted in Spain, irrespective of the claimant's

28 Grahl-Madsen, note 3, 249.
29 Grahl-Madsen cites Zink as an author supportive of this view: Ibid., 220–221.
30 Ibid., 233.
31 See also Caroline Lantero (2013) 'La notion de groupe social au sens de la convention de Genève dans la jurisprudence française', 41 *Actualités Juridiques – Droit Administratif* 2364–2370, 2367.

actual identity.[32] This approach becomes restrictive because it slides into the nexus analysis; rather than concluding from context and circumstances of differential treatment that the harm was inflicted due to the sexual orientation, written evidence is required to prove it.

This persecutor's perception approach has in particular one weakness, which is discussed in Grahl-Madsen's book, namely the 'bad faith' concern of people committing acts in order to cause political persecution without in fact holding the opinion that is then attributed to them by the persecutor.[33] Grahl-Madsen cites a German case from 1962 to illustrate this problem, which held:

> Such a broad right cannot be attributed to the person who, for reasons of self-interest, puts himself at risk of being 'politically' persecuted, but rather, one's own attitude and conviction, even if they are expressed only by belonging to a certain group which is fought by the state, must have triggered the political threat.[34]

Without forming a determined position on the point, Grahl-Madsen concluded that one '*may* have to draw a distinction … between those who unwittingly or unwillingly have committed a politically pertinent act, and those who have done it for the sole purpose of getting a pretext for claiming refugeehood'.[35] At this point, the analysis slides back into the assessment of the claimant's 'true' identity, rather than relying on the persecutor's perception, in order to create a 'possibility for screening out those unworthy ones whose claim to refugeehood goes back to their own' decision, which is not always based on recognisable motives.[36] This is a response to the concern that asylum 'might be devaluated at its core' if it were so easy to achieve that joining an emigrant organisation was sufficient to warrant protection.[37]

A 'good faith' requirement was subsequently regularly rejected, both by scholars[38] and in the jurisprudence.[39] The rationale is that the claimant would be at risk *for*

32 See Chapter 6.

33 Grahl-Madsen, note 3, 222.

34 Ibid., 221–222 ['Ein derartig weites Recht … kann nicht dem jenigen zustehen, der aus eigennützigen Motiven sich in die Gefahr begibt, "politisch" … verfolgt zu werden, vielmehr muss die eigene Einstellung und Überzeugung, mag sie auch nur durch die Zugehörigkeit zu einer bestimmten, vom Staate bekämpften Gruppe zum Ausdruck kommen, die politische Bedrohung ausgelöst haben'].

35 Ibid., 252.

36 Ibid. [Their own 'nicht stets auf anerkennenswerten Motiven beruhenden Willensentschluss'].

37 Ibid., 247 ['Wenn die Erreichung der Anerkennung so einfach ist, dass sie mit hoher Sicherheit durch den blossen Eintritt in eine Emigrantenorganisation … zu erlangen ist, so muss man die Frage stellen, ob nicht dadurch das Asyl in seinem Kern entwertet ist'].

38 See e.g. Guy Goodwin-Gill and Jane McAdam (2007) *The Refugee in International Law* (3rd ed.), Oxford: Oxford University Press, 65–67.

39 See the line of cases concerning religion and political opinion in the United Kingdom, cited in the introduction, in particular: *Danian* v. *Secretary of State for the Home Department (Appeal)*, [2000] Imm AR 96, United Kingdom: Court of Appeal (England and Wales), 28 October 1999; *Ahmed (Iftikhar)* v. *Secretary of State for the Home Department*, [2000] INLR 1, United Kingdom: Court of Appeal (England and Wales), 5 November 1999.

reasons of the Convention ground nonetheless, if the persecutor – wrongly – attributed the characteristic to them. It is in this line that the UK Supreme Court in *HJ (Iran) and HT (Cameroon)* ruled that those who 'will live openly' are entitled to protection, and refrained from distinguishing protected from unprotected acts.[40]

But it points to the core challenge of a persecutor approach, which lies in the future-focused nature of the assessment. If a claimant has not yet been 'found out' or, rather, if the persecuted characteristic has not yet been imputed to them, on what basis can it be assessed whether this will likely occur in the future? This is reflected in French and Spanish jurisprudence, in that they essentially conduct a backward assessment based on *having* been discovered/attributed the characteristic. In Germany, where a future-focused assessment is conducted, the analysis is made dependent on the strength of the claimant's identity, based on the assumption that it will inevitably become visible – and the UK Supreme Court undertakes a 'factual' assessment of what the claimant 'will do'.

This is where Hathaway and Pobjoy's triviality concern comes in. Their approach to limiting 'protected acts' in order to exclude 'trivial' claims in some ways constitutes a reinvented future-focused 'good faith' requirement; even if a claimant *were* subject to persecution following a so-called trivial act – because the persecutor now viewed them as a group member – they would not be entitled to protection.[41]

7.3.2 *The 'Liberal Doctrine': Focus on the Claimant*

What Grahl-Madsen named the liberal doctrine, in contrast, relies on the political motivation of the claimant. As such, any offence could be relevant, but only provided it was committed because of a genuine political opinion. According to Grahl-Madsen, this interpretation is based on 'instinct' and historical development, but 'rests on solid ground'.[42] The logic is that if someone commits an offence, they can be refugees if they acted out of deep conviction.[43] According to Grahl-Madsen, in both religious and political cases, acts beyond mere expressions of opinion warrant protection if the claimants' convictions put them in a position of the 'constant plight' ('ständige Zwangslage') of having to dissemble or lie. If a claimant

40 *HJ (Iran) and HT (Cameroon)* v. *Secretary of State for the Home Department*, [2010] UKSC 31, United Kingdom: Supreme Court, 7 July 2010.

41 Hathaway and Pobjoy, note 27, 315–389, 388: 'And no, it is not the case that refugee status is owed whenever serious harm is threatened by reason only of an applicant having engaged in some activity that is vaguely or stereotypically associated with homosexuality (or any other protected ground).'

42 Grahl-Madsen, note 3, 249.

43 Ibid., 229–230: 'Such action is punished in every state. [He is still a refugee if] the person has committed the crime out of political conviction.' ['Solches Tun wird in jedem Staat bestraft. [Er ist dennoch ein Flüchtling wenn] der Betreffende aus einer politischen Überzeugung heraus die Straftat begangen hat'].

was subject to severe conflicts of conscience ('schwere Gewissenskonflikte') and decided against state orders and in favour of their own convictions, they were entitled to asylum.[44] So the claimant's motivation is decisive for eligibility.[45]

Note that, again, Grahl-Madsen develops this approach mainly with a view to laws of general application. In fact, there are some indications that the approach was invented in order to be able to include conscientious objectors – it is in this typical Cold War context that it was developed by Grahl-Madsen. But the focus on the 'deep conviction' of the claimant re-emerges in the German requirement that the sexual orientation must be 'identity-defining', or of particular importance for the claimant, in order to warrant protection. It also underlies the energies invested in finding out the 'real' sexual orientation of persons who make asylum claims based on sexual orientation, applying physical[46] or psychiatric[47] examinations and other problematic means, which have led to the CJEU judgment in *A, B and C*.[48] Under this approach, it is the claimant who establishes group membership.

The paradoxical nature of this undertaking is neatly encapsulated in the German government's statement following the judgment in *Y and Z*, according to which the BAMF would now abstain from any assessment of the claimant's sexual orientation, 'particularly as the latter can only be assumed by the persecutor as well'.[49] In other words, it matters little whether or not the claimant actually possesses the characteristic or whether they feel strongly about it, if the persecutor attributes it to them. This is the crux of the issue and the point where both approaches intersect. Does this mean that claimants are not persecuted until they have been imputed to be gay? Or does it mean that anyone in the respective country is at risk, regardless of their sexual orientation, because they could possibly be perceived to be gay ('imputed') in the future? If only those who 'actually' are gay make up the group, how is it determined who is really gay? Does it depend on the claimant's self-ascription, an 'external', 'objective' standard applied by the decision-maker, or the persecutor's concept of

44 Ibid., 237.

45 Ibid., 231.

46 For some time, the Czech Republic submitted claimants to so-called phallometric tests, in an attempt to scientifically quantify male sexual arousal by measuring physiological responses to visual stimuli through attachment of electrodes to the penis; the counterpart used on women is called 'vaginal photoplethysmography'. For an analysis and criticism of that practice, see Organization for Refuge, Asylum & Migration (2011) *Testing Sexual Orientation: A Scientific and Legal Analysis of Plethysmography in Asylum and Refugee Status Proceedings*, San Francisco: ORAM, December 2011.

47 It was common practice in Germany that claimants provide psychiatric evidence of their sexual orientation, see e.g. VG Neustadt/Weinstraße, Urteil vom 8.9.2008, 3 K 753/07.NW; but see VG Chemnitz, Urteil vom 11.7.2008, A 2 K 304/06 rejecting the use of such evidence to support the claimant's sexual orientation; and discussion in Chapter 5.

48 *A, B, C v. Staatssecretaris van Veiligheid en Justitie*, Joined Cases C-148/13 to C-150/13, European Union: Court of Justice of the European Union, 2 December 2014, rejecting 'tests' at 65.

49 Manfred Schmidt (2012) 'Kriterien der Flüchtlingsanerkennung. Hier: Sexuelle Orientierung', 424 –7313/05 – 12 (5506046-286) *Brief an Volker Beck MdB*, Nürnberg, 27 December 2012, 1–2.

gayness? Those different notions will frequently not fully coincide – and the question then becomes one of deciding which is given precedence. Does the protected group differ from the persecuted group?

Notably, the claimant's self-ascription is rarely used as the benchmark in the assessment of asylum claims.[50] It can only be speculated that a 'bad faith' concern is at the root of this. The claimant's 'claim' is generally considered insufficient and needs to be corroborated in one way or another. The conflict therefore tends to be between the other two – a standard applied by the country of asylum and the persecutor's own definition. The case law analysis conducted by Grahl-Madsen throughout his book, for example, shows that the focus continually shifts in the judgments he reviewed. In some judgments, one act was taken to have made the claimant a political opponent in the eyes of the regime, whether he was or not;[51] in others, it was relevant whether they acted out of political conviction;[52] and in yet others, the act had to be 'doubly political': committed out of political conviction, *and* perceived as such by the authorities.[53] The issue of the shifting focus is sometimes located in the establishment of the Convention ground, other times in the assessment of risk – and in yet others in the discussion of the connection between harm and reason (the nexus). In the latter context, it is a question of who provides the nexus. The malleability contained in this tension can work in favour of claimants, as it allows for a broad, inclusive approach, or against them, depending on the situation.

7.4 CONCLUSION: DEFINING GROUPS, ESTABLISHING MEMBERSHIP

The tensions involved in the question of how the protected group is defined and how group membership of individuals can be established can be traced back to the earliest contributions to refugee law scholarship. Both questions are caught between capturing what the persecutor considers and what has motivated the claimant. There are important power dynamics at play, since whatever the position of the

50 Although for sexuality-based claims, one of the claimants had made an argument in favour of this approach in the proceedings before the CJEU in A, B, C v. *Staatssecretaris van Veiligheid en Justitie*, note 48.

51 Grahl-Madsen, note 3, 230: 'He had good reason to fear that this statement would not only be used as a basis for his conviction for facilitating the escape, but also for the evaluation of his actions in general.' ['Mit Grund musste er in der Folge befürchten, dass diese Erklärung nicht nur seiner Verurteilung wegen Beihilfe zur Flucht, sondern über diesen Rahmen hinaus der Bewertung seines Handelns ganz allgemein zu Grunde gelegt werde'].

52 Ibid., 229–230.

53 Ibid., 230: 'The decisive factor for the assessment of the plaintiff's conduct is that it was carried out for political reasons and that it was perceived as political by the authorities.' ['Entscheidend für die Beurteilung des klägerischen Handelns ist, dass es aus politischen Gründen erfolgte und von den Machthabern politisch aufgefasst wurde'.]

claimant, the persecutor will have the last word concerning the parameters of what – and who – is persecuted. As a consequence, a particular person positions themselves towards this persecuted group, but irrespective or their own identification with it (assuming or rejecting membership, fully or somewhat), they can be persecuted when the persecutor perceives them to possess that characteristic, whether or not there is a rational basis for this assumption.

It is, therefore, generally accepted that refugee protection also extends to those with an imputed political, religious or sexual identity.[54] But what, then, is the role of the claimant's 'actual' membership, that is, their own motives? In Grahl-Madsen's analysis, they acquire particular relevance in cases of 'acts beyond the mere expression' of the Convention grounds, though it remains unclear how these may be defined. Grahl-Madsen identified two approaches, the 'restrictive' approach, with its focus on the persecutor, and the 'liberal' approach, focusing on the claimant. The flexibility this dual conception involves, which permits shifts between the claimant's own conviction and the persecutor's perception, reproduces the tension identified in the introduction; the vulnerable position of the claimant who is at once entitled to, and restricted from, the expression of the characteristic that gives rise to persecution. A claimant cannot be asked to forego their political opinion, yet maybe they can a little bit, if their situation is not so serious. 'Discretion' cannot be required, but triviality cannot be protected. The protected group does not necessarily neatly align with the persecuted group.

This situation is compounded for sexuality-based claims, which are generally considered under the 'membership of a particular social group' ground. Although the fact that sexual orientation claims are encompassed by the Refugee Convention is generally accepted, the question of how to define the social group and on what basis has achieved much less consensus, and the struggles outlined by Grahl-Madsen concerning claims based on political opinion are neatly reflected in the ongoing controversy over how to define the social group ground.

[54] See e.g. UNHCR (2001) *The International Protection of Refugees: Interpreting Article 1 of the 1951 Convention Relating to the Status of Refugees*, April 2001, 25. See also: UNHCR (1979, re-edited 1992) *Handbook on Procedures and Criteria for Determining Refugee Status under the 1951 Convention and the 1967 Protocol Relating to the Status of Refugees*, HCR/IP/4/Eng/REV.1 Re-edited, Geneva, January 1992, 80; Supreme Court of Canada: *Canada (Attorney General) v. Ward*, [1993] 2 S.C.R. 689, 30 June 1993, at 747; University of Michigan Law School (2015) *The Michigan Guidelines on Risk for Reasons of Political Opinion*, April 2015, para 6, www.refworld.org/docid/555de15b4.html.

8

Mind the Gap

Particular Social Group and the Limits of Protection

'Membership of a particular social group' has repeatedly been described as the Convention ground with the least clarity.[1] After playing a subordinated role for years, its significance increased with the end of the Cold War and the advent of gender- and sexuality-based claims. 'Fitting' these claims into the Refugee Convention has propelled the conceptualisation of the social group ground. Its evolution is said to have advanced the understanding of the refugee definition as a whole[2] by inciting a broader engagement with the Convention grounds. And yet, no single accepted conceptual approach has been reached. With the 'protected characteristics' and the 'social perception' approaches, two major interpretations continue to compete.[3] They essentially echo Grahl-Madsen's 'liberal' and 'restrictive' doctrines concerning political opinion. The 'protected characteristics' approach is based on an ex ante definition of what can constitute a group, and looks for the elements of that in the claimant. It places limits on the *reason* for persecution in order to prevent seemingly trivial claims. It defines the protected group. In contrast, the 'social perception' approach is based on an ex post definition. Rather than establishing in general terms what can or cannot constitute a group, it is based on

[1] Global Consultations on International Protection (2003) *Summary Conclusions: Membership of a Particular Social Group*, adopted at the expert roundtable organized by the United Nations High Commissioner for Refugees and the International Institute of Humanitarian Law, San Remo, Italy, 6–8 September 2001, www.refworld.org/pdfid/470a33b40.pdf, 312; see also: Michelle Foster (2012) *The 'Ground with the Least Clarity': A Comparative Study of Jurisprudential Developments Relating to 'Membership of a Particular Social Group'*, UNHCR Division of International Protection, Geneva, August 2012, PPLA/2012/02; and Michelle Foster (2014) 'Why We Are Not There Yet: The Particular Challenge of "Particular Social Group"', in Efrat Arbel, Catherine Dauvergne and Jenni Millbank (eds.) *Gender in Refugee Law: From the Margins to the Centre*, London: Routledge, 17–45.

[2] Global Consultations on International Protection, note 1, 312.

[3] Foster, *The 'Ground with the Least Clarity'*, note 1, 2–23.

an assessment of what is viewed as a group by the surrounding society, thus potentially allowing what may appear as trivial claims. It relies on the persecuted group. The tension between the two approaches, and the difficulty in reaching consensus, reflect the fact that a conceptualisation of the Convention grounds raises complex questions at the core of refugee protection: there is uncertainty as to how to identify or define the limits of the Convention grounds such that the triviality concern is met while at the same time avoiding protection gaps (the 'fundamentality concern'). Further confusion arises with a view to the role of the claimant and the persecutor. This chapter juxtaposes the two competing approaches to defining 'membership of a particular social group' and places them in the context of the concealment controversy: it draws out how each of the approaches responds to, and is incapable of dissolving, the central tension between the principle that the Convention grounds should not be hidden (fundamentality principle) and the notion that refugee protection is for particularly serious situations (severity rationale). The contentious question here essentially takes the form of whether any type of associations, including for trivial pastimes such as bridge clubs or rollerbladers, would be encompassed by the notion of particular social group.

8.1 THE PROTECTED CHARACTERISTICS APPROACH

When the United States Board of Immigration Appeals was faced with the case of *Matter of Acosta*[4] in the mid-1980s, it first developed what came to be called the 'protected characteristics' approach. Drawing on the seminal decisions in *Acosta* and the 1993 Canadian Supreme Court case in *Ward* v. *Canada*,[5] as well as subsequent case law that has since applied and refined the protected characteristics approach, Foster summarises this approach as including:

(i) groups defined by an innate or unchangeable characteristic;
(ii) groups defined by a characteristic that is fundamental to human dignity such that a person should not be forced to relinquish it; and
(iii) groups defined by a former status, unalterable due to its historical permanence.[6]

4 *Matter of Acosta*, 19 I. & N. Dec. 11 (B.I.A. 1985), United States Board of Immigration Appeals, 1 March 1985. Acosta was a Salvadoran taxi driver who refused to take part in strikes. It is not entirely clear why the case was not considered under the political opinion ground; see also on this point Maryellen Fullerton (1993) 'A Comparative Look at Refugee Status Based on Persecution due to Membership in a Particular Social Group', 26(3) *Cornell International Law Journal* 505–563, footnote 238.

5 *Canada (Attorney General)* v. *Ward*, [1993] 2 SCR 689, Canada: Supreme Court, 30 June 1993.

6 Foster, *The 'Ground with the Least Clarity'*, note 1, 7.

When approaching the social group analysis, the United States Board of Immigration Appeals (BIA) advanced the

> well-established doctrine of *ejusdem generis*, meaning literally, 'of the same kind', as most helpful in construing the phrase 'membership of a particular social group'. This doctrine holds that general words used in an enumeration with specific words should be construed in a manner consistent with the specific words.[7]

Considering the other four grounds – race, nationality, religion and political opinion – the BIA identified immutability as a unifying characteristic between those grounds: 'a characteristic that is either beyond the power of an individual to change or is so fundamental to individual identity or conscience that it ought not to be required to be changed'.[8] On this basis, the BIA understood the other four grounds of persecution to 'restrict refugee status to individuals who are either unable by their own actions, or as a matter of conscience should not be required, to *avoid persecution*'.[9] Notably, this passage is constructed around the possibility of avoiding persecution. It clearly differentiates between characteristics that are generally immediately visible and therefore largely impossible to hide, let alone change (un*able* to avoid persecution), and other characteristics, which require expression and are more susceptible to being changed or remaining unexpressed (should not be *required* to avoid persecution, in spite of a supposed *ability*). The distinction resonates with Grahl-Madsen's concept of characteristics beyond the control of a claimant on the one hand and those of 'individual' character on the other.

In his seminal 1991 book, James Hathaway adopted and articulated the *ejusdem generis* approach as one that avoids both redundancy and all-inclusiveness.[10] The 'protected characteristics' approach claims to be one that does not make the other grounds superfluous by designing the social group ground as an all-encompassing residual category.[11] Ironically, though, precisely because it aims to identify the unifying principles of the other grounds, these would also be covered by the 'protected characteristics' definition and, hence, race, nationality, religion and political opinion do become redundant, in the sense that they are innate or fundamental characteristics applying to groups of people. Furthermore, the 'either/or' (*either* innate *or* fundamental) definition for a 'protected characteristic' is somewhat awkward in itself. As noted by Aleinikoff, it is artificial because it needs to reach beyond immutable characteristics in order to cover political opinion and religion. Aleinikoff concludes: 'Once that conceptual move is made, it is not clear

7 *Matter of Acosta*, note 4, 37–39.
8 Ibid.
9 Ibid.; emphasis added.
10 James Hathaway (1991) *The Status of Refugees in International Law*, Toronto: Butterworths, 161.
11 Ibid., 157–159.

why an additional element could not be added to extend to social group; so the common element could logically be described as "immutable characteristic, fundamental characteristic or shared characteristic of a group."'[12]

8.2 SEARCH FOR LIMITS: THE TRIVIALITY CONCERN

The concern not to make the social group category all-inclusive is grounded in a deliberate search for limits. According to Hathaway, the 'drafters of the Convention did not wish to avoid drawing distinctions among various types of putative refugees, but rather intended to establish a demarcation between those whose fear was attributable to civil or political status (refugees) and those whose concern to flee was prompted by other concerns (not refugees)'.[13] The awkward 'protected characteristics' construction is effectively, and explicitly, designed to exclude 'groups defined by a characteristic which is changeable or from which disassociation is possible, so long as neither option requires renunciation of basic human rights'.[14] Thus, the purpose of the 'protected characteristics' definition is the concern not to protect 'triviality', ensuring that recognised groups are united by a 'truly important trait'.[15] In this way, the approach reflects Grahl-Madsen's 'liberal doctrine' with its focus on the claimant's true identity.

Hathaway illustrates this concern with the following example: 'Surely, it would be more reasonable to expect ... roller-bladers [if they were persecuted as a group] to take off their skates than to insist that they be granted a "trump card" on migration control to enable them to continue to roll'.[16] While this is an invented, and most likely unhelpful, example, Aleinikoff replies that most trivial associations are not likely to attract persecutory acts, even if they constitute a social group. Though, if they were subject to persecution, then clearly the persecutor would see them as a group that constitutes a threat and would therefore be willing to inflict unjustifiable harm to accomplish the goal of suppression: 'The Convention is aimed at preventing the infliction of serious abuses based on group membership, not at preserving membership in groups that are deemed important or worthy.'[17] Similarly, Goodwin-Gill observed that '[c]learly, there are social groups other than those that share

[12] T. Alexander Aleinikoff (2003) 'Protected Characteristics and Social Perceptions: An Analysis of the Meaning of "Membership of a Particular Social Group"', in Erika Feller, Volker Türk and Frances Nicholson (eds.) *Refugee Protection in International Law: UNHCR's Global Consultations on International Protection*, Cambridge: Cambridge University Press, 263–311, 290; footnote 116.

[13] Hathaway, note 10, 159.

[14] *Canada (Attorney General)* v. *Ward*, [1993] 2 S.C.R. 689, Canada: Supreme Court, 30 June 1993, 739, citing Hathaway, note 10, 161.

[15] Aleinikoff, note 12, 263–311, 299.

[16] James Hathaway, cited in Ibid.

[17] Aleinikoff, note 12, 263–311, 299.

immutable characteristics, or which combine for reasons fundamental to their human dignity'.[18]

Indeed, there is a risk of protection gaps in this approach: 'to adopt a "non-triviality" requirement would be to give the persecutor a *carte blanche* for groups that associate for "non-fundamental" reasons'.[19] That is, an a priori or external 'objective' definition of what constitutes a social group bears the risk of not mapping onto the persecutor's idea of what constitutes the undesired social group. The triviality concern, however, pretends that persecution is caused by and aimed at the external manifestation of the Convention ground (be that rollerblades, multi-coloured cocktails or the wrong hair style), rather than what the persecutor takes this 'trivial' sign to stand for. Moreover, and significantly, '[s]uch an approach puts things backwards – imposing a burden on members of a group to change in order to avoid persecution rather than providing protection to those at risk of serious unjustifiable harm'.[20] In other words, it entails 'discretion reasoning' – it is based on the idea that under certain circumstances the claimant has to participate in their own protection and behave reasonably to avoid harm that would otherwise ensue due to their group membership. Hathaway makes this clear:

> The central question, therefore, in examining wealth-based categories or classes is whether the group's defining characteristic is either innate or unchangeable, or if subject to voluntary alienation, whether it is premised on the realization of basic human rights. In all other cases, it would be *reasonable to expect an applicant to accommodate herself to less privileged circumstances* as an alternative to the invocation of international protection.[21]

In their joint 2014 book, Hathaway and Foster reiterate this position, considering the *ejusdem generis* approach to be a 'standard that is capable of principled evolution but not so vague as to admit persons *without a serious basis* for [a] claim to international protection'.[22]

8.3 THE SOCIAL PERCEPTION APPROACH

Conscious of possible protection gaps, most other commentators favour what has been termed a 'social perception approach' to membership of a particular social group. Already Grahl-Madsen in his groundbreaking 1966 book was concerned with

[18] Guy Goodwin-Gill (1996) *The Refugee in International Law* (2nd ed.), Oxford: Clarendon Press, 365.

[19] Aleinikoff, note 12, 263–311, 300.

[20] Ibid.

[21] Hathaway, note 10, 167; emphasis added.

[22] James Hathaway and Michelle Foster (2014) *The Law of Refugee Status* (2nd ed.), Cambridge: Cambridge University Press, 427; emphasis added.

preventing gaps. According to Grahl-Madsen, many cases falling under the social group ground are also covered by the other Convention grounds, 'but the *notion of "social group" is of broader application* than the combined notions of racial, ethnic, and religious groups, and in order to stop a possible gap, the Conference [of Plenipotentiaries] felt that it would be as well to mention this reason for persecution explicitly'.[23] Overall, Grahl-Madsen was of the view that it is 'appropriate to give the phrase a liberal interpretation': 'Whenever a person is likely to suffer persecution *merely because of his background*, he should get the benefit of the present provision.'[24]

The 1979 UNHCR Handbook on Procedures and Criteria for Determining Refugee Status builds on this notion and defines as follows: 'A "particular social group" normally comprises persons of similar background, habits or social status.'[25] The Handbook further explains:

> Membership of such a particular social group may be at the root of persecution because there is no confidence in the group's loyalty to the Government or because the political outlook, antecedents or economic activity of its members, or the very existence of the social group as such, is held to be an obstacle to the Government's policies.[26]

Thus, the Handbook gives a political cast to the social group term. As Fullerton notes, seen in this manner, it bears a resemblance to the nationality, race, and religion categories of persecution, as well as to the political opinion category:

> [A]lthough the political dimension is often not explicitly acknowledged, people persecuted on account of race, religion, or nationality generally become targets for persecution because *the persecuted group as a whole* – whether it be a racial, religious, or ethnic group – *is perceived by the government* as unreliable or disloyal.[27]

Similarly, in her discussion rejecting the 'voluntary association' element that was first required to establish a social group according to the Canadian Supreme Court decision in *Ward*[28] (although quickly rejected by subsequent authority), Audrey Macklin argues that an anti-discrimination approach should look at the social consequences of possessing certain attributes:

> After all, it hardly matters to a racist whether a person of colour sees himself or herself as united with other people of colour … *As long as perpetrators of*

[23] Atle Grahl-Madsen (1966) *The Status of Refugees in International Law – Volume I: Refugee Character*, Leyden: A. W. Sijthoff, 219; emphasis added.

[24] Ibid., 220; emphasis added.

[25] UNHCR (1979, re-edited 1992) *Handbook on Procedures and Criteria for Determining Refugee Status under the 1951 Convention and the 1967 Protocol Relating to the Status of Refugees*, HCR/IP/4/Eng/REV.1 Re-edited, Geneva, January 1992, at 77.

[26] Ibid.

[27] Fullerton, note 4, 505–563, 551; emphasis added.

[28] *Canada (Attorney General)* v. *Ward*, note 14.

> *persecution treat people with a shared attribute as comprising a group by virtue of that common characteristic*, whether individuals so identified would choose to see themselves as united in any meaningful sense has little impact.[29]

Although this approach has been termed 'social perception' test, all of these definitions appear to focus on the perception of the (potential) persecutor. The approach would therefore more appropriately be called persecutor's perception test – which turns out to be surprisingly similar to Grahl-Madsen's 'restrictive doctrine', with its reliance on the persecutor and imputation.

In jurisprudence, the social perception test has most emphatically been embraced by Australia and France.[30] The High Court of Australia eschewed the protected characteristics test in the 1997 judgment concerning *Applicant* A,[31] and developed an approach based on the ordinary meaning of the text, which was later refined in *Applicant* S.[32] According to this approach, three factors must be satisfied:

> First, the group must be identifiable by a characteristic or attribute common to all members of the group. Secondly, the characteristic or attribute common to all members of the group cannot be the shared fear of persecution. Thirdly, the possession of that characteristic or attribute must distinguish the group from society at large.[33]

This rationale is outlined by McHugh J in *Applicant* A, where he established the so-called left-handed test:

> While persecutory conduct cannot define the social group, the actions of the persecutors may serve to identify or even cause the creation of a particular social group in society. Left-handed men are not a particular social group. But, if they were persecuted because they were left-handed, they would no doubt quickly become recognisable in their society as a particular social group. Their persecution for being left-handed would create a public perception that they were a particular social group. But it would be the attribute of being left-handed and not the persecutory acts that would identify them as a particular social group.[34]

The Australian definition closely relates to the concept of particular social group put forth by Guy Goodwin-Gill in his 1983 book. In discussing the social group ground, Goodwin-Gill states that a fully comprehensive definition is both impracticable and impossible. Goodwin-Gill identifies two essential elements for the determination of

[29] Audrey Macklin (1994) 'Ward v. Canada: A Review Essay', 6(3) *International Journal of Refugee Law* 362–381, 375; emphasis added.

[30] See Foster, *The 'Ground with the Least Clarity'*, note 1.

[31] *Applicant A and Another* v. *Minister for Immigration and Ethnic Affairs and Another*, (1997) 190 CLR 225, Australia: High Court, 24 February 1997.

[32] *Applicant S* v. *Minister for Immigration and Multicultural Affairs* [2004] HCA 25, Australia: High Court, 27 May 2004.

[33] Ibid., per Gleeson C. J. and Gummow and Kirby JJ at 36.

[34] *Applicant A and Another* v. *Minister for Immigration and Ethnic Affairs and Another*, note 31, at 21.

a particular social group. The first is the presence of uniting factors such as ethnic, cultural and linguistic origin; education; family background; economic activity; or shared values, outlook, aspirations. The second is the attitude towards the putative social group of other groups in the same society and, in particular, the treatment accorded to it by state authorities: 'The importance, and therefore the identity, of a social group may well be in direct proportion to the notice taken of it by others, *particularly the authorities of the state*'.[35] In the later editions of his book from 1996 and 2007 (the latter with Jane McAdam), Goodwin-Gill's basic notion of particular social group remains unchanged.[36] He does acknowledge the 'protected characteristics approach' that has emerged in the meantime resulting from *Acosta* and *Ward* and supported by Hathaway, noting that this test, while designed as a 'limiting' approach, is not in fact as restrictive as it may appear.[37] However, he favours a perception approach with a particular focus on the persecutor's perception:

> The experience of 1951 is also illustrative, for its implicit reference to the perception or attitude of the persecuting authority. It is still not unusual for governments publicly to write off sections of their population – the petty bourgeoisie, for example, or the class traitors; and even more frequent will be those occasions on which the identification of groups to be neutralised takes place covertly. In eastern Europe in the late 1940s and the 1950s, groups and classes and their descendants were *perceived* to be a threat to the new order, whatever their individual qualities or beliefs.[38]

Referring to the former capitalists of eastern Europe, Goodwin-Gill notes that what counted at the time was the fact that they were 'not only internally linked by having engaged in a particular type of (past) economic activity, but also externally defined, *partly if not exclusively, by the perception of the new ruling class*'.[39] In this context, Goodwin-Gill notes favourably the particular social group definition from the 1979 UNHCR Handbook, which is based on such a 'conjunction of "internal" characteristics and "external" perceptions' by the state.[40]

In an article published in the same year as the first edition of Goodwin-Gill's book, Arthur Helton similarly argues that the social group ground is to be interpreted broadly: 'the contours of a social group for purposes of refugee status are *limited only by the imagination of the persecutor*'.[41] In his view, 'the "social group" category was meant to be a catch-all which could include all bases for and types of persecution

[35] Guy Goodwin-Gill (1983) *The Refugee in International Law* (1st ed.), Oxford: Clarendon Press, 30; emphasis added.

[36] Guy Goodwin-Gill and Jane McAdam (2007) *The Refugee in International Law* (3rd ed.), Oxford: Oxford University Press, 75–76.

[37] Goodwin-Gill, note 18, 360–361.

[38] Ibid., 47; emphasis added.

[39] Ibid., 361; emphasis added.

[40] Ibid., 47.

[41] Arthur Helton (1983) 'Persecution on Account of Membership in a Social Group as Basis for Refugee Status', 15 *Columbia Human Rights Law Review* 39–67, 66; emphasis added.

which an imaginative despot might conjure up'.[42] Helton, too, argues in favour of a persecutor's perception approach to the question of what constitutes a social group.

8.3.1 *Avoiding Protection Gaps?*

With the exception of Hathaway and Foster, who defend the 'protected characteristics' approach,[43] there is a tendency in the literature to favour the social perception approach in the form of a persecutor's perception approach. While he was critical of this approach in the context of membership of a particular social group, Hathaway clearly supported the persecutor's perception approach in the context of religion and political opinion, where he has repeatedly stated that the crucial test is that the applicant is perceived by the authorities in power as political opposition.[44] In response to criticism of this view potentially being overinclusive and the necessity to apply some external standard for what can be considered a political opinion, he stated: 'This reasoning, however, assumes that the rationale for refugee law is in some sense the protection of persons on the basis of personal merit, e.g., those who possess a particular political opinion, rather than the establishment of a surrogate protection system for those whose membership in the national community has been fundamentally denied.'[45] If the same standard were to be applied to the particular social group ground, the persecutor's perception test would result.

In contrast, in relation to membership of a particular social group, Hathaway and Foster disapprove of the persecutor's perception approach. In view in particular of attempts by the UNHCR[46] and the EU *Qualification Directive*,[47] and, accordingly, state practice to combine both approaches, Hathaway and Foster emphatically reject the social perception approach for being unprincipled and unworkable:

42 Ibid., 45; emphasis added.

43 See James Hathaway and Michelle Foster (2003) 'Membership of a Particular Social Group' Discussion Paper No. 4, Advanced Refugee Law Workshop, International Association of Refugee Law Judges, Auckland, New Zealand, October 2002, 15(3) *International Journal of Refugee Law* 477–491, 487; Hathaway and Foster, note 22, 423–461; Foster, 'Why We Are Not There Yet', note 1, 17–45.

44 See Hathaway, note 10, 153–157; and more recently in the Michigan Guidelines on Risk for Reasons of Political Opinion, which are the result of a colloquium he convened and chaired: University of Michigan Law School (2015) *The Michigan Guidelines on Risk for Reasons of Political Opinion*, April 2015, www.refworld.org/docid/555de15b4.html.

45 Hathaway, note 10, 157.

46 UNHCR (2002) *Guidelines on International Protection No. 2: 'Membership of a Particular Social Group' within the Context of Article 1A(2) of the 1951 Convention and/or Its 1967 Protocol Relating to the Status of Refugees*, 7 May 2002, HCR/GIP/02/02, www.refworld.org/docid/3d36f23f4.html, at 10–11.

47 Article 10, Directive 2011/95/EU of the European Parliament and of the Council of 13 December 2011 on standards for the qualification of third-country nationals or stateless persons as beneficiaries of international protection, for a uniform status for refugees or for persons eligible for subsidiary protection, and for the content of the protection granted (recast), oj L 337/9, 20 December 2011 (*Recast Qualification Directive*).

> In sum, we believe that the only principled and sustainable method of interpreting the membership of a particular social group ground is to adopt the *ejusdem generis* principle … In our view, it is time for the global interpretative community to relinquish the unprincipled and fundamentally unworkable social perception test, and reclaim the dominant *ejusdem generis* test as the sole method of assessing membership of a particular social group for Convention purposes.[48]

In Foster's view, the 'elegant simplicity' of the protected characteristics approach risks being undermined by the import of 'additional hurdles' through the 'nebulous' social perception test.[49] In an earlier piece, both authors had criticised the social perception approach for being too broad and privileging claims by persons at risk 'simply because they belong to a group', thus deeming the fact of experiencing risk as a group somehow 'inherently more egregious or protection-worthy' than experiencing the same risk individually.[50] Yet, in contrast to random violence, persecution means that a person is harmed *for a reason.* If there is a reason for which the harm is inflicted, then this reason will necessarily apply to other persons as well; the Convention grounds are group characteristics, and indeed, the Convention privileges claims by persons who are at risk simply because they belong to a – political, ethnic, religious, national or social – group.[51] The point is not, therefore, the protection of groups per se, but rather the protection of people persecuted for sharing a political, religious, ethnic, national or social background, whichever it may be. In this sense, the persecutor perception test encompasses a non-discrimination approach – one Hathaway and Foster argue is best captured in the protected characteristics approach.[52]

Since the persecutor's perception test operates without an a priori, external definition (but on the basis of the persecutor's notion of the persecuted characteristic), it applies a very broad concept of the Convention grounds. In response to the concern that the social perception test might create too broad an interpretation of social group, opening the floodgates to any number of groups and claimants (the triviality concern), Aleinikoff states that, as long as adjudicators observe the rule that the group must exist outside the persecution, the category will be significantly limited and other elements of the refugee definition such as the 'nexus' requirement will supply additional limits.[53] This chimes with Helton's observation that adoption of the 'social group' category does not impose limitless obligations on

48 Hathaway and Foster, note 22, 460–461.

49 Foster, 'Why We Are Not There Yet', note 1, 17–45, 38.

50 Hathaway and Foster, 'Membership of a Particular Social Group', note 43, 477–491, 487; see also Hathaway and Foster, note 22, 432–433.

51 John Tobin (2012) 'Assessing GLBTI Refugee Claims: Using Human Rights Law to Shift the Narrative of Persecution within Refugee Law', 44(2) *New York University Journal of International Law and Politics* 447–484, 476.

52 Hathaway and Foster, note 22, 427.

53 Aleinikoff, note 12, 263–311, 300.

the contracting states.[54] Rather, 'the most important limitation on the scope of the definition is the requirement of a showing of "well-founded fear of persecution"'.[55]

8.3.2 A *New Limit: The Singling Out Requirement*

A broad concept of social group is in line with broad concepts of the other Convention grounds. In principle, it has the capacity to circumvent 'discretion reasoning' as there is no distinction between the claimant's act and identity and no particular conduct is excluded from protection; if the persecutor views a claimant as part of a persecuted group – irrespective of whether that assessment is based on behaviour or identity – then they are entitled to protection.[56] To be sure, for the future-focused assessment, the claimant would have to show that they possess what Goodwin-Gill named the internally linking element, or that it has been or will be attributed to them. But it is broader in that it allows any type of element to qualify in order to be in line with what the persecutor decides to persecute. Yet Hathaway and Foster criticise the lack of clarity inherent in the social perception test as one that 'has often paradoxically produced a narrowing – not widening – in the range and types of claim that can fall within the social group ground'.[57]

Indeed, the limiting element often drawn on in those cases is the notion that a claimant needs to be 'singled out' for persecution. This seems illogical per se, as it essentially requires individual persecution for a group characteristic. An important way in which this can be found is by way of 'discretion reasoning'; people with the persecuted characteristic are only safe from persecution if they are able to 'pass unnoticed' – and if they do hide, these people would then not be entitled to protection. Perception is equated with visibility or perceptibility. This can apply both to the establishment of the group in general terms (the group can only be said to exist if there is evidence that it is generally set apart in society) or to the identifiability of the claimant as a group member. As discussed, although France

[54] Helton, note 41, 39–67, 53.

[55] Ibid., 54.

[56] There is a risk in this context that the social perception approach may be misunderstood to be a 'social visibility' approach as was the case in the United States since 2006, though that view was rejected in two Board of Immigration Appeals decisions: *Matter of* M-E-V-G-, 26 I & N Dec. 227 (BIA 2014), United States Board of Immigration Appeals, 7 February 2014; and *Matter of* W-G-R-, 26 I & N Dec. 208 (BIA 2014), United States Board of Immigration Appeals, 7 February 2014. For a discussion of the reformulated 'social distinction' standard, see Isaac T. R. Smith (2015) 'Searching for Consistency in Asylum's Protected Grounds', 100 *Iowa Law Review* 1891–1915; Reagan Greenberg (2017) 'The Particular Social Group Requirement: How the Asylum Process Is Consistently Failing LGB Applicants and How an Evidentiary Standard of Self-Attestation Can Remedy These Failures', 17 *University of Maryland Law Journal of Race, Religion, Gender & Class* 147–172; Bernardo M. Velasco (2017) 'Who Are the Real Refugees: Labels as Evidence of a Particular Social Group', 59 *Arizona Law Review* 235–262.

[57] Hathaway and Foster, note 22, 433.

and Spain can be said to apply a version of the persecutor perception approach, 'singling out' logics were the basis of Spanish jurisprudence, and also intrinsic in the French public manifestation approach. Both apply the perception requirement not to the question of whether the persecutor differentially harms people with the characteristic, but to the particular claimant. Strikingly, the 2002 UNHCR Guidelines on membership of a particular social group also make that distinction, stating that 'not all members' need be 'singled out' for persecution, as 'certain members of the group may not be at risk if, for example, they *hide* their shared characteristic, they *are not known to the persecutors*, or they cooperate with the persecutor'.[58] Clearly, these people would still be at risk; the fact that they try to reduce that risk as much as possible does not change the nature of the risk, but is, rather, demonstrative of the existence of such risk.[59] Therefore, if an individual can show that they are (perceived to be) a member of a group that is persecuted in their country of origin, then they should logically be entitled to protection without further requirements. Goodwin-Gill's conclusion comes down to exactly that when he notes:

> If a sociological approach is adopted to the notion of groups in society, then apparently unconnected and unallied individuals may indeed satisfy the criteria ... Whether they then qualify as refugees having a well-founded fear of persecution by reason of their membership in a particular social group will depend on answers to related questions, including the perceptions *of the group* shared by other groups or the State authorities, policies and practices *vis-à-vis the group*, and the risk, if any, of treatment amounting to persecution.[60]

Yet even the most radically inclusive commentator appears to be hesitant to embrace this principle. Helton notes that '"mere membership" in a particular social group is not normally enough to substantiate a claim for refugee status', though under 'special circumstances' such membership alone may be sufficient.[61] These 'special circumstances' cannot be anything other than a well-founded fear of being persecuted on account of that group membership, which would be satisfied if the claimant can show that they belong (or are perceived to belong) to that group and that the group is persecuted in their country of origin. Aleinikoff similarly points to the requirement of 'something more': 'Importantly, this analysis does not suggest that every case of domestic abuse establishes a refugee claim ... The claimant would have to show "something more"'.[62] But he is careful to explicitly connect this

58 UNHCR, note 46, at 17; emphasis added.

59 The reason for the inclusion of this somewhat surprising distinction in the Guidelines may be the concern to ensure that the particular social group stays recognised. If it seemed too broad, decision-makers would be more reluctant to apply it.

60 Goodwin-Gill, note 18, 366; emphasis added.

61 Helton, note 41, 39–67, 63.

62 Aleinikoff, note 12, 263–311, 303.

'something more' to the (non-)availability of protection for the group as a whole, rather than to the individual claimant.[63]

Nonetheless, Spain and France are prime examples of instances where the 'special circumstances' or 'something more' requirement turns from the group to the individual claimant and, therefore, into a 'singling out' requirement. The 'individual persecution' requirement varieties outlined constitute a version of 'discretion reasoning', and thus an additional hurdle for claimants. If a person possesses a characteristic that is persecuted, they are at risk; the only way they can reduce that risk is if they hide or collaborate, or if the fact that they are members of the persecuted group is not known for other reasons – in other words, if they are 'discreet'.

8.4 CONCLUSION: SKETCHING THE BOUNDARIES OF THE SOCIAL GROUP

The two competing definitions of membership of a particular social group both in principle un-controversially encompass sexuality-based claims. The controversial questions arise with a view to the *scope* of protected sexual orientation in each of the concepts. A review of the literature on the conceptualisation of membership of particular social group shows that the 'protected characteristics' approach is designed to exclude what appears to be 'trivial' claims, and bears the risk of protection gaps where the receiving country's notion of social group is not in line with the persecutor's. If claimants fear harm for what is considered a non-fundamental aspect, they must hide it. Germany's understanding, according to which protection can only be granted if the sexual orientation is 'identity-defining' for the claimant, reflects this concern.

The 'social perception' approach, in contrast, is more broadly designed to avoid such protection gaps that may result from excluding certain groups *per definitionem*. A closer reading of the literature further reveals that the 'social perception' test would more appropriately be called 'persecutor's perception' test, as the relevant perception is that of the (potential) persecutor, be that private actors or the authorities. The persecutor's perception approach in principle precludes any a priori exclusion of certain 'particular social groups', just as there can be no exclusion of certain political opinions.[64] Rather, if the persecutor views a certain social group as

[63] Citing the Australian case of *Khawar*, he states that this requirement 'would be satisfied at least by a sustained or systemic absence of state protection for members of a particular social group attributable to a perception of them by the state as not deserving equal protection under the law with other members of the society'; Ibid., citing *Minister for Immigration and Multicultural Affairs* v. *Khawar* [2002] HCA 14, Australia: High Court, 11 April 2002.

[64] See the UK case of *RT (Zimbabwe)*, where the claimant received protection for *not* holding a political opinion: *RT (Zimbabwe) and others* v. *Secretary of State for the Home Department*, [2012] UKSC 38, United Kingdom: Supreme Court, 25 July 2012.

an obstacle such that persecution ensues, (imputed) members of those groups are entitled to protection. This broad approach to social groups is, in principle, in line with approaches to other Convention grounds such as political opinion and religion.

But even this broader approach is prone to 'discretion' logics. The limit that is often reverted to is the 'singling out' requirement. If persecution occurs for group membership, then distinctions among group members can be drawn on the basis of 'discretion reasoning' between those whose group membership is made public (either by their own choice or by accident) and those who try to avoid persecution by hiding it and 'passing unnoticed' – such that the group is divided into an 'open' and a 'discreet' group, as evidenced in both France and Spain.

In different ways, both approaches entail 'discretion' logics grounded in the concern to delimit the 'beneficiary class' of the Refugee Convention – and thus undermine the principle that claimants do not have to hide the characteristic for which they are persecuted. The persistence of the competing definitions and the confusion arising from them can be attributed to a different weighting of the two fundamental notions of refugee law identified in the introduction. Those subscribing to the protected characteristics approach slightly favour the severity argument, whereas those supporting the persecutor perception approach prefer the fundamentality principle. However, because everyone also backs the other notion respectively, neither of the approaches can remain stable; the protected characteristics approach cannot be read so as to require 'discretion', and the social perception approach cannot be read so as to protect entirely trivial claims. Both approaches simultaneously succumb and persist, as neither is able to dissolve the insoluble tension.

The same tension that troubled Grahl-Madsen's conceptualisation of political opinion thus also sows dissent in the cohesion of a notion of particular social group. Given the difficulties that emerge from the different approaches to defining both political opinion, as outlined in the previous chapter, as well as particular social group, as discussed in the present chapter, the following chapter explores the use of human rights as a benchmark for defining the Convention grounds, with a focus on religion. It will reveal that, rather than making the analysis more principled, by grounding the definition of the Convention grounds in established legal principles, a human rights approach makes it even messier by further shrouding the central tension.

9

Human Rights

Messing with the Definition

Given the complex questions that arise in the context of defining the Convention grounds, some decision-makers and scholars, seeking interpretative guidance, have drawn upon a human rights framework to determine the scope of protection.[1] As Lord Dyson put it in a UK Supreme Court decision:

> The Convention reasons reflect characteristics or statuses which either the individual cannot change or cannot be expected to change because they are so closely linked to his identity *or are an expression of fundamental rights*.[2]

This is an interesting suggestion to explore, given that the basic tension that was identified in this study is partly grounded in human rights. This tension consists in the clash between the notion that, on the one hand, the Convention grounds are so fundamental to human identity that claimants should not be compelled to hide, change or renounce them, and, on the other hand, the notion that the Refugee Convention is not there to provide a 'world wide guarantee' of freedoms. Both notions can be framed in terms of human rights.

Indeed, a jumbled handling of human rights arguments is one observation that emerges from the review of jurisprudence. Conspicuously, human rights arguments are mostly made in those jurisdictions with traditions of more detailed judicial reasoning. Very prominent in the common law jurisdictions, it emerges much more visibly from German practice than from the case law in France or Spain. As the analysis of decision-making practice revealed, references to human rights are well established in German case law in the context of religion-based claims (which is also reflected in the German referral for a preliminary ruling in the case of Y *and* Z) and

[1] Some of the main arguments of this chapter were previously published in Janna Wessels (2016) '"Discretion", Persecution and the Act/Identity Dichotomy', *VU Migration Law Series No. 12*, Vrije Universiteit Amsterdam.

[2] *RT (Zimbabwe) and others* v. *Secretary of State for the Home Department*, [2012] UKSC 38, United Kingdom: Supreme Court, 25 July 2012, per Lord Dyson at 25.

have, more recently, also been applied to claims based on sexuality.[3] The question is, do human rights arguments help in addressing the questions concerning the conceptualisation of the Convention grounds identified in the preceding chapters?

Remarkably, the application of a human rights framework to the Convention grounds is rarely explicitly spelled out. In contrast to persecution, which is regularly explicitly defined by reference to human rights, a human rights-based understanding of the Convention grounds is usually implicit and remains underdeveloped. The process of conceiving of the Convention grounds as expressions of human rights apparently seems so straightforward for religion, which is mapped onto the freedom of religion, and for political opinion, which is interpreted as an expression of the freedom of thought,[4] that it is simply taken for granted. It is already much less clear for cases based on membership of a particular social group – the uncertainty of what fundamental right to draw on for sexuality-based claims (e.g. privacy vs. equality)[5] suggests that this approach, in addition to being problematic for all Convention grounds, disproportionally affects social group claims, such as sexuality- or gender-based claims, because in these cases it is often not even clear which human right to link the group to. This chapter, therefore, explores the ways in which human rights are drawn on, and add another layer of complexity, in the context of the intricate questions surrounding the scope of protection. It examines how the human rights–based approach affects the conception of the Convention grounds in refugee law and explores the consequences of reframing the Convention grounds *as* human rights with a view to the tensions identified in the preceding analysis.

The argument advanced in this chapter is that the human rights-based understanding of refugee law fails to clearly and consistently distinguish the ways in which rights are applied. The effect is that persecution and Convention ground tend to be conflated. In order to fully grasp this effect, it is necessary to elaborate on the interrelationship between human rights and refugee law, which is shaped by a 'distinction' problem. This helps explain the 'lesser scope' rationale that determines refugee law doctrine and is at the core of the severity concern described in the introduction. Building on this, the chapter argues that the human rights approach tends to create a mess by conflating persecutory harm and Convention ground.

3 See Chapter 5 on German jurisprudence.

4 See e.g. Vincent Chetail (2014) 'Are Refugee Rights Human Rights? An Unorthodox Questioning of the Relations between Refugee Law and Human Rights Law', in Ruth Rubio-Marin (ed.) *Human Rights and Immigration*, Collected Courses of the Academy of European Law, Oxford: Oxford University Press, 19–72, 27.

5 See James Hathaway and Jason Pobjoy (2012) 'Queer Cases Make Bad Law', 44(2) *New York University Journal of International Law and Politics* 315–389. See also John Tobin's discussion of the persecution analysis in the UK Supreme Court case of *HJ (Iran) and HT (Cameroon)*, where he notes that each Lord relies on the breach of a different 'human right' that is not actually expressed in human rights treaties ('the right to be who they are', the 'right to live openly' and the 'right to dignity'); John Tobin (2012) 'Assessing GLBTI Refugee Claims: Using Human Rights Law to Shift the Narrative of Persecution within Refugee Law', 44(2) *New York University Journal of International Law and Politics* 447–484, 456–457.

In conceiving of the Convention grounds as human rights, the focus shifts away from the persecutory harm feared and turns refugee status determination into an assessment of the applicant's entitlements, the *value* they place on them and how they *exercise* these rights. Rather than making the assessment more principled by 'grounding' the elements of the Refugee definition, a human rights approach may thus *reduce* the scope of protection by opening up the space for 'discretion' logics. As the following will show, the human rights approach is therefore similarly unable to settle the dispute.

9.1 THE INTERRELATIONSHIP BETWEEN HUMAN RIGHTS AND REFUGEE LAW

The question of whether and how international refugee law forms part of international human rights law remains deeply contested. While the preamble to the 1951 Convention states a commitment to the equal enjoyment of fundamental human rights, scholars and decision-makers have struggled to understand and conceptualise the interplay between the two bodies of law.[6] The literature on the interrelationship between human rights and refugee law essentially reveals two main trends. First, the more 'dominant view'[7] is that characterised as the 'human rights approach' to refugee law, calling for an alignment of the two bodies of law. Second, and less prominent, is a more critical view, conscious of the 'uneasy relationship'[8] of the two fields. Both will be reviewed here with the aim of drawing out the 'distinction problem' that is inherent in a human rights-based understanding of refugee law.

9.1.1 *The Context: The Human Rights Approach to Refugee Law*

Since Hathaway's seminal 1991 book *The Law of Refugee Status*,[9] a human rights approach to refugee status has been the dominant view. Moving beyond the previously common 'dictionary approach', Hathaway drew on human rights in order to interpret and define 'key elements' of the Refugee Convention. Most notably, he offered an understanding of persecution grounded in human rights and based on the basic tenets of the Convention, which he identified as 'a liberal sense of the types of past or anticipated harm which might warrant protection abroad' as well as 'a fundamental preoccupation to identify forms of harm demonstrative of a breach

6 Jenni Millbank (2004) 'The Role of Rights in Asylum Claims on the Basis of Sexual Orientation', 4(2) *Human Rights Law Review* 193–228.

7 Michelle Foster (2007) *International Refugee Law and Socio-economic Rights – Refuge from Deprivation*, Cambridge Studies in International and Comparative Law, Cambridge: Cambridge University Press, 31.

8 Catherine Dauvergne (2013) 'Refugee Law as Perpetual Crisis', in Satvinder Juss and Colin Harvey (eds.) *Contemporary Issues in Refugee Law*, Cheltenham: Edward Elgar, 13–30, 23.

9 James Hathaway (1991) *The Law of Refugee Status*, Toronto: Butterworths, 104–124.

by a state of its basic obligations of protection'.[10] Drawing on these precepts, he then proposed the following definition: 'persecution may be defined as the sustained or systemic violation of basic human rights demonstrative of a failure of state protection'.[11]

In order to define such basic human rights, Hathaway turned this around and stated that, where there is a breach of those core entitlements that the state should protect, this constitutes persecution.[12] Hathaway distinguished different types of rights and proposed an understanding of persecution as a violation of *basic* human rights: 'Persecution is most appropriately defined as the sustained or systemic failure of state protection in relation to one of the core entitlements which has been recognized by the international community.'[13] These 'core entitlements' are defined by reference to the different international human rights instruments. First- and second-tier rights are those contained in the Universal Declaration on Human Rights (UDHR), which are made binding by their inclusion in the ICCPR and ICESCR. First-tier rights (freedom from arbitrary deprivation of life, freedom from torture and cruel inhuman and degrading treatment, etc.) are non-derogable; second-tier rights (such as freedom from arbitrary arrest, right to family life) are derogable in cases of national emergency. The third tier comprises rights enunciated in the UDHR that are also codified in the ICESCR, which pose less immediate obligations on states (right to work, entitlement to food, etc.). The fourth tier is composed of rights that are found in the UDHR but not contained in other instruments (such as the right to own property). Hathaway argues that breaches of first- and second-tier rights (the latter in non-emergency cases only) would always constitute persecution, whereas breaches of third-tier rights would only be considered persecutory in particularly severe or discriminatory cases, and breaches of fourth-tier rights would very rarely be considered as persecution.[14]

This understanding of persecution was widely received as a helpful 'principled approach'[15] and was subsequently adopted as authoritative. It has strongly influenced refugee law doctrine. Since then, it has become conventional wisdom in legal doctrine to define persecution by reference to human rights.[16] Its great contribution is that it prompted a shift beyond the previously common 'dictionary approach',

[10] Ibid., 104.
[11] Ibid., 104–105.
[12] See also Noll's distinction between negative and positive obligations: Gregor Noll (2006) 'Asylum Claims and the Translation of Culture into Politics', 41(3) *Texas International Law Journal* 491–501, 495.
[13] Hathaway, note 9, 112.
[14] Ibid., 108–112.
[15] See *Canada (Attorney General)* v. *Ward*, [1993] 2 S.C.R. 689, Canada: Supreme Court, 30 June 1993 as an early decision drawing heavily on Hathaway's framework and often relied on by other judgments in a range of jurisdictions.
[16] Chetail, note 4, 19–72, 26.

which often tended to restrict persecution to purely physical harms, and opened up a more complex understanding of persecution.

And yet, this approach has obvious drawbacks. The main one is the inevitable construction of a hierarchy within the body of human rights law, which purports to be universal, indivisible, interdependent and interrelated.[17] In particular, Hathaway's four-tiered system had been criticised for prioritising certain types of rights over others in a hierarchical human rights structure. As Catherine Dauvergne notes, '[d]ecision makers are usually clever enough to stop short of saying that certain human rights abuses are simply ok, but this structure of analysis invites an invidious line of reasoning nevertheless'.[18]

In her 2007 book *International Refugee Law and Socio-economic Rights – Refuge from Deprivation*, Michelle Foster responded to this central concern and developed Hathaway's human rights approach further.[19] Foster chose a different angle and developed what she characterises as a 'core obligations approach'. She considers this a

> more principled method of explaining the common-sense notion developed in the refugee case law that not all violations of human rights are equally serious, and thus provides a useful tool for conceptualising what it is that refugee judges are attempting to do when they undertake the persecution assessment.[20]

Foster's approach circumvents hierarchies between different *types* of rights, treating all human rights as equally important. Rather, the threshold for persecution is drawn at the level of the *quality of the breach*: whereas breaches affecting the 'core' of a right would lead to refugee protection, breaches on the 'periphery' of the right would not entail an obligation to protect. While not ruling out violations for particular sets of rights as not persecutory per se, the 'core/periphery' distinction still accounts for the 'lesser' scope of protection in refugee law that the term 'being persecuted' requires.

In their joint 2014 book, which appeared as the second edition of *The Law of Refugee Status*, Hathaway and Foster combined and further refined their previous approaches. They now explicitly reject any hierarchies of rights[21] and argue that all violations of human rights codified in international law amount to persecution

17 Hathaway and Foster recognised this in their co-authored second edition of *The Law of Refugee Status*: James Hathaway and Michelle Foster (2014) *The Law of Refugee Status* (2nd ed.), Cambridge: Cambridge University Press, 203.

18 Catherine Dauvergne (2008) *Making People Illegal: What Globalization Means for Migration and Law*, Cambridge: Cambridge University Press, 63–64.

19 Foster, note 7, 123–155.

20 Ibid., 198.

21 'There is, in truth, no convincing conceptual framework that is capable of distinguishing on an absolute basis between those rights that are "basic", "fundamental", or "important" and those that are not'; Hathaway and Foster, note 17, 204. Hathaway here clearly distances himself from the 'basic' human rights approach he had introduced twenty-five years earlier.

unless they are warranted by the limitations on the scope of that right – though the idea of marginal breaches persists, it is now reduced to what they term *de minimis* harm in exceptional cases.[22]

The human rights paradigm has been described as critical in the understanding of refugee law,[23] and many refugee and human rights scholars clearly endorse it. Deborah Anker, for example, argues that '[n]ot only are states interpreting key criteria of the refugee definition in the light of human rights principles, but international human rights law is providing the unifying theory binding different bodies of national jurisprudence'.[24] Alice Edwards similarly argues that, conceptually, international refugee law and international human rights law form part of the 'same legal schema and tradition' – and that 'keeping refugee law distinct from human rights law has played into the hands of governments choosing to flout minimum standards'.[25] Brian Gorlick also advocates the use of international, regional and national human rights standards and structures to provide refugees broader legal protection.[26] A particularly strong rejection of the 'unhelpful and unfounded dualist approach' of regarding 'international refugee law and international human rights law as separate and distinct bodies of jurisprudence addressing quite different problems' was presented by Louise Arbour in her introduction to the *Refugee Studies Quarterly* 60th anniversary of the UDHR special issue.[27] In her view, the notion that the two disciplines occupy two different *champs d'application* has proven surprisingly resilient and does a disservice to both, as they are 'cut from the same legal and jurisprudential cloth':[28] 'judges, advocates, practitioners, scholars, and policymakers' should therefore not allow themselves 'to be unduly fettered by counterproductive distinctions or excessive focus on certain parts of the law'.[29]

9.1.2 *The Distinction Problem: The Awkward Fit of Human Rights and Refugee Law*

Upon closer inspection, however, the resilience identified by Arbour is not so surprising. Rather, as critical scholars have noted, it accounts for the contrasts that

22 Hathaway and Foster, note 17, 204–206.

23 See e.g. Deborah Anker (2002) 'Boundaries in the Field of Human Rights: Refugee Law, Gender and the Human Rights Paradigm', 15 *Harvard Human Rights Journal* 133–154; Louise Arbour (2008) 'Message from Louise Arbour: United Nations High Commissioner for Human Rights', 27(3) *Refugee Studies Quarterly* 13–15.

24 Anker, note 23, 133–154, 136.

25 Alice Edwards (2005) 'Human Rights, Refugees, and the Right "To Enjoy" Asylum', 17(2) *International Journal of Refugee Law* 293–330, 294.

26 Brian Gorlick (2000) 'Human Rights and Refugees: Enhancing Protection through International Human Rights Law', *New Issues in Refugee Research*, Working Paper No. 30, www.refworld.org/docid/4ff581592.html, 7.

27 Arbour, note 23, 13–15, 13.

28 Ibid., 13–15, 14.

29 Ibid., 13–15, 15.

do exist between international human rights law and refugee law, which lead to an 'awkward fit',[30] exemplified in the fact that not all breaches of human rights – to which anyone is entitled as a person – are understood to lead to refugee status, and that refugee protection is therefore necessarily lesser in scope. This difference in scope has been described as 'the most palpable difference' between the two branches of international law.[31] As Dauvergne observed:

> Ironically . . . refugee law is either the mother-of-all-human-rights law, or not about human rights at all, as human rights refer to a different kind of thing that everyone can claim on the basis of being human, regardless of other circumstances. Refugee status is most explicitly *not* available to everyone and *not* regardless of other circumstances.[32]

The central issue is that refugee protection is only granted when a certain level of severity is reached that cannot be found in *any* breach of *any* human right. In reflecting 'why human rights can cause refugee law such trouble',[33] Colin Harvey emphasises that there is a clash between the human rights regime, which focuses on the protection of the human *person*, and international refugee law, as a legal mechanism that 'is particularly concerned with a designated *status*'[34] and which carries 'elements of the ghostly substance of citizenship elsewhere (until normality is restored, wherever that may be)'.[35] He suggests that, rather than being a challenge to it, refugee law may in fact be seen to be securely anchored within the instrumentalist logic of a profoundly statist model.[36] Given that it is 'evident that refugee law remains a secure part of the broader international human rights field', however, 'it is possible to overplay these contrasts'.[37] In other words, the focus in refugee law is on the state. This leads to a fundamental difference in the starting point – *status* as linking an individual to a state versus *person* qua person – which may at least partly

30 Dauvergne, note 8, 13–30, 30.
31 Chetail, note 4, 19–72, 23.
32 Dauvergne, note 18, 61–62; emphasis in original.
33 Colin Harvey (2013) 'Is Humanity Enough? Refugees, Asylum Seekers and the Rights Regime', in Satvinder Juss and Colin Harvey (eds.) *Contemporary Issues in Refugee Law*, Cheltenham: Edward Elgar, 68–89, 73.
34 Ibid., 68–89, 88.
35 Ibid.
36 Note that the argument that refugee law is entrenched in state-based thought also aligns with the drafting history of the right to seek and enjoy asylum in Article 14 of the Universal Declaration of Human Rights. While there was a tension during the drafting process between States that regarded asylum as their sovereign prerogative and those that saw it as a duty of the international community, the view that ultimately prevailed was that asylum was primarily a right of States; see Jane McAdam (2008) 'Introduction: Asylum and the Universal Declaration of Human Rights', 27(3) *Refugee Survey Quarterly* 3–13; see also: Guy Goodwin-Gill and Jane McAdam (2007) *The Refugee in International Law* (3rd ed.), Oxford: Oxford University Press, 358–359.
37 Harvey, note 33, 68–89, 88.

account for the 'uneasy relationship'[38] of refugees with international human rights law: though an entitlement to human rights protection ought to be based simply on being human, the fact that 'this is not, and has never been, enough, is the reason for refugee law'.[39] As a consequence, refugee law 'provides *surrogate* protection, at a *lesser* level'.[40] This is reflected in the principle that the Refugee Convention does not guarantee the same level of rights and freedoms to all – the severity argument. Inherent in the idea of the surrogacy of refugee status, there is a distinction problem when it comes to a human rights understanding of refugee status. There must be some degree of line-drawing, which excludes as much as it includes. The crucial question is where to locate the distinction and how to draw that line.

In this sense, the refugee regime 'is both within the wider tradition of international human rights and also acts as a subtle internal critique of it'.[41] According to Harvey, this need not be an 'intrinsic negative', but human rights discourse appears to have a 'positively disruptive impact' on refugee law.[42] While this chimes with the literature advocating a 'human-rights based approach' to refugee law, it remains open to question whether the disruption is indeed always positive. Dauvergne warned:

> Over the past two decades, as states have been cracking down on migration and as numbers of asylum seekers have been rising, refugee law has been drawing closer to human rights law. This is a useful and important development for individual protection, but it tends towards implosion. There is much contested ground here. Implosion is a long way off, but it is a pinpoint on the horizon – a vanishing point.[43]

Refugee law tends towards implosion, in the sense that the closer the understanding of persecution comes to any breach of any human right, eventually the raison d'être of refugee law vanishes. As research such as that by Dauvergne and Millbank has shown,[44] however, this implosion is indeed still looming in the far distance. They showed that there is a discrepancy – particularly in the United Kingdom – between the understanding of forced marriage outside the refugee context (where it is seen as a severe human rights abuse) and forced marriage within the refugee context (where most claims based on forced marriage fail, often based on a cultural relativity reasoning). Notably, in the refugee context human rights instruments on forced marriage are simply ignored.

38 Dauvergne, note 8, 13–30, 30.
39 Ibid.
40 Ibid.; emphasis in original.
41 Harvey, note 33, 68–89, 74–75.
42 Ibid., 68–89, 73.
43 Dauvergne, note 8, 13–30, 30 (internal citation omitted).
44 Catherine Dauverge and Jenni Millbank (2010) 'Forced Marriage as a Harm in Domestic and International Law', 73(1) *The Modern Law Review* 57–88.

But there is also a risk of *explosion* of refugee law resulting from a human rights approach, arising from overplaying the different foci of the two fields – *status* versus *person* – and uncritically reconceiving refugee law *as* human rights protection. Explosion becomes imminent when the fundamental differences are disregarded; attempts to simultaneously understand all elements of the refugee definition in terms of human rights leads to a wild mess of inextricably contradictory assumptions.

In order to avoid explosion, it is of utmost importance to have a clear understanding of which human rights are applied to which element of the Convention definition and what consequences this entails. Looking more closely at authors who defend a 'human-rights based approach'[45] to refugee law, however, it becomes clear that they often do not explicitly distinguish between the elements of the definition and fail to assess their interplay.

9.1.3 *Locating the Lesser Scope: Human Rights and Persecution*

While the literature is overwhelmingly supportive of a human rights approach to refugee law, there is a general lack of clarity as to which human rights standards apply and where. Thus, while refugee law 'is only ever partially about human rights protection',[46] this seems to back up Millbank's finding that refugee decision-making cannot be instantly improved by the use of international human rights standards, as reference to these does not automatically translate into a thoughtful analysis and application. Rather, she states that they may also be utilised to restrict, rather than expand, an understanding of the rights of asylum-seekers.[47] In other words, much depends on the way the distinction problem is addressed – how the difference in scope between the two fields is reconciled.

Hathaway, who is credited with introducing the 'human rights' approach to refugee law, and later Foster, who drew on and developed his approach, both located the 'lesser' scope of refugee law in the quality of persecution. Though ostensibly calling for a human rights approach to 'refugee law' in general terms, the authors consistently referred to a human rights-based understanding of the 'being persecuted' element only.[48] In her very comprehensive and concise analysis of the 'human rights approach' to 'refugee law' extending over more than eighty pages, for example, Foster repeatedly refers to 'key elements of the refugee

45 Foster, note 7, 31.
46 Dauverge and Millbank, note 44, 57–88.
47 Millbank shows how Australia has used international human rights to restrict an understanding of the rights of lesbians and gay men – whereas Canada has successfully and positively integrated the human rights framework into refugee determinations of lesbians and gay men, Millbank, note 6, 193–228.
48 See also Chetail, note 4, 19–72, 26–27. Note that some scholars analyse procedural issues such as minimum standards outside refugee status determination as such in a human rights context, e.g., Edwards, note 25, 293–330.

convention, *such as persecution*',[49] though her discussion is then effectively limited to persecution. Similarly, Hathaway's seminal *The Law of Refugee Status* developed the human rights argument most comprehensively when introducing the four-tiered human rights approach to defining persecution. To be sure, Hathaway has further expanded the argument that refugee law should be reconceived as human rights protection in subsequent work;[50] for example, in addition to conceptualising the 'being persecuted' inquiry by reference to international human rights law, he drew on international human rights standards to limit the reach of the 'internal protection alternative' doctrines,[51] to consider the circumstances when risk following from behaviour will warrant refugee status,[52] and to sketch the scope of the obligations that a state owes to refugees.[53] But as Pobjoy observed, '[a]lthough Hathaway advocates this vision in a more general sense, the link has been most readily embraced by domestic courts in the context of the "being persecuted" inquiry'.[54] This is likely due to the fact that Hathaway's analysis of other 'key elements in the light of human rights' was initially only undertaken in passing and in no consistent manner, particularly in relation to the Convention grounds. For example, in the discussion of Convention grounds in *The Law of Refugee Status*, Hathaway briefly referred to the Universal Declaration of Human Rights when introducing 'religion'[55] but not the other grounds, although he mentioned 'basic human rights' generally as a yardstick for determining a particular social group, without further discussion.[56] It was not until the second edition of *The Law of Refugee Status* appeared in 2014 that Hathaway and Foster submitted an analysis laying out the human rights approach to each of the elements in a more principled manner. Yet their analysis does not

[49] Foster, note 7, 1–86, e.g. 39, 49; emphasis added.

[50] See e.g. James Hathaway (1991) 'Reconceiving Refugee Law as Human Rights Protection' 4(2) *Journal of Refugee Studies* 113–131; James Hathaway (1998) 'The Relationship between Human Rights and Refugee Law: What Refugee Judges Can Contribute', in *International Association of Refugee Law Judges: The Realities of Refugee Determination on the Eve of a New Millennium: The Role of the Judiciary*, 3rd Conference, Ottawa, October 1998, 80–90; see also Jason Pobjoy (2013) 'A Child Rights Framework for Assessing the Status of Refugee Children', in Satvinder Juss and Colin Harvey (eds.) *Contemporary Issues in Refugee Law*, Cheltenham: Edward Elgar, 91–137, 122.

[51] James Hathaway and Michelle Foster (2003) 'Internal Protection/Relocation/Flight Alternative as an Aspect of Refugee Status Determination', in Erika Feller, Frances Nicholson and Volker Türk (eds.) *Refugee Protection in International Law: UNHCR's Global Consultations on International Protection*, Cambridge: Cambridge University Press, 357–417.

[52] Rodger Haines, James Hathaway and Michelle Foster (2003) 'Claims to Refugee Status Based on Voluntary but Protected Actions – Discussion Paper No. 1, Advanced Refugee Law Workshop, International Association of Refugee Law Judges, Auckland, New Zealand, October 2002', 15(3) *International Journal of Refugee Law* 430–443; Hathaway and Pobjoy, note 5, 315–389.

[53] James Hathaway (2005) *The Rights of Refugees under International Law*, Cambridge University Press.

[54] Pobjoy, note 50, 91–137, 122.

[55] Hathaway, note 9, 145.

[56] Ibid., 161.

reconcile all the different human rights arguments with each other. Since the authors proceed by elements of the definition, a potential clash or conflation resulting from understanding both the persecutory harm and the Convention ground by reference to human rights does not become apparent in their analysis.[57]

Both the 'four-tiered' and the 'core/periphery' human rights approach were developed to account for the 'lesser scope' of refugee law by providing a distinction between human rights breaches reaching the severity of persecutory harm and those not of that quality. This has been received as a useful tool in addressing the often difficult and contentious question of whether the harm that a claimant faces amounts to persecution. It aims to make *the persecution analysis* more principled by grounding it in human rights norms. Thus, the distinction in scope between human rights and refugee protection was initially identified in the quality of persecution. This appears to be a clear and relatively straightforward matter.

However, as a result of moving beyond purely physical harms when considering persecution, breaches of those human rights that can be mapped onto the Convention grounds – such as, for example, a violation of the freedom of religion – are also capable of amounting to persecution. This, in turn, is the source of much confusion, including the risk of conflating persecutory harm and Convention ground. To illustrate, under a human rights–based approach, in theory, the harms that a political opposition party or gay people might face could include, for example, denial of participation in religious services, among other harms.[58] But the situation easily gets muddled up in claims *based* on religion, where the infringement of freedom of religion itself is considered to amount to persecution. In that case, freedom of religion adopts the double role of providing the framework both to assess the severity of the harm *and* the scope of the Convention ground. The logic of this approach is that the question of the ground is automatically answered if the harm is found in the infringement of freedom of religion. Thus, this approach effectively merges both elements into one, leading to a range of complications to which 'discretion' logics tend to be the response. The balance of the chapter discusses these.

9.2 A HUMAN RIGHTS UNDERSTANDING OF THE CONVENTION GROUNDS?

Framing the Convention grounds as expressions of human rights appears so self-explanatory in the context of a human rights paradigm in refugee law that it has seldom been questioned or critically reflected upon; rather, it is often just assumed in passing. However, the 'danger in transplanting approaches developed in an area

[57] Hathaway and Foster, note 17.
[58] See Ibid., 260–287.

with one set of objectives into a field that has quite different policy aims' has long been recognised.[59] The notions of political opinion or religion may *not* have the same meaning and purpose as Convention grounds in refugee law as may be attributed to them in certain international human rights instruments. John Tobin pointed out that distinctive interpretative communities have developed autonomous meanings for the terms within each of the regimes, which creates the potential for confusion when terms and concepts are imported into one regime from another.[60] Indeed, it is not unreasonable to wonder whether the primary purpose of the Refugee Convention is the protection of certain characteristics (the Convention grounds) or the protection from harm (persecution). This question is, in some ways, a reformulation of the central tension between the fundamentality principle and the severity argument. As the following analysis will show, the answer given to this question tips the balance one way or another but never gets around the paradox.

9.2.1 *Conceiving Sexual Orientation in Terms of Human Rights: Hathaway & Pobjoy*

Hathaway and Pobjoy are among the few scholars who have engaged in attempts to conceive of the Convention grounds in terms of human rights law. In their article in response to the judgment in *HJ (Iran) and HT (Cameroon)*, they argue that the 'beneficiary class' of the Refugee Convention is delimited and the necessary limitation of the Convention grounds is best achieved by 'grounding interpretation of both protected forms of civil or political status and the activities inherent therein in international human rights law'.[61] They reason:

> Reliance on international human rights law, of course, denies the possibility of immediate assertion that all activities in any way associated with sexuality are necessarily protected. We nonetheless believe that it affords the most principled basis for drawing a line between behaviour or actions included within a form of protected civil or political status, and those which are not.[62]

Hathaway and Pobjoy buttress this position by reference to cases based on political opinion and religion, where 'courts have been quite prepared to engage in line-drawing to separate protected from unprotected forms of activity'.[63] According to them, 'the ICCPR offers clear, if nascent, textual guidance on the scope of protected activities' to carry out the task of line-drawing, though they concede with respect to

59 Foster, note 7, 57.
60 Tobin, note 5, 447–484, 454.
61 Hathaway and Pobjoy, note 5, 315–389, 384.
62 Ibid., 315–389, 382.
63 Ibid., 315–389, 378.

the evidence they cite that 'the line drawing of courts in relation to religion and political opinion . . . has at times been problematic'.[64]

Hathaway and Pobjoy go on to note that the 'difficulty is accentuated in the sexual orientation context where . . . the absence of any express mention of sexual orientation in international instruments means that guidance must be derived indirectly from the understandings of non-discrimination law, and international human rights law more generally'.[65] Hathaway and Pobjoy do not offer any particular human right to draw on for this task. Instead, they refer to a range of different human rights judgments, which, in turn, based their reasoning on a variety of different norms.[66] On this basis, Hathaway and Pobjoy settle on a standard that is itself unknown to human rights law: they conclude that 'the protected status of sexual orientation ought more generally to encompass any activity reasonably required to reveal or express an individual's sexual identity'.[67] So Hathaway and Pobjoy are at pains to ground sexual orientation in human rights law in order to establish that it is protected at all, while simultaneously seeking to ground legitimate *restrictions* on sexual orientation in the right to privacy, the right to equality and the prohibition of torture and cruel and degrading treatment.[68] This confusing approach – which turns to a wide variety of human rights in order to undertake the delicate task of defining both those aspects of sexuality refugee law protects and those it does not – has many drawbacks, which have been extensively discussed elsewhere.[69]

The situation is much clearer in the context of religion-based claims, since, for this class of cases, freedom of religion provides a specific human right to rely on. German practice concerning religion-based claims, which gave rise to the CJEU judgment in *Y and Z*, is instructive in this context, since what Hathaway and Pobjoy seek to define has long been established practice in Germany. The effects that reverting to human rights in order to conceptualise the Convention grounds has on 'discretion' reasoning and the scope of protection are, therefore, best assessed with regards to these claims. Such effects will only be compounded in the context of sexuality-based claims, where they are shrouded by the uncertainty of which human right to rely on.

64 Ibid., 315–389, 379.

65 Ibid.; see also Hathaway and Foster, note 17, 445, stating that '[a]ny attempt to delimit the broad reach of this ground [claims founded in sexual orientation], for example on the basis that the applicant can legitimately be expected to refrain from engaging in certain conduct on return, must be undertaken *in accordance with international human rights principles*'; emphasis added.

66 Hathaway and Pobjoy, note 5, 315–389, 380–381.

67 Ibid., 315–389, 382.

68 Ibid., 315–389, 346–371.

69 See criticism in particular in Jenni Millbank (2012) 'The Right of Lesbians and Gay Men to Live Freely, Openly, and on Equal Terms Is Not Bad Law: A Reply to Hathaway and Pobjoy', 44(2) *New York University Journal of International Law and Politics* 497–527; Tobin, note 5, 447–484; and Ryan Goodman (2012) 'Asylum and the Concealment of Sexual Orientation: Where Not to Draw the Line', 44(2) *New York University Journal of International Law and Politics* 407–446.

9.2.2 *Conceiving Religion in Terms of Human Rights: Germany and the CJEU in* Y and Z

The decision of the Court of Justice of the European Union in *Y and Z* is a clear illustration of the range of complications following from a human rights understanding of the Convention grounds. To recap, Y and Z were two Pakistani nationals of Ahmadi faith. The Ahmadiyya community is an Islamic reformist movement, contested by the Sunni Muslim majority in Pakistan. Ahmadi religious activities are severely restricted by the Pakistan Penal Code; public profession of this faith is liable to be considered blasphemous, a charge punishable by a sentence of imprisonment or even the death penalty.[70] Accordingly, Y and Z claimed refugee protection on religious grounds, based on their fear of imprisonment and death.

When conducting the persecution analysis, however, rather than focusing on the right to life and liberty, the German courts turned to assessing the scope of freedom of religion. That is, rather than considering imprisonment as an infringement of the right to liberty and death as an infringement of the right to life in the persecution analysis, they turned to assessing whether 'not being able to profess their religion in public' constituted an infringement of the freedom of religion amounting to persecution. This twist, which is well established in German case law,[71] exposes a slip in the analysis that confuses two of the central elements of the refugee definition: Convention ground and persecution. This is clearly reflected in the questions referred by the Bundesverwaltungsgericht (Federal Administrative Court of Germany), which framed the infringement of the freedom of religion itself (i.e. the impossibility of practising their religion in public) as the persecution feared.[72] Notably, in its questions to the CJEU, the referring Court clearly frames

[70] See *Federal Republic of Germany* v. *Y and Z (Opinion of Advocate General Bot)*, Joined Cases C-71/11 and C-99/11, European Union: Court of Justice of the European Union, 19 April 2012, at 2.

[71] See e.g. Julian Lehmann (2014) 'Persecution, Concealment and the Limits of a Human Rights Approach in (European) Asylum Law – The Case of Germany v. Y and Z in the Court of Justice of the European Union' 26(1) *International Journal of Refugee* Law 65–81, 66–70.

[72] The questions referred:

'1. *Is Article 9(1)(a) of the directive … to be interpreted as meaning that not every interference with religious freedom which infringes Article 9 of the ECHR constitutes an act of persecution within the meaning of [the former provision], and that a severe violation of religious freedom as a basic human right arises only if the core area of that religious freedom is adversely affected?*

2. *If Question 1 is to be answered in the affirmative:*

(a) *Is the core area of religious freedom limited to the profession and practice of faith in the areas of the home and neighbourhood, or can there be an act of persecution, within the meaning of article 9(1)(a) of the directive … also in cases where, in the country of origin, the observance of faith in public gives rise to a risk to life, physical integrity or freedom and the applicant accordingly abstains from such practice?*

(b) *If the core area of religious freedom can also comprise the public observance of certain religious practices:*

religion as a basic human right and places the discussion of religion squarely in the context of persecution, as the reference to Article 9(1)(a) of the *Qualification Directive*,[73] defining persecution, indicates. It is *not* framed in the context of the Convention grounds, for which Article 10(1)(b) states:

> the concept of religion shall in particular include the holding of theistic, non-theistic and atheistic beliefs, the participation in, or abstention from, formal worship in private or in public, either alone or in community with others, other religious acts or expressions of view or forms of personal or communal conduct based on or mandated by any religious belief.[74]

So, rather than focusing on the fear of imprisonment or death and then asking whether the claimants feared these harms because of their Ahmadi religion, the litigation revolved around the acceptability of limiting their public expression of their faith.

Figure 9.1 represents this shift: turning from imprisonment and death (and consequently, the right to life and liberty) to the public profession of faith (and freedom of religion), essentially turns from persecution to the Convention ground, to the effect that the claimant's acts are assessed, rather than the harm inflicted by the persecutor. What is portrayed as the persecution assessment takes place in the sphere of the Convention ground; the limitations that are placed on the Convention

- *Does it suffice in that case, in order for there to be a severe violation of religious freedom, that the applicant feels that such observance of his faith is indispensable in order for him to preserve his religious identity?*
- *Or is it further necessary that the religious community to which the applicant belongs should regard that religious observance as constituting a central part of its doctrine?*
- *Or can further restrictions arise as a result of other circumstances, such as the general conditions in the country of origin?*

3. *If Question 1 is to be answered in the affirmative:*
Is there a well-founded fear of persecution, within the meaning of article 2(c) of the directive ... if it is established that the applicant will carry out certain religious practices – other than those falling within the core area – after returning to the country of origin, even though they will give rise to a risk to his life, physical integrity or freedom, or can the applicant reasonably be expected to abstain from such practices?'; *Federal Republic of Germany* v. *Y and Z (Opinion of Advocate General Bot)*, note 70, at 18.

73 Article 9(1)(a) *Recast Qualification Directive*: 'In order to be regarded as an act of persecution within the meaning of Article 1(A) of the Geneva Convention, an act must: (a) be sufficiently serious by its nature or repetition as to constitute a severe violation of basic human rights, in particular the rights from which derogation cannot be made under Article 15(2) of the European Convention for the Protection of Human Rights and Fundamental Freedoms.'

74 Article 10(1)(b) Directive 2011/95/EU of the European Parliament and of the Council of 13 December 2011 on standards for the qualification of third-country nationals or stateless persons as beneficiaries of international protection, for a uniform status for refugees or for persons eligible for subsidiary protection, and for the content of the protection granted (recast), oj L 337/9, 20 December 2011 (*Recast Qualification Directive*).

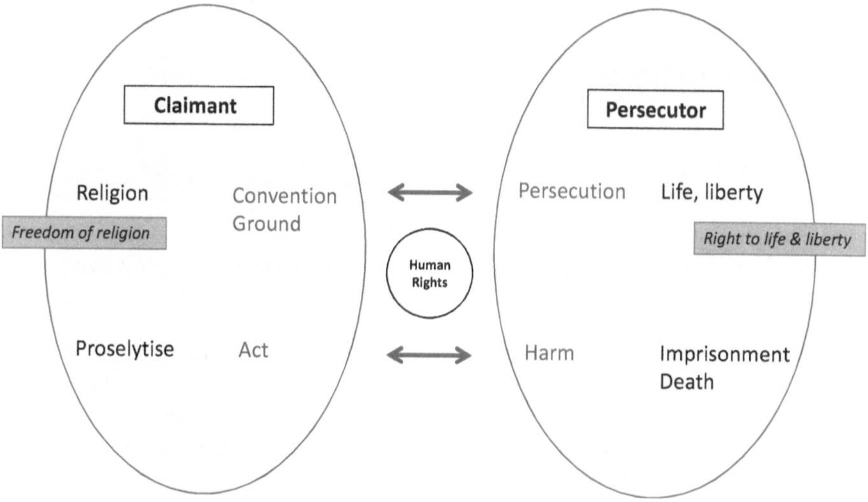

FIGURE 9.1. Shifting the focus between claimant and persecutor

ground are assessed to determine whether they are 'tolerable' or amount to persecution, and persecution becomes an 'interference in a person's religion or sexual identity'.[75] It is at this stage, where the focus turns onto the claimant's behaviour and expression of the Convention ground, that the human rights approach becomes restrictive and gives rise to 'discretion' logics.

The slip was, of course, invested in the referral. As noted, the framing of the questions referred for preliminary ruling is important, as the Court is bound to reply to the specific questions presented. But the Court does have the ability to restate questions in the interest of clarity without subverting them, and often does so ('the referring court in essence wants to know whether . . .').[76] However, the CJEU decided not to make use of that option here. In his opinion presented to the CJEU,[77] Advocate General Bot appears to have noted the slip, stating that 'persecution is characterised not by the fact that it occurs in the sphere of freedom of religion, but by the nature of the repression inflicted on the individual and its consequences'.[78] This point was similarly taken up in the judgment of the Court:

> It follows that acts which, on account of their intrinsic severity as well as the severity of their consequences for the person concerned, may be regarded as constituting

[75] Harald Dörig (2014) 'German Courts and Their Understanding of the Common European Asylum System (Opinion)', 25(4) *International Journal of Refugee Law* 768–778, 778.

[76] For details on the preliminary rulings procedure, please refer to Annex I.

[77] The Court of Justice of the European Union has one judge per EU country and is helped by eight 'advocates-general' whose job is to present opinions on the cases brought before the Court. They must do so publicly and impartially; see Annex I for further details.

[78] *Federal Republic of Germany* v. *Y and Z (Opinion of Advocate General Bot)*, note 70, at 52, see also paragraphs 44–46.

> persecution must be identified, not on the basis of the particular aspect of religious freedom that is being interfered with but on the basis of the nature of the repression inflicted on the individual and its consequences.[79]

It appears, however, that both the Advocate General and the Court stop short of entirely rejecting the relevance of freedom of religion, as they still refer to the 'repression inflicted' (arguably the prohibitions on the public profession of the faith) and 'its consequences' (arguably the prospect of imprisonment and death). The conclusions of both Advocate General Bot and the court indicate some continued confusion when they state in very similar terms that

> a violation of the right to freedom of religion may constitute persecution within the meaning of Article (9)(1)(a) of the Directive where an applicant for asylum, as a result of exercising that freedom in his country of origin, runs a genuine risk of, in alia, being prosecuted or subjected to inhuman or degrading treatment or punishment.[80]

This convoluted formulation appears to break down to a person facing persecutory harm (prosecution or inhuman or degrading treatment or punishment) for reasons of religion. Adding the 'violation of the right to freedom of religion' to the equation does nothing but confuse the assessment by shifting the focus onto the claimant and linking the persecutory harm to a violation of the wrong human right.

9.3 TWO DISTINCT NEW APPROACHES TO PERSECUTION

As a result of the concern to address persecution as encompassing harms beyond physical injuries, two distinct new approaches to persecution have emerged. On the basis of a conflation between harm and reason, both give rise to 'discretion'. The logic is that, in such situations, Convention ground and persecutory harm coincide, so that the question of Convention ground is *automatically answered* when the harm

79 *Federal Republic of Germany* v. Y *and* Z, Joined Cases C-71/11 and C-99/11, Court of Justice of the European Union, 5 September 2012, at 65.

80 Ibid., at 67, see also Opinion of Advocate General Bot, *Federal Republic of Germany* v. Y *and* Z *(Opinion of Advocate General Bot)*, note 70, at 86: '… a severe violation of freedom of religion, regardless of which component of that freedom is targeted by the violation, is likely to amount to an "act of persecution" where the asylum seeker, by exercising that freedom or infringing the restrictions placed on the exercise of that freedom in his country of origin, runs a real risk of being executed or subjected to torture, or inhuman or degrading treatment, or being reduced to slavery or servitude or of being prosecuted or imprisoned arbitrarily'.

Note that the wording of the definition of persecution in Article 9(1)(a) of the EU *Qualification Directive* bears similarities to Hathaway's approach, making reference to 'basic human rights': '1. Acts of persecution within the meaning of article 1A of the Geneva Convention must: (a) Be sufficiently serious by their nature or repetition as to constitute a severe violation of basic human rights, in particular the rights from which derogation cannot be made under Article 15(2) of the [ECHR].' It does not, however, require both a breach of a right underlying the Convention ground *and* another breach deemed persecutory.

feared is an infringement of the freedom of religion. But this approach bears the risk of overlooking the *other* harms that the claimant would face and enters into complex relationships with these.

1 *Alternative approach: Focus on the Claimant (and the Convention ground)*
   The *prohibition* of, or impossibility for the claimant to exercise, certain practices related to the Convention ground – i.e., the limitation of the right underlying the Convention ground – is in itself the persecutory act. In other words, the persecutory harm here *consists in* the fact that the relevant Convention ground may not be publicly proclaimed.
2 *Additional approach: Focus on the Persecutor (and persecution)*
   Certain practices (acts, behaviour) of the claimant may be *triggers* of persecutory harm (exercised by the persecutor), which may be imprisonment, death or any other sustained or systematic violation of human rights. In other words, persecutory harm *follows* the public proclamation *or any other form of revelation* of the relevant Convention ground, which itself must respond to the fundamentality concern.

Both approaches and their implications will be discussed in turn in order to show how the well-intentioned move of opening up the notion of persecution to a wider range of harms grounded in human rights law rebounds and becomes potentially restrictive. In both the alternative and the additional view, the focus shifts away from an applicant seeking protection from persecutory harm to an applicant who is 'seeking to exercise a human right', that is, asking for permission to act in a particular way, *even though* this would entail persecutory harm. This allows for situations where the answer is 'no' – the claimant cannot act in that way and must exercise 'discretion'.

9.3.1 *Alternative Approach: Focus on Claimant and Convention Ground*

The first view, labelled here 'the alternative approach', focuses on the Convention ground and makes a series of problematic assumptions. An example of this kind of reasoning can be found in the New Zealand case *Refugee Appeal No. 74665/03*:

> A *prohibition* is to be understood to be within the ambit of a risk of 'being persecuted' if it infringes basic standards of international human rights law. Where, however, *the substance of the risk* does not amount to a violation of a right under applicable standards of international law, it is difficult to understand why it should be recognised as sufficient to give rise to a risk of 'being persecuted.[81]

[81] *Refugee Appeal* No. 74665/03, New Zealand: Refugee Status Appeals Authority, 7 July 2004, at 115; emphasis added.

This view suggests that the infringement of the right that is mapped onto the applicable Convention ground has to amount to persecution. The inability to proselytise itself would have to fulfil the criteria of persecution. At the same time, the adverse consequences, which would *otherwise* materialise (i.e. if the person did not respect the infringement or limitation and proselytised irrespectively) and which are the actual substance of the risk, such that *they* have to reach the threshold of persecutory harm, are overlooked. If the infringement of the right is not found to amount to persecution, the applicant would be expected to avoid the adverse consequences precisely by respecting the limitation (being 'discreet') – without consideration of the consequences that would ensue if they did not respect it, or, for that matter, if their identity were revealed in any other way. It assumes that persecution is directed at acts and that it is therefore within the power of the applicant to *avoid* the adverse consequences through 'discretion' and, based on that assumption, ignores these adverse consequences, or, more to the point, the feared persecution. As such, it is conceived as an *alternative* way to establish persecution where secrecy is taken as synonymous with safety; if behaving 'discreetly' is understood to obviate the risk of imprisonment or death, according to this view the relevant risk becomes that of having to bear the limitation on the freedom of religion, or, in other words, 'discretion'.

Viewing the infringement of a fundamental right as the relevant persecutory harm then swiftly turns into an assessment of the applicant's behaviour. Through the detour of what a state is required to protect, the inquiry turns into an assessment of the ways in which the claimant is entitled to draw attention to their status.[82] Yet it would seem that applying the 'infringement of a fundamental human right' standard to the 'being persecuted' analysis in this way, the relevant human right would almost always be found to be 'fundamental'. The rights that the Convention grounds are mapped onto, such as freedom of religion and freedom of thought for claims based on religion and political opinion respectively, are clearly fundamental human rights. Note that the case is not as clear for claims based on membership of a particular social group, as Hathaway and Pobjoy's article plainly demonstrates.

In this broad definition, however, in order to delimit those applicants who are genuinely entitled to protection from those who are not, courts and scholars have then engaged in determining the 'metes and bounds' of the fundamental right the claimant 'seeks to exercise'. In this line, Haines, Hathaway and Foster suggested that, for persons at risk of being prohibited from engaging in public or overt activities, the denial of public exercise is unlikely to be within the ambit of a fear of 'being persecuted' where the relevant right encompasses no public dimension.[83]

82 Ibid., at 115.

83 Haines et al., note 52, 430–443, 439–440.

In one notable case in particular, *Refugee Appeal No. 74665/03*, the New Zealand Refugee Status Appeals Authority engaged with this question. According to the Authority, for the purpose of refugee determination the focus must be on 'the minimum core entitlement conferred by the relevant right'.[84] The examples that the Authority lists for the kind of activity deemed to be at the margin of a 'protected right' provide an idea of the sort of exercise this task would require. The Authority enumerates: the prohibition on a gay person adopting a child, the denial to post-operative transsexuals of the right to marry, the prosecution of gay people for sado-masochistic acts. The Authority suggested that, whether or not any of these involved breaches of human rights, they could not be said to amount to persecution since the prohibited activities in each case were at the margin of the protected right – where it remains unclear *which* right that would be.[85] This is expressed in strong terms in the end of *Refugee Appeal No. 74665/03*:

> Once those boundaries have been identified it is possible to determine whether the *proposed action* by the claimant is at the core of the right or at its margins and whether the prohibition or restriction imposed by the state is lawful in terms of international human rights law. If the proposed action is at the core of the right and the restriction unlawful, we would agree that the claimant has no duty to avoid the harm by being discreet or by complying with the wishes of the persecutor. If, however, the proposed activity is at the margin of the protected interest, then *persistence in the activity in the face of the threatened harm is not a situation of 'being persecuted'* for the purposes of the Refugee Convention. *The individual can choose to carry out the intended conduct or to act 'reasonably' or 'discreetly' in order to avoid the threatened serious harm. None of these choices, however, engages the Refugee Convention.*[86]

According to this view, 'a fundamental human right' cannot be forfeited, but the 'simple act' of participating in a gay rights march possibly can – because the act may not be a 'fundamental human right', or rather, not 'covered' by the relevant fundamental right. The right appears to become a stand-in for identity; nobody disputes that the claimant has a right to *be* gay, but acts are viewed as separate from that identity, which has repercussions for the persecution analysis as decision-makers seem to veer from the actual question. This approach reproduces Grahl-Madsen's blurry notion of acts beyond mere expression. It is also reminiscent of the fundamental characteristics approach to defining membership of a particular social group – and replicates Hathaway and Pobjoy's concept of limiting protection of those acts 'reasonably required to express' the protected characteristic.

In *HJ (Iran) and HT (Cameroon)*, though a unanimous decision, the judges were split on the question of whether the limitation on the right mapped onto the

[84] *Refugee Appeal No. 74665/03*, note 81, at 82.
[85] Ibid., at 99–102.
[86] Ibid., at 120; emphasis added.

Convention ground (i.e. 'discretion') had to amount to persecution itself. Lord Walker, for example, considered that a focus on the harm occasioned by modification of behaviour 'may be an unnecessary complication, and lead to confusion'.[87] In contrast both Lords Rodger[88] and Dyson[89] agreed with the position of the New Zealand Refugee Status Appeals Authority, finding that a determination of whether the applicant's proposed or intended action lay at the core of the right or at its margins was useful in deciding whether or not the prohibition of it amounted to persecution. Lord Rodger 'respectfully [saw] the attractions' of the approach and summarised it as follows:

> [T]he authority ... preferred to use a human rights framework in order to determine the limits of what an individual is *entitled to do and not to do*. That approach might, for instance, be relevant if an applicant were claiming asylum on the ground that he feared persecution *if he took part in a gay rights march*.[90]

So in this view, suddenly, the issue under scrutiny for decision-makers becomes the analysis of whether the 'proposed actions' of a claimant are 'protected' by international human rights law – it becomes a situation where a person asks permission to 'do' something or behave in a certain way, and squarely places the issue in the context of the central tension between fundamentality and triviality, making it an exercise in 'discretion' reasoning. In the words of Spijkerboer, '[t]o formulate this as the question of whether one's hairstyle is protected by international human rights law reflects a fundamental misunderstanding of what refugee protection means in situations such as these'.[91] Indeed, it insinuates that the claimant is somehow inconvenienced by the fact that they cannot 'do' something and 'live as freely and as openly ... as he would be able to if he were not returned'.[92] This then drives decision-makers to reflexively defend the position that the 'purpose [of the Convention is] not to guarantee to asylum-seekers when they are returned all the freedoms that are available in the country where they seek refuge'.[93] For example, in *RT (Zimbabwe) and others*, a political opinion case, Lord Dyson confirmed his

[87] *HJ (Iran) and HT (Cameroon)* v. *Secretary of State for the Home Department*, [2010] UKSC 31, United Kingdom: Supreme Court, 7 July 2010, per Lord Walker at 96.

[88] Ibid., at 72.

[89] Ibid., at 114–115, though he sees no scope for it for sexual orientation cases, but, rather, for political opinion and religion cases.

[90] Ibid., per Lord Rodger at 72; emphasis added.

[91] Thomas Spijkerboer (2012) 'Two Remarks on Queer Law and Queer Politics: Thomas Spijkerboer Responds to Jenni Millbank & Guglielmo Verdirame', Panel 3 of the Online Symposium of the *NYU Journal of International Law and Politics*, Vol. 44(2), http://opiniojuris.org/2012/03/09/two-remarks-on-queer-law-and-queer-politics-thomas-spijkerboer-responds-to-jenni-millbank-guglielmo-verdirame.

[92] *HJ (Iran) and HT (Cameroon)* v. *Secretary of State for the Home Department*, note 87, per Lord Rodger at 35c.

[93] Ibid., at 15.

earlier support for the New Zealand approach, finding that it facilitated a determination of whether *the proposed action* by the claimant was 'at the *core* of the right or at its *margins*',[94] and noting that the 'distinction is valuable because it focuses attention on the important point that persecution is more than a breach of human rights'.[95] In other words, the tension between severity and fundamentality resurfaces, and variants on the 'discretion' theme serve to remedy it. 'Discretion' is vested in a human rights cloak.

9.3.2 *Additional Approach: Focus on Persecutor and Harm*

Rather than an alternative, the persecutory infringement of the Convention ground may also be viewed as an *additional* requirement to establish persecution. In this approach, characterised here as the 'additional approach' to persecution, the analysis also slides into the nexus analysis, resulting in a complex confusion of Convention ground, 'being persecuted' and 'for reasons of'. This approach assumes that the claimant is responsible for the risk and asks under what circumstances they can also be *held* responsible.[96] Thus, the claimant will have to show that the 'right proposed to be exercised ... is at the core of the relevant entitlement' and that having to forfeit it would therefore be serious enough to amount to persecution. It is only once this has been established that the additional 'serious harm threatened' will become relevant. Only if the breach of the Convention ground is persecutory can the 'other' serious harm be said to be 'for reasons of' that Convention ground; the threshold of persecution must be met twice.

Such reasoning can be found in the decision of the UK Supreme Court in *RT (Zimbabwe) and others*, where Lord Dyson, by reference to the earlier cases *HJ (Iran)* (UK), *Appellant S395/2002* (Australia) and *Refugee Appeal No. 74665/03* (New Zealand), found that 'refugee status cannot be denied by requiring of the claimant that he or she avoid being persecuted by forfeiting a fundamental human right'.[97] Inversely, this would suggest that refugee status *can* be denied by requiring of the claimant that he or she avoid being persecuted (i.e. change her behaviour and be 'discreet') if that is *not* deemed to involve forfeiting a fundamental human right. Accordingly, the New Zealand Refugee Status Appeals Authority, notably represented among others by Rodger Haines QC, found in *Refugee Appeal No. 74665/03* that 'if the right sought to be exercised by the applicant is not a core human right,

94 *RT (Zimbabwe) and others* v. *Secretary of State for the Home Department*, note 2, per Lord Dyson at 114; emphasis added.

95 Ibid., at 50.

96 Jenni Millbank called 'discretion' reasoning a 'particularly invidious form of victim blaming', because it makes the claimant responsible for the harm suffered; Millbank, note 69, 497–527, 504.

97 *RT (Zimbabwe) and others* v. *Secretary of State for the Home Department*, note 2, per Lord Dyson at 20.

the "being persecuted" standard of the Convention is not engaged'.[98] The Authority concluded:

> Understanding the predicament of 'being persecuted' as the sustained or systemic violation of basic human rights demonstrative of a failure of state protection means that the refugee definition is to be approached not from the perspective of what the refugee claimant can do to avoid being persecuted, but from the perspective of the fundamental human right in jeopardy *and the resulting harm.* If the right proposed to be exercised by the refugee claimant in the country of origin is at the core of the relevant entitlement *and serious harm is threatened,* it would be contrary to the language context, object and purpose of the Refugee Convention to require the refugee claimant to forfeit or forego that right and to be denied refugee status on the basis that he or she could engage in self-denial or discretion on return to the country of origin.[99]

In other words, in addition to the 'serious harm threatened', the claimant will also have to show that the 'right proposed to be exercised . . . is at the core of the relevant entitlement'. This formulation is rather cryptic. Arguably, it means that the 'proposed action' by the claimant must be at the core of the fundamental right and that in addition, serious harm will result. This indicates that the idea of protected and unprotected (or core and marginal) acts is also applied to the 'additional approach' to understanding persecutory harm. Haines, Hathaway and Foster state: 'Similarly, where the risk of a *broader range of persecutory harm ensues* only from taking such marginal actions, the risk is unlikely to be "for reasons of" religion, political opinion, sexual identity, or whatever other Convention ground is relied upon.'[100] Here, acts are analysed in the context of the nexus requirement and the analysis of the act becomes an additional hurdle for a claimant, such as illustrated by Haines QC in *Refugee Appeal* No. 74665/03:

> There is no right to same-sex marriage in international human rights law and the claimed right is at, if not beyond, the margin of what international human rights law regards as being the protection owed to homosexuals. On the other hand, a prohibition of consensual homosexual acts, *if accompanied by penal sanctions of severity which are in fact enforced*, may well found a refugee claim. There is no easy formulation. It cannot be said that *criminalisation of consensual homosexual acts is on its own* sufficient to establish a situation of 'being persecuted'.[101]

In essence, this approach holds that a wider range of persecutory harm only warrants protection if the claimant's *act* triggering that persecution can be viewed as being 'covered' by a fundamental human right (i.e. the right that the Convention grounds are mapped onto). The logic is that if this is not the case, the persecution cannot be

98 *Refugee Appeal* No. 74665/03, note 81, at 82.
99 Ibid., at 114; emphasis added.
100 Haines et al., note 52, 430–443, 437–438; emphasis added.
101 *Refugee Appeal* No. 74665/03, note 81, at 103; emphasis added.

said to be 'for reasons of' religion/political opinion/sexual orientation. After splitting the Convention ground into act and identity, the act is moved to the nexus element. This is an artificial move: if the act is not 'covered', the Convention ground is by definition not met, and therefore failure to meet the nexus requirement necessary follows. As Millbank pointed out, the nexus element requires a connection between the persecution feared and the Convention ground.[102] They are separate elements; the membership of a particular social group element is satisfied when the claimant is or is perceived to be gay – an identity disclosed/perceived in multitudinous ways, including, but not limited to, conduct of the claimant or the lack thereof. The nexus requirement is satisfied either when the harm is directed at the person because they are perceived to be gay or when the state fails to protect the person because they are perceived to be gay. So the 'for reasons of' element reflects the perspective of the persecutor and/or state. The nexus requirement is not intended to address any conduct on the part of the applicant. Rather, it requires that the applicant must be persecuted because the persecutor thinks or will think they are gay – for whatever reason.[103] Again, the view shifts between persecutor and persecuted. The flexibility inherent in these shifts makes the scope of protection very malleable. The view that persecution is restricted to a core area of freedom involves the idea that claimants should exercise restraint in their 'conduct' and be 'discreet' about 'marginal conduct' and that only persons persecuted for their 'identity per se' or 'activities at the core of a fundamental right' are entitled to protection. The jurisprudence of the United Kingdom with its triviality concern in the form of the 'why question' as well as German case law with its preoccupation with irreversibility are examples of this type of reasoning.

And yet, this is an unreal and impossible distinction; it is unclear what risk accruing 'simply from status' means in real terms for political opinion, religion or sexual orientation and it is impossible to know which 'signifiers'[104] (whether the applicant's own conduct or otherwise) will draw attention to the identity and trigger persecutory harm. This approach is also problematic because in a persecutory environment, where persons seek to reduce the risk by concealing their identities, it is likely to be marginal or inadvertent conduct only loosely associated with the status that will then reveal the same. As Spijkerboer pointed out,

> [i]t may be sheer stupidity that made a hair get out from under a chador which brought the religious police to believe an Iranian woman was a loose woman. Hiding forbidden political or religious materials in stupid places may expose someone's political or religious convictions.[105]

[102] See Millbank, note 69, 497–527, 510–512.
[103] See also UNHCR (2001) *The International Protection of Refugees: Interpreting Article 1 of the 1951 Convention Relating to the Status of Refugees*, April 2001, 25.
[104] See Spijkerboer, note 91.
[105] Ibid.

To say that these people are then not at risk of persecution for a Convention ground is absurd. In the words of Gummow and Hayne JJ in the Australian case of S395:

> Addressing the question of what an individual is *entitled* to do … leads on to the consideration of what modifications of behaviour it is reasonable to require that individual to make without entrenching on the right. This type of reasoning … leads to error. It distracts attention from the fundamental question … considering what an individual is entitled to do is of little assistance in deciding whether that person has a well-founded fear of persecution.[106]

Again, this approach is another materialisation of the conflict resulting from the requirement that persecution must be for a reason – and the tension between the fundamentality principle and the severity rationale. In this version, the dilemma is patched by moving the act to the nexus requirement. But the result remains the same: it is another way to provide for and justify a measure of 'discretion' on the part of the claimant.

9.4 RESPONDING TO THE PARADOX: LEGITIMISING 'DISCRETION'

The focus on the consequences of hiding a fundamental characteristic was explicitly intended as an answer to what Hathaway and Pobjoy termed the 'conundrum'[107] created when 'discretion' is taken to mean that there is no real chance for the risk to accrue. Lord Dyson in *HJ (Iran)* put the question this way:

> How can a gay man, who would have a well-founded fear of persecution if he were to live openly as a gay man on return to his country, be said to have a well-founded fear of persecution if on return he would in fact live discreetly, thereby probably escaping the attention of those who might harm him if they were aware of his sexual orientation?[108]

Or, as Hathaway and Pobjoy termed it, 'how can an implausible risk be real?'[109] It would thus provide an alternative basis to establish persecutory harm for applicants who will 'behave discreetly'. This becomes clear in the New Zealand case *Refugee Appeal* No. 74665/03, where Rodger Haines QC found:

> If he returns to Iran the appellant will not be able to live openly as a homosexual and will have to choose between denying his sexual orientation or facing the risk of severe judicial or extra-judicial punishment.[110]

[106] *Appellant S395/2002* v. *Minister for Immigration and Multicultural Affairs*; *Appellant S396/2002* v. *Minister for Immigration and Multicultural Affairs*, [2003] HCA 71, Australia: High Court, 9 December 2003, at 83; emphasis added.

[107] Hathaway and Pobjoy, note 5, 315–389, 331.

[108] *HJ (Iran) and HT (Cameroon)* v. *Secretary of State for the Home Department*, note 87, per Sir Dyson at 109.

[109] Hathaway and Pobjoy, note 5, 315–389, 340.

[110] *Refugee Appeal* No. 74665/03, note 81, at 129.

When presented as interchangeable alternatives as in this case, it appears to be an approach that would strengthen the case for many applicants. However, it *builds on* 'discretion reasoning'; it still draws a line between open and 'discreet' (those 'denying their sexual orientation') behaviour and assumes that if a person will 'deny his sexual orientation', in other words, behave 'discreetly', then the 'severe judicial or extra-judicial punishment' will not be the relevant risk anymore (alternative approach) or becomes relevant only on condition that 'discretion' itself amounts to persecution (additional approach). This involves an assumption that risks are activity-based. This focus on the act provides the means to respond to the central paradox, because it offers the possibility of distinguishing between people sharing the persecuted characteristic on the basis of 'discretion' logics.

9.4.1 *The Assumptions: Activity-Based Risks and the Unsafe Closet*

An assumption that risk of persecution arises from a person's behaviour – and that it is therefore entirely within the power of that person to manage that risk by 'simply' desisting from that behaviour – is particularly recurrent in sexual orientation, religion and political opinion cases. This assumption has given rise to Haines, Hathaway and Foster's discussion paper on the question of whether it matters that a risk 'accrues from action, rather than *simply from the applicant's civil or political status*'.[111] They chose three 'commonly encountered factual contexts' for their study – 'practice of a non-majoritarian religion, oppositional political activism, and living an openly homosexual life'.[112] Haines et al. reject the idea that a claim should not be recognised where the 'risk accrues only to a subset of persons within the protected group who undertake a particular form of *action*'.[113] The authors offer three examples for this sort of scenario, for each of their case studies, where a claim should be recognised (note that these examples are not substantiated by case law or other sources):

> Thus, not all Jews may be at risk, but only those who wear a yarmulke; not all socialists may be threatened, but only those who advocate publically for an end to privatization of public corporations; and not all homosexuals are targeted, but only those who routinely cohabit as a same-sex couple.[114]

In this context, the authors concede that 'it is often the case that it is the activities undertaken which reveal the status of the applicant as a member of a protected group'.[115] However, the authors fail to conversely provide examples for cases where risk would accrue 'simply from the applicant's civil or political status' as they term

[111] Haines et al., note 52, 430–443.
[112] Ibid., 431.
[113] Ibid., 432; emphasis in original.
[114] Ibid.
[115] Ibid.

it.[116] Arguably, this would be the case if all members of the protected group were targeted, regardless of the way in which their group membership is revealed. It remains unclear whether in their view this *includes* those 'triggers' (ways of exposure or revelation) that can be attributed to the applicant's own conduct where that conduct is not deemed to be 'protected' – since it is precisely this question of whether the 'action in question is, or is not, within the ambit of the protected interest' that in their view becomes 'the relevant question' (see discussion of 'core' and 'marginal' acts shortly).[117]

As discussed throughout, the view that risks are activity-based and, thus, within the power of the applicant to manage is empirically flawed: the closet is a very unsafe place.[118] Queer theory reveals that acts and identity are mutually constitutive and disclosure and 'discretion' are never entirely in the hands of the person concerned. Acts may disclose or hide an identity, and identity can be expressed or suppressed through acts. Importantly, this may be conscious or unconscious, intended or unintended and does not only depend on the person him or herself but also on the 'recipient' of the message. The latter may view certain acts or other small signifiers (or the lack thereof) as indications of an identity – or not. So, to repeat the observation by Sedgwick quoted in the introduction, while the persecuted individual has at least notionally some discretion over other people's knowledge of her or his membership in the group, importantly, it is never to be taken for granted how much.[119] The door of the closet is never quite shut – there is no universal 'on/off switch'.[120] Millbank and Dauvergne observed that '[t]he question of being "out" is never answered once and for all, it is a decision made over and over, each day and in each new social situation'[121] and that 'even an individual who wishes to hide, who desperately wishes – and takes all possible steps – to remain closeted does, in fact become increasingly "visible" with the passage of time'.[122]

[116] Ibid., 430–443, 430. This distinction was reiterated by Hathaway and Pobjoy: '[The judgment in *HJ (Iran) and HT (Cameroon)*] fails to interrogate the extant scope of "sexual orientation" as a protected interest to determine when there is a duty to protect on the basis of associated activities, rather than *simply as a function of identity per se*'; emphasis added; Hathaway and Pobjoy, note 5, 315–389, 336.

[117] Haines et al., note 52, 430–443, 432.

[118] Sabine Jansen and Thomas Spijkerboer (2011) *Fleeing Homophobia, Asylum Claims Related to Sexual Orientation and Gender Identity in Europe*, Vrije Universiteit Amsterdam, September 2011, 8. See also Nora Markard (2013) 'Sexuelle Orientierung als Fluchtgrund – Das Ende der "Diskretion" – Aktuelle Entwicklungen beim Flüchtlingsschutz aufgrund der sexuellen Orientierung', *Asylmagazin* 3/2013, 74–84, 81.

[119] Eve Kosofsky Sedgwick (1990) *Epistemology of the Closet*, Berkeley: University of California Press, 75.

[120] Cf Hathaway and Pobjoy, note 5, 315–389, 326.

[121] Catherine Dauvergne and Jenni Millbank (2003) 'Before the High Court: Applicants S396/2002 and S395/2002, a Gay Refugee Couple from Bangladesh', 25 *Sydney Law Review* 97–124, 122.

[122] Ibid.

The assumption of activity-based risks does not take into account the fact that, although the applicant might in fact seek to live in a 'discreet' way, persecution may still be imminent as soon as the applicant's identity is discovered or is outed against their will by others.[123] There is a permanent risk that this will happen, be it by accident, through rumours or through growing suspicion.[124] Also, the absence of certain expected activities and behaviour may identify a difference between them and other people and place them at risk of harm.[125] So the state of 'closeted-ness' is 'always a potentially permeable one'.[126] This implies a permanent risk of persecution. The case of HT, the Cameroonian claimant from the UK Supreme Court judgment in *HJ (Iran) and HT (Cameroon)* illustrates this situation. HT had been in a relationship for five years, during which time he had successfully concealed his sexual orientation – until neighbours spotted him kissing his partner in his own garden.[127] He was then the victim of serious violence by mob justice (he was beaten with sticks, stones were thrown at him, his clothes were pulled off and the mob tried to cut off his penis with a knife), and police officers joined in when they arrived at the scene.[128] Ironically, French and Spanish jurisprudence take account of the permeability of 'discretion' in their focus on past outing. But they limit the scope of protection by cutting out the future-focused element of the inquiry, restricting protection to assessments based on a backward-looking analysis.

It is thus clear that to understand risks as 'activity-based' confines the examination. To draw on an observation by Gummow and Hayne JJ in the Australian case of S395/2002, asking whether a particular behaviour on the part of the applicant would put them at risk would be a narrow inquiry that would

> be relevant to whether an applicant had a well-founded fear of persecution for a Convention reason only if the description given to what the applicant would do on return was not only comprehensive, but exhaustively described the circumstances

[123] Jansen and Spijkerboer, note 118, 38.

[124] This point has been made by many scholars, see e.g. Dauvergne and Millbank, note 121, 97–124; Ghassan Kassisieh (2008) 'From Lives of Fear to Lives of Freedom: A Review of Australian Refugee Decisions on the Basis of Sexual Orientation', *Gay & Lesbian Rights Lobby*, Glebe, 69; Jansen and Spijkerboer, note 118, 8; Janna Wessels (2012) 'HJ (Iran) and HT (Cameroon) – Reflections on a New Test for Sexuality-Based Asylum Claims in Britain', 24(4) *International Journal of Refugee Law* 815–839, 830–831; see also UNHCR (2012) *Guidelines on International Protection No. 9: Claims to Refugee Status Based on Sexual Orientation and/or Gender Identity within the Context of Article 1A(2) of the 1951 Convention and/or Its 1967 Protocol Relating to the Status of Refugees*, 23 October 2012, HCR/GIP/12/01, www.refworld.org/docid/50348afc2.html, at 32.

[125] See UNHCR (2012) *Guidelines on International Protection No. 9, note 124, at* 32. See also: SW *(lesbians – HJ and HT applied) Jamaica* v. *Secretary of State for the Home Department*, UK, CG [2011] UKUT 00251(IAC), United Kingdom: Upper Tribunal (Immigration and Asylum Chamber), 24 June 2011.

[126] Dauvergne and Millbank, note 121, 97–124, 122.

[127] *HJ (Iran) and HT (Cameroon)* v. *Secretary of State for the Home Department*, note 87, per Lord Hope at 38.

[128] Ibid., per Lord Rodger at 44.

> relevant to the fear that the applicant alleged. On its face it appears to be an incomplete, and therefore inadequate, description.[129]

Such an incomplete – and inadequate – description of the claimant's situation serves as a means to respond to the tension that inhabits the space between the protection of fundamental characteristics and the protection against serious harm. Attaching the risk of persecution to the claimant's activity allows for the assumption that 'discretion' obviates the risk – and, as in Spanish and French jurisprudence, will continue to do so in the future.

9.4.2 *The Focus: Anne Frank and Endogenous Harms*

Not only can a person merely *reduce* (rather than entirely manage and *avoid*) a risk, the fact that she can and will *try to* avoid it does not change the nature of the risk in the sense that the substance of the risk changes. This can be illustrated by reference to what has been termed the 'Anne Frank principle'.[130] This – contested – comparison was proposed by Madgwick J in the Australian political opinion case of *Win v. Minister for Immigration and Multicultural Affairs* [2001][131] and has since often been relied upon in the context of 'discretion' reasoning. Madgwick J said:

> [U]pon the approach suggested by counsel for the respondent, Anne Frank, terrified as a Jew and hiding for her life in Nazi-occupied Holland, would not be a refugee: if the Tribunal were satisfied that the possibility of her being discovered by the authorities was remote, she would be sent back to live in the attic. It is inconceivable that the framers of the Convention ever did have, or should be imputed to have had, such a result in contemplation.[132]

To be sure, Madgwick used this 'historical example' to illustrate the point that there 'appears to be no reason why . . . a denial of freedom to express one's political opinion *may* not, of itself, constitute persecution', that is, the problematic alternative approach to persecution just discussed.[133] However, this view was rejected when the same question was discussed in the course of the litigation of the UK case of *HJ (Iran)*. Lord Dyson in *HJ (Iran)* found it to be absurd and unreal:

> In this case the Secretary of State argued that had Anne Frank escaped to the United Kingdom, and had it been found (improbably, as the Secretary of State

[129] *Appellant S395/2002* v. *Minister for Immigration and Multicultural Affairs*; *Appellant S396/2002* v. *Minister for Immigration and Multicultural Affairs*, note 106, per Gummow and Hayne JJ at 83.
[130] *HJ (Iran) and HT (Cameroon)* v. *Secretary of State for the Home Department*, note 87, per Lord Walker at 96.
[131] *Win* v. *Minister for Immigration and Multicultural Affairs* [2001] FCA 132, Australia: Federal Court, 23 February 2001 at 18.
[132] Ibid.
[133] Ibid.; emphasis in original.

> recognised) that on return to Holland she would successfully avoid detection by hiding in the attic, then she would not be at real risk of persecution by the Nazis, and the question would be whether permanent enforced confinement in the attic would itself amount to persecution. Simply to re-state the Secretary of State's argument shows that it is not possible to characterise it as anything other than absurd and unreal. It is plain that it remains the threat to Jews of the concentration camp and the gas chamber which constitutes the persecution.[134]

Though controversial, as it may be viewed as abusing the plight of Anne Frank, the example neatly picks up on the metaphor of the closet taken from queer theory in its application to other situations of persecution, such as political opinion or religion. It uses the image of an actual closet to refer to the consequences of a constant state of hiding. The fervour of the rejection is striking taking into account the ease with which less blatant versions of the closet are not only accepted, but required – it suffices to look at the alternative approach to persecution, the fundamental characteristics approach to membership of a particular social group, Grahl-Madsen's acts beyond mere expression; but also the irreversibility requirement in Germany or the singling out logics in France and Spain. Lord Dyson went on:

> [T]he phrase 'being persecuted' in article 1A(2) refers to the harm caused by the acts of the state *authorities* or those for whom they are responsible. The impact of those acts on the *asylum-seeker* is only relevant to the question whether they are sufficiently harmful to amount to persecution. But the phrase 'being persecuted' does not refer to what the asylum-seeker does in order to avoid such persecution. The response by the victim to the threat of serious harm is not itself persecution (whether tolerable or not) within the meaning of the article.[135]

Not only does it come down to 'an unnecessary complication, and lead[s] to confusion',[136] it is also perverse to say that a risk is not real when a person who genuinely (and objectively) fears it and therefore seeks to *reduce* it as best as possible by hiding is thus not at risk. That person remains persecuted – which is why they remain in hiding. If anything, the fact that they endure the hiding is an indication of their genuine fear of a real risk.[137] Otherwise, the worse the persecutory

[134] *HJ (Iran) and HT (Cameroon)* v. *Secretary of State for the Home Department*, note 87, per Lord Collins at 107, citing *Win* v. *Minister for Immigration and Multicultural Affairs*, note 131. See also Sir Dyson at 116–118. Importantly, Anne Frank's own story demonstrates the permanent unreliability of the state of hiding, as the family was discovered and deported to a concentration camp, where they were killed.

[135] *HJ (Iran) and HT (Cameroon)* v. *Secretary of State for the Home Department*, note 87, per Sir John Dyson at 120; emphasis added.

[136] *HJ (Iran) and HT (Cameroon)* v. *Secretary of State for the Home Department*, note 87, per Lord Walker at 96.

[137] See also Jenni Millbank (2013) 'Sexual Orientation and Refugee Status Determination over the Past 20 Years: Unsteady Progress through Standard Sequences?', in Thomas Spijkerboer (ed.) *Fleeing Homophobia: Sexual Orientation, Gender Identity and Asylum*, London: Routledge, 32–54, 40.

environment gets, and the more deeply the affected persons have to hide their fundamental characteristic, the less well founded would be their fear. In fact, this seems to be the basis of much German jurisprudence, as reflected in the mathematical calculations to assess the 'persecution density' in order to establish a 'real risk'.[138]

In response to the absurdity of this situation, Hathaway and Pobjoy propose to focus on what they term 'endogenous harms' in such types of cases.[139] The notion attempts to capture the harm that arises from the fact of having to hide in terms of human rights. While the approach might provide protection for some claimants who would be excluded under the German 'persecution density' approach, it establishes these 'endogenous' harms arising from 'discretion' as an alternative harm, thus exemplifying the 'alternative approach' to persecution. Not the reason for hiding, but its effect, is assessed. Drawing on activity-based risk logics, this reasoning allows for distinctions between those sharing the characteristic on the basis of their assumed visibility to the persecutor. For those who 'will hide', the state of hiding becomes the harm to be assessed (labelled 'endogenous harm' in this case). In line with the observations in preceding chapters, the malleability inherent in the use of human rights to conceptualise the Convention grounds thus allows for different types of restrictions on the scope of protection, which, each in their own way, entail 'discretion' reasoning.

9.5 CONCLUSION: HUMAN RIGHTS AND REFUGEE LAW – AN UNHOLY ALLIANCE?

The human rights approach to refugee law has helped expand the central notion of the refugee definition – persecution – to include harms reaching beyond purely physical injuries. This win, however, comes at a price: mapping human rights onto refugee law is not a straightforward calculation, since refugee protection requires a certain level of severity.[140] Accordingly, a 'distinction' problem emerges from the understanding that not all human rights breaches are considered to warrant protection under the Refugee Convention. Similarly, it is generally accepted that claimants cannot be required to forego the reason for which they are persecuted, as it would undermine the very essence of refugee protection to tell claimants to eliminate the reason that led to their persecution. This double rationale, however – protecting from persecution and protecting the Convention grounds – creates a tension, as previous chapters have shown. Some decision-makers and scholars have, therefore, turned to human rights for guidance. The main argument is that drawing on internationally accepted standards to understand the core notions of the refugee definition would help ground their interpretation. As the preceding discussion

138 VGH Baden Württemberg, Urteil vom 7.3.2013, A 9 S 1872/12, 36–37.
139 Hathaway and Pobjoy, note 5, 315–389, 346–352.
140 Otherwise, there is a risk of implosion, see Dauvergne, note 8, 13–30, 30.

reveals, however, much like other responses attempting to solve the tension in a principled manner, recourse to human rights law is unable to undo the knot arising from the central paradox. It achieves no more than glossing over its core by conflating persecutory harm and Convention ground.

This conflation occurs as follows: in order to assess whether the requisite level of severity is reached, the human rights framework that was developed to understand which breaches of rights reach the threshold of persecution is applied to the question of the extent to which a claimant is *entitled to* the characteristic described by the Convention ground, rather than focusing on what the claimant is *seeking protection from*, that is, the persecution feared.[141] In this view, the persecutory act consists in the limitation of the right underlying the Convention ground, as in the prohibition of publicly proclaiming the relevant (religious, political, sexual, etc.) identity. In essence, the claimant's negative right does not matter if they do not have the positive right in the first place; if a claimant does not have a right to drink multicoloured cocktails, being put to death on account of it does not lead to refugee status. This conception of the persecutory act shifts the focus from the persecutor to the persecuted, where the latter has to defend their right to 'act' in a certain way. If the claimant's act is deemed not to be covered by core human rights, the claim fails, even though the harm is still imminent and even though the harm is triggered by a persecution ground that was made known to the persecutor, albeit through what is considered a 'non-protected' act. Thus, it is easy to argue that wearing lipstick or drinking cocktails are not acts at the 'core' of the 'protected interest' (which is what? Being a woman? Being gay?) and are, therefore, not protected by the Convention. This does not change the fact that the woman still faces stoning for transgressing social norms and that the man still faces hanging for being gay. Through the focus on their acts, applicants are made at least partly responsible for their persecution as the act/identity dichotomy turns the refugee status determination into a 'particularly invidious form of victim blaming'[142] that assumes that if only the claimant didn't 'act' that way they wouldn't have a problem. So the persecution analysis is twisted and confined to assessing the likely behaviour of the applicant rather than the actual persecution feared. Inspired by the triviality concern, this then leads to calls for circumspection.

Just like any other 'external' definition of the reason for persecution, a human rights–based understanding of the Convention grounds sets limits that do not necessarily correlate with the persecuted group. It draws a restrictive line between insiders and outsiders[143] at the level of the Convention ground, which enables and

[141] 'Refugee recognition is restricted to situations in which there is a risk of a type of injury that is inconsistent with the basic duty of protection owed by a state to its population', *Refugee Appeal No. 74665/03*, note 81, at 124.

[142] Millbank, note 69, 497–527, 504.

[143] Compare Chetail, note 4, 19–72, 23.

allows for some sort of 'discretion' reasoning. As a result of understanding the Convention grounds as expressions of human rights, the 'metes and bounds'[144] of those rights in international human rights law are also transposed to refugee law. As a consequence, some religious, sexual and political conduct falls outside of Convention protection – even though it may be precisely this conduct that indicates the religion, political opinion or sexual orientation to the persecutor, and even though it is the religion, political opinion or sexual orientation as a characteristic that is persecuted and protected. Whichever boundaries international human rights law may provide for the Convention grounds, the persecutor does not draw on such standards when considering which conduct or behaviour (or lack thereof) indicates a particular religion or sexual orientation. There is no escaping the tension.

In light of the aforementioned, is the union of human rights and refugee law an 'unholy alliance'? This may be going too far, but certainly the link between human rights and refugee law creates a complicated relationship. The human rights approach has opened up the persecution analysis to incorporate a wider of range of harms, in this sense broadening the scope of protection. But it comes with important pitfalls. First, by conflating harm and reason, it risks reducing the scope of protection through 'discretion' logics at a different point of the definition. This demonstrates that human rights law is just as incapable as other approaches of resolving the central conundrums of the refugee definition. Second, because of the positive, inclusionary connotation of human rights law generally, such exclusionary effects are particularly difficult to see. As a consequence, they are difficult to uncover and require particular attention.

[144] *Refugee Appeal* No. 74665/03, note 81, at 82.

Conclusion

10

Conundrums, Paradoxes and Productive Instability

In its January 2017 *Country Policy and Information Note* on 'Afghanistan: Sexual Orientation and Gender Identity', the UK Home Office advised decision-makers that 'a practicing homosexual on return to Kabul who *would not attract or seek to cause public outrage* would not face a real risk of persecution'.[1] This guidance caused some irritation in the refugee activist community. Critics argued that the guidance was contrary to both the UNHCR's and the CJEU's rejections of the 'discretion' requirement.[2] Against the backdrop of the preceding analysis, however, it

[1] UK Home Office (2017) 'Afghanistan: Sexual Orientation and Gender Identity', *Country Policy and Information Note*, 6; emphasis added. The section in full reads:

> However it should be noted that in the country guidance case of AJ (Risk to Homosexuals) the Tribunal found that:
>
> – Some conduct that would be seen in the West as a manifestation of homosexuality is not necessarily interpreted in such a way in Afghan society (Headnote point 2 and paragraph 57).
> – So far as non-state actors are concerned, a practising homosexual on return to Kabul who would not attract or seek to cause public outrage would not face a real risk of persecution (Headnote point 4 and paragraphs 58 and 61).
> – If some individual, or some gay lobby, tried to make a political point in public or otherwise behaved in a way such as to attract public outrage, then there might be a sharp response from the Government (Headnote point 5 and paragraph 54).
> – The evidence shows that a considerable proportion of Afghan men may have had some homosexual experience without having a homosexual preference. A careful assessment of the credibility of a claim to be a practising homosexual and the extent of it is particularly important. The evaluation of an appellant's behaviour in the UK may well be significant (Headnote point 8 and paragraph 57).

[2] ECRE (2017) 'UK Home Office Guideline: Afghan Gay Asylum-Seekers Expected to Conceal Their Sexual Orientation to Avoid Persecution When Sent Back', *News*, 3 March 2017, www.ecre.org/uk-home-office-guideline-afghan-gay-asylum-seekers-expected-to-conceal-their-sexual-orientation-to-avoid-persecution-when-sent-back; see also 'Afghan LGBT Asylum Seekers in UK Among Most Vulnerable – At Risk of Imprisonment, Violence If Deported to Afghanistan', *Human Rights Watch News*, 26 February 2017, www.hrw.org/news/2017/02/26/afghan-lgbt-asylum-seekers-uk-among-most-vulnerable.

should come as no surprise – it is but another materialisation of the concealment controversy, which is at the heart of the book.

Moreover, looking at the text of the country guidance closely, it is in fact in line with both the UNHCR Guidelines on sexual orientation claims[3] and CJEU case law (in *X, Y and Z*), which merely rejected the normative requirement of 'discretion' (see Chapter 3), whereas the Home Office Country Note talks about a factual finding ('*would* not attract' rather than '*should* not attract'). This new country guidance supports the observation that triggered the present study, namely the resilience of 'discretion' in spite of its repeated rejections in refugee law.

This puzzling situation – the persistence of 'discretion' reasoning despite continuously being refuted – constitutes the centre of one of most heated discussions in refugee law doctrine in recent years, and simultaneously formed the starting point for this research. Seeking out both the shapes and the origins of 'discretion' reasoning, the central puzzle that the study addressed was the question of why 'discretion' reasoning is so difficult to get rid of. How does it inform the construction and definition of the scope of protection? What are the role and responsibilities of the claimant in this negotiation process? These questions combined into the underlying exploration of what is protected under refugee law – and why. To tackle these questions, the book employed the act/identity dichotomy drawn from queer theory as a lens. The adoption of this subdominant perspective uncovered a fundamental tension at the core of the refugee concept. The book concludes that 'discretion' reasoning is a site where the scope of refugee protection is negotiated in response to a fundamental tension between two competing principles of refugee law: the notion that claimants cannot be required to hide the characteristic they are persecuted for, and the principle that the purpose of refugee protection is to protect from persecution and not to provide full human rights protection.

This concluding chapter synthesises the insights of the book and reflects on their implications. Drawing together the findings from the preceding analysis, it argues that the insights from analysis come together to form a complex picture of instability. Due to the refugee definition's double rationale – Convention grounds and persecution – and the consequent conundrum of whether to focus on persecutor or persecuted, the scope of protection is subject to a variety of tensions and ambiguities which overlap and intersect in significant and complex ways.

The remainder of this chapter unfolds in four main steps. First, it sums up the main findings of the preceding chapters and concludes that 'discretion' is omnipresent across time, places and approaches. This lays the groundwork for broader reflections on the conceptual implications of the analysis. In this vein, the second

[3] UNHCR (2012) *Guidelines on International Protection No. 9: Claims to Refugee Status Based on Sexual Orientation and/or Gender Identity within the Context of Article 1A(2) of the 1951 Convention and/or Its 1967 Protocol Relating to the Status of Refugees*, 23 October 2012, HCR/GIP/12/01, www.refworld.org/docid/50348afc2.html, at 30–33.

section attributes the omnipresence of 'discretion' to the fundamentality/severity paradox that shapes refugee law doctrine and reflects on the role and place of the Convention grounds within that tension. This section concludes that the conceptualisation of the Convention grounds is inextricably wound up in the operating logics of refugee law. On this basis, thirdly, the chapter suggests that the Convention grounds must be seen in context with the other elements of the definition and concludes that together, they form a complex web of instabilities. Finally, the chapter discusses the implications of these findings for decision-making, current debates and further research.

10.1 THE OMNIPRESENCE OF 'DISCRETION'

As the book has been at pains to show, not only has 'discretion' reasoning withstood repeated high-level judgments rejecting it, but it is a much broader issue, spanning jurisdictions, time and Convention grounds. Rather than being a marginal annoyance, if the present analysis is correct, it shapes refugee law doctrine in all its facets.

Firstly, 'discretion' reasoning is not confined to the English-speaking common law jurisdictions. As outlined in Chapter 1, previous research on case law had mainly focused on the United Kingdom, Australia, New Zealand and Canada. The empirical findings from Part I of the present analysis indicate that such reasoning is also deeply entrenched in the civil law jurisdictions of France, Germany and Spain. Recognising the multitudinous shapes of 'discretion' as well as the range of its occurrences avoids a reductive understanding of the phenomenon.

Queer theory, and in particular the related binary distinctions between act and identity, and between 'discretion' and disclosure, proved apt for the task of opening up a fuller understanding of the workings of concealment in refugee status determinations (Chapter 2). Conceptualising 'discretion' as based on the separation of acts and identities enabled the analysis to grasp a wider variety of its materialisations. Previously, the debate on 'discretion' mainly centred on an explicit *requirement* to be discreet. This approach was unable to encompass different, often much subtler, but nonetheless significant, versions of 'discretion' logics. Understanding 'discretion' reasoning as based on an unstable binary distinction between the claimant's acts and identity permitted reaching beyond the established notion of 'discretion'.

Thus equipped, the book demonstrated that the three high-level European judgments that rejected 'discretion' in recent years – the UK Supreme Court in its 2010 judgment *HJ (Iran) and HT (Cameroon)* and the CJEU in its twin decisions Y *and* Z from 2012 and X, Y, Z from 2013 – were fixed on an explicit requirement and did not address other variants of 'discretion' (Chapter 3). In the jurisdictions that served as case studies, namely France, Germany and Spain, in contrast, 'discretion' took a different form (Chapters 4–6). That is, whereas 'discretion' logics significantly dominated jurisprudence in these three civil law jurisdictions, they were not formulated as a *requirement* and, therefore, the judgments rejecting such requirements did not resonate strongly. In each of the case studies, 'discretion' logics were based on a distinction between the claimant's act and identity and emerged from the preference of one of these elements over the other. That is, in France, 'discretion' logics were traditionally based on a focus on the claimant's past behaviour – irrespective of their actual or presumed gay identity, it was their past public behaviour that was relevant for whether the claimant was entitled to protection. In Germany, the opposite was true: regardless of their open or 'discreet' behaviour, it was relevant that the claimant had a stable gay identity. In Spain, though less evidently, 'discretion' logics emanated from a focus on behaviour, as the claimant had to have been singled out for persecution by the persecutor. These specific versions of 'discretion' reasoning were barely affected by the high-level rejections of the discretion requirement of the CJEU – or, for that matter, the UK Supreme Court. Such change as did occur in the decision-making of these jurisdictions was mostly triggered by the Europeanisation of asylum (the *Qualification Directive* which entered into force in 2006) rather than the CJEU judgments. And although reasoning *was* transformed in all three countries, the essence of the jurisprudence has remained the same. In France, the public manifestation requirement was converted into a requirement to claim the sexual orientation (Chapter 4). In Germany, the Courts transformed their previous requirement of an irreversible identity into a requirement that their identity must be of particular importance to the claimant (Chapter 5). In Spain, the singling out requirement was followed up by the notion of significant transcendence of harm (Chapter 6). Just as previous research found in the common law jurisdictions, therefore, the present study confirms that 'discretion' was not only prevalent but also resilient in all three case studies. In other words, it turned out that 'discretion' reasoning is not limited to any particular jurisdictions (such as the common law countries) or particular doctrinal forms (i.e. the 'reasonable requirement'); it is an issue that takes a wide variety of shapes and affects a range of different jurisdictions.

Secondly, the book has demonstrated that 'discretion' reasoning is by no means a new phenomenon. Rather, it has haunted refugee law doctrine since its beginnings and continues to accompany new doctrinal developments. This was demonstrated on two levels – both in case law, where 'discretion' logics survive even far-ranging changes, and in refugee law doctrine more generally. German jurisprudence distinctly exemplifies the evolution of 'discretion' logics from the earliest reported sexuality-based asylum claim in 1983 to present decisions (Chapter 5). But importantly, the same robustness is inherent in broader doctrine. The findings from Part II indicate that the struggles around 'discretion' logics extend from the earliest doctrinal developments in the 1960s, to long-standing unsettled doctrinal quarrels, as well as to contemporary refugee law doctrine. A line can be drawn that connects Grahl-Madsen's 1966 *The Status of Refugees in International Law* (Chapter 7) with the competing approaches to conceptualising membership of a particular social group, a debate that remains unresolved since the first such cases emerged in the late 1980s (Chapter 8), and also with the human rights–based approach to understanding persecution that forms the basis of current debates (Chapter 9). The tension Grahl-Madsen identified in his work is still reflected in today's discussions; the question of whether acts beyond the 'mere expression' of a characteristic are protected is not only the bone of contention in the conceptualisation of particular social group, but also one of the things that the so-called human rights–based approach to refugee law seeks to answer.

In respect of the latter, the book has shown that the deployment of human rights as a standard to define elements of the refugee definition has added a new layer of complication. The human rights–based approach has clarified *some* things, but muddied others. Refugee law is necessarily lesser in scope than human rights. While a human rights–based understanding has broadened the notion of persecution, this structural incoherence in the human rights–based approach to refugee law has also caused new confusion. As discussed in Chapter 9, by expanding the notion of persecution to a wider range of harms, the human rights approach conceptually merges Convention ground and persecution. In the process, it blurs the location of the 'lesser' scope that refugee law provides vis-à-vis human rights law: prohibitions on the expression of the Convention grounds (such as religion or political opinion or sexual orientation) *in themselves* can be considered persecutory – but only if they are an essential element of that expression (Chapter 9). Otherwise, the claimant must endure those prohibitions, that is, maintain 'discretion'. This is precisely the question that the competing definitions of the social group ground are split over – is it possible to separate fundamental from trivial groups, or at least fundamental from trivial forms of expression of group membership (Chapter 8)? It is here that Grahl-Madsen's notion of acts beyond the 'mere expression' resurfaces; although claimants whose behaviour is considered to fall into the space beyond 'mere expression' would be persecuted, they are not protected and are instead required to hide their protected characteristic (Chapter 7). Thus, 'discretion' reasoning spans time and re-emerges both in the oldest and modern approaches to refugee law.

Thirdly, 'discretion' is far from being confined to sexuality-based claims. Instead, the present analysis drew out many parallels, across all types of claims based on Convention grounds reflecting characteristics that are not necessarily immediately visible and require expression. In spite of differences regarding assumptions about their publicness and privateness, the conceptual questions that arise are very similar across the different Convention grounds. The distinction between the focus on the persecutor and the focus on the claimant that Grahl-Madsen identified in relation to political opinion (Chapter 7) is neatly reproduced in the two competing definitions for 'particular social group' (Chapter 8) as well as the two approaches to persecution identified in the context of religion-based claims (discussed in Chapter 9). It is also the guiding tension in the jurisprudence on sexuality-based asylum claims in the civil law jurisdictions reviewed here: whereas Spain and France focus on the persecutor (Chapters 4 and 6), Germany focuses on the claimant (Chapter 5). Although the discourses on sexual orientation on the one hand and political opinion and religion on the other have evolved quite independently, the present analysis strongly underlines the emerging recognition that the various Convention grounds are subject to very similar definitional challenges. This is a fundamental concern for refugee law more broadly. While their outer appearance evolves, the core rationale of 'discretion' logics remains remarkably stable as they travel across time, places and Convention grounds.

10.2 FUNDAMENTALITY, SEVERITY AND THE CONVENTION GROUNDS

The omnipresence of 'discretion' drawn out in this research invites reflections at the conceptual level. The book asserts that the pervasiveness and pliability of 'discretion' can be explained by the paradoxical relationship between two widely held but contradictory notions of refugee law doctrine, namely the fundamentality principle and the severity concern, which in turn both have a bearing on the ways in which the Convention grounds are conceptualised.

10.2.1 *Caught in the Fundamentality/Severity Paradox*

The two notions that form the basis of the controversy have been referred to here as the fundamentality principle and the severity argument (see Chapter 1 and throughout). The fundamentality principle consists in the generally accepted idea that no one should be required to hide, change or renounce the attributes or opinions that are persecuted. The rationale is that if hiding were required, then there would be no need for refugee law at all. Such reasoning generally takes precedence for example in French jurisprudence (Chapter 4), as well as in the social perception approach to particular social group (Chapter 8). The severity concern, in turn, is based on the shared understanding that refugee law provides surrogate protection for serious harms. The logic is that the task of refugee law is not to guarantee the same level of rights and freedoms everywhere in the world and, therefore, to remedy even minimal or trivial harms. Rather, refugee protection extends only to injuries of a certain quality. This concern appears to be commonly foregrounded for example in German decision-making practice (Chapter 5) as well as in the context of the human rights–based approach to refugee law (as discussed in Chapter 9). These two notions are in principle un-controversially shared in refugee law doctrine. The problem is that they are in fact in tension. 'No hiding' on the one hand, but 'not the same freedoms' on the other is difficult to reconcile. 'Not the same freedoms' requires some measure of hiding. And 'no hiding' requires the same freedoms.

This tension creates an intricate situation for the Convention grounds: hiding is required *and* forbidden at the same time. The analysis demonstrated that the different variants of 'discretion' logics based on an act/identity dichotomy serve to respond to this incoherence. The persecuted characteristic is split into act and identity. Either at times can serve as the Convention ground – and therefore, to uphold the fundamentality principle, and the rejection of 'discretion'. This simultaneously allows the other element to float free such that it can expand or limit the definition elsewhere, and thus ensure that the severity concern is met through a degree of 'discretion'. The claimant is thus entitled to the Convention ground and restricted from it in conflicting ways. Certain identities may be deemed protected, whereas some related conduct may be understood to fall outside the scope of protection – and vice versa. The preference of one element over the other as the basis for the Convention ground opens up a margin of manoeuvre, in particular because the preference can be flipped. It follows that while the circumscribed range of protection offered under the Convention reflects assumptions that certain act/identity patterns are deemed worthy of protection, these patterns are not fixed but highly volatile (Chapter 2). These insights point to the finding that the role and place of the Convention grounds are little understood. The volatility of the act/identity dichotomy causes conceptual trouble and makes 'discretion' difficult to grasp.

10.2.2 *Understanding the Convention Grounds*

A broader finding of this book at the conceptual level is that the Convention grounds remain under-theorised. It argues that a better understanding of the functions of the Convention grounds permits a better understanding of the workings of 'discretion' reasoning, and, hence, the mechanisms of inclusion and exclusion it conveys.

In refugee law doctrine, the Convention grounds have traditionally been somewhat neglected. Most scholarship and much of the jurisprudence has focused on persecution as the core notion of the refugee concept. This has culminated in positions such as that the question of the Convention ground is 'automatically answered' when the persecutory harm is found to lie in restrictions on the freedom of religion (as described in Chapter 9) – an assumption of full conflation. The present analysis proposes that 'discretion' logics contribute to bringing broader conceptual questions regarding the Convention grounds to the fore, which have repercussions for the scope of refugee protection.

In this context, the closet, which is a familiar trope in queer theory, proved to be a useful lens through which to look at refugee law (Chapter 2). In analogy with homophobia, persecution was conceived to create a 'closet' for refugees fearing persecution on the basis of one of the Convention grounds: in their countries of origin, the management of information about the persecuted characteristic is highly delicate and risky. 'Discretion' equals the notion of closetedness, and disclosure the concept of 'outing'. The persecutory closet and the resulting dynamics of 'discretion' and disclosure rely on a distinction between act and identity. Specifically, if it only appears 'sensible' that gay people would seek to hide their sexual orientation in a generalised anti-gay climate – then by analogy, a persecutory environment may function as a 'closet' also for political opinion and religion cases in the context of asylum. It is 'rational' that the religious zealot keeps their faith within their home. It is 'reasonable' for the opposition politician to keep their views to themselves. 'Discretion' – and its opposite, disclosure – are a product of the 'closet' that persecution creates. The closet of persecution thus emphasises the distinction between an internal and an external dimension, not only of sexual orientation, but also of characteristics such as religion or political opinion.

However, whereas homophobia has always been a shaping presence for homosexuality (Chapter 2), political opinion and religion are generally considered to be characteristics that are collectively expressed in the public sphere. There are thus different starting points: sexual orientation is traditionally thought to be mainly an internal, 'private' thing, whereas political opinion and religion are un-controversially assumed to be public attributes. Their internal dimension is presupposed but generally not the centre of attention (see e.g. Chapter 7). The persecutory closet shifts the focus: the need to hide one's 'true beliefs' from persecutors, or society at large, emphasises the internal dimension of such characteristics as well. In the refugee decision-making process, it explicitly raises the question of how much publicness must be provided for – and, simultaneously, how much privateness, or conviction, is required to justify such publicness. The internal dimension arguably manifests itself to varying degrees; and more prominently in the context of religion than in political opinion cases, for example – after all, religion can be construed at least partly as an 'intimate relationship' with God. The German jurisprudence on the religious subsistence level (see Chapters 5 and 9) has grappled with this question and essentially confined religion-based claimants to the closet, although this has been rejected by the CJEU (see Chapter 3). The internal dimension transpires less clearly in the context of political opinion; Grahl-Madsen's distinction between the protected expression of opinions and unprotected acts beyond the 'mere expression' of opinions is a case in point (see Chapter 7) – here, even the 'internal' dimension comprises an external element, and he struggled to devise a standard to separate these two categories.

But the strength of the conviction or belief often figures in the refugee context – although characteristics such as political opinion can unquestionably be fleeting, the refugee law context develops an invitation to establish the 'essence' of a person and their group: have they really converted? Do they really object military service? Theoretical elements from queer theory such as the closet, and the act/identity dichotomy, allow for an analysis of the dynamics that come along with this: assumptions of immutability, which strongly affect the idea of 'particular social group' (Chapter 8), thus recur in religion and also political opinion claims.

At the same time, the resistance against confining religion and political opinion to the internal dimension is stronger than in the context of sexual orientation. Beyond homophobia and the generalised assumption that closetedness is the 'natural' position for gay people, this is partly due to the fact that the recognition of public expression as an essential part of both religion and political opinion is laid down in specifically formulated human rights. In contrast, there is no specifically formulated human right that protects (the expression of) sexual orientation (see Chapter 9).

It was only when sexual orientation cases were considered in the light of religious and political opinion cases both in the common law jurisdictions and in Europe (Chapter 1) that this was seen as a dissonance. The UK Supreme Court brought sexuality-based claims in line with religion when drawing on the Australian High Court judgment in *NABD* in order to decide the case of *HJ (Iran) and HT (Cameroon)*, and the CJEU dealt with religion in *Y and Z* before it was concerned with sexuality in *X, Y and Z*, which was then considered in the light of and by analogy with the ruling on religion (Chapter 3). Sexuality-based claims were therefore fitted into a scheme that had been developed for other grounds for which reference to the closet did not seem natural to the same extent, and human rights warranted public expression.

Whereas this approach established that much like for the other grounds, 'discretion' cannot be *required* in sexuality-based claims, other things got lost along the way. Integrating sexuality-based claims into the poorly developed framework for claims based on political opinion and religion allowed brushing over much of the insights concerning 'discretion' logics that had been developed on sexuality-based claims (see Chapter 1). The reference to human rights appears to have allowed much of the detailed analysis necessary for sexuality-based claims to be glossed over. As a result, the 'discretion' logics inherent in the approach remain elusive. This book proposes to reintroduce some of the complication.

Indeed, the analysis in this book suggests that beyond establishing that public expression is in principle part of the Convention grounds, human rights are not very helpful in defining the contours of the reasons for persecution. Human rights law is not equipped to do the definitional work on the Convention grounds that refugee law requires. In this sense, it echoes previous findings from other scholars. Tobin, for example, found that '[h]uman rights tend to lack the precision and determinacy being sought by refugee lawyers and academics when they draw upon them to resolve the interpretative dilemmas that arise under the Refugee Convention'.[4] For the specific context of political opinion, Dauvergne noted, following an extensive review of case law on key cases: 'All of this leads to the conclusion that political opinion is not a term of art in refugee or international human rights law. It has been consistently treated, over a sixty-year span, as a straightforward expression used in its ordinary sense. The interpretive dilemmas it has posed within refugee law are not

4 John Tobin (2012) 'Assessing GLBTI Refugee Claims: Using Human Rights Law to Shift the Narrative of Persecution within Refugee Law', 44(2) *New York University Journal of International Law and Politics* 447–484, 480.

mirrored elsewhere in international human rights law.'[5] The analysis in this book supports these findings. As Chapter 9 extensively laid out, by failing to properly separate Convention ground and harm, human rights even create new interpretative difficulties within the refugee definition.

But beyond the limited applicability of human rights law to defining the Convention grounds, the book shows something else. It shows that due to the interpretative dilemmas of refugee law, the human rights approach was bound to fail in attempting to provide a principled basis for defining the Convention grounds as much as any other attempt to do the same in abstract or objective terms (Chapter 7). Defining the Convention grounds places limits on them which risk not being in line with the persecutor's notion of the persecuted characteristic. They are a distinct element but inherently connected to the persecution that is addressed at them. The definitional knot is this: due to the operating logics of refugee law, the Convention grounds must be *something*, but at the same time be open to being *anything*. Their contours remain blurry. The book therefore submits that the Convention grounds cannot be conceptualised in isolation; they have a contextual function. To understand the Convention grounds is to understand their interplay with the other elements – in particular persecution.

10.3 THE TROUBLE WITH THE SCOPE OF PROTECTION

What can be made of these insights with a view to the scope of protection of refugee law? The main theme running through the entire analysis is the uncertainties concerning the limits of protection. This book submits that these uncertainties can be attributed to and explained by the Refugee Convention's paradoxical double rationale: protection *of the Convention grounds* and *from persecution*. The issue runs deep. It raises complex questions at the heart of refugee law, involving the role of the claimant, the scope of the Convention grounds and the place of human rights in the analysis. A recognition of this double rationale can be employed productively to rethink refugee law more broadly.

10.3.1 *The Double Rationale of Refugee Protection: Persecution and Convention Grounds*

The tentative conclusion of the present analysis is that 'discretion' logics originate from a tension that is built into the refugee definition's double rationale: it protects *from persecution*, carried out by persecutors, on account of a *reason*, located with the claimant, and over which the claimant in many cases has a degree of control. This is in and of itself a conundrum. Is the main motivation of refugee law to be

[5] Catherine Dauvergne (2016) 'Toward a New Framework for Understanding Political Opinion', 37 *Michigan Journal of International Law* 243–298, 252.

seen in the protection *of the Convention grounds* (given that persecution for *other* reasons is not protected)? Or is it the protection *from persecution* (given that other harms on the basis of the Convention grounds are not protected)? The fact that *both* are laid out in the definition as necessary conditions creates a dilemma in situations of conflict; persecution is relevant only if it is due to the Convention ground and the Convention ground is relevant only if it is met with persecutory harm.

The balance can tip one way or another. As noted, the conflict is reflected in the clash of the severity argument and the fundamentality principle. These notions are in tension, because they interact. The claimant is in a position to reduce the prospects of serious harm precisely by exercising control over the reason which triggers this harm. But the claimant is never in full control (Chapter 2). Because persecution must be for a reason, the persecutor will only submit the claimant to harm relevant under the Refugee Convention if they identify and take them to possess that characteristic, but it remains the persecutor who determines the parameters of what (and therefore who) is persecuted.

To stipulate the paradox in this way evinces a certain degree of interaction between Convention ground and harm. Each of the two notions – the fundamentality principle and the severity rationale – is derived from the elements of the refugee definition. The fundamentality principle foregrounds the reason for persecution, whereas the severity argument prioritises the persecutory harm. Yet the 'not the same freedoms' logic of the severity concern also connects with the ability of the claimant to express the Convention ground and 'live freely and openly' (in the words of the UK Supreme Court, see Chapter 3). This includes the idea that the harm occasioned by some small limitations on this expression – that is, 'discretion' – is not sufficient to reach the threshold of persecution, or in other words, the degree of severity necessary to warrant international protection (see e.g. Chapter 9). Some hiding is ok. On the other hand, the 'no hiding' rationale of the fundamentality principle invokes the triviality concern: in this logic, whereas it is not the appropriate response to a refugee situation to tell the claimant to simply hide, the severity principle might not be met as accepting some minor restrictions on the forms of expression cannot be considered to cause persecutory harm.

The four variables – persecutor, persecution, claimant, Convention grounds – are wound up in a web of interconnected relationships. While there are important power dynamics at play, the whole set-up is inherently unstable. 'Discretion' is merely the flip side, or the mirror image, of the uncertainties related to the scope of what it is that is protected in refugee law. In that sense, 'discretion' reasoning is the *expression* of the struggles over defining what is protected and why.

10.3.2 *The Central Conundrum: Between Persecutor and Persecuted*

One way in which this tension between Convention ground and persecution plays out in terms of the scope of protection relates to the question of how group

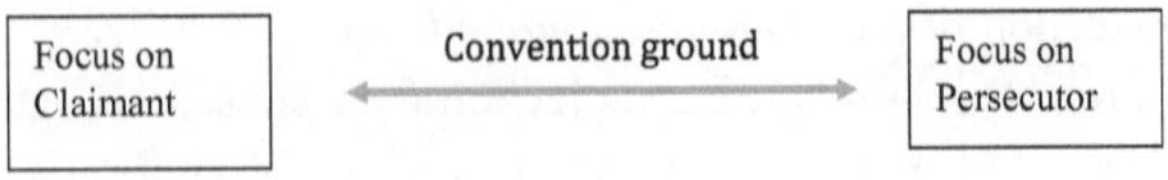

FIGURE 10.1. Claimant/persecutor continuum

membership is established, that is, whether it is the claimant themselves or the persecutor who assigns the Convention ground to the claimant, as discussed in Chapter 7. On the one hand, it may be the persecutor who defines what and who is persecuted. In this case, it is relevant whether harm is differentially inflicted due to the fact that the persecutor *imputes* or *assumes* a political opinion, social background or religious belief – irrespective of the claimant's 'actual' group membership. On the other hand, it may be the claimant who defines group membership. Here, it is relevant whether the claimant has a *deeply held* political conviction or religious belief, for example – or whether their sexual orientation is identity-defining for them. In this approach, it is the claimants themselves who provide the nexus to the persecuted group. The approaches do not necessarily map onto each other.

To make things even more complex, this communication process between claimant and persecutor is evaluated by a third party. In the refugee status determination context, it is the decision-maker, lawyer or academic, who makes a judgment on the ways the characteristic was, is or, importantly, will be expressed (or not) by the claimant and the extent to which it was, or rather, will be perceived by the persecutor. These third-party observers present themselves as neutral arbiters, but are obliged to position themselves in relation to this tension.

Thus, there is a continuum the two poles of which are a complete focus on the claimant and a complete focus on the persecutor (Figure 10.1).

As Chapter 9 demonstrated, the question of focus is an important one. It has significant consequences for the assessment of the claim. If the focus is on the claimant rather than the persecutor, then the correlating assumption is that it is in the hands of the claimant to manage and avoid the risk – secrecy is understood to equal safety. If, on the other hand, the focus is on the persecutor, the options available to the claimant are greatly reduced: because the persecutor establishes the link between the claimant and the persecuted group, the equation *secrecy = safety* breaks down. If anything, the claimant can attempt to reduce, but never avoid risk – in fact, they do not even have to identify with the persecuted group in any way to be at risk. There were brief glimpses of a recognition of this breakdown in various jurisdictions. One example is the broad French definition of particular social group, requiring no identification of the claimant whatsoever (Chapter 4). Another example is the position of the German administrative decision-making body, BAMF, in (briefly) refraining from any tests concerning the claimant's sexual orientation on the basis that the persecutor can only assume it as well (Chapter 5).

TABLE 10.1. *Assumptions: Focus on claimant versus focus on persecutor*

Focus on claimant	*Focus on persecutor*
Assumption that claimant attributes membership of persecuted group (through self-ascription)	Assumption that persecutor attributes membership of the persecuted group (through imputation)
The claimant needs to be an 'actual' group member	Claimant needs not be a group member (imputed group membership)
Secrecy = safety: If the claimant is 'discreet' there is no risk	Secrecy ≠ safety: Even if not a group member, can be at risk
Claimant can manage and avoid risk	Claimant can reduce, but not avoid risk

Table 10.1. illustrates the different assumptions that correlate with the focus on the claimant on the one hand, and the focus on the persecutor on the other.

The dilemma is this: focusing entirely on the claimant results in a *reductio ad absurdum* vis-à-vis refugee status. If it is entirely in the hands of the claimant to manage and avoid the risk, then there is no need for refugee law. This is the classical 'discretion' reasoning approach, which is generally rejected.

Importantly, however, the opposite – focusing entirely on the persecutor – is equally unworkable. If what counts is the persecutor's establishment of a link between the claimant and the persecuted group, irrespective of 'actual' group membership, anyone could potentially be imputed to be a group member. If no link whatsoever is required between the claimant and the persecuted group, the refugee concept becomes so broad that it tends towards implosion. It would be relinquished to the remote possibilities of the persecutors' whims. Under such an approach, the entire population of a country could qualify on the basis that they could possibly be thought to belong to a persecuted group one day – for example, in the event an ill-intentioned neighbour might allege that they are gay (or supporters of an opposition movement, or adhere to a minority religion). There must, therefore, be more of a link between the claimant and the Convention ground. This link can either be established through actual membership or through membership having already been imputed. Figure 10.2 illustrates the different ways of establishing group membership – either through the focus on the persecutor and 'perceived' membership or through the focus on the claimant ('actual' membership) – and the ways in which they interact.

The case is relatively straightforward for those situations where 'actual' and 'perceived' membership overlaps, that is, for those claimants who self-identify as gay and have been outed (box D). In both German and French practice, group membership was no issue in such cases. Notably, rejections still took place, but on the basis of disbelief (Chapters 4 and 5). It is much less clear for the other situations. If a claimant is gay but has not been outed, that is, the persecutor does not know

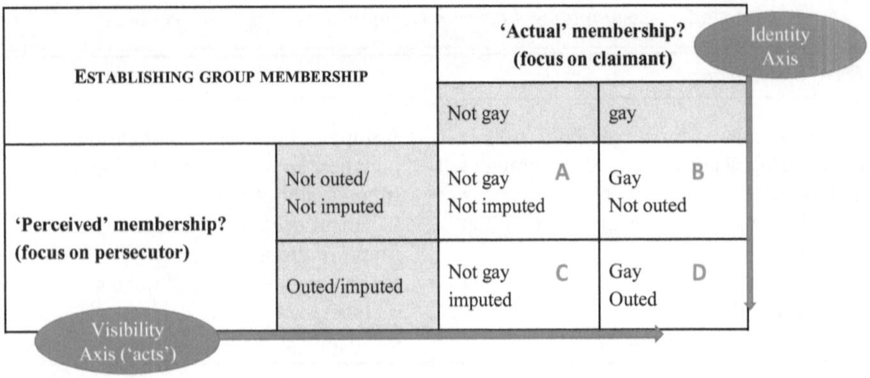

FIGURE 10.2. Establishing group membership

about the claimant's group membership – is the claimant entitled to protection (box B)? If the balance tips towards the protection of the Convention ground, this person is protected. If the protection from persecution is given preference, the person might not be – since the harm only occurs if the Convention ground becomes known (which presumably can be avoided through 'discretion'). French jurisprudence would likely tend towards this interpretation (Chapter 4).

If, on the other hand, a person does *not* self-identify as gay but has been taken to be so – are they entitled to protection (box C)? Here, if protection from persecution is the determining element, the claimant is protected. On the other hand, if the main rationale is sought in protection of the Convention grounds, the person might not be (and told to return to a different part of the country, denounce or conceal). This position is neatly reflected in German jurisprudence, with its focus on identity (Chapter 5), and can also be found in the Spanish 'significant transcendence' criterion (Chapter 6).

If a person neither self-identifies as gay nor has been taken to be so (box A), they would never be entitled to protection if protection of the Convention ground guides the assessment (there is nothing to protect), but might be if protection from persecution was the main concern (on the basis of possible future imputation).

All these different aspects come together to form a complex picture of instability; 'discretion' reasoning is the flip side of the scope of protection. Both are subject to a variety of tensions and ambiguities that overlap and intersect in significant and complex ways. These complex connections make everything unstable – not only 'discretion' itself but also its rejection. As a result, 'discretion' functions as a patch for all these instabilities that emerge from the refugee definition. As such, it is an unresolvable issue that surfaces at different layers, in different locations and in different ways – if it is put down in one place and form, it will resurface in another place and in another form. The material analysed in this study provides ample evidence for this; each of the rejections of 'discretion' proved to be unsuccessful or incomplete.

The argument advanced here is that the different shapes and forms 'discretion' reasoning takes in various contexts and jurisdictions reflect attempts to find a, more-or-less principled, but, in any case, necessary way of dealing with the incoherence that forms part of the refugee definition. They are different approaches to finding a position on the continuum and balancing the focus on the persecutor and the persecuted – and simultaneously, between the protection of the Convention grounds and protection from persecutory harm. 'Discretion' thus provides these 'arbiters' with quite some discretion. In this sense, 'discretion' may not be a misnomer at all (see Chapter 2), but, in fact, the most accurate and succinct denomination that the phenomenon could have been given.

10.4 SO WHAT? IMPLICATIONS FOR DRAWING LINES

In an answer to the guiding question of this book, this research has shown that 'discretion' is so difficult to get rid of because it functions as the patch for the tensions that arise from the clash between the protection of the Convention grounds and the protection from persecution. It is both a necessity and a risk for refugee law – it stabilises and destabilises protection. Due to this function, it will not disappear; the concealment controversy is an insoluble element of the refugee definition. It covers the space beyond the boundaries of protection that are drawn up in each particular case.

What are the implications of these findings for refugee decision-making? The complex instabilities inscribed in the refugee definition mean that there is no single solution as the scope of protection of refugee law is unstable. But the question remains as to how to work within this system to devise the best possible solution, that is, where to draw the lines of refugee protection.

10.4.1 *Reconsidering the Scope of Refugee Protection*

The present analysis produced a number of insights that allow for a reconsideration of the scope of refugee protection. Firstly, the analysis reveals that there is no coherent refugee law discourse on the scope of protection with a compelling inner logic. The scope of refugee protection is, in fact, utterly unclear. The idea of what constitutes persecution is vague, the contours of the Convention grounds remain blurry and just what the point of protection is, is uncertain.

Secondly, 'discretion' ties back to the very rationale of refugee protection. This explains why the concealment controversy is argued so vehemently. The fury in some of the submissions cited in Chapter 1 exposes profound concerns regarding approaches that putatively misunderstood the fundamental purpose of refugee law.

Thirdly, this implies that it is futile to raise the pitch of the debate. It is a fantasy that there is a 'right' answer. The scope of refugee protection is, by its very nature, wound up in double and contradictory meanings. In this web of contradictions, a range of parameters may be reverted to in order to ground the process and give it a semblance of coherence. Some such attempts to control the instability may appear more legitimate, adequate or logical than others, but none of them relieve the 'arbiter' from the arbitration exercise. Rather, they adapt the mechanism of exclusion and inclusion to the necessities of the day.[6]

Fourthly, on a positive note, this process can work in favour of claimants too. In a given situation the various tensions can be controlled in a claimant's favour. The 'master of the double bind' (Chapter 2) is in a position to offset not only limiting but also expanding functions.

It is this aspect that can be used strategically as a point of departure for conscious strategies to develop approaches that would be the most inclusive for each claimant. Such strategies consist in attempting to make the instabilities work in the claimants' favour. Importantly, there is no general solution, but rather, the approach is necessarily different for each claimant and dependent on their specific circumstances. In particular, it is relevant whether the claimant actually holds the persecuted characteristic or whether it is a case of imputation, and whether they have already been outed.

Referring back to the aforementioned classification of cases, in rough terms, a most inclusive approach might look as follows. Claimants who do possess the persecuted characteristic and where this has already come to the knowledge of the persecutor (box D) constitute largely uncomplicated cases. This type of claims likely involves experiences of past persecution. While disbelief becomes an issue here (see Chapters 4 and 5), which is a major concern for refugee status determination generally, 'discretion' logics are not the main consideration.

But the insights from the previous analysis become relevant for the more complicated cases classified in boxes B and C. In the case of a claimant who does not self-identify with the persecuted characteristic that has been imputed to them (box C), subscription to the persecutor's perspective would lead to the most favourable outcome for the claimant. In the process, it would be important to beware of singling out logics and requirements of past persecution (see e.g. in Spain, Chapter 6).

In contrast, in the particular case of a claimant who does self-identify, although this has not yet come to the attention of the persecutor (box B), it would lead to the most favourable result for the claimant to subscribe to the claimant's perspective, while resisting disbelief and requirements of visibility (see e.g. in France, Chapter 4).

Finally, claimants who do not self-identity, and who have not been imputed with a persecuted characteristic (box A) constitute the most difficult cases, and would, for the most part, not be protected. There must be *something*. However, if such a

6 See, making a similar point, Thomas Spijkerboer (2000) *Gender and Refugee Status*, Aldershot: Ashgate, 192.

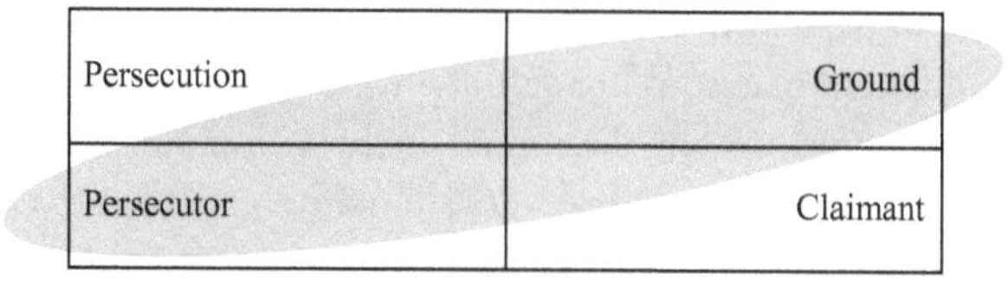

FIGURE 10.3. Working on the dyads

claimant does have fear of possible future imputation, it is most promising to rely on the persecutor's perspective.

In more abstract terms, to resist 'discretion' reasoning involves working on the dyads persecution-ground and persecutor-claimant in order to attempt flipping the discourses (Figure 10.3). Generally, the focus in doctrine and also case law often remains reductive, with an overall tendency of looking either at persecution and the claimant (such as in Germany, Chapter 5) or at the Convention ground and the persecutor (such as in France, Chapter 4). Such a limited focus creates an imbalance, submerging the relevant counterparts. It makes 'discretion' difficult to grasp, which necessarily remains elusive. A conscious strategy to counter this in order to adapt the scope of protection to the needs of a particular claimant may consist in matching each element with its counterpart. Where in a particular case, or jurisdiction, or doctrinal figure, the primary focus is on persecution, reference to the Convention ground may open up new space for manoeuvre in legal argumentation. Likewise, if the focus is on the claimant, reintegrating the persecutor into the picture may unsettle an exclusive interpretation and turn it into an inclusive one.

A principled attempt to control 'discretion' with a view to enhancing the scope of protection in each particular case reintegrates the submerged element into the picture respectively. Matching the prioritised elements with their counterparts permits for a productive use of the interplay of the various elements. It may help shift the perspective and flip the discourses. As a result, there are more levers to shift, and the range of options to achieve protection for each particular claimant increases substantially.

Nonetheless, it is important to reiterate that such an approach, due to the nature of the refugee definition, is never safe. Precisely because of the instabilities inherent in the tensions that are inbuilt into the refugee definition, the discourse always remains vulnerable to being flipped (back).

10.4.2 *Revisiting the Controversy around Hathaway and Pobjoy*

What does this analysis mean for the storm triggered by Hathaway and Pobjoy's response to the UK Supreme Court judgment in *HJ (Iran) and HT (Cameroon)*, as laid out in the introduction? The quarrel is a stalemate: neither the UK Supreme Court nor the refugee scholars have found a definitive answer. They merely suggest different variants to deal with the question of acceptable limitations: they include and exclude in different places. Whereas the UK Supreme Court would allow those claimants whose motivation for 'discretion' is the persecutor, and disallow those whose motivation is family disapproval, the 'alternative approach to conceptualizing the relevant persecutory harm in cases of enforced concealment' advanced by Hathaway and Pobjoy[7] would permit those claimants who suffer severely from 'discretion' and forbid those who do not experience 'discretion' as so psychologically harmful. The protected group is differently constructed in each approach – those falling *outside*, and therefore, those having to bear 'discretion' – are differently situated. Though both measure degrees of triviality, which warrants 'discretion' in each approach, they hook onto different arguments. A claimant whose motivation for 'discretion' is family disapproval, but whose suffering arising from concealment is so severe that it amounts to persecution, would be included in Hathaway and Pobjoy's proposal but not in the UK Supreme Court's. Conversely, a claimant who hides for fear of persecution, but without that occasioning severe mental suffering, would be included in the UK Supreme Court's approach, but not necessarily in Hathaway and Pobjoy's. In both cases, some gay people are excluded and sent back to 'discretion' – the difference lies only in the question of *how* to isolate the protected from the persecuted group, that is, where to draw the line. The balance is flipped between the approaches; the UK Supreme Court slightly favours the protection of the Convention grounds and the requirement that the protected characteristics should not be hidden, whereas Hathaway and Pobjoy lean towards protection from persecution and the severity argument.

Note that Hathaway and Pobjoy flag that there might be force in an approach based on equal treatment before the law as laid down in Art 26 ICCPR,[8] although they do not develop this line of thought in their paper on the basis that 'while the duty of "equal protection of the law" might one day come to be understood as mandating an affirmative "right to be different," there is not yet a normative consensus in favor of such a meaning'.[9] Other participants to the controversy have more positively endorsed equality or non-discrimination approaches. Tobin, for example, advanced an 'alternative nexus test which would be to inquire whether there is the risk of differential treatment on the basis of sexual orientation (as defined and identified by the potential persecutor) that cannot be reasonably justified'.[10] Arguably, this is a reformulated version of the refugee definition: persecution must be differentially inflicted on the claimant because of their sexual orientation.

7 James Hathaway and Jason Pobjoy (2012) 'Queer Cases Make Bad Law', 44(2) *New York University Journal of International Law and Politics* 315–389, 358.

8 Ibid., 356–357.

9 Ibid., 358.

10 Tobin, note 4, 447–484, 483; see also Jenni Millbank (2012) 'The Right of Lesbians and Gay Men to Live Freely, Openly, and on Equal Terms Is Not Bad Law: A Reply to Hathaway and Pobjoy', 44(2) *New York University Journal of International Law and Politics* 497–527, 511–512.

Tobin's formulation explicitly reintegrates the persecutor perspective into the picture. Combined with an approach based on equality, which integrates the claimant perspective, and which is what other scholars, such as Millbank[11] call for, or dignity – in a fuller version than that advanced in German case law – there might indeed be force in such arguments. This type of human rights approach abstains from attempts to carve out exact definitions for single terms of the refugee definition (and thus avoids inevitably getting caught in the interpretative dilemmas of refugee law), and instead takes place at a more global level. Further research might establish whether an equality/non-discrimination or a dignity approach holds the requisite flexibility to accommodate the various malleabilities of the refugee definition while at the same time grounding it in a more principled framework.

10.5 THE WAY FORWARD: PRODUCTIVE INSTABILITY

The present analysis does not produce the missing piece to solve the puzzle. But what it does reveal is that that piece does not exist – and refugee protection is not a puzzle. There is more than one way to make it seem right. Therefore, there can be no general guidance on how to conciliate the dispute. Instead, the significance of this study lies in having uncovered some of the variables, paradoxes and conundrums that shape the discursive struggles. Awareness of these may open up an understanding of alternative approaches – and of the levers that can be shifted in each particular case.

Being prepared for 'discretion' to continue to come up – and an understanding of its functions – equips us to manage its pitfalls. A very broad, inclusive notion of protection is possible, and so is a very narrow, exclusive one. Importantly, arguments drawing on human rights are not automatically more inclusive. Moreover, the same notion will not be inclusive or exclusive for all claimants – depending on their specific situation, the inclusive notion for one may turn out to be exclusive for another. This requires constantly questioning the strategies that are reverted to and their effects.

The aim must not be one common understanding. Rather, the instability inherent in the refugee definition can be used productively in favour of each particular claimant. In order to achieve this, it is necessary to recognise the required balancing exercise between the focus on the claimant and the focus on the persecutor, and between the fundamentality principle and the severity argument, to consciously struggle for inclusion. This is not a safe strategy – as the double bind situation can be exploited, such that the preferences tip – but it is the best one available.

[11] Millbank, note 10, 497–527, 525.

ANNEX

ANNEX I

European and International Refugee Law

The European Union has been in the process of establishing a Common European Asylum System (CEAS) since 1999, aiming to unify standards relating to asylum.[1] Previously an intergovernmental matter, the Treaty of Amsterdam instituted asylum as a community (EU) competence.[2] The rationale was to avoid an uneven distribution of asylum seekers due to different levels of protection after the Schengen Agreement had removed internal border controls.[3]

The harmonisation efforts produced six legislative acts, only two of which – concerning the distribution of asylum seekers – are Regulations and therefore are directly applicable as soon as they enter into force (the *Dublin* and *Eurodac Regulations*).[4] All protection-related acts are Directives which – unlike

[1] European Commission (2015) 'Common European Asylum System', https://ec.europa.eu/home-affairs/what-we-do/policies/asylum/index_en.htm.

[2] Treaty of Amsterdam Amending the Treaty on European Union, the Treaties Establishing the European Communities and Certain Related Acts of 2 October 1997, oj C 340, 10 November 1997 (entry into force 1 May 1999).

[3] Vincent Chetail (2016) 'The Common European Asylum System: Bric-à-brac or System?', in Vincent Chetail, Philippe De Bruycker and Francesco Maiani (eds.) *Reforming the Common European Asylum System – The New European Refugee Law*, Leiden: Brill Nijhoff, 3–38, 4.

[4] Council Regulation No. 343/2003 of 18 February 2003 establishing the criteria and mechanisms for determining the Member State responsible for examining an asylum application lodged in one of the Member States by a third-country national, oj L 50/1, 25 February 2003 (*2003 Dublin Regulation*) and Regulation No. 2725/2000 of 11 December 2000 concerning the establishment of 'Eurodac' for the comparison of fingerprints for the effective application of the Dublin Convention, oj L 31/1, 15 December 2000 (*2000 Eurodac Regulation*) – both recast on 26 June 2013: Regulation (EU) No. 604/2013 of the European Parliament and of the Council of 26 June 2013 establishing the criteria and mechanisms for determining the Member State responsible for examining an application for international protection lodged in one of the Member States by a third-country national or a stateless person (recast), oj L 180/31, 29 June 2013 (*Recast Dublin Regulation*) and Regulation (EU) No. 603/2013 of the European Parliament and of the Council of 26 June 2013 on the establishment of 'Eurodac' for the comparison of fingerprints for the effective application of Regulation (EU) No. 604/2013 establishing the criteria and mechanisms for determining the Member State responsible for examining an application for

Regulations – are binding only regarding the outcome and need to be transposed into national legislation by EU member states (*Qualification*, *Asylum Procedures*, *Reception Conditions* and *Temporary Protection Directives*).[5] In this way, member states retain substantial discretion to establish procedures for granting and withdrawing protection, which has led to much-criticised disparities across member states.[6]

The establishment of the CEAS consists of a 'first phase', from 1999 to 2004, with a first generation of legislative acts establishing 'minimum' standards,[7] and a 'second phase' from 2004 to 2013, with a second generation of 'recast' Directives and Regulations, now establishing 'common' or 'uniform' standards.[8] However, the

international protection lodged in one of the Member States by a third-country national or a stateless person and on requests for the comparison with Eurodac data by Member States' law enforcement authorities and Europol for law enforcement purposes, and amending Regulation (EU) No. 1077/2011 establishing a European Agency for the operational management of large-scale IT systems in the area of freedom, security and justice (recast), oj L 180/1, 29 June 2013 (*Recast Eurodac Regulation*).

5 Although the European Commission has proposed converting the *Qualification Directive* and the *Asylum Procedures Directive* into more detailed and binding regulations in July 2016, see: European Commission (2016) 'Completing the Reform of the Common European Asylum System: Towards an Efficient, Fair and Humane Asylum Policy', European Commission – Press Release, Brussels, 13 July 2016, together with proposed texts for Regulations, https://ec.europa.eu/commission/presscorner/detail/en/IP_16_2433.

6 See e.g. Catherine Teitgen-Colly (2006) 'The European Union and Asylum: An Illusion of Protection', 43(6) *Common Market Law Review* 1503–1566, 1512–1513.

7 According to Article 63 TEC (Treaty of Amsterdam Amending the Treaty on European Union, the Treaties Establishing the European Communities and Certain Related Acts of 2 October 1997, oj C 340, 10 November 1997 (entry into force 1 May 1999)); see Council Directive 2004/83/EC of 29 April 2004 on minimum standards for the qualification and status of third-country nationals or stateless persons as refugees or as persons who otherwise need international protection and the content of the protection granted, oj L 304/12, 30 September 2004 (2004 *Qualification Directive*); Council Directive 2005/85/EC of 1 December 2005 on minimum standards on procedures in Member States for granting and withdrawing refugee status, oj L 326/13, 13 December 2005 (2005 *Asylum Procedures Directive*); and Council Directive 2003/9/EC of 27 January 2003 laying down minimum standards for the reception of asylum seekers, oj L 31/18, 6 February 2003 (2003 *Reception Conditions Directive*).

8 According to Article 78(2) of the *Treaty on the Functioning of the European Union (TFEU) as Amended by the Treaty of Lisbon*; see Directive 2011/95/EU of the European Parliament and of the Council of 13 December 2011 on standards for the qualification of third-country nationals or stateless persons as beneficiaries of international protection, for a uniform status for refugees or for persons eligible for subsidiary protection, and for the content of the protection granted (recast), oj L 337/9, 20 December 2011 (*Recast Qualification Directive*), transposition date 21 December 2013; Directive 2013/33/EU of the European Parliament and of the Council of 26 June 2013 laying down standards for the reception of applicants for international protection (recast), oj L 1980/96, 29 June 2013 (*Recast Reception Conditions Directive*), transposition date 20 June 2015; Directive 2013/32/EU of the European Parliament and of the Council of 26 June 2013 on common procedures for granting and withdrawing international protection (recast), oj L 180/160, 29 June 2013 (*Recast Asylum Procedures Directive*), with varying transposition deadlines in 2015 and 2018 depending on provisions.

second phase instruments are 'neither a revolution nor an evolution', but rather a reformulation of the previous legislation in the interest of clarity.[9]

This is reflected in the *Qualification Directive*, where most of the operative provisions, as well as the Article numbering, remain entirely or essentially unchanged.[10] The *Qualification Directive* constitutes the most relevant element of the CEAS for the purposes of this study, as it lays out the standards for the recognition of refugee status, thus principally covering the same ground as the 1951 Convention. It amounts to a translation of the Refugee Convention into European law, adding more detail and definitions in some instances, and thus giving up some of the malleability that allowed for the continual reinterpretation of the key terms of the Refugee Convention.[11]

An important step forward for the CEAS was the new legal frame that resulted from the Treaty of Lisbon.[12] Signed in December 2007, it entered into force on 1 December 2009 and legally endorsed the Common European Asylum System in Article 78(2) of the of the *Treaty on the Functioning of the European Union* (TFEU). Thus, the general policy objective of establishing a common asylum system was turned into a specific – and binding – legal duty.[13] Notably, this entailed a full role for the Court of Justice of the European Union (CJEU) in matters of European asylum law.[14] This created a somewhat ambiguous situation; because the Convention is only open to accession for states, the EU itself is not a signatory. Therefore, the 1951 Refugee Convention is not formally part of EU law, and the CJEU does not have the jurisdiction to rule on it directly.[15] Still, the Convention

[9] Chetail, note 3, 3–38, 27.

[10] UNHCR (2015) *The Case Law of the European Regional Courts: The Court of Justice of the European Union and the European Court of Human Rights. Refugees, Asylum-Seekers, and Stateless Persons* (1st ed.), June 2015, 43. Distinctions between the 2004 and the 2011 *Qualification Directive* are therefore only made where necessary.

[11] Catherine Dauvergne (2008) *Making People Illegal: What Globalization Means for Migration and Law*, Cambridge: Cambridge University Press, 149–150.

[12] *Treaty of Lisbon Amending the Treaty on European Union and the Treaty Establishing the European Community*, oj C 306, 17 December 2007 (entry into force 1 December 2009).

[13] Chetail, note 3, 3–38, 20.

[14] Cathryn Costello and Emily Hancox (2014) 'The UK, the Common European Asylum System and EU Immigration Law', *Policy Primer*, Oxford: The Migration Observatory, www.migrationobservatory.ox.ac.uk/wp-content/uploads/2016/04/PolicyPrimer-UK_EU_Asylum_Law.pdf.

[15] See the CJEU case of *Mohammad Ferooz Qurbani*, Case C-481/13, European Union: Court of Justice of the European Union, 17 July 2014, where the Court held at 23–24: 'It is only where and in so far as the European Union has assumed the powers previously exercised by the Member States in the field to which an international convention not concluded by the European Union applies and, therefore, the provisions of the convention have the effect of binding the European Union that the Court has jurisdiction to interpret such a convention. In the present case, although several pieces of EU legislation have been adopted in the field to which the Geneva Convention applies as part of the implementation of a Common European Asylum System, it is undisputed that the Member States have retained certain powers falling within that field, in particular relating to the subject-matter covered by Article 31 of that

occupies a special role in EU law. Article 78 of the *Treaty on the Functioning of the European Union* (TFEU) – formerly Article 63 of the *Treaty Establishing the European Community* (TEC) – as well as Article 18 of the *EU Charter of Fundamental Rights*, require that the CEAS and the right to asylum must be in accordance with the 1951 *Refugee Convention*.[16] In particular, when asked to interpret the criteria for refugee status as defined by the *Qualification Directive*, the CJEU may be called upon to interpret the 1951 Refugee Convention in order to be able to answer the question – and consequently became the first ever supranational court applying and interpreting provisions of the Geneva Convention.[17]

The first judgments of the CJEU on the refugee definition were passed in 2010.[18] CJEU rulings are legally binding only for EU law – that is, they are authoritative for the member states of the EU.[19] This amounts to 27 of the 148 signatories of the 1951 Convention and/or its 1967 Protocol.[20] They thus represent a substantial proportion, such that their approach can be assumed to carry some weight beyond its strictly authoritative value, developing 'jurisprudential glow'.[21]

Such a 'ripple effect' even outside the EU, particularly with regards to the interpretation of the 1951 Convention[22] also carries a risk. In certain ways, the *Qualification Directive* 'wrest[s] international law away from the international and ... reframe[s] it'.[23] Commentators have pointed to the risk of the vanishing, at least in Europe, of the 1951 Convention 'refugee'.[24] Even early on, doubts were voiced as to whether the EU framework complied with obligations from

convention. Therefore, the Court does not have jurisdiction to interpret directly Article 31, or any other article, of that convention.'

16 UNHCR, note 10, 5–6.

17 Hélène Lambert (2013) 'Introduction: European Refugee Law and Transnational Emulation', in Hélène Lambert, Jane McAdam and Maryellen Fullerton (eds.) *The Global Reach of European Refugee Law*, Cambridge: Cambridge University Press, 1–24, 18–19.

18 *Salahadin Abdulla and Others* v. *Bundesrepublik Deutschland*, Joined Cases C-175/08, C-176/08, C-178/08 and C-179/08, European Union: Court of Justice of the European Union, 2 March 2010; *Nawras Bolbol* v. *Bevándorlási és Állampolgársági Hivatal*, Case C-31/09, European Union: Court of Justice of the European Union, 17 June 2010; *Bundesrepublik Deutschland* v. *B and D*, Joined Cases C-57/09 and C-101/09, European Union: Court of Justice of the European Union, 9 November 2010.

19 Out of twenty-eight EU member states, Denmark is the only state that opted out entirely of the asylum package; both the United Kingdom and Ireland opted out of most of the second phase (recast) of EU legislation, but the first generation remains applicable.

20 As of April 2015, see: UNHCR (2015) *States Parties to the 1951 Convention Relating to the Status of Refugees and the 1967 Protocol*, www.unhcr.org/protect/PROTECTION/3b73b0d63.pdf.

21 Dauvergne, note 11, 150.

22 Lambert, note 17, 1–24, 1.

23 Dauvergne, note 11, 150.

24 Jean-François Durieux (2013) 'The Vanishing Refugee: How EU Asylum Law Blurs the Specificity of Refugee Protection', in Hélène Lambert, Jane McAdam and Maryellen Fullerton (eds.) *The Global Reach of European Refugee Law*, Cambridge: Cambridge University Press, 225–257.

international law.[25] Such digressions from international refugee law are all the more consequential as the application of the *Qualification Directive* in twenty-seven states will provide a vital interpretive source for international law that leads to a re-export of departures from the 1951 Refugee Convention.[26] And whereas the European Union has a corrective, in the form of a constant 'double-judicial check' by the Court of Justice of the European Union and the European Court of Human Rights, this 'safety net' is unique to Europe.[27]

So the institutional context is as follows: like all EU member states, France, Germany and Spain are signatories to the 1951 Refugee Convention (and its 1967 Protocol). Before asylum was Europeanised, they had developed their own reception and status determination procedures, based on their own interpretations of the 1951 Geneva Convention. Germany and France both also guarantee a right to asylum in their national constitutions, but in view of the 1951 Convention and, particularly, the Common European Asylum System, constitutional asylum has become obsolete.[28] Since the Treaty of Lisbon, the jurisdiction of the Court of Justice for preliminary rulings on the interpretation of EU primary or secondary law at the request of a national court or tribunal also extends to matters of asylum.[29]

The preliminary ruling procedure operates as follows. When a national court considers that a question concerning the interpretation (or validity) of EU law is necessary to give judgment on a case, it has the right to request a preliminary ruling from the CJEU. Highest national courts or those against whose decisions there is no judicial remedy under national law have the obligation to do so when such a question arises.[30] The court then submits an 'order for reference' to the CJEU for preliminary ruling on a question or series of questions concerning EU law. The CJEU decides that question and the referring national court uses the Court's ruling to give ruling in the proceedings that gave rise to the question.

The question must be necessary in order to give judgment in the case and cannot merely ask for an advisory opinion on general or hypothetical questions. The CJEU can reformulate the questions that have been asked ('in essence, the question is . . .') without subverting them. Preliminary rulings on interpretation are final and cannot be appealed, although – while it cannot contest the validity of the ruling – another

[25] See e.g. Geoff Gilbert (2004) 'Is Europe Living Up to Its Obligations to Refugees?', 15(5) *European Journal of International Law* 963–987; Elspeth Guild (2004) 'Seeking Asylum: Storm Clouds between International Commitments and EU Legislative Measures', 29(2) *European Law Review* 198–218.

[26] Dauvergne, note 11, 150.

[27] Hélène Lambert (2013) 'Conclusion: Europe's Normative Power in Refugee Law', in Hélène Lambert, Jane McAdam and Maryellen Fullerton (eds.) *The Global Reach of European Refugee Law*, Cambridge: Cambridge University Press, 258–266, 265.

[28] For a discussion see: Hélène Lambert, Francesco Messineo and Paul Tiedemann (2008) 'Comparative Perspectives of Constitutional Asylum in France, Italy, and Germany: *Requiescat In Pace?*', 27(3) *Refugee Survey Quarterly* 16–32.

[29] Article 267 *TFEU*.

[30] Ibid.

preliminary ruling procedure is possible in order to ask the Court to interpret its own previous ruling. The Court's jurisdiction extends only to answering the question concerning EU law, not to deciding the case, and its rulings are very exact, limited to those points that are necessary for the referring court in order to decide the case that gave rise to the procedure. The judgment is binding for the national court with regard to that case, as well as generally for the courts and tribunals of all member states. The binding character extends not only to the ruling at the end of the judgment but to the body of the judgment as well. Preliminary rulings are declaratory and have *ex tunc* effect. All member states, as well as the Commission, the EU institution that adopted the act in issue and the parties to the main proceedings before the national court, including third-party interveners, are entitled to submit 'observations' to the Court on the answer it should give. An oral hearing may be held at the reasoned request of the interested parties.

The CJEU is assisted by Advocates General who – unless the Court decides to dispense with it – deliver an Opinion on how the case should be decided, which is not legally binding in any way. Though it cannot be assumed that the Court agrees with the Advocate General unless it explicitly states so, the Opinions are often more detailed and discursive than the Court's judgments, and can therefore provide valuable insights.[31]

[31] On the preliminary ruling procedure see for a good summary: UNHCR, note 10, 22–38; and for more detail: Koen Lenaerts, Ignace Maselis and Kathleen Gutman (2014) *EU Procedural Law*, Oxford: Oxford University Press; Morten Broberg and Niels Fenger (2014) *Preliminary References to the European Court of Justice* (2nd ed.), Oxford: Oxford University Press.

ANNEX II

Table of Cases

The following tables list those cases that compose the case collection upon which the country analyses in Chapters 4 (France), 5 (Germany) and 6 (Spain) draw. For information on the collection, please refer to the respective chapter.

1 FRANCE

#	Case No.	Date	Country of Origin	Court	Gender	Sexual Orientation
Conseil d'Etat (CE)						
1	CE, 171858, Ourbih	23 juin 1997	Algeria	Conseil d'Etat	MTF	? (Trans)
2	CE, 207241	19 juin 2000	Philippines	Conseil d'Etat	Male	Gay
3	CE, 244208	20 décembre 2002	Egypt	Conseil d'Etat	Male	Gay
4	CE, 229043, M. L.	10 janvier 2003	China	Conseil d'Etat	Male	Gay
5	CE, 245405	28 avril 2003	Algeria	Conseil d'Etat	Male	Gay
6	CE, 244362	19 novembre 2003	Algeria	Conseil d'Etat	Male	Gay
7	CE, 242294	9 avril 2004	Algeria	Conseil d'Etat	Male	Gay
8	CE, 250379	25 juin 2004	Morocco	Conseil d'Etat	Male	Gay

(*continued*)

(*continued*)

#	Case No.	Date	Country of Origin	Court	Gender	Sexual Orientation
9	CE, 258133	21 septembre 2005	Algeria	Conseil d'Etat	Male	Gay
10	CE, 260223	20 avril 2005	Algeria	Conseil d'Etat	Male	Gay
11	CE, 242002	30 mars 2005	Armenia	Conseil d'Etat	Female	Lesbian
12	CE, 272679, Olena	23 août 2006	Ukraine	Conseil d'Etat	Female	Lesbian
13	CE, 281294	7 août 2007	Iran	Conseil d'Etat	Male	Gay
14	CE, 336953	17 décembre 2010	?	Conseil d'Etat	Male	Gay
15	CE, 351079	22 juin 2012	Gambia	Conseil d'Etat	Male	Gay
16	CE, 375618	28 février 2014	Lithuania	Conseil d'Etat	Female	Lesbian
17	CE, 369178	15 octobre 2014	Rwanda	Conseil d'Etat	Male	Gay
18	CE, 383198 C, M. C.	1 octobre 2015	Comores	Conseil d'Etat	Male	Gay
19	CE, 391534	17 juin 2016	Nigeria	Conseil d'Etat	Male	Gay
20	CE, 350369	7 juillet 2011	Nigeria	Conseil d'Etat	Male	Gay
21	CE, 342552, O. A.	27 juillet 2012	Mongolia	Conseil d'Etat	Female	Lesbian
22	CE, 349824, A. B.	27 juillet 2012	DRC	Conseil d'Etat	Male	Gay
Commission des Recours des Réfugiés (CRR) (predecessor of CNDA)						
23	CRR 328310, Djellal	12 mai 1999	Algeria	Commission des Recours des Réfugiés	Male	Gay
24	CRR 343157, M. A	22 février 2000	Algeria	Commission des Recours des Réfugiés	Male	Gay
25	CRR 347330, M. A.	3 avril 2000	Romania	Commission des Recours des Réfugiés	Male	Gay
26	CRR 340068, M. E.	22 mai 2000	Algeria	Commission des Recours des Réfugiés	Male	Gay

#	Case No.	Date	Country of Origin	Court	Gender	Sexual Orientation
27	CRR 330627, M. M.	4 octobre 2000	Iran	Commission des Recours des Réfugiés	Male	Gay
28	CRR 363200, M. H.	18 janvier 2001	Yemen	Commission des Recours des Réfugiés	?	?
29	CRR 359001, M. B.	6 février 2001	Jordan	Commission des Recours des Réfugiés	Male	Gay
30	CRR 364711, M. D.	29 mars 2001	Mali	Commission des Recours des Réfugiés	Male	Gay
31	CRR 357662, M. G.	5 juin 2001	Ecuador	Commission des Recours des Réfugiés	?	? (Trans)
32	CRR 364910, Mlle M.	20 juin 2001	Armenia	Commission des Recours des Réfugiés	Female	Lesbian
33	CRR 367645, M. K.	29 juin 2001	Ukraine	Commission des Recours des Réfugiés	Male	Gay
34	CRR 379319, M. N.	13 septembre 2001	Morocco	Commission des Recours des Réfugiés	Male	Gay
35	CRR 388492, M. K.	23 mai 2002	Algeria	Commission des Recours des Réfugiés	Male	Gay
36	CRR 394788, M. H.	23 juillet 2002	Ethiopia	Commission des Recours des Réfugiés	Male	Gay
37	CRR 402381, M. T.	26 novembre 2002	Russia	Commission des Recours des Réfugiés	Male	Gay
38	CRR 483808, M. A.	12 octobre 2004	Turkey	Commission des Recours des Réfugiés	Male	Gay
39	CRR 487069, M. K.	28 janvier 2005	Ukraine	Commission des Recours des Réfugiés	Male	?
40	CRR 496775, M. B.	15 février 2005	Algeria	Commission des Recours des Réfugiés	MTF?	? (Trans)
41	CRR 513547, Mlle G.	25 mars 2005	Moldova	Commission des Recours des Réfugiés	Female	Lesbian

(*continued*)

(*continued*)

#	Case No.	Date	Country of Origin	Court	Gender	Sexual Orientation
42	CRR 498570, Mme. AGB	12 septembre 2005	Mongolia	Commission des Recours des Réfugiés	Female	Lesbian
43	CRR 495394, M. K	21 octobre 2005	Russia	Commission des Recours des Réfugiés	Male	Gay
44	CRR 27 480235	27 avril 2006	Cameroon	Commission des Recours des Réfugiés	Male	Gay
45	CRR 555672, M. S.	12 mai 2006	Bosnia-Herzegovina	Commission des Recours des Réfugiés	Male	Gay
46	CRR 497803, M. B.	3 juillet 2006	Gaboun	Commission des Recours des Réfugiés	Male	Gay
47	CRR 568157, M.	4 septembre 2006	Mali	Commission des Recours des Réfugiés	Male	Gay
48	CRR 571707, Mlle O.	12 octobre 2006	Kazakhstan	Commission des Recours des Réfugiés	Female	?
49	CRR 579547 Mlle ML	1 décembre 2006	Mauritania	Commission des Recours des Réfugiés	Female	Lesbian
50	CRR 569392, M. MMB	11 décembre 2006	Mauritania	Commission des Recours des Réfugiés	Male	Gay
51	CRR 584531, Melle EK	19 janvier 2007	Sierra Leone	Commission des Recours des Réfugiés	Female	Lesbian
52	CRR 578257 S	2 mars 2007	Cameroon	Commission des Recours des Réfugiés	Male	Gay
53	CRR 585858, Mlle L. alias M. L.	18 avril 2007	Argentina	Commission des Recours des Réfugiés	MTF	? (Trans)
54	CRR 589676, D	18 mai 2007	Senegal	Commission des Recours des Réfugiés	Male	Gay
55	CRR 589257, Z	23 mai 2007	Afghanistan	Commission des Recours des Réfugiés	Male	Gay

#	Case No.	Date	Country of Origin	Court	Gender	Sexual Orientation
Cour Nationale du Droit d'Asile (CNDA)						
56	CNDA 607063, A	9 janvier 2008	Turkey	Cour Nationale du Droit d'Asile	MTF	? (Trans)
57	CNDA 602367	29 janvier 2008	Morocco	Cour Nationale du Droit d'Asile	Male	Gay
58	CNDA 571886, G	11 avril 2008	Algeria	Cour Nationale du Droit d'Asile	Male	Gay
59	CNDA 571904, K	1 juillet 2008	Uganda	Cour Nationale du Droit d'Asile	Male	Gay
60	CNDA 605398, H	7 mai 2008	Albania	Cour Nationale du Droit d'Asile	Male	Gay
61	CNDA 588107	11 décembre 2008	Bangladesh	Cour Nationale du Droit d'Asile	Male	Gay
62	CNDA 588108	11 décembre 2008	Bangladesh	Cour Nationale du Droit d'Asile	Male	Gay
63	CNDA 473648, Mlle S.	16 décembre 2008	Ukraine	Cour Nationale du Droit d'Asile	Female	Lesbian
64	CNDA 602026	18 décembre 2008	Nigeria	Cour Nationale du Droit d'Asile	Male	Gay
65	CNDA 616907, K	6 avril 2009	Kosovo	Cour Nationale du Droit d'Asile	Male	Gay
66	CNDA 610542, Y.	7 mai 2009	Cameroon	Cour Nationale du Droit d'Asile	Male	Gay
67	CNDA 621093	27 mai 2009	Cameroon	Cour Nationale du Droit d'Asile	Male	Gay
68	CNDA 634565/ 08015025 C	7 juillet 2009	Tunisia	Cour Nationale du Droit d'Asile	Male	Gay
69	CNDA 08017195	9 novembre 2009	Cameroon	Cour Nationale du Droit d'Asile	Female	Lesbian

(continued)

(*continued*)

#	Case No.	Date	Country of Origin	Court	Gender	Sexual Orientation
70	CNDA 08018574	10 decembre 2009	Albania	Cour Nationale du Droit d'Asile	Male	Gay
71	CNDA 09012138	23 décembre 2009	Kosovo	Cour Nationale du Droit d'Asile	Male	Gay
72	CNDA 09018078 O	3 novembre 2010	Nigeria	Cour Nationale du Droit d'Asile	Male	Gay
73	CNDA 10009346 & 10009345	2 décembre 2010	Kosovo	Cour Nationale du Droit d'Asile	Male	Bisexual
74	CNDA 10013721	7 décembre 2010	Kosovo	Cour Nationale du Droit d'Asile	Male	Gay
75	CNDA 09012710 C+	10 janvier 2011	Cameroon	Cour Nationale du Droit d'Asile	Male	Gay
76	CNDA 09023968 C (M. I.)	1 mars 2011	Mauritania	Cour Nationale du Droit d'Asile	Male	Gay
77	CNDA 10002367 M	7 mars 2011	Guinea	Cour Nationale du Droit d'Asile	Male	Gay
78	CNDA 10015959 C (Mlle N.)	1 juin 2011	DRC	Cour Nationale du Droit d'Asile	Female	Lesbian
79	CNDA 10025142 C (M. V.)	24 juin 2011	Colombia	Cour Nationale du Droit d'Asile	Male	Gay
80	CNDA 11002234 C (M. K.)	4 juillet 2011	Pakistan	Cour Nationale du Droit d'Asile	Male	Gay
81	CNDA 10020448 C (M. M.)	11 juillet 2011	Uganda	Cour Nationale du Droit d'Asile	Male	Gay
82	CNDA 08015548 C (M. W.)	29 juillet 2011	Jamaica	Cour Nationale du Droit d'Asile	Male	Gay
83	CNDA 09004056 C (M. B.)	29 juillet 2011	Sierra Leone	Cour Nationale du Droit d'Asile	Male	Gay
84	CNDA 11010972 C (M. A.)	3 novembre 2011	Sudan	Cour Nationale du Droit d'Asile	Male	Gay

#	Case No.	Date	Country of Origin	Court	Gender	Sexual Orientation
85	CNDA 11010494 C (Mlle M)	21 novembre 2011	Cameroon	Cour Nationale du Droit d'Asile	Female	Lesbian
86	CNDA 10019216 C (M. C.)	28 novembre 2011	Senegal	Cour Nationale du Droit d'Asile	Male	Gay
87	CNDA 11009260 C (M. D.)	4 mai 2012	Georgia	Cour Nationale du Droit d'Asile	Male	Gay
88	CNDA 1201364 C (M. B. N.)	18 octobre 2012	Cameroon	Cour Nationale du Droit d'Asile	Male	Straight (imputed gay)
89	CNDA 12013647 C (M. B. N.)	18 octobre 2012	Cameroon	Cour Nationale du Droit d'Asile	Male	Gay
90	CNDA 13018825 C (M. A.)	29 novembre 2013	Bangladesh	Cour Nationale du Droit d'Asile	Male	Gay
91	CNDA 13025005 (M. J.-J.)	10 juillet 2014	Haiti	Cour Nationale du Droit d'Asile	Male	Gay
92	CNDA 14017576 C (Mme W.)	19 décembre 2014	DRC	Cour Nationale du Droit d'Asile	Female	Lesbian
93	CNDA 13021072 C	4 novembre 2014	Ghana	Cour Nationale du Droit d'Asile	Male	Gay
94	CNDA 15006472 C+	29 octobre 2015	Bangladesh	Cour Nationale du Droit d'Asile	Male	Gay
95	CNDA 15031443 C (M. K.)	18 mars 2016	Ivory Coast	Cour Nacionale du droit d'asile	Male	Gay
96	CNDA 15030258 C (Mme E.)	14 juin 2016	DRC	Cour Nacionale du droit d'asile	Female	Lesbian
97	CNDA 15004721 C (Mme T.)	27 septembre 2016	Cameroon	Cour Nacionale du droit d'asile	Female	Lesbian

2 GERMANY

#	Case No.	Date	Country of Origin	Court	Gender	Sexual Orientation
Bundesverwaltungsgericht (Federal Administrative Court)						
1	BVerwG 9 C 278/86	15.3.1988	Iran	Bundesverwaltungsgericht	Male	Gay
2	BVerwG, – 9 C 25–89 (München)	17.10.1989	Iran	Bundesverwaltungsgericht	Male	Bisexual
3	BVerwG 10 C 20.12	20.2.2013	Pakistan	Bundesverwaltungsgericht	Male	unknown
4	BVerwG 10 C 23.12	20.2.2013	Pakistan	Bundesverwaltungsgericht	Male	unknown
Oberverwaltungsgerichte/Verwaltungsgerichtshöfe (Higher Administrative Courts)						
5	VGH München – 19 ZB 98.33916	12.11.1998	Iran	Verwaltungsgerichtshof München	Male	Gay
6	OVG Berlin – Brandenburg 3 S 120.09	4.2.2010	Morocco	Oberverwaltungsgericht Berlin-Brandenburg	Male	Gay
7	VGH Baden-Württemberg A 9 S 1873/12	7.3.2013	Nigeria	Verwaltungsgerichtshof Baden-Württemberg	Male	Gay
8	OVG Lüneburg 8 LA 221/12	18.10.2013	Kosovo	Oberverwaltungsgericht Lüneburg	Female	Lesbian
9	OVG Nordrhein–Westfalen A324/14.A	05.01.2016	Guinea	Oberverwaltungsgericht Nordrhein-Westfalen	Male	Gay
10	VGH Baden–Württemberg A 9 S 908/13	26.10.2016	Gambia	Verwaltungsgerichtshof Baden-Württemberg	Male	Gay
Verwaltungsgerichte (Administrative Courts)						
11	VG Wiesbaden IV/I E 06244/81	26.4.1983	Iran	Verwaltungsgericht Wiesbaden	Male	Gay
12	VG Neustadt a.d. Weinstraße, – 9 K 2122/95.NW	16.12.1996	Syria	Verwaltungsgericht Neustadt/Weinstraße	Male	Gay
13	VG Ansbach – AN 17 K 97.33376	20.04.2000	Ethiopia	Verwaltungsgericht Ansbach	Male	Gay/ Bisexual
14	VG Würzburg, – W 7 K 01.30170	16.07.2002	Iran	Verwaltungsgericht Würzburg	male	Gay
15	VG München Gerichtsbescheid M 12 K 05.50666	9.1. 2006	Nigeria	Bayrisches Verwaltungsgericht München	Male	Gay
16	VG Bremen 7 K 632/05.A	28.4.2006	Iraq	Verwaltungsgericht Bremen	Male	Gay
17	VG Köln 18 K 9030/ 03.A	8.9.2006	Iraq	Verwaltungsgericht Köln	Male	Gay
18	VG Potsdam 9K189/ 03.A	11.9.2006	Sudan	Verwaltungsgericht Potsdam	Male	Gay
19	VG Hamburg 21 A 311/05	18.12.2006	Iraq	Verwaltungsgericht Hamburg	Male	Gay

#	Case No.	Date	Country of Origin	Court	Gender	Sexual Orientation
20	VG München M 21 K 04.51494	30.1.2007	Nigeria	Verwaltungsgericht München	Male	Gay
21	VG Berlin VG 38 X 79.05	27.3.2007	Bangladesh	Verwaltungsgericht Berlin	Male	Gay
22	VG Münster Beschluss 9 L 381/07.A	4.7.2007	Cameroon	Verwaltungsgericht Münster	Male	Gay
23	VG Düsseldorf 11 K 2432/07.A	21.2.2008	Egypt	Verwaltungsgericht Düsseldorf	Male	Gay
24	VG Chemnitz A 2 K 304/06	11.7.2008	Afghanistan	Verwaltungsgericht Chemnitz	Male	Gay
25	VG Ansbach AN 18 K 08.30201	21.8.2008	Iran	Verwaltungsgericht Ansbach	Male	Gay
26	VG Neustadt/Weinstraße 3 K 753/07.NW	8.9.2008	Iran	Verwaltungsgericht Neustadt/Weinstraße	Female	Lesbian
27	VG Regensburg RN 8 K 08.30020	15.9.2008	Algeria	Verwaltungsgericht Regensburg	Male	Gay
28	VG Berlin 23 X 30.06	3. 12. 2008	Iran	Verwaltungsgericht Berlin	Male	Gay
29	VG Düsseldorf 5 K 1875/08.A	11.3.2009	Iran	Verwaltungsgericht Düsseldorf	Male	Gay
30	VG Dresden A1 K 30157/07	15.5.2009	Venezuela	Verwaltungsgericht Dresden	Male	? (Trans)
31	VG Schleswig-Holstein 6 B 32/09	7.9.2009	Iran	Schleswig-Holsteinisches Verwaltungsgericht	Male	Gay
32	VG Chemnitz A 4K1453/08	17. 12.2009	Tunisia	Verwaltungsgericht Chemnitz	Female	Lesbian
33	VG Düsseldorf 11 K 6778/09/A	14.1.2010	Morocco	Verwaltungsgericht Düsseldorf	Male	Gay
34	VG Potsdam 11 K 397/06.A	19.1.2010	Cameroon	Verwaltungsgericht Potsdam	Female	Lesbian
35	VG Sigmaringen A 1 K 1911/09	26.4.2010	Iraq	Verwaltungsgericht Sigmaringen	Male	Gay
36	VG Trier Beschluss 1 L 928/10.TR	9. 9.2010	Algeria	Verwaltungsgericht Trier	Male	Gay
37	VG Münster 4 K 2514/09.A	14.9.2010	Morocco	Verwaltungsgericht Münster	Male	Gay
38	VG Frankfurt/Oder 4 K 772/10.A	11.11.2010	Cameroon	Verwaltungsgericht Frankfurt/Oder	Male	Gay
39	VG Köln 15 K 6103/10.A	15.9.2011	Guinea	Verwaltungsgericht Köln	Male	Gay
40	VG Regensburg Beschluss Az. RO 7 S 11.30513	31.10.2011	Ethiopia	Bayrisches Verwaltungsgericht Regensburg	Male	Gay
41	VG Düsseldorf 13 K 1217/11.A	23.3.2012	Guinea	Verwaltungsgericht Düsseldorf	Male	Gay
42	VG Sigmaringen A 6 K 737/12	14.6.2012	Cameroon	Verwaltungsgericht Sigmaringen	Male	Gay

(*continued*)

(*continued*)

#	Case No.	Date	Country of Origin	Court	Gender	Sexual Orientation
43	VG Meiningen 8 K 20174/11 Me	9.8.2012	Afghanistan	Verwaltungsgericht Meiningen	Male	Gay
44	VG Köln 13 K 1011/09.A	16.8.2012	Uzbekistan	Verwaltungsgericht Köln	Male	Gay
45	VG Baden-Württemberg A 9 S 1681/12	11.9.2012	Nigeria	Verwaltungsgericht Baden-Württemberg	Male	Gay
46	VG Sigmaringen A 1 K20111	17.10.2012	Gambia	Verwaltungsgericht Sigmaringen	Male	Gay
47	VG Würzburg W 6 K 12.30072	14.11.2012	Iran	Verwaltungsgericht Würzburg	Male	Gay
48	VG Ansbach AN 11 K 12.30387	20.12.2012	Pakistan	Verwaltungsgericht Ansbach	Male	Gay
49	VG Meiningen 8 K 20272/11 Me	7.2.2013	Afghanistan	Verwaltungsgericht Meiningen	Male	Gay
50	VG Potsdam VG 6 K 1657/12.A	19.2.2013	Kenya	Verwaltungsgericht Potsdam	Male	Gay
51	VG Augsburg Au 6 K 12.30387	19.3.2013	Kosovo	Verwaltungsgericht Augsburg	Male	Bisexual
52	VG Augsburg Au 6K13.30158	29.7.2013	Afghanistan	Bayrisches Verwaltungsgericht Augsburg	Male	Gay
53	VG Ansbach AN 11 E 13.30587	5.9.2013	Afghanistan	Verwaltungsgericht Ansbach	Male	Gay
54	VG Ansbach AN 11 K 13.30497	10.10.2013	Afghanistan	Verwaltungsgericht Ansbach	Male	Gay
55	VG Berlin Beschluss 34 L 89.13	29.10.2013	Uganda	Verwaltungsgericht Berlin	Male	Gay
56	VG Düsseldorf 13 K 3683/13.A	13.12.2013	Guinea	Verwaltungsgericht Düsseldorf	Male	Gay
57	VG München M 17 K 13.31074	19.2.2014	Serbia	Verwaltungsgericht München	Male	Gay
58	VG Stuttgart A 7 K 4000/13	20.2.2014	Nigeria	Verwaltungsgericht Stuttgart	Male	Gay
59	VG Potsdam VG 6 K 435/13.A	27.2.2014	Russia	Verwaltungsgericht Potsdam	Female	Lesbian
60	VG Hamburg 10 A 465/12	2.4.2014	Iran	Verwaltungsgericht Hamburg	Male	Gay
61	VG München M 4 K 13.30114	24.4.2014	Iraq	Bayrisches Verwaltungsgericht München	Male	Gay
62	VG Potsdam VG 6 K 3802/13.A	13.5.2014	Kenya	Verwaltungsgericht Potsdam	Male	Gay
63	VG Würzburg Beschluss W 1 S 14.30384	21.8.2014	Macedonia	Verwaltungsgericht Würzburg	Male	Gay
64	VG Augsburg Au 3 K 14.30222	31.10.2014	Pakistan	Bayrisches Verwaltungsgericht Augsburg	Male	Gay

#	Case No.	Date	Country of Origin	Court	Gender	Sexual Orientation
65	VG Aachen 2 K 1477/13.A	12.12.2014	Nigeria	Verwaltungsgericht Aachen	Male	Gay
66	VG Saarland 5 K 534/13	23.01.2015	Algeria	Verwaltungsgericht des Saarlandes	Male	Bisexual
67	VG Hannover 1 A 109/13	18.02.2015	Georgia	Verwaltungsgericht Hannover	Male	Gay
68	VG Braunschweig 7 A 68/15	02.09.2015	Nigeria	Verwaltungsgericht Braunschweig	Female	Lesbian
69	VG Frankfurt/Oder 4 K 109912.A	19.11.2015	Cameroon	Verwaltungsgericht Frankfurt/Oder	Male	Gay
70	VG Gelsenkirchen 9a K 3162/15.A	18.12.2015	Nigeria	Verwaltungsgericht Gelsenkirchen	Female	Lesbian
71	VG Minden	21.01.2016	Bangladesh	Verwaltungsgericht Minden	Male	Gay
72	VG Würzburg W 6 K 15.30116	1.7.2016	Iran	Verwaltungsgericht Würzburg	Male	Gay
73	VG Düsseldorf 23 K 8700/16.A	21.12.2016	Morocco	Verwaltungsgericht Düsseldorf	Male	Gay
Bundesamt für Migration und Flüchtlinge (Federal Office for Migration and Refugees, BAMF)						
74	BAMF Bescheid Gesch-Z 5377307 – 262	13.7. 2010	Cameroon	Bundesamt für Migration und Fluechtlinge Aussenstelle Bremen	Male	Gay
75	BAMF Bescheid Gesch-Z 5359496 – 262	3.9.2010	Cameroon	Bundesamt für Migration und Fluechtlinge Aussenstelle Bremen	Male	Gay

3 SPAIN

#	Case No.	Year	Country of Origin	Court	Gender	Sexual Orientation
Tribunal Supremo						
1	STS 6515/ 2004	14 octubre 2004	Romania	Tribunal Supremo	Male	Gay
2	STS 4171/ 2005	23 junio 2005	Cuba	Tribunal Supremo	Male	Gay
3	STS 7098/2005	30 noviembre 2005	Moldova	Tribunal Supremo	Male	Gay
4	STS 2266/ 2006	30 marzo 2006	Colombia	Tribunal Supremo	Male	Gay
5	STS 2331/ 2006	21 abril 2006	Cuba	Tribunal Supremo	Male	Gay
6	STS 3122/ 2006	19 mayo 2006	Cuba	Tribunal Supremo	Male	Gay
7	STS 5782/ 2006	29 septiembre 2006	Cuba	Tribunal Supremo	Male	Gay
8	STS 8650/2006	14 diciembre 2006	Cuba	Tribunal Supremo	Male	Gay
9	STS 8248/ 2006	22 diciembre 2006	Cuba	Tribunal Supremo	Female	Lesbian
10	STS 149/ 2007	18 enero 2007	Cuba	Tribunal Supremo	Male	Gay
11	STS 5650/2007	25 julio 2007	Cuba	Tribunal Supremo	Male	Gay
12	STS 6674/2007	4 octubre 2007	Russia	Tribunal Supremo	Male	Gay
13	STS 8251/ 2007	13 diciembre 2007	Cuba	Tribunal Supremo	Male	Gay
14	STS 27/ 2008	09 enero 2008	Cuba	Tribunal Supremo	Male	Bisexual
15	STS 6142/ 2008	28 noviembre 2008	Cuba	Tribunal Supremo	Male	Gay
16	STS 6881/ 2008	19 diciembre 2008	Cuba	Tribunal Supremo	Male	Gay
17	STS 2330/ 2011	29 abril 2011	Cameroon	Tribunal Supremo	Male	Gay
18	STS 3284/ 2011	30 mayo 2011	Algeria	Tribunal Supremo	Male	Gay

#	Case No.	Year	Country of Origin	Court	Gender	Sexual Orientation
19	STS 3854/2011	16 junio 2011	Cuba	Tribunal Supremo	Male	Gay
20	STS 3901/2011	16 junio 2011	Eritrea	Tribunal Supremo	Male	Gay
21	STS 4985/2011	14 julio 2011	Bangladesh	Tribunal Supremo	Male	Gay
22	STS 2352/2012	27 marzo 2012	Iran	Tribunal Supremo	Male	Gay
23	STS 5907/2012	21 septiembre 2012	Nicaragua	Tribunal Supremo	Male	Gay
24	STS 5908/2012	21 septiembre 2012	DRC	Tribunal Supremo	Male	Gay
25	STS 3906/2013	18 julio 2013	Algeria	Tribunal Supremo	Male	Gay
26	STS 4500/2013	16 septiembre 2013	Mexico	Tribunal Supremo	Male	Gay
27	STS 376/2014	12 febrero 2014	Cameroon	Tribunal Supremo	Male	Gay
28	STS 1257/2014	31 Marzo 2014	Cameroon	Tribunal Supremo	Female	Lesbian
29	STS 4492/2015	2 noviembre 2015	Senegal	Tribunal Supremo	Male	Gay
30	STS 124/2016	25 enero 2016	Algeria	Tribunal Supremo	Male	Gay
31	STS 3847/2016	18 julio 2016	Cameroon	Tribunal Supremo	Male	Gay
Audiencia Nacional						
32	SAN 5109/1998	4 diciembre 1998	Cuba	Audiencia Nacional	Male	Gay
33	SAN 3500/1998	29 septiembre 1998	Kazakhstan	Audiencia Nacional	Male	Gay
34	SAN 4388/1998	6 noviembre 1998	Ecuador	Audiencia Nacional	Male	Gay
35	SAN 4278/1999	25 junio 1999	Ecuador	Audiencia Nacional	MTF	? (Trans)
36	SAN 6483/1999	29 octubre 1999	Ecuador	Audiencia Nacional	MTF	? (Trans)
37	SAN 1606/2000	10 marzo 2000	Ecuador	Audiencia Nacional	Male	Gay/Trans
38	SAN 1890/2001	23 marzo 2001	Romania	Audiencia Nacional	Male	Bisexual

(continued)

(*continued*)

#	Case No.	Year	Country of Origin	Court	Gender	Sexual Orientation
39	SAN 3708/2001	8 junio 2001	Cuba	Audiencia Nacional	Male	Gay
40	SAN 4464/2002	12 julio 2002	Russia	Audiencia Nacional	Female	Lesbian
41	SAN 6584/2002	29 noviembre 2002	Cuba	Audiencia Nacional	Male	Gay
42	SAN 2628/2003	11 noviembre 2003	Cuba	Audiencia Nacional	Male	Gay
43	SAN 4473/2003	11 junio 2003	Cuba	Audiencia Nacional	Female	Lesbian
44	SAN 2717/2004	21 abril 2004	Venezuela	Audiencia Nacional	Male	Gay
45	SAN 7020/2004	10 noviembre 2004	Nigeria	Audiencia Nacional	Female	Lesbian
46	SAN 1790/2005	30 marzo 2005	Cuba	Audiencia Nacional	Male	Gay
47	SAN 3039/2005	7 junio 2005	Cuba	Audiencia Nacional	Unclear	"Homosexual"
48	SAN 318/2006	20 enero 2006	Kenia	Audiencia Nacional	Male	Gay
49	SAN 5515/2006	30 noviembre 2006	Guinea	Audiencia Nacional	Male	Gay
50	SAN 200/2007	30 enero 2007	Cuba	Audiencia Nacional	Male	Gay
51	SAN 3139/2007	4 julio 07	Croatia	Audiencia Nacional	Male	Gay
52	SAN 2491/2007	23 mayo 2007	Georgia	Audiencia Nacional	Male	Gay
53	SAN 5372/2008	10 diciembre 2008	Algeria	Audiencia Nacional	Male	Gay
54	SAN 5321/2008	7 noviembre 2008	Algeria	Audiencia Nacional	Male	Gay
55	SAN 1003/2009	25 febrero 2009	Algeria	Audiencia Nacional	Female	Lesbian
56	SAN 1138/2009	11 marzo 2009	'Africa' (sic)	Audiencia Nacional	Female	Lesbian
57	SAN 1234/2010	24 marzo 2010	Cameroon	Audiencia Nacional	Female	Lesbian
58	SAN 4536/2010	23 septiembre 2010	Colombia	Audiencia Nacional	MTF	? (Trans)

#	Case No.	Year	Country of Origin	Court	Gender	Sexual Orientation
59	SAN 842/ 2011	18 febrero 2011	Russia	Audiencia Nacional	Male	Gay
60	SAN 379/ 2011	31 enero 2011	Iran	Audiencia Nacional	Male	Bisexual
61	SAN 1584/ 2011	24 marzo 2011	Iran	Audiencia Nacional	Male	Gay
62	SAN 3674/2012	12 septiembre 2012	Algeria	Audiencia Nacional	Female	Lesbian
63	SAN 4025/2012	10 octubre 2012	Nicaragua	Audiencia Nacional	Male	Gay
64	SAN 1256/ 2013	21 marzo 2013	Venezuela	Audiencia Nacional	Male	Gay
65	SAN 1490/2013	11 abril 2013	DRC	Audiencia Nacional	Male	Gay
66	SAN 2530/2014	30 mayo 2014	Cameroon	Audiencia Nacional	Male	Gay
67	SAN 2122/ 2014	22 mayo 2014	Venezuela	Audiencia Nacional	Male	Gay
68	SAN 2340/2014	12 mayo 2014	Cameroon	Audiencia Nacional	Male	Gay
69	SAN 1832/ 2014	30 abril 2014	Nigeria	Audiencia Nacional	Male	Gay
70	SAN 2523/ 2014	18 mayo 2014	Nigeria	Audiencia Nacional	Male	Gay
71	SAN 2530/2014	30 mayo 2014	Cameroon	Audiencia Nacional	Male	Gay
72	SAN 2533/2014	30 mayo 2014	Nigeria	Audiencia Nacional	Male	Gay
73	SAN 2793/2014	12 junio 2014	Cameroon	Audiencia Nacional	Male	Gay
74	SAN 1903/2015	13 mayo 2015	Cameroon	Audiencia Nacional	Male	Gay
75	SAN 4282/2015	20 noviembre 2015	Cameroon	Audiencia Nacional	Male	Gay
76	SAN 142/ 2016	1 febrero 2016	Senegal	Audiencia Nacional	Male	Gay
77	SAN 4869/2016	7 diciembre 2016	Morocco	Audiencia Nacional	Male	Gay

Bibliography

LEGISLATION AND GUIDELINES

Council of Europe

European Convention for the Protection of Human Rights and Fundamental Freedoms, as amended by Protocols Nos. 11 and 14, 4 November 1950, ETS 5 (*European Convention of Human Rights, ECHR*).

European Union

Treaties

Charter of Fundamental Rights of the European Union, 26 October 2012, 2012/C 326/02 (*EU Charter*).

Treaty of Amsterdam Amending the Treaty on European Union, the Treaties Establishing the European Communities and Certain Related Acts of 2 October 1997, oj C 340, 10 November 1997 (entry into force 1 May 1999).

Treaty of Lisbon Amending the Treaty on European Union and the Treaty Establishing the European Community, oj C 306, 17 December 2007 (entry into force 1 December 2009).

Directives

Council Directive 2003/9/EC of 27 January 2003 laying down minimum standards for the reception of asylum seekers, oj L 31/18, 6 February 2003 (2003 *Reception Conditions Directive*).

Council Directive 2004/83/EC of 29 April 2004 on minimum standards for the qualification and status of third-country nationals or stateless persons as refugees or as persons who otherwise need international protection and the content of the protection granted, oj L 304/12, 30 September 2004 (2004 *Qualification Directive*).

Council Directive 2005/85/EC of 1 December 2005 on minimum standards on procedures in Member States for granting and withdrawing refugee status, oj L 326/13, 13 December 2005 (2005 *Asylum Procedures Directive*).

Directive 2011/95/EU of the European Parliament and of the Council of 13 December 2011 on standards for the qualification of third-country nationals or stateless persons as beneficiaries of international protection, for a uniform status for refugees or for persons eligible for subsidiary protection, and for the content of the protection granted (recast), oj L 337/9, 20 December 2011 (*Recast Qualification Directive*).

Directive 2013/32/EU of the European Parliament and of the Council of 26 June 2013 on common procedures for granting and withdrawing international protection (recast), oj L 180/160, 29 June 2013 (*Recast Asylum Procedures Directive*).

Directive 2013/33/EU of the European Parliament and of the Council of 26 June 2013 laying down standards for the reception of applicants for international protection (recast), oj L 1980/96, 29 June 2013 (*Recast Reception Conditions Directive*).

Regulations

Regulation No. 2725/2000 of 11 December 2000 concerning the establishment of 'Eurodac' for the comparison of fingerprints for the effective application of the Dublin Convention, oj L 31/1, 15 December 2000 (2000 *Eurodac Regulation*).

Council Regulation No. 343/2003 of 18 February 2003 establishing the criteria and mechanisms for determining the Member State responsible for examining an asylum application lodged in one of the Member States by a third-country national, oj L 50/1, 25 February 2003 (2003 *Dublin Regulation*).

Regulation (EU) No. 603/2013 of the European Parliament and of the Council of 26 June 2013 on the establishment of 'Eurodac' for the comparison of fingerprints for the effective application of Regulation (EU) No. 604/2013 establishing the criteria and mechanisms for determining the Member State responsible for examining an application for international protection lodged in one of the Member States by a third-country national or a stateless person and on requests for the comparison with Eurodac data by Member States' law enforcement authorities and Europol for law enforcement purposes, and amending Regulation (EU) No. 1077/2011 establishing a European Agency for the operational management of large-scale it systems in the area of freedom, security and justice (recast), oj L 180/1, 29 June 2013 (*Recast Eurodac Regulation*).

Regulation (EU) No. 604/2013 of the European Parliament and of the Council of 26 June 2013 establishing the criteria and mechanisms for determining the Member State responsible for examining an application for international protection lodged in one of the Member States by a third-country national or a stateless person (recast), oj L 180/31, 29 June 2013 (*Recast Dublin Regulation*).

France

Constitutions

Constitution of the Year I – First Republic – 24 June 1793 (Constitution de l'An I – Première République – 24 juin 1793).

Constitution of the IVth Republic from 1946 – 27 October 1946 (Constitution de 1946, IVe République – 27 octobre 1946).

Constitution of the Vth Republic from 1958 – 4 October 1958 (Constitution de 1958, Ve République – 4 octobre 1958).

Legislation

Code on the entry and residence of aliens and the right of asylum (Code de l'entrée et du séjour des étrangers et du droit d'asile, *CESEDA*).

Law No. 52–893 of 25 July 1952 establishing a French Office for the Protection of Refugees and Stateless Persons (Loi n°52–893 du 25 juillet 1952 portant création d'un office français de protection des réfugiés et des apatrides, JORF du 27 juillet 1952, p. 7642).

Law No. 98–349 of 11 May 1998 on the entry and residence of foreigners in France and the right of asylum (Loi n° 98–349 du 11 mai 1998 relative a l'entrée et au séjour des étrangers en France et au droit d'asile (*RESEDA*), JORF n°109 du 12 mai 1998, p. 7087).

Law No. 2003–1176 of 10 December 2003 amending Law 52–893 of 25 July 1952 on the right of asylum (Loi n° 2003–1176 du 10 décembre 2003 modifiant la loi n° 52–893 du 25 juillet 1952 relative au droit d'asile, JORF n°286 du 11 décembre 2003, p. 21080).

Law No. 2007–1631 of 20 November 2007 on the control of immigration, integration and asylum (Loi n° 2007–1631 du 20 novembre 2007 relative à la maîtrise de l'immigration, à l'intégration et à l'asile, JORF n°270 du 21 novembre 2007, p. 18993).

Law No. 2015–925 of 29 July 2015 on the reform of asylum law (Loi n° 2015–925 du 29 juillet 2015 relative à la réforme du droit d'asile, JORF n°0174 du 30 juillet 2015, p. 12977).

Germany

Constitution

Basic Law for the Federal Republic of Germany of 23 May 1949 (Grundgesetz für die Bundesrepublik Deutschland vom 23. Mai 1949 (BGBl. S. 1)).

Legislation

Act concerning the legal status of refugees of 1 September 1953 (Gesetz betreffend das Abkommen vom 28. Juli 1951 über die Rechtsstellung der Flüchtlinge vom 1. September 1953, BGBl. II 559).

Order on the Recognition and Distribution of Foreign Refugees (Asylum Ordinance) of 6 January 1953 (Verordnung über die Anerkennung und die Verteilung von ausländischen Flüchtlingen (Asylverordnung) vom 6. Januar 1953, BGBl 1953 Abs. 1 3).

Aliens Act of the Federal Republic of Germany of 28 April 1965 (Ausländergesetz der Bundesrepublik Deutschland vom 28. April 1965; BGBl. I 1965 353).

Law on the residence, employment and the integration of foreigners in the federal territory of 30 July 2004 (Residence Act) (Gesetz über den Aufenthalt, die Erwerbstätigkeit und die Integration von Ausländern im Bundesgebiet vom 30. Juli 2004 (*Aufenthaltsgesetz, AufenthG*); BGBl. I 2004 1950).

Act implementing the European Union directives on residence and asylum of 19 August 2007 (Gesetz zur Umsetzung aufenthalts- und asylrechtlicher Richtlinien der Europäischen Union vom 19. August 2007, BGBl. I 2007 1970, '*Richtlinienumsetzungsgesetz*').

Act implementing the Directive 2011/95/EU of 28 August 2013 (Gesetz zur Umsetzung der Richtlinie 2011/95/EU vom 28. August 2013, BGBl. I 2013 3473).

Spain

Constitution

Spanish Constitution of 1978 (Constitución española de 1978; B.O.E. núm. 311, de 29 de diciembre de 1978, páginas 29313 a 29424).

Legislation

Law 5/1984, of 26 March, regulating the right of asylum and refugee status (Ley 5/1984, de 26 de marzo, reguladora del derecho de asilo y de la condición de refugiado; B.O.E. núm. 74, de 27 de marzo de 1984, páginas 8389 a 8392).

Law 9/1994, of 19 May, amending Law 5/1984, of 26 March, regulating the right to asylum and refugee status (Ley 9/1994, de 19 de mayo, de modificación de la Ley 5/1984, de 26 de marzo, reguladora del derecho de asilo y de la condición de refugiado; B.O.E. núm. 122, de 23 de mayo de 1994, páginas 15796 a 15800).

Law 12/2009 of 30 October, regulating the right of asylum and subsidiary protection (Ley 12/2009 de 30 de octubre, reguladora del derecho de asilo y de la protección subsidiaria; B.O.E. núm. 263 del 31 de Octubre de 2009).

Royal Decree 203/1995, of 10 February, which approves the Regulation implementing Law 5/1984, of 26 March, regulating the right to asylum and refugee status, as amended by Law 9/1994, of 19 May (Real Decreto 203/1995, de 10 de febrero, por el que se aprueba el Reglamento de aplicación de la Ley 5/1984, de 26 de marzo, reguladora del derecho de asilo y de la condición de refugiado, modificada por la Ley 9/1994, de 19 de mayo; B.O.E. núm. 52, de 2 de marzo de 1995, páginas 7237 a 7246).

United Nations

Conventions

UN General Assembly, *Convention Relating to the Status of Refugees*, 28 July 1951, United Nations, Treaty Series, vol. 189, p. 137.

UN General Assembly, *Protocol Relating to the Status of Refugees*, 31 January 1967, United Nations, Treaty Series, vol. 606, p. 267.

Guidelines

UNHCR (2002) *Guidelines on International Protection No. 1: Gender-Related Persecution within the Context of Article 1A(2) of the 1951 Convention and/or Its 1967 Protocol Relating to the Status of Refugees*, 7 May 2002, HCR/GIP/02/01, www.refworld.org/docid/3d36f1c64.html.

UNHCR (2002) *Guidelines on International Protection No. 2: 'Membership of a Particular Social Group' within the Context of Article 1A(2) of the 1951 Convention and/or Its 1967 Protocol Relating to the Status of Refugees*, 7 May 2002, HCR/GIP/02/02, www.refworld.org/docid/3d36f23f4.html.

UNHCR (2003) *Guidelines on International Protection No. 4: 'Internal Flight or Relocation Alternative' within the Context of Article 1A(2) of the 1951 Convention and/or 1967 Protocol Relating to the Status of Refugees*, 23 July 2003, HCR/GIP/03/04, www.refworld.org/docid/3f2791a44.html.

UNHCR (2004) *Guidelines on International Protection No. 6: Religion-Based Refugee Claims under Article 1A(2) of the 1951 Convention and/or the 1967 Protocol Relating to the Status of Refugees*, 28 April 2004, HCR/GIP/04/06, www.refworld.org/docid/4090f9794.html.

UNHCR (2008) *UNHCR Guidance Note on Refugee Claims Relating to Sexual Orientation and Gender Identity*, 21 November 2008, www.refworld.org/docid/48abd5660.html.

UNHCR (2012) *Guidelines on International Protection No. 9: Claims to Refugee Status Based on Sexual Orientation and/or Gender Identity within the Context of Article 1A(2) of the 1951 Convention and/or Its 1967 Protocol Relating to the Status of Refugees*, 23 October 2012, HCR/GIP/12/01, www.refworld.org/docid/50348afc2.html.

CASES

Judgments are listed in ascending chronological order (by date of decision).

Australia

High Court

Applicant A and Another v. *Minister for Immigration and Ethnic Affairs and Another*, [1997] 190 CLR 225, Australia: High Court, 24 February 1997.

Minister for Immigration and Multicultural Affairs v. *Khawar* [2002] HCA 14, Australia: High Court, 11 April 2002.

Appellant S395/2002 v. *Minister for Immigration and Multicultural Affairs; Appellant S396/2002* v. *Minister for Immigration and Multicultural Affairs*, [2003] HCA 71, Australia: High Court, 9 December 2003.

Applicant S v. *Minister for Immigration and Multicultural Affairs* [2004] HCA 25, Australia: High Court, 27 May 2004.

Applicant NABD of 2002 v. *Minister for Immigration and Multicultural and Indigenous Affairs*, [2005] HCA 29, Australia: High Court, 26 May 2005.

Federal Court

Win v. *Minister for Immigration and Multicultural Affairs* [2001] FCA 132, Australia: Federal Court, 23 February 2001.

Federal Magistrates Court

SZJSL v. *Minister for Immigration & Another* [2007] FCMA 313, Australia: Federal Magistrates Court, 19 February 2007.

Refugee Review Tribunal

RRT Case No. V95/03527, [1998] RRTA 246, Australia: Refugee Review Tribunal, 9 February 1996.

RRT Reference No. N97/14768 (Unreported, P Thomson, 29 April 1998); case cited from: Jenni Millbank (2002) 'Imagining Otherness: Refugee Claims on the Basis of Sexuality in Canada and Australia', 26 *Melbourne University Law Review* 144, 145–146.

Canada

Supreme Court

Canada (Attorney General) v. *Ward*, [1993] 2 S.C.R. 689, Canada: Supreme Court, 30 June 1993.

Federal Court

Khrystych v. *Canada* (Minister of Citizenship and Immigration), 2005 FC 498, Canada: Federal Court, 12 April 2004.

Immigration and Refugee Board

MA5-04358, Canadian Immigration and Refugee Board, 19 January 2006.

TA1-11498, Canadian Immigration and Refugee Board, 7 February 2006.
MA6-01843, Canadian Immigration and Refugee Board, 1 November 2006.
Re S. (I.Q.) [1994] C.R.D.D. No. 323 (QL); case cited from: Nicole LaViolette (1997) 'The Immutable Refugees: Sexual Orientation in *Canada (A.G.) v. Ward*', 55(1) *University of Toronto Law Review* 1–41, 35.

European Union

Judgments

Salahadin Abdulla and Others v. *Bundesrepublik Deutschland*, Joined Cases C-175/08, C-176/08, C-178/08 and C-179/08, European Union: Court of Justice of the European Union, 2 March 2010.
Nawras Bolbol v. *Bevándorlási és Állampolgársági Hivatal*, Case C-31/09, European Union: Court of Justice of the European Union, 17 June 2010.
Bundesrepublik Deutschland v. *B and D*, Joined Cases C-57/09 and C-101/09, European Union: Court of Justice of the European Union, 9 November 2010.
Federal Republic of Germany v. *Y and Z*, Joined Cases C-71/11 and C-99/11, Court of Justice of the European Union, 5 September 2012.
X, Y *and* Z v. *Minister voor Immigratie, Integratie en Asiel*, Joined Cases C-199/12, C-200/12 and C-201/12, European Union: Court of Justice of the European Union, 7 November 2013.
Mohammad Ferooz Qurbani, Case C-481/13, European Union: Court of Justice of the European Union, 17 July 2014.
A, *B*, *C* v. *Staatssecretaris van Veiligheid en Justitie*, Joined Cases C-148/13 to C-150/13, European Union: Court of Justice of the European Union, 2 December 2014.

Advocate General Opinions

Federal Republic of Germany v. *Y and Z (Opinion of Advocate General Bot)*, Joined Cases C-71/11 and C-99/11, European Union: Court of Justice of the European Union, 19 April 2012.
X, Y *and* Z v. *Minister voor Immigratie, Integratie en Asiel (Opinion of Advocate General Sharpston)*, Joined Cases C-199/12, C-200/12 and C-201/12, European Union: Court of Justice of the European Union, 11 July 2013.

Orders

Order of the President of the Court of 11 March 2011 (Reference for a preliminary ruling from the Oberverwaltungsgericht für das Land Nordrhein-Westfalen, Germany), *Kashayar Khavand* v. *Bundesrepublik Deutschland* (Case C-563/10), 'Removal'.
Order of the President of the Court of 24 March 2011 (References for preliminary rulings from the Bundesverwaltungsgericht, Germany), *Federal Republic of Germany* v. Y *(Case C-71/11)* and *Federal Republic of Germany* v. Z *(Case C-99/11)*, 'Joining' [Beschluss des Präsidenten des Gerichtshofs vom 24. März 2011, 'Verbindung' in der Rechtssache C-71/11 und in der Rechtssache C-99/11].
Order of the President of the Court of 15 April 2016 (Reference for a preliminary ruling from the Sächsisches Oberverwaltungsgericht, Germany), *Federal Commissioner for Asylum Affairs* v. N (Case C-150/15), 'Removal' [Beschluss des Präsidenten des Gerichtshofs 15. April 2016 'Streichung' In der Rechtssache C-150/15].

References for a Preliminary Ruling

Reference for a preliminary ruling from the Oberverwaltungsgericht für das Land Nordrhein-Westfalen (Germany) lodged on 1 December 2010, *Kashayar Khavand* v. *Federal Republic of Germany (Case C-563/10)*.

Reference for a preliminary ruling from the Bundesverwaltungsgericht (Germany) lodged on 18 February 2011, *Federal Republic of Germany* v. *Y (Case C-71/11)*.

Reference for a preliminary ruling from the Bundesverwaltungsgericht (Germany) lodged on 2 March 2011, *Federal Republic of Germany* v. *Z (Case C-99/11)*.

Reference for a preliminary ruling from the Raad van State (Netherlands) lodged on 27 April 2012, *Minister voor Immigratie en Asiel* v. *X (Case C-199/12)*.

Reference for a preliminary ruling from the Sächsisches Oberverwaltungsgericht (Germany) lodged on 30 March 2015, *Federal Commissioner for Asylum Affairs* v. *N (Case C-150/15)*.

France

Conseil Constitutionnel

CC, décision no. 93–325 DC du 12 août 1993.

CC, décision no. 97–389 DC du 22 avril 1997.

Conseil d'Etat

CE, 23 juin 1997, 171858, *Ourbih*.

CE, 23 août 2006, 272679, *Olena*.

CE, 27 juillet 2012, 342552, O.A.

CE, 27 juillet 2012, 349824.

CE, 17 juin 2016, 391534.

Cour Nationale du Droit d'Asile/Commission des Recours des Réfugiés

CRR 17 décembre 1993, *Koloskov*, Documentation réfugiés no. 245, cited in Virginie Fraissinier-Amiot (2011) 'Les homosexuels étrangers et le droit d'asile en France: un octroi en demi-teinte', 27(2) *Revue française de droit administratif* 291–300 at 293.

CRR 12 mai 1999, 328310, *Djellal*.

CRR 22 mai 2000 340068, M. E.

CRR 4 octobre 2000, 330627, M. M.

CRR 6 février 2001, 359001, M. B.

CRR 29 juin 2001, 367645, M. K.

CRR 13 septembre 2001, 379319, M. N.

CRR 23 mai 2002, 388492, M. K.

CRR 23 juillet 2002, 394788.

CRR 26 novembre 2002, 402381, M. T.

CRR 12 octobre 2004, 483808, M. A.

CRR 25 mars 2005, 513547, Mlle G.

CRR 12 septembre 2005, 498570, Mme. AGB.

CRR 12 mai 2006, 555672, MS.

CRR 2 mars 2007, 578257 S.

CRR 18 mai 2007, 589676 D.

CNDA 11 avril 2008, 571886 G.

CNDA 7 mai 2008, 605398 H.

CNDA 1er juillet 2008, 571904, K.
CNDA 7 juillet 2009, 634565/08015025, C.
CNDA 3 novembre 2010, 09018078 O.
CNDA 10 janvier 2011, 09012710 C+, M. N.
CNDA 1er mars 2011, 09023968 C, M. I.
CNDA 7 mars 2011, 10002367 M.
CNDA 1er juin 2011, 10015959 C, Mlle N.
CNDA 24 juin 2011, 10025142 C, M. V.
CNDA 4 juillet 2011, 11002234 C, M. K.
CNDA 11 juillet 2011, 10020448 C, M. M.
CNDA 29 juillet 2011, 09004056 C, M. B.
CNDA 3 novembre 2011, 11010972 C, M. A.
CNDA 21 novembre 2011, 11010494 C, Mlle M.
CNDA 28 novembre 2011, 10019216 C, M. C.
CNDA 4 mai 2012, 11009260 C, M. D.
CNDA 18 octobre 2012, 12013647 C, M. B. N.
CNDA 12 février 2013, 11029513 C, M. M.
CNDA 4 novembre 2013, 13007332 C, M. F.
CNDA 29 novembre 2013, 13018825 C, M. A.
CNDA 10 juillet 2014, 13025005 C, M. J-J.
CNDA 19 décembre 2014, 14017576 C, Mme W.
CNDA 29 octobre 2015, 15006472 C+, M. H.
CNDA 18 mars 2016, 15031443 C, M. K.
CNDA 14 juin 2016, 15030258 C, Mme E.
CNDA 27 septembre 2016, 15004721 C, Mme T.

Germany

Bundesverfassungsgericht

BVerfGE 54, 341, Urteil vom 02.07.1980.
BVerfGE 74, 51, Urteil vom 26.11.1986.
BVerfGE 76, 143, Beschluss vom 01.07.1987.
BverfGE 80, 315, Urteil vom 10.07.1989.

Bundesverwaltungsgericht

BVerwG Urteil vom 15.3.1988, 9 C 278/86.
BverwG, Urteil vom 17.10.1989, 9 C 25/89.
BVerwGE 88, 367, Urteil vom 23.7.1991, 9 C 154/90.
BVerwGE 92, 278, Urteil vom 13.05.1993, 9 C 49/92.
BVerwGE 95, 42, Urteil vom 18.01.1994, 9 C 48/92.
BVerwG Urteile vom 20.2.2013, 10 C 20.12; 10 C 21.12; 10 C 22.12; 10 C 23.12.

Oberverwaltungsgerichte/Verwaltungsgerichtshöfe

Hess. VGH, Urteil vom 21.08.1986, 10 OE 69/83.
VGH München, Beschluss vom 12.11.1998, 19 ZB 98.33916.
OVG Münster, Beschluss vom 23.11.2010, 13 A 1013/09.A.
VGH Baden Württemberg, Urteile vom 7.3.2013, A 9 S 1872/12; A 9 S 1873/12.

Verwaltungsgerichte

VG Wiesbaden, Urteil vom 26.4.1983, IV/I E 06244/81, cited from Maryellen Fullerton (1990) 'Persecution Due to Membership in a Particular Social Group: Jurisprudence in the Federal Republic of Germany', 4 *Georgetown Immigration Law Journal* 381–444 at 408–410.
VG Ansbach, Urteil vom 11.10.2000, AN 3 K 00.31628.
VG Würzburg, Urteil vom 16.7.2002, W 7 K 01.30170.
VG Bremen, Urteil vom 28.4.2006, 7 K 632/05.A.
VG Köln, Urteil vom 8.9.2006, 18 K 9030/03.A.
VG München, Urteil vom 30.1.2007, M 21 K 04.51494.
VG Münster, Beschluss vom 4.7.2007, 9 L 381/07.A.
VG Düsseldorf, Urteil vom 21.2.2008, 11 K 2432/07.A.
VG Chemnitz, Urteil vom 11.7.2008, A 2 K 304/06.
VG Ansbach, Urteil vom 21.8.2008, AN 18 K 08.30201.
VG Neustadt/Weinstraße, Urteil vom 8.9.2008, 3 K 753/07.NW.
VG Regensburg, Urteil vom 15.9.2008, RN 8 K 08.30020.
VG Berlin, Urteil vom 3.12.2008, 23 X 30.06.
VG Düsseldorf, Urteil vom 11.3.2009, 5 K 1875/08.A.
VG Düsseldorf, Urteil vom 14.1.2010, 11 K 6778/09.A.
VG Sigmaringen, Urteil vom 26.4.2010, A 1 K 1911/09.
VG Trier, Beschluss vom 9.9.2010, 1 L 928-10.TR.
VG Frankfurt/Oder, Urteil vom 11.11.2010, VG 4 K 772/10.A.
VG Düsseldorf, Urteil vom 23.3.2012, 13 K 1217/11.A.
VG Berlin, Beschluss vom 29.10.2013, 34 L 89.13 A.
VG Düsseldorf, Urteil vom 13.12.2013, 13 K 3683/13.A.
VG Potsdam, Urteil vom 27.2.2014, VG 6 K 435/13.A.
VG München, Urteil vom 24.4.2014, M 4 K 13.30114.
VG Potsdam, Urteil vom 13.5.2014, VG 6 K 3802/13.A.
VG Würzburg, Beschluss vom 21.8.2014, W 1 S 14.30384.
VG Augsburg, Urteil vom 31.10.2014, Au 3 K 14.30222.
VG Aachen, Urteil vom 12.12.2014, 2 K 1477/13.A.
VG Saarland, Urteil vom 23.1.2015, 5 K 534/13.
VG Braunschweig, Urteil vom 2.9.2015, 7 A 68/15.
VG Frankfurt/Oder, Urteil vom 19.11.2015, 4 K 109912.A.
VG Würzburg, Urteil vom 1.7.2016, W 6 K 15.30116.

New Zealand

Refugee Status Appeals Authority

Re GJ, *Refugee Appeal* No. 1312/93, New Zealand: Refugee Status Appeals Authority, 30 August 1995.
Refugee Appeal No. 74665/03, New Zealand: Refugee Status Appeals Authority, 7 July 2004.

Spain

Tribunal Supremo

STS 7098/2005 de 30 de noviembre de 2005.
STS 2331/2006 de 21 de abril de 2006.
STS 4511/2003 de 29 de septiembre de 2006.

STS 8650/2006 de 14 de diciembre de 2006.
STS 8248/2006 de 22 de diciembre de 2006.
STS 5650/2007 de 25 de julio de 2007.
STS 6674/2007 de 4 de octubre de 2007.
STS 8251/2007 de 13 de diciembre de 2007.
STS 5265/2005 de 28 de noviembre de 2008.
STS 3901/2011 de 16 de junio de 2011.
STS 5907/2012 de 21 de septiembre de 2012.
STS 1957/2013 de 27 de marzo de 2013.
STS 1971/2013 de 27 de marzo de 2013.
STS 376/2014 de 12 de febrero de 2014.
STS 4492/2015 de 2 de noviembre de 2015.
STS 124/2016 de 25 de enero de 2016.
STS 3847/2016 de 18 de julio de 2016.

Audiencia Nacional

SAN 3500/1998 de 29 de septiembre del 1998.
SAN 4388/1998 de 6 de noviembre del 1998.
SAN 6483/1999 de 29 de octubre del 1999.
SAN 1890/2001 de 23 de marzo de 2001.
SAN 4464/2002 de 12 de julio de 2002.
SAN 2628/2003 de 11 de noviembre de 2003.
SAN 1790/2005 de 30 de marzo de 2005.
SAN 5515/2006 de 30 de noviembre 2006.
SAN 200/2007 de 30 de enero de 2007.
SAN 2491/2007 de 23 de mayo de 2007.
SAN 3139/2007 de 4 de julio de 2007.
SAN 5321/2008 de 7 de noviembre de 2008.
SAN 5372/2008 de 10 de diciembre de 2008.
SAN 1003/2009 de 25 de febrero de 2009.
SAN 379/2011 de 31 de enero de 2011.
SAN 842/2011 de 18 de febrero de 2011.
SAN 1584/2011 de 24 de marzo de 2011.
SAN 1832/2014 de 30 de abril de 2014.
SAN 2340/2013 de 12 de mayo de 2014.
SAN 2523/2014 de 18 de mayo de 2014.
SAN 2122/2014 de 22 de mayo de 2014.
SAN 2530/2014 de 30 de mayo de 2014.
SAN 2533/2014 de 30 de mayo de 2014.
SAN 2793/2014 de 12 de junio de 2014.

United Kingdom

Supreme Court

HJ (Iran) and HT (Cameroon) v. *Secretary of State for the Home Department*, [2010] UKSC 31, United Kingdom: Supreme Court, 7 July 2010.

RT (Zimbabwe) and others v Secretary of State for the Home Department, [2012] UKSC 38, United Kingdom: Supreme Court, 25 July 2012.

Court of Appeal

Mendis v. *Immigration Appeal Tribunal and Secretary of State for the Home Department*, [1989] Imm AR 6, United Kingdom: Court of Appeal (England and Wales), 17 June 1988.

Ahmad and Others v. *Secretary of State for the Home Department*, [1990] Imm AR 61, United Kingdom: Court of Appeal (England and Wales), 6 October 1989.

Danian v. *Secretary of State for the Home Department (Appeal)*, [2000] Imm AR 96, United Kingdom: Court of Appeal (England and Wales), 28 October 1999.

Ahmed (Iftikhar) v. *Secretary of State for the Home Department*, [2000] INLR 1, United Kingdom: Court of Appeal (England and Wales), 5 November 1999.

Demirkaya v. *Secretary of State for the Home Department* [1999] Imm AR 498, United Kingdom: Court of Appeal (England and Wales), 23 July 1999.

Upper Tribunal

SW *(lesbians – HJ and HT applied) Jamaica* v. *Secretary of State for the Home Department*, UK, CG [2011] UKUT 00251(IAC), United Kingdom: Upper Tribunal (Immigration and Asylum Chamber), 24 June 2011.

United States

Supreme Court

Bowers v. *Hardwick*, 478 U.S. 186 (1986), United States Supreme Court, 30 June 1986.

Board of Immigration Appeals

Matter of Acosta, 19 I. & N. Dec. 11 (B.I.A. 1985), United States Board of Immigration Appeals, 1 March 1985.

In re Toboso-Alfonso, 20 I. & N. Dec. 819 (B.I.A. 1990), United States Board of Immigration Appeals, 12 March 1990.

In re Fauziya Kasinga, 21 I. & N. Dec. 357 (B.I.A. 1996), United States Board of Immigration Appeals, 13 June 1996.

Matter of M-E-V-G-, 26 I&N Dec. 227 (BIA 2014), United States Board of Immigration Appeals, 7 February 2014.

Matter of W-G-R-, 26 I&N Dec. 208 (BIA 2014), United States Board of Immigration Appeals, 7 February 2014.

LITERATURE

All online sources were last accessed on 25 April 2021.

Akin, Deniz (2015) 'Assessing Sexual Orientation-Based Persecution – A Closer Look at the Norwegian Practices of Asylum Evaluation of Gay and Lesbian Claimants', 1 *Föreningen Lambda Nordica* 19–42.

(2017) 'Queer Asylum Seekers: Translating Sexuality in Norway', 43(3) *Journal of Ethnic and Migration Studies* 458–474.

Aleinikoff, T. Alexander (2003) 'Protected Characteristics and Social Perceptions: An Analysis of the Meaning of "Membership of a Particular Social Group"', in Erika Feller, Volker Türk and Frances Nicholson (eds.) *Refugee Protection in International Law: UNHCR's*

Global Consultations on International Protection, Cambridge: Cambridge University Press, 263–311.

Amnesty International (2008) *Love, Hate and the Law: Decriminalizing Homosexuality*, London: Amnesty International Publications, www.amnesty.org/en/documents/POL30/003/2008/en.

Anker, Deborah (2002) 'Boundaries in the Field of Human Rights: Refugee Law, Gender and the Human Rights Paradigm', 15 *Harvard Human Rights Journal* 133–154.

Anker, Deborah and Sabi Ardalan (2012) 'Escalating Persecution of Gays and Refugee Protection: Comment on Queer Cases Make Bad Law', 44(2) *New York University Journal of International Law and Politics* 529–557.

Annicchino, Pasquale (2015) 'The Persecution of Religious and LGBTI Minorities and Asylum Law: Recent Trends in the Adjudication of European Supranational Courts', 21(3) *European Public Law* 571–590.

Arbel, Efrat, Catherine Dauvergne and Jenni Millbank (2014) 'Introduction', in Efrat Arbel, Catherine Dauvergne and Jenni Millbank (eds.) *Gender in Refugee Law: From the Margins to the Centre*, London: Routledge, 1–16.

Arbour, Louise (2008) 'Message from Louise Arbour: United Nations High Commissioner for Human Rights', 27(3) *Refugee Studies Quarterly* 13–15.

Astaix, Anthony (2012) 'Réfugié: le statut doit être accordé en raison de persécutions religieuses', *Dalloz Actualité* 14 September 2012.

Bank, Roland (2016) 'Refugee Law Jurisprudence from Germany and Human Rights: Cutting Edge or Chilling Effect?', in Bruce Burson and David Cantor (eds.) *Human Rights and the Refugee Definition – Comparative Legal Practice and Theory*, Leiden: Brill Nijhoff, 156–179.

Battjes, Hemme (2013) 'Accommodation: Sur Place Claims and the Accommodation Requirement', in Thomas Spijkerboer (ed.) *Fleeing Homophobia – Sexual Orientation, Gender Identity and Asylum*, London: Routledge, 82–97.

Bauer, Greta and David Brennan (2013) 'The Problem with "Behavioral Bisexuality": Assessing Sexual Orientation in Survey Research', 13(2) *Journal of Bisexuality* 148–164.

Berg, Laurie and Jenni Millbank (2009) 'Constructing the Personal Narratives of Lesbian, Gay and Bisexual Asylum Claimants', 22(2) *Journal of Refugee Studies* 195–223.

(2013) 'Developing a Jurisprudence of Transgender Particular Social Group', in Thomas Spijkerboer (ed.) *Fleeing Homophobia: Sexual Orientation, Gender Identity and Asylum*, London: Routledge, 121–153.

Berlit, Uwe, Harald Dörig and Hugo Storey (2015) 'Credibility Assessment in Claims Based on Persecution for Reasons of Religious Conversion and Homosexuality: A Practitioners Approach', 27(4) *International Journal of Refugee Law* 649–666.

Broberg, Morten and Niels Fenger (2014) *Preliminary References to the European Court of Justice* (2nd ed.), Oxford: Oxford University Press.

Budd, Michael Carl (2009) *Mistakes in Identity: Sexual Orientation and Credibility in the Asylum Process*, MA thesis, The American University in Cairo [unpublished].

Bundestags-Drucksache 17/1505, 'Antwort der Bundesregierung auf die Kleine Anfrage der Abgeordneten Ulla Jelpke, Jan Korte, Dr. Barabara Höll, weiterer Abgeordneter und der Fraktion DIE LINKE: Aufnahme von Flüchtlingen aus dem Iran und Umgang mit homosexuellen Flüchtlingen', Deutscher Bundestag 17. Wahlperiode, 2010.

Buxton, Richard (2012) 'A History from across the Pond', 44(2) *New York University Journal of International Law and Politics* 391–406.

Cantor, David (2014) *Introductory Remarks*, ICJ Second Expert Roundtable on Asylum Claims Based on Sexual Orientation or Gender Identity, Friday 3 October 2014, London.

de Castro Sánchez, Claribel (2015) 'La condición sexual como razón de la concesión de asilo. ¿Una nueva puerta de entrada a Europa? Reflexiones a la luz de la sentencia del Tribunal de Justicia de la UE de 7 de noviembre de 2013, Minister Voor Inmigratie en Asiel/X, Y y Z. (RI §415704)', 35 *Revista General de Derecho Europeo* 3–25.

Cheikh Ali, Hana, Christel Querton and Élodie Soulard (2012) *Gender Related Asylum Claims in Europe – A Comparative Analysis of Law, Policies and Practice Focusing on Women in Nine EU Member States* ('GENSEN Report'). Brussels: European Parliament, Directorate General for Internal Policies, Department of Citizens' Rights and Constitutional Affairs.

Chelvan, S. (2011) 'Put Your Hands Up (If You Feel Love)', 25(1) *Journal on Immigration, Asylum and Nationality Law* 56–66.

Chetail, Vincent (2014) 'Are Refugee Rights Human Rights? An Unorthodox Questioning of the Relations between Refugee Law and Human Rights Law', in Ruth Rubio-Marin (ed.) *Human Rights and Immigration, Collected Courses of the Academy of European Law*, Oxford: Oxford University Press, 19–72.

(2016) 'The Common European Asylum System: Bric-à-brac or System?', in Vincent Chetail, Philippe de Bruycker and Francesco Maiani (eds.) *Reforming the Common European Asylum System – The New European Refugee Law*, Leiden: Brill Nijhoff, 3–38.

Choi, Venice (2010) 'Living Discreetly: A Catch 22 in Refugee Status Determinations on the Basis of Sexual Orientation', 36(1) *Brooklyn Journal of International Law* 241–263.

Cores, Arsenio (2011) *Fleeing Homophobia Questionnaire: Best Practices on the (Legal) Position of LGBT Asylum Seekers in the EU Member States – Spain*, Fleeing Homophobia Project, www.rechten.vu.nl/nl/Images/Spain_questionnaire_tcm247-240407.pdf.

Costello, Cathryn and Emily Hancox (2014) 'The UK, the Common European Asylum System and EU Immigration Law', *Policy Primer*, Oxford: The Migration Observatory, www.migrationobservatory.ox.ac.uk/wp-content/uploads/2016/04/PolicyPrimer-UK_EU_Asylum_Law.pdf.

Council of Australian Law Deans (2005) *CALD Statement on the Nature of Research* (May and October 2005), https://cald.asn.au/wp-content/uploads/2017/11/cald-statement-on-the-nature-of-legal-research-20051.pdf.

Cowen, Tim, Francesca Stella, Kirsty Magahy, Kendra Strauss and James Morton (2011) 'Sanctuary, Safety and Solidarity: Lesbian, Gay, Bisexual, Transgender Asylum Seekers and Refugees in Scotland', Glasgow: Equality Network, BEMIS and GRAMNe, online: University of Glasgow, www.equality-network.org/wp-content/uploads/2013/05/Sanctuary-Safety-and-Solidarity.pdf.

Dauvergne, Catherine (2008) *Making People Illegal: What Globalization Means for Migration and Law*, Cambridge: Cambridge University Press.

(2013) 'Refugee Law as Perpetual Crisis', in Satvinder Juss and Colin Harvey (eds.) *Contemporary Issues in Refugee Law*, Cheltenham: Edward Elgar, 13–30.

(2016) 'Toward a New Framework for Understanding Political Opinion', 37 *Michigan Journal of International Law* 243–298.

Dauvergne, Catherine and Jenni Millbank (2003) 'Before the High Court: Applicants S396/2002 and S395/2002, a Gay Refugee Couple from Bangladesh', 25 *Sydney Law Review* 97–124.

(2010) 'Forced Marriage as a Harm in Domestic and International Law', 73(1) *The Modern Law Review* 57–88.

Dawson, Jasmine and Paula Gerber (2017) 'Assessing the Refugee Claims of LGBTI People: Is the DSSH Model Useful for Determining Claims by Women for Asylum Based on Sexual Orientation?', 29(2) *International Journal of Refugee Law* 292–322.

Defossez, Alexandre (2014) 'Arrêt "X, Y et Z": les homosexuels persécutés dans leur pays d'origine peuvent-ils bénéficier du statut de "réfugié"?', 206 *Journal de droit européen* 54–55.

Delouvin, Patrick (2000) 'The Evolution of Asylum in France', 13(1) *Journal of Refugee Studies* 61–73.

Díaz Lafuente, José (2014) 'El Derecho de Asilo por Motivos de Orientación Sexual e Identidad de Género', 89 *Revista de Derecho Público* 345–388.

(2014) 'Estudio de la doctrina jurisprudencial española sobre la protección internacional por motivos de orientación sexual e identidad de género', *Libertad de circulación, asilo y refugio en la Unión Europea* 69–92.

(2014) *Refugio y asilo por motivos de orientación sexual y/o identidad de género en el ordenamiento constitucional español*, doctoral thesis, Faculty of Law, University of Valencia.

Dienelt, Klaus (2008) 'Vermeidungsverhalten zur Abwendung von Verfolgung – Vereinbarkeit mit der Qualifkationsrichtlinie', *Nachrichten zum Schwerpunkt Asylrecht, Migrationsrecht.net*, www.migrationsrecht.net/nachrichten-asylrecht/1178-eu-qualifikationsrichtlinie-rl-200483eg-religion-verfolgung.html.

Dodet-Cauphy, Isabelle (1999) 'La difficile reconnaissance du droit d'asile constitutionnel. Commentaire de la loi du 11 mai 1998 relative à l'entrée et au séjour des étrangers en France et au droit d'asile', 15(3) *Revue française de droit administratif* 469–484.

Dolk, Klaudia and Andreas Schwandtner (2007) 'Homosexualität und (Abschiebungs)schutz in Deutschland', 7–8 *amnesty international – asyl-info* 4–15.

Dörig, Harald (2014) 'German Courts and Their Understanding of the Common European Asylum System (Opinion)', 25(4) *International Journal of Refugee Law* 768–778.

Drywood, Eleanor (2014) 'Who's In and Who's Out? The Court's Emerging Case Law on the Definition of a Refugee', 51 *Common Market Law Review* 1093–1124.

Durieux, Jean-François (2013) 'The Vanishing Refugee: How EU Asylum Law Blurs the Specificity of Refugee Protection', in Hélène Lambert, Jane McAdam and Maryellen Fullerton (eds.) *The Global Reach of European Refugee Law*, Cambridge: Cambridge University Press, 225–257.

ECRE (2014) *Agentes de Protección y Aplicación de la Alternativa de Protección Interna – Informe de País España*, APAIPA, www.refworld.org.es/pdfid/543bc5424.pdf.

(2016) *ECRE Comments on the Commission Proposal for a Qualification Regulation COM (2016) 466*, www.ecre.org/wp-content/uploads/2016/07/ECRE-Comments-EU-Asylum-Agency_July-2016-final_2.pdf.

(2017) 'UK Home Office Guideline: Afghan Gay Asylum-Seekers Expected to Conceal Their Sexual Orientation to Avoid Persecution When Sent Back', *News*, 3 March 2017, www.ecre.org/uk-home-office-guideline-afghan-gay-asylum-seekers-expected-to-conceal-their-sexual-orientation-to-avoid-persecution-when-sent-back.

Edwards, Alice (2003) 'Age and Gender Dimensions in International Refugee Law', in Erika Feller, Volker Türk and Frances Nicholson (eds.) *Refugee Protection in International Law: UNHCR's Global Consultations on International Protection*, Cambridge: Cambridge University Press, 46–80.

(2005) 'Human Rights, Refugees, and the Right "To Enjoy" Asylum', 17(2) *International Journal of Refugee Law* 293–330.

(2012) 'Distinction, Discretion, Discrimination: The New Frontiers of Gender-Related Claims to Asylum', *paper delivered at the Gender, Migration and Human Rights Conference at the European University Institute*, Florence, Italy, 19 June 2012, www.refworld.org/docid/4ffd430c2.html.

(2014) 'X, Y and Z: The "A, B, C" of Claims Based on Sexual Orientation and/or Gender Identity?', UN High Commissioner for Refugees (UNHCR), International Commission of Jurists: Expert Roundtable on Asylum Claims Based on Sexual Orientation or Gender Identity or Expression Brussels, 27 June 2014, www.refworld.org/docid/53bb99984.html.

Escribano Testaut, Pedro and Margarita Diana Fernández Sánchez (n.d.) *Doctrina jurisprudencial sobre protección internacional (asilo, y refugio, protección subsidiaria y autorización de permanencia en España por razones humanitarias) 2009–2012*. Tribunal Supremo, Sala de lo Contencioso-Administrativo, Gabinete Técnico.

European Commission (2015) 'Common European Asylum System', https://ec.europa.eu/home-affairs/what-we-do/policies/asylum/index_en.htm.

(2016) 'Completing the Reform of the Common European Asylum System: Towards an Efficient, Fair and Humane Asylum Policy', European Commission – press release, Brussels, 13 July 2016, together with proposed texts for regulations, https://ec.europa.eu/commission/presscorner/detail/en/IP_16_2433.

Ferreira, Nuno (2015) 'Portuguese Refugee Law in the European Context: The Case of Sexuality-Based Claims', 27(3) *International Journal of Refugee Law* 411–432.

Foster, Michelle (2007) *International Refugee Law and Socio-Economic Rights: Refuge from Deprivation, Cambridge Studies in International and Comparative Law*, Cambridge: Cambridge University Press.

(2012) *The 'Ground with the Least Clarity': A Comparative Study of Jurisprudential Developments relating to 'Membership of a Particular Social Group'*, UNHCR Division of International Protection, Geneva, August 2012, PPLA/2012/02.

(2014) 'Why We Are Not There Yet: The Particular Challenge of "Particular Social Group"', in Efrat Arbel, Catherine Dauvergne and Jenni Millbank (eds.) *Gender in Refugee Law: From the Margins to the Centre*, London: Routledge, 17–45.

Foucault, Michel (1972) *The Archaeology of Knowledge and the Discourse on Language*, New York: Pantheon Books.

(1976) *Histoire de la sexualité I: La volonté de savoir*, Paris: Gallimard.

Fouquet-Lapar, Thomas and Flor Tercero (2011) *Fleeing Homophobia Questionnaire Best Practices on the (Legal) Position of LGBT Asylum Seekers in the EU Member States – France*, Fleeing Homophobia Project, www.rechten.vu.nl/nl/Images/France_FINAL_tcm247-240411.pdf.

Fraissinier-Amiot, Virginie (2011) 'Les homosexuels étrangers et le droit d'asile en France: un octroi en demi-teinte', 27(2) *Revue française de droit administratif* 291–300.

Frank, David John (2012) 'Making Sense of LGBT Asylum Claims: Change and Variation in Institutional Contexts', 44(2) *New York University Journal of International Law and Politics* 485–495.

Fullerton, Maryellen (1990) 'Persecution Due to Membership in a Particular Social Group: Jurisprudence in the Federal Republic of Germany', 4 *Georgetown Immigration Law Journal* 381–444.

(1993) 'A Comparative Look at Refugee Status Based on Persecution Due to Membership in a Particular Social Group', 26(3) *Cornell International Law Journal* 505–563.

Garden Court Chambers (2010) 'Future Behaviour and the Refugee Convention', *Free Movement Blog*, 12 July 2010, www.freemovement.org.uk/future-behaviour-and-the-refugee-convention.

Gay & Lesbian Alliance against Defamation (2016) *Media Reference Guide* (10th ed.), New York, October 2016.

Gil-Bazo, María-Teresa (2010) '"Thou Shalt Not Judge" ... Spanish Judicial Decision-Making on Asylum and the Role of Judges in Interpreting the Law', in: Guy Goodwin-

Gil and Hélène Lambert (eds.) *The Limits of Transnational Law – Refugee Law, Policy Harmonization and Judicial Dialogue in the European Union*, 107–124.

Gilbert, Geoff (2004) 'Is Europe Living Up to Its Obligations to Refugees?', 15(5) *European Journal of International Law* 963–987.

Global Consultations on International Protection (2003) *Summary Conclusions: Membership of a Particular Social Group*, adopted at the expert roundtable organized by the United Nations High Commissioner for Refugees and the International Institute of Humanitarian Law, San Remo, Italy, 6–8 September 2001, www.refworld.org/pdfid/470a33b40.pdf.

Goodman, Ryan (2012) 'Asylum and the Concealment of Sexual Orientation: Where Not to Draw the Line', 44(2) *New York University Journal of International Law and Politics* 407–446.

Goodwin-Gill, Guy (1983) The Refugee in International *Law* (1st ed.), Oxford: Clarendon Press.

(1996) *The Refugee in International Law* (2nd ed.), Oxford: Clarendon Press.

(2014) 'Editorial – The Dynamic of International Refugee Law', 25(4) *International Journal of Refugee Law* 651–666.

Goodwin-Gill, Guy and Hélène Lambert, eds. (2010) *The Limits of Transnational Law: Refugee Law, Policy Harmonization and Judicial Dialogue in the European Union*, Cambridge: Cambridge University Press.

Goodwin-Gill, Guy and Jane McAdam (2007) *The Refugee in International Law* (3rd ed.), Oxford: Oxford University Press.

Gorlick, Brian (2000) 'Human Rights and Refugees: Enhancing Protection through International Human Rights Law', *New Issues in Refugee Research*, working paper no. 30, www.refworld.org/docid/4ff581592.html.

Gossman, Patricia (2017) 'Afghan LGBT Asylum Seekers in UK among Most Vulnerable – At Risk of Imprisonment, Violence If Deported to Afghanistan', *Human Rights Watch News*, 26 February 2017, www.hrw.org/news/2017/02/26/afghan-lgbt-asylum-seekers-uk-among-most-vulnerable.

Grahl-Madsen, Atle (1966) *The Status of Refugees in International Law – Volume I: Refugee Character*, Leyden: A. W. Sijthoff.

Greenberg, Reagan (2017) 'The Particular Social Group Requirement: How the Asylum Process Is Consistently Failing LGB Applicants and How an Evidentiary Standard of Self-Attestation Can Remedy These Failures', 17 *University of Maryland Law Journal of Race, Religion, Gender & Class* 147–172.

Guild, Elspeth (2004) 'Seeking Asylum: Storm Clouds between International Commitments and EU Legislative Measures', 29(2) *European Law Review* 198–218.

Haines, Rodger, James Hathaway and Michelle Foster (2003) 'Claims to Refugee Status based on Voluntary but Protected Actions – Discussion Paper No. 1, Advanced Refugee Law Workshop, International Association of Refugee Law Judges, Auckland, New Zealand, October 2002', 15(3) *International Journal of Refugee Law* 430–443.

Hall, Mark A. and Ronald F. Wright (2008) 'Systematic Content Analysis of Judicial Opinions', 96(1) *California Law Review* 63–122.

Halley, Janet (1993) 'Reasoning about Sodomy: Act and Identity in and after Bowers v. Hardwick', 79(7) *Virginia Law Review* 1721–1780.

Harvey, Colin (2013) 'Is Humanity Enough? Refugees, Asylum Seekers and the Rights Regime', in Satvinder Juss and Colin Harvey (eds.) *Contemporary Issues in Refugee Law*, Cheltenham: Edward Elgar, 68–89.

Hathaway, James (1991) *The Law of Refugee Status*, Toronto: Butterworths.

(1991) 'Reconceiving Refugee Law as Human Rights Protection' 4(2) *Journal of Refugee Studies* 113–131.

(1998) 'The Relationship between Human Rights and Refugee Law: What Refugee Judges Can Contribute' in International Association of Refugee Law Judges: *The Realities of Refugee Determination on the Eve of a New Millennium: The Role of the Judiciary*, 3rd Conference, Ottawa, October 1998, 80–90.

(2005) *The Rights of Refugees under International Law*, Cambridge: Cambridge University Press.

(2014) 'The Conundrum of Concealment: Minister for Immigration and Border Protection v SZSCA [2013] FCAFC 155', *Melbourne Law School High Court Blog: Opinions on High*, 9 November 2014, https://blogs.unimelb.edu.au/opinionsonhigh/2014/11/09/hathaway-szsca-fcafc.

Hathaway, James and Michelle Foster (2003) 'Internal Protection/Relocation/Flight Alternative as an Aspect of Refugee Status Determination', in Erika Feller, Frances Nicholson and Volker Türk (eds.) *Refugee Protection in International Law: UNHCR's Global Consultations on International Protection*, Cambridge: Cambridge University Press, 357–417.

(2003) 'Membership of a Particular Social Group' Discussion Paper No. 4, Advanced Refugee Law Workshop, International Association of Refugee Law Judges, Auckland, New Zealand, October 2002, 15(3) *International Journal of Refugee Law* 477–491.

(2014) *The Law of Refugee Status* (2nd ed.), Cambridge: Cambridge University Press.

Hathaway, James and Jason Pobjoy (2012) 'Queer Cases Make Bad Law', 44(2) *New York University Journal of International Law and Politics* 315–389.

den Heijer, Maarten (2014) 'Persecution for Reason of Sexual Orientation: X,Y and Z', 51(4) *Common Market Law Review* 1217–1234.

Helton, Arthur (1983) 'Persecution on Account of Membership in a Social Group as Basis for Refugee Status', 15 *Columbia Human Rights Law Review* 39–67.

Hersh, Nicholas (2015) 'Challenges to Assessing Same-Sex Relationships under Refugee Law In Canada', 60(3) *McGill Law Journal* 527–571.

Hudson, Jeffrey H. (2013) 'Comprehensive Literature Review Pertaining to Married Men Who Have Sex with Men (MMSM)', 13(4) *Journal of Bisexuality* 417–601.

Hutchinson, Terry (2010) *Researching and Writing in Law* (3rd ed.), Pyrmont: Lawbook.

Hutchinson, Terry and Nigel Duncan (2012) 'Defining and Describing What We Do: Doctrinal Legal Research', 17(1) *Deakin Law Review* 83–119.

ILGA Europe (2015) *Glossary*, www.ilga-europe.org/media/2431.

International Commission of Jurists (2007) *Yogyakarta Principles on the Application of International Human Rights Law in relation to Sexual Orientation and Gender Identity*, March 2007, www.yogyakartaprinciples.org.

(2014) 'X, Y and Z: A Glass Half Full for "Rainbow Refugees"?', *The International Commission of Jurists' Observations on the Judgment of the Court of Justice of the European Union in X, Y and Z v. Minister voor Immigratie en Asiel*, ICJ, Geneva.

Jansen, Sabine and Joël Le Déroff (2014) *Good Practices Related to LGBTI Asylum Applicants in Europe*, International Lesbian, Gay, Bisexual, Trans and Intersex Association (ILGA), May 2014.

Jansen, Sabine and Thomas Spijkerboer (2011) *Fleeing Homophobia, Asylum Claims Related to Sexual Orientation and Gender Identity in Europe*, Vrije Universiteit Amsterdam, September 2011.

Johnson, Toni (2007) 'Flamers, Flaunting and Permissible Persecution', 15(1) *Feminist Legal Studies* 99–111.

(2011) 'On Silence, Sexuality and Skeletons: Reconceptualizing Narrative in Asylum Hearings', 20(1) *Social & Legal Studies* 57–78.

Juss, Satvinder (2015) 'Sexual Orientation and the Sexualisation of Refugee Law', 22 *International Journal on Minority and Group Rights* 128–153.

Kalkmann, Michael (2011) *Fleeing Homophobia Questionnaire: Best Practices on the (Legal) Position of LGBT Asylum Seekers in the EU Member States – Germany*, Fleeing Homophobia Project, www.rechten.vu.nl/nl/Images/Germany_questionnaire_tcm247-240406.pdf.

Kassisieh, Ghassan (2008) 'From Lives of Fear to Lives of Freedom: A Review of Australian Refugee Decisions on the Basis of Sexual Orientation', *Gay & Lesbian Rights Lobby*, Glebe.

Keil, Rainer (2016) 'Sexuelle Orientierung im Flüchtlingsrecht und im allgemeinen Migrationsrecht der Bundesrepublik Deutschland', in Claus Dieter Classen, Dagmar Richter and Bernard Łukanko (eds.) *'Sexuelle Orientierung' als Diskriminierungsgrund: Regelungsbedarf in Deutschland und Polen?*, Tübingen: Mohr Siebeck, 293–315.

Kendall, Christopher (2003) 'Lesbian and Gay Refugees in Australia: Now That "Acting Discreetly" Is No Longer an Option, Will Equality Be Forthcoming?', 15(4) *International Journal of Refugee Law* 715–749.

Kobelinsky, Carolina (2012) 'L'asile gay: jurisprudence de l'intime a la Cour nationale du droit d'asile', 3(82) *Droit et Société* 583–601.

(2012) 'Ver o no ver al refugiado. La evaluación de las solicitudes de asilo (por motivos sexuales) en Francia', 4 *Revista Temas de Antropología y Migración* 13–29.

(2015) 'Judging Intimacies at the French Court of Asylum', 38(2) *Political and Legal Anthropology Review* 338–355.

Kolinsky, Heather (2016) 'The Shibboleth of Discretion: The Discretion, Identity, and Persecution Paradigm in American and Australian LGBT Asylum Claims, 31(2) *Berkeley Journal of Gender, Law & Justice* 206–240.

Ku Wei Bin, Gabriel (2014) *No Freedom in a Closet: The Persistence of Discretion Reasoning in the Refugee Status Determination Process for Lesbian, Gay, and Bisexual Asylum Applications to the European Union*, master's thesis, Lund University, Faculty of Law, Spring 2014, Lund University Student Papers, https://lup.lub.lu.se/student-papers/search/publication/4500056.

Labayle, Henri (1997) 'Le droit d'asile en France: normalisation ou neutralisation?', 13(2) *Revue française de droit administratif* 242–269.

Lambert, Hélène (2009) 'Transnational judicial dialogue, harmonization and the Common European Asylum System', 58(3) *International and Comparative Law Quarterly* 519–543.

(2013) 'Conclusion: Europe's Normative Power in Refugee Law', in Hélène Lambert, Jane McAdam and Maryellen Fullerton (eds.) *The Global Reach of European Refugee Law*, Cambridge: Cambridge University Press, 258–266.

(2013) 'Introduction: European Refugee Law and Transnational Emulation', in Hélène Lambert, Jane McAdam and Maryellen Fullerton (eds.) *The Global Reach of European Refugee Law*, Cambridge: Cambridge University Press, 1–24.

Lambert, Hélène and Janine Silga (2010) 'Transnational Refugee Law in the French Courts: Deliberate or Compelled Change in Judicial Attitudes?', in Guy Goodwin-Gil and Hélène Lambert (eds.) *The Limits of Transnational Law – Refugee Law, Policy Harmonization and Judicial Dialogue in the European Union*, 35–56.

Lambert, Hélène, Francesco Messineo and Paul Tiedemann (2008) 'Comparative Perspectives of Constitutional Asylum in France, Italy, and Germany: Requiescat In Pace?', 27(3) *Refugee Survey Quarterly* 16–32.

Lambert, Hélène, Jane McAdam and Maryellen Fullerton, eds. (2013) *The Global Reach of European Refugee Law*, Cambridge: Cambridge University Press.

Lantero, Caroline (2013) 'La notion de groupe social au sens de la convention de Genève dans la jurisprudence française', 41 *Actualités Juridiques – Droit Administratif* 2364–2370.

Lantero, Caroline and Marie-Laure Basilien-Gainche (2013) 'Statut de réfugié et appartenance à un groupe social (Directive 2004/83/CE): Une victoire à la Pyrrhus pour les personnes homosexuelles', *La Revue des droits de l'homme [En ligne], Actualités Droits-Libertés*, mis en ligne le 13 novembre 2013.

Lasa, Leire, Izaro López de Lacalle, Estefanía Pasarín and Iñaki Ramírez de Olano (2009) *Persecución por motivos de género y derecho de asilo: del contexto global al compromiso local – El sistema de asilo español frente a la violación de los derechos humanos de las mujeres y de lesbianas, gays, bisexuales y transexuales*. Comisión Española de Ayuda al Refugiado en Euskadi (CEAR-Euskadi), Bilbao.

LaViolette, Nicole (1997) 'The Immutable Refugees: Sexual Orientation in Canada (A.G.) v. Ward', 55(1) *University of Toronto Law Review* 1–41.

(2013) 'Sexual Orientation, Gender Identity and the Refugee Determination Process', report prepared for the Immigration and Refugee Board of Canada, online: Social Science Research Network, http://papers.ssrn.com/sol3/papers.cfm?abstract_id=2276049.

(2017) 'Sexual Orientation, Gender Identity and the Refugee Determination Process in Canada', 18(1) *Annals of Spiru Haret University Journalism Studies* 5–55.

Leboeuf, Luc and Evangelia (Lilian) Tsourdi (2013) 'Towards a Re-definition of Persecution? Assessing the Potential Impact of Y and Z', 13(2) *Human Rights Law Review* 402–415.

Lehmann, Julian (2014) 'Persecution, Concealment and the Limits of a Human Rights Approach in (European) Asylum Law – The Case of Germany v. Y and Z in the Court of Justice of the European Union', 26(1) *International Journal of Refugee Law* 65–81.

Lenaerts, Koen, Ignace Maselis and Kathleen Gutman (2014) *EU Procedural Law*, Oxford: Oxford University Press.

Lübbe, Anna (2011) 'Zielgerichtetheit des Akteursverhaltens und Unterlassen im Flüchtlingsrecht', *Zeitschrift für Ausländerrecht und Ausländerpolitik* 2011, 164–167.

(2012) 'Verfolgungsvermeidende Anpassung an menschenrechtswidrige Verhaltenslenkungen als Grenze der Flüchtlingsanerkennung?', *Zeitschrift für Ausländerrecht und Ausländerpolitik* 2012, 7–13.

(2013) 'Flüchtlingsanerkennung in Verhaltenslenkungsfällen nach den Ahmadi-Entscheidungen des BVerwG', *Zeitschrift für Ausländerrecht und Ausländerpolitik* 2013, 272–278.

Macklin, Audrey (1994) 'Ward v. Canada: A Review Essay', 6(3) *International Journal of Refugee Law* 362–381.

Markard, Nora (2007) 'Fortschritte im Flüchtlingsrecht? Gender Guidelines und geschlechtsspezifische Verfolgung', 40(4) *Kritische Justiz* 373–390.

(2011) '60 Jahre Genfer Flüchtlingskonvention: Verantwortung für den Flüchtlingsschutz – 11. Berliner Symposium zum Flüchtlingsschutz, 21–22. Juni 2011, Berlin – Tagungsbericht', 8 *Zeitschrift für Ausländerrecht und Ausländerpolitik* 241–280.

(2013) 'Sexuelle Orientierung als Fluchtgrund – Das Ende der "Diskretion" – Aktuelle Entwicklungen beim Flüchtlingsschutz aufgrund der sexuellen Orientierung', 3 *Asylmagazin* 74–84.

Markard, Nora and Laura Adamietz (2011) 'Keep It in the Closet? Flüchtlingsanerkennung wegen Homosexualität auf dem Prüfstand', 44(3) *Kritische Justiz* 294–302.

McAdam, Jane (2008) 'Introduction: Asylum and the Universal Declaration of Human Rights', 27(3) *Refugee Survey Quarterly* 3–13.

Merino Sancho, Victor (2012) *Tratamiento Jurídico de las Demandas de Asilo por Violencia contra las Mujeres en el Ordenamiento Jurídico Español: Perspectivas y Prospectivas*, Pamplona: Thomson Reuters.

Middelkoop, Louis (2013) 'Normativity and Credibility of Sexual Orientation in Asylum Decision Making', in Thomas Spikerboer (ed.) *Fleeing Homophobia: Sexual Orientation, Gender Identity and Asylum*, London: Routledge, 154–175.

Millbank, Jenni (1995) 'Fear of Persecution or Just a Queer Feeling? Refugee Status and Sexual Orientation in Australia', 20(6) *Alternative Law Journal* 261–265.

(2002) 'Imagining Otherness: Refugee Claims on the Basis of Sexuality in Canada and Australia', 26 *Melbourne University Law Review* 144–177.

(2004) 'The Role of Rights in Asylum Claims on the Basis of Sexual Orientation', 4(2) *Human Rights Law Review* 193–228.

(2005) 'A Preoccupation with Perversion: The British Response to Refugee Claims on the Basis of Sexual Orientation 1989–2003', 14(1) *Social Legal Studies* 115–138.

(2009) 'From Discretion to Disbelief: Recent Trends in Refugee Determinations on the Basis of Sexual Orientation in Australia and the United Kingdom', 13(2/3) *International Journal of Human Rights* 391–414.

(2012) 'The Right of Lesbians and Gay Men to Live Freely, Openly, and on Equal Terms Is Not Bad Law: A Reply to Hathaway and Pobjoy', 44(2) *New York University Journal of International Law and Politics* 497–527.

(2013) 'Sexual Orientation and Refugee Status Determination over the Past 20 Years: Unsteady Progress through Standard Sequences?', in Thomas Spijkerboer (ed.) *Fleeing Homophobia: Sexual Orientation, Gender Identity and Asylum*, London: Routledge, 32–54.

Mohr, Richard D. (1992) *Gay Ideas: Outing and Other Controversies*, Boston: Beacon Press.

Mullally, Siobhán (2013) 'Gender and Asylum Law: Providing Transformative Remedies?', in Satvinder Juss and Colin Harvey (eds.) *Contemporary Issues in Refugee Law*, Cheltenham: Edward Elgar, 196–225.

Muñoz, Elena (2013) *Personal Interview*, CEAR Madrid, 18 June 2013.

Murray, David A. B. (2016) 'Queer Forms: Producing Documentation in Sexual Orientation Refugee Cases', 89(2) *Anthropological Quarterly* 465–484.

(2017) 'The Homonational Archive: Sexual Orientation and Gendered Identity Refugee Documentation in Canada and the USA', 82(3) *Ethnos* 520–544.

New York University Journal of International Law and Politics (2012) *Vol. 44:2 Online Symposium*, http://opiniojuris.org/2012/03/07/new-york-university-journal-of-international-law-and-politics-vol-442-opinio-juris-online-symposium.

Noll, Gregor (2006) 'Asylum Claims and the Translation of Culture into Politics', 41(3) *Texas International Law Journal* 491–501.

O'Dwyer, Paul (2008) 'A Well-Founded Fear of Having My Sexual Orientation Asylum Claim Heard in the Wrong Court', 52(2) *New York Law School Law Review* 185–212.

Okisai, Kizitos Charloz (2015) *Sexual Orientation and Gender Identity Asylum Claims and Refugee Protection under South African Law*, LLM Dissertation, Faculty of Law, Unviersity of Pretoria, South Africa, https://repository.up.ac.za/handle/2263/46231.

Organization for Refuge, Asylum & Migration (2011) *Testing Sexual Orientation: A Scientific and Legal Analysis of Plethysmography in Asylum and Refugee Status Proceedings*, San Francisco: ORAM.

Pathela, Preeti, Anjum Hajat, Julia Schillinger, Susan Blank, Randall Sell and Farzad Mostashari (2006) 'Discordance between Sexual Behavior and Self-Reported Sexual

Identity: A Population-Based Survey of New York City Men', 145(6) *Annals of Internal Medicine* 416–425.
Perret, Hélène (2000) *La Règle de droit à la Commission des recours des réfugiés*, mémoire de DEA en sociologie du droit, université Panthéon-Assas (Paris 2), dir. J.-P. Heurtin.
Phillips, Marianne and Louise J. Jorgensen (2002) *Discourse Analysis as Theory and Method*, London: Sage Publications.
Pobjoy, Jason (2013) 'A Child Rights Framework for Assessing the Status of Refugee Children', in Satvinder Juss and Colin Harvey (eds.) *Contemporary Issues in Refugee Law*, Cheltenham: Edward Elgar, 91–137.
Posner, Richard (2007) 'In Memoriam: Bernard D. Meltzer (1914–2007)', 74(2) *University of Chicago Law Review* 435, 437, cited in Terry Hutchinson and Nigel Duncan (2012) 'Defining and Describing What We Do: Doctrinal Legal Research', 17(1) *Deakin Law Review* 83–119, 107.
Potter, Jonathan and Margaret Wetherell (1987) *Discourse and Social Psychology – Beyond Attitudes and Behaviour*, London: Sage Publications.
Rehaag, Sean (2008) 'Patrolling the Borders of Sexual Orientation: Bisexual Refugee Claims in Canada', 53 *McGill Law Journal* 59–102.
(2009) 'Bisexuals Need Not Apply: A Comparative Appraisal of Refugee Law and Policy in Canada, the United States, and Australia', 13(2) *International Journal of Human Rights* 415–436.
Rodrigues Araújo, Alexandra Maria (2014) 'The Qualification for Being a Refugee under EU Law: Religion as a Reason for Persecution – Court of Justice of the European Union (Grand Chamber), Judgment of 5 September 2012, Joined Cases C-71/11 and C-99/11, Bundesrepublik Deutschland v. Y and Z', 16(4) *European Journal of Migration and Law* 535–558.
Rodríguez Moya, Almudena (2015) 'Asylum and Religious Freedom: The ECJ Position', 94 *Revista de Derecho Político* 115–140.
Sahliu Braimah, Tim (2015) 'Divorcing Sexual Orientation from Religion and Politics: Utilizing the Convention Grounds of Religion and Political Opinion in Same-Sex Oriented Asylum Claims', 27(3) *International Journal of Refugee Law* 481–497.
Schmidt, Manfred (2012) 'Kriterien der Flüchtlingsanerkennung. Hier: Sexuelle Orientierung', 424–7313/05 – 12 (5506046-286) *Brief an Volker Beck MdB*, Nürnberg, 27 December.
Schmitz, Lisa (2015) *The 'True' Homosexual Refugee – An Archaeology of the Becoming and Governing of Refugees through Scientific-Legal Categories of Sexuality in German Legal Decision-Making*, master's thesis, Lund University, Sociology of Law Department, Autumn 2015, Lund Student University Papers, https://lup.lub.lu.se/student-papers/search/publication/8568341.
Schutzer, Mathew (2012) 'Bringing the Asylum Process Out of the Closet: Promoting the Acknowledgment of LGB Refugees', 13(3) *Georgetown Journal of Gender & the Law* 669–707.
Sedgwick, Eve Kosofsky (1990) *Epistemology of the Closet*, Berkeley: University of California Press.
Smeulders, Max (2016) *Somewhere over the Rainbow: The Contemporary Situation for LGBTI Asylum Seekers in the Netherlands*, master's thesis, Tilburg Law School, Tilburg Univesrsity. International and European law, track International law and Human Rights, 2015–2016, http://arno.uvt.nl/show.cgi?fid=141905.
Smith, Isaac T. R. (2015) 'Searching for Consistency in Asylum's Protected Grounds', 100 *Iowa Law Review* 1891–1915.

Spijkerboer, Thomas (2000) *Gender and Refugee Status*, Aldershot: Ashgate.

(2012) 'Two Remarks on Queer Law and Queer Politics: Thomas Spijkerboer Responds to Jenni Millbank & Guglielmo Verdirame', Panel 3 of the Online Symposium of the *NYU Journal of International Law and Politics*, 44(2), http://opiniojuris.org/2012/03/09/two-remarks-on-queer-law-and-queer-politics-thomas-spijkerboer-responds-to-jenni-millbank-guglielmo-verdirame.

(2013) 'Sexual Identity, Normativity and Asylum', in Thomas Spijkerboer (ed.) *Fleeing Homophobia: Sexual Orientation, Gender Identity and Asylum*, London: Routledge, 217–238.

Stein, Jeffrey D. (2012) 'A Brief Introduction to the Conversation', 44(2) *New York University Journal of International Law and Politics* 313–314.

Szczensny, Jerzy (2009) 'Sexuelle Selbstbestimmung und das Recht auf Asyl in Deutschland', in Claudia Lohrenscheit (ed.) *Sexuelle Selbstbestimmung als Menschenrecht*, Berlin: Nomos, 169–181.

Teitgen-Colly, Catherine (1994) 'Le droit d'asile: la fin des illusions', *L'Actualité juridique – Droit administratif* 97–114.

(2006) 'The European Union and Asylum: An Illusion of Protection', 43(6) *Common Market Law Review* 1503–1566.

Teitgen-Colly, Catherine and François Julien-Lafèrriere (1998) 'La réforme du droit d'asile', *L'Actualité juridique – Droit administratif*, 1002–1004.

The Equality and Human Rights Commission (2010) *HJ (Iran) and HT (Cameroon) v Secretary of State for the Home Department – Case for the Equality and Human Rights Commission*, copy on file with author.

Tiedemann, Paul (2010) 'The Use of Foreign Asylum Jurisprudence in the German Administrative Courts', in Guy Goodwin-Gil and Hélène Lambert (eds.) *The Limits of Transnational Law – Refugee Law, Policy Harmonization and Judicial Dialogue in the European Union*, 57–84.

(2014) *Flüchtlingsrecht – Die materiellen und verfahrensrechtlichen Grundlagen*, Berlin: Springer.

Tissier-Raffin, Marion (2015) 'L'orientation sexuelle comme motif de persécution doit être appréciée dans la dignité', *La Revue des droits de l'homme [En ligne], Actualités Droits-Libertés*, mis en ligne le 15 janvier 2015.

Titze, Anngeret (2012) 'Sexuelle Orientierung und die Zumutung der Diskretion', *Zeitschrift für Ausländerrecht und Ausländerpolitik* 2012, 93–102.

Tobin, John (2012) 'Assessing GLBTI Refugee Claims: Using Human Rights Law to Shift the Narrative of Persecution within Refugee Law', 44(2) *New York University Journal of International Law and Politics* 447–484.

Topel, Kimberly D. (2017) '"So, What Should I Ask Him to Prove That He's Gay?": How Sincerity, and Not Stereotype, Should Dictate the Outcome of an LGB Asylum Claim in the United States', 102 *Iowa Law Review* 2357–2384.

Türk, Volker (2013) 'Ensuring Protection to LGBTI Persons of Concern', opinion delivered at the *Invisible in the City: Urban Protection Gaps Facing Sexual Minorities Fleeing Persecution*, HIAS LGBTI Symposium, 20–21 September 2012, 25(1) *International Journal of Refugee Law* 120–129.

UK Home Office (2006) *Explanatory Memorandum to the Refugee or Person in Need of International Protection (Qualification) Regulations* 2006, No. 2525, www.legislation.gov.uk/uksi/2006/2525/pdfs/uksi_20062525_en.pdf.

(2017) 'Afghanistan: Sexual Orientation and Gender Identity', *Country Policy and Information Note*.

UNHCR (1979, re-edited 1992) *Handbook on Procedures and Criteria for Determining Refugee Status under the 1951 Convention and the 1967 Protocol Relating to the Status of Refugees*, HCR/IP/4/Eng/REV.1 Reedited, Geneva, January 1992.

(2001) *The International Protection of Refugees: Interpreting Article 1 of the 1951 Convention Relating to the Status of Refugees*, April 2001.

(2005) *Conclusion on the Provision on International Protection Including through Complementary Forms of Protection*, Executive Committee of the High Commissioner's Programme 7 October 2005, No. 103 (LVI).

(2011) *HJ (Iran) and HT (Cameroon) v Secretary of State for the Home Department – Case for the first intervener (the United Nations High Commissioner for Refugees)*, 19 April 2010, http://www.unhcr.org/refworld/docid/4bd1abbc2.html.

(2013) *Beyond Proof, Credibility Assessment in EU Asylum Systems: Full Report*, May 2013.

(2015) *States Parties to the 1951 Convention relating to the Status of Refugees and the 1967 Protocol*, www.unhcr.org/protect/PROTECTION/3b73b0d63.pdf.

(2015) *The Case Law of the European Regional Courts: The Court of Justice of the European Union and the European Court of Human Rights. Refugees, asylum-seekers, and stateless persons* (1st ed.), June 2015.

University of Michigan Law School (2015) *The Michigan Guidelines on Risk for Reasons of Political Opinion*, April 2015, www.refworld.org/docid/555de15b4.html.

Vanheule, Dirk (1997) 'A Comparison of the Judicial Interpretations of the Notion of Refugee', in Jean-Yves Carlier and Dirk Vanheule (eds.) *Europe and Refugees: A Challenge?*, The Hague: Kluwer Law International, 98–103.

Velasco, Bernardo M. (2017) 'Who Are the Real Refugees: Labels as Evidence of a Particular Social Group', 59 *Arizona Law Review* 235–262.

Verdirame, Guglielmo (2012) 'A Friendly Act of Socio-cultural Contestation: Asylum and the Big Cultural Divide', 44(2) *New York University Journal of International Law and Politics* 559–572.

Vogler, Stefan (2016) 'Legally Queer: The Construction of Sexuality in LGBQ Asylum Claims', 50(4) *Law & Society Review* 856–889.

Wagner, Neva (2016) 'B Is for Bisexual: The Forgotten Letter in U.K. Sexual Orientation Asylum Reform', 26 *Transnational Law & Contemporary Problems* 205–227.

Walker, Kristen (1996) 'The Importance of Being Out: Sexuality and Refugee Status', 18 *Sydney Law Review* 568–597.

(2000) 'Sexuality and Refugee Status in Australia' 12(2) *International Journal of Refugee Law* 175–211.

Watson, Alan (1993) *Legal Transplants: An Approach to Comparative Law (2nd ed.)*, Athens: The University of Georgia Press.

Wayne, Adena L. (2016) 'Unique Identities and Vulnerabilities: The Case for Transgender Identity as a Basis for Asylum', 102 *Cornell Law Review* 241–270.

Wessels, Janna (2011) 'Sexual Orientation in Refugee Status Determination', RSC Working Paper Series No. 74, University of Oxford.

(2012) 'HJ (Iran) and HT (Cameroon) – Reflections on a New Test for Sexuality-Based Asylum Claims in Britain', 24(4) *International Journal of Refugee Law* 815–839.

(2013) '"Discretion" in Sexuality-Based Asylum Cases: An Adaptive Phenomenon', in Thomas Spijkerboer (ed.) *Fleeing Homophobia: Sexual Orientation, Gender Identity and Asylum*, London: Routledge, 55–81.

(2016) '"Discretion", Persecution and the Act/Identity Dichotomy', *VU Migration Law Series No 12*, Vrije Universiteit Amsterdam.

(2017) 'Publicly Manifested—Fatefully Determined—Invariably "Discreet": The Assessment of Sexuality-Based Asylum Claims in Germany and France' 29(2) *Canadian Journal of Women and the Law* 343–374.

Young, Rebecca M. and Ilan H. Meyer (2005) 'The Trouble with "MSM" and "WSW": Erasure of the Sexual-Minority Person in Public Health Discourse', 95(7) *American Journal of Public Health* 1144–1149.

Index